Royalists and royalism
during the Interregnum

MANCHESTER
1824

Manchester University Press

Politics, culture and society in early modern Britain

General editors

PROFESSOR ANN HUGHES
PROFESSOR ANTHONY MILTON
PROFESSOR PETER LAKE

This important series publishes monographs that take a fresh and challenging look at the interactions between politics, culture and society in Britain between 1500 and the mid-eighteenth century. It counteracts the fragmentation of current historiography through encouraging a variety of approaches which attempt to redefine the political, social and cultural worlds, and to explore their interconnection in a flexible and creative fashion. All the volumes in the series question and transcend traditional interdisciplinary boundaries, such as those between political history and literary studies, social history and divinity, urban history and anthropology. They thus contribute to a broader understanding of crucial developments in early modern Britain.

Royalists and royalism during the Interregnum

Edited by
JASON McELLIGOTT
and DAVID L. SMITH

Manchester
University Press
Manchester and New York

distributed exclusively in the USA by Palgrave Macmillan

Published by Manchester University Press
Oxford Road, Manchester M13 9NR, UK
and Room 400, 175 Fifth Avenue, New York, NY 10010, USA
www.manchesteruniversitypress.co.uk

Distributed exclusively in the USA by
Palgrave Macmillan, 175 Fifth Avenue, New York, NY 10010, USA

Distributed exclusively in Canada by
UBC Press, University of British Columbia, 2029 West Mall,
Vancouver, BC, Canada V6T 1Z2

British Library Cataloguing-in-Publication Data
A catalogue record for this book is available from the British Library

Library of Congress Cataloging-in-Publication Data applied for

ISBN 978 0 7190 8161 3 *hardback*

First published 2010

19 18 17 16 15 14 13 12 11 10   10 9 8 7 6 5 4 3 2 1

Typeset in Scala with Pastonchi display
by Koinonia, Manchester

Printed in Great Britain
by TJ International Ltd, Padstow

Contents

List of illustrations

Notes on contributors

Lloyd Bowen is Senior Lecturer in Early Modern and Welsh History at Cardiff University and author of *The Politics of the Principality: Wales, c.1603–42* (2007). He is currently working on aspects of royalism, political speech and popular culture in the 1640s and 1650s.

Jan Broadway is Technical Director of the Centre for Editing Lives and Letters, Queen Mary, University of London. She is the author of *'No historie so meete': Gentry Culture and the Development of Local History in Elizabethan and Early Stuart England* (2006) and is currently writing a biography of William Dugdale.

D'Maris Coffman received her MA and PhD in History from the University of Pennsylvania and her BSc in Economics from the Wharton School, University of Pennsylvania. She is currently a Junior Research Fellow at Newnham College, Cambridge, where she is revising her PhD dissertation on the fiscal revolution of the Interregnum for publication.

Kenneth Fincham is Professor of Early Modern History at the University of Kent. His first book, *Prelate as Pastor: The Episcopate of James I*, appeared in 1990, and since then he has published two volumes of *Visitation Articles and Injunctions of the Early Stuart Church*, edited two collections of essays and, most recently, co-authored with Nicholas Tyacke *Altars Restored: The Changing Face of English Religious Worship, 1547–c.1700* (2007). He is also a co-director of the Clergy of the Church of England Database 1540–1835, funded by the Arts and Humanities Research Council.

Ann Hughes is Professor of Early Modern History at the University of Keele and the author of several articles and books on mid-seventeenth century English history, most recently *Gangraena and the Struggle for the English Revolution* (2004).

James Loxley is Senior Lecturer in English Literature at the University of Edinburgh. He is the author of *Royalism and Poetry in the English Civil Wars* (1997), *Ben Jonson* (2002) and *Performativity* (2007). He has also published articles and essays on various aspects of seventeenth-century English literature and on some of the methodological issues implicit in historicist literary criticism. He is currently completing a co-authored book entitled *Shakespeare, Jonson and the Claims of the Performative*, and editing a collection of essays on the work of Stanley Cavell.

Jason McElligott works at the Trinity Long Room Hub, the arts and humanities research institute at Trinity College Dublin. He is the author of *Royalism, Print and Censorship in Revolutionary England* (2007), *A Biographical Companion to the Entring Book of Roger Morrice, 1677–1691* (2007) and *Censorship and the Press, 1640–1660* (2009), and the editor of *Fear, Exclusion and Revolution: Roger Morrice and*

Britain in the 1680s (2006) and (with David L. Smith) of *Royalists and Royalism during the English Civil Wars* (2007).

Anthony Milton is Professor of History at the University of Sheffield. His publications include *Laudian and Royalist Polemic in Seventeenth-Century England: The Career and Writings of Peter Heylyn* (2007). He was recently awarded a Leverhulme Major Research Fellowship to work on a monograph provisionally entitled 'England's Second Reformation: The Battle for the Church of England 1636–1666'.

Marcus Nevitt is Lecturer in Renaissance Literature at the University of Sheffield. He is the author of *Women and the Pamphlet Culture of Revolutionary England* (2006) as well as numerous articles on early modern pamphlet culture. He is currently working on a book about the Cromwellian afterlives of Elizabethan poets.

Helen Pierce is a Postdoctoral Research Fellow at the University of York's Centre for Renaissance and Early Modern Studies, where her work focuses on the relationship between politics and visual culture in seventeenth-century England. Her book *Unseemly Pictures: Graphic Satire and Politics in Early Modern England* was published in 2008.

Julie Sanders is Professor of English Literature and Drama at the University of Nottingham. She is the author of several books and articles on early seventeenth-century drama and culture, as well as scholarly editions of plays, and the co-editor with Ian Atherton of an interdisciplinary collection of essays on the 1630s.

David L. Smith is Fellow and Director of Studies in History at Selwyn College, Cambridge. His books include *Constitutional Royalism and the Search for Settlement, c.1640–1649* (1994), *A History of the Modern British Isles, 1603–1707: The Double Crown* (1998), *The Stuart Parliaments, 1603–1689* (1999) and (with Patrick Little) *Parliaments and Politics during the Cromwellian Protectorate* (2007).

Geoffrey Smith is an Honorary Research Fellow in the School of History in the University of Melbourne. He is the author of *The Cavaliers in Exile, 1640–1660* (2003) and of several articles on the Royalists. He is currently working on a study of Royalist agents, spies and conspirators during the period of the Civil Wars and the Interregnum.

Stephen Taylor is Professor of Early Modern History at the University of Reading, where he has taught since 1988. Most of his research hitherto has been on the religious and political history of England in the late seventeenth and early eighteenth centuries. He is one of the directors of the Clergy of the Church of England Database 1540–1835, and the collaboration with Kenneth Fincham on this project provided the stimulus for his chapter in this collection. He is now planning, with Professor Fincham, a study entitled 'Shifting Conformities: Clergy, Laity and Parish Religion 1640–1665'.

Preface

This book is the second collection of essays to emerge from an international conference entitled 'Royalists and Royalism: Politics, Religion, and Culture, 1640–60' that we organised at Clare College, Cambridge, in July 2004. The first edited collection was published by Cambridge University Press in 2007 as *Royalists and Royalism during the English Civil Wars*. In exploring the subject of royalism during the Interregnum we have had even less prior historiography to engage with than was the case with the volume on the 1640s. Yet, as we argue in Chapter 1, it is precisely this longstanding neglect that makes the subject all the more exciting and compelling.

We raised close to £10,000 to pay for the 2004 conference. We are deeply grateful to the Centre for Research in the Arts, Humanities and Social Sciences (CRASSH) in Cambridge for its generous financial support of the conference, and for providing us with invaluable administrative assistance. The British Academy paid for the flights of a number of scholars from the United States. We also gratefully acknowledge the generous financial help that we received from the Trevelyan Fund of the Cambridge History Faculty, the Royal Stuart Society, the Royal Historical Society and Christ Church, Oxford. John Morrill has, as always, been a great source of support and encouragement, as have Ronald Hutton and Quentin Skinner. Thanks are also due to Mark Goldie, Steve Gunn, David Norbrook, Jane Ohlmeyer and Julia Walworth.

In the notes, place of publication is London unless otherwise stated. Spelling in quotations from primary sources has been modernised and the standard abbreviated forms have been expanded. Dates are given in old style, except that the year is taken to begin on 1 January rather than 25 March.

Jason McElligott
David L. Smith

List of abbreviations

Add. MS	Additional Manuscript
AGR	Archives Générales du Royaume, Brussels
AHR	*American Historical Review*
A&O	C.H. Firth and R.S. Rait (eds), *Acts and Ordinances of the Interregnum*, 3 vols (1911)
BL	British Library, London
Bodl.	Bodleian Library, Oxford
CCA	Cheshire and Chester Archives
CClSP	O. Ogle, W.H. Bliss, W. D. Macray and F. J. Routledge (eds), *Calendar of the Clarendon State Papers*, 5 vols (Oxford, 1869–1970)
CHR	W.D. Macray (ed.), *The History of the Rebellion and Civil Wars in England by Edward, Earl of Clarendon*, 6 vols (Oxford, 1888)
CJ	Commons' Journals
CSP	Richard Scrope and Thomas Monckhouse (eds), *State Papers Collected by Edward, Earl of Clarendon*, 3 vols (Oxford, 1767–86)
CSPD	*Calendar of State Papers Domestic*
CTB	W.A. Shaw, *Calendar of Treasury Books and Papers Preserved in the Record Office* (1904)
CUL	Cambridge University Library
EEBO	Early English Books Online
EHR	*English Historical Review*
HJ	*Historical Journal*
HLQ	*Huntington Library Quarterly*
HMC	Historical Manuscripts Commission
HR	*Historical Research*
HWJ	*History Workshop Journal*
KB	Koninklijke Bibliotheek, The Hague
LJ	Lords' Journals
LMA	London Metropolitan Archives
NP	F. Warner (ed.), *The Nicholas Correspondence: The Correspondence of Sir Edward Nicholas*, 4 vols (Camden Society, 1886–1920)
OED	*Oxford English Dictionary*
Oxford DNB	*Oxford Dictionary of National Biography* (Oxford, 2004)
P&P	*Past & Present*
RO	Record Office
SP	State Papers
TNA	The National Archives, Kew
TSP	Thomas Birch (ed.), *A Collection of the State Papers of John Thurloe, Esq.*, 7 vols (1742)
TRHS	*Transactions of the Royal Historical Society*
WMQ	*William and Mary Quarterly*

Chapter 1

Introduction:
rethinking Royalists and royalism
during the Interregnum

Jason McElligott and David L. Smith

I

In the vast scholarly literature on the English Revolution, more has been written about the 1640s than about the 1650s, and more attention has been given to the Parliamentarians than to the Royalists. As a result, royalism during the 1650s is the most sparsely populated sector of this historiographical quadrant and represents a significantly under-studied aspect of the period. Over the past half-century, there have been only three book-length treatments of Royalist politics during the period from the Regicide to the Restoration. The first, Paul H. Hardacre's *The Royalists during the Puritan Revolution* (1956),[1] devotes 80 of its 169 pages to the period from 1649 to 1660. It is an important and pioneering study, all the more commendable as Hardacre had very little historiography to build upon other than a posthumously published article by Sir Charles Firth.[2] Hardacre's book does, however, have its limitations. As John Morrill has written, it 'is not so much about the Royalists as about the policies and practices of their victorious opponents towards them'. The book's principal contribution lies in the fact that it 'is an important study of the processes of sequestration and composition (i.e. the confiscation of Royalist estates and their return on payment of heavy fines) and of the Major-Generals'.[3] In 1960, four years after the appearance of Hardacre's book, David Underdown's *Royalist Conspiracy in England, 1649–1660* was published.[4] John Morrill has observed that Underdown's book complements Hardacre's in that it 'explores the reasons why Royalist conspiracies were so ineffectual, and finds the reasons in the divisions within the exiled court, in the English provinces and in the brilliance of Cromwell's intelligence service'.[5] Indeed, Underdown himself admitted that he had not 'written a complete history of the English Royalist party' and had only discussed 'the Royalists abroad ... insofar as is necessary for a full understanding of the [home-grown] conspiracies'.[6] The book nevertheless offers what is still the fullest account of what it was like to live as a Royalist in England during the Interregnum.

One would have expected two fine studies produced within a few years of each other to have stimulated much further research on the Royalist experience of the 1650s, but over the next forty years scholars of the English Revolution came to be enchanted, besotted and beguiled by Parliamentarians, Puritans and so-called 'radicals' of every imaginable hue.[7] Scholars are often among the most dedicated followers of fashion, and royalism was, quite simply, distinctly unfashionable. Indeed, these works by Hardacre and Underdown remained the only books devoted to Royalist politics during the Interregnum until the very welcome appearance in 2003 of Geoffrey Smith's *The Cavaliers in Exile, 1640–1660*.[8] Smith presents the most detailed treatment yet published of the experience of those Royalists who went into exile on the continent during the Interregnum. His study is particularly notable for its reconstruction of the varied experiences of exiled Royalists, and also for his demonstration that the conventional factional divisions sometimes applied to the exiles – the 'Old Royalists', 'Louvrians' and 'Swordsmen' – rapidly dissolve under closer examination. Smith shows that the exiles represented a broad social, religious and political cross-section that defies simple categorisation: diversity was the most striking characteristic of the Royalists in exile, as it was of those who remained behind in Britain.

The existing literature leaves many aspects of royalism during the Interregnum explored only briefly, if at all. This neglect is partly a function of the traditional indifference of scholars of the English Revolution to royalism in general, but it is also due to the surprising lack of attention paid in recent decades to the Interregnum as a whole, and to the Protectorate in particular. When, in 1971, Anthony Cotton completed a ground-breaking DPhil dissertation at Oxford on the growth and development of London newsbooks during the Civil War, he claimed that he had chosen to write about the 1640s rather than the 1650s because the journalism of the Interregnum was 'extremely dull'.[9] This disregard for the 1650s has changed little, if at all, over the four decades since Cotton submitted his dissertation. Indeed, Ronald Hutton has recently written that 'the 1650s have always lacked an appeal for historians of both the preceding and succeeding ages, seeming to belong neither to one nor the other. Revisionists tended to ignore them simply because there seemed to be nothing much there to revise.'[10] Although greater attention is now belatedly being paid to the Cromwellian Protectorate, current research has so far tended to concentrate mainly on its political and parliamentary history rather than on Royalist reactions to it.[11] This neglect of royalism in the 1650s may have come about partly because the sources that throw light on it during this period are often diffuse and unsystematic, but also because our understanding of what royalism was, and what it meant to be a Royalist, has until recently been decidedly unsophisticated and lacking in nuance. Scholars have traditionally been content to describe Royalist politics in terms of a simplistic dichotomy between 'absolutists' and 'constitutionalists', and they have also studiously ignored the hundreds of thousands of men and women outside the rarefied milieu of the court and the upper echelons of the clergy and the military who supported the Stuart cause.[12] Is it any wonder that so little has been written about royalism during the 1650s when so many of the scholars interested in the topic have unwittingly created the impression that the Royalist party consisted of nothing more than a few dozen squabbling grandees with very few followers among the wider population?

The essays in this volume are an important milestone in the recovery of the Royalist experience of the 1650s. They offer a variety of fresh and exciting perspectives on Royalist politics, religion and culture during these years. Royalism emerges from this collection as a much more variegated, complex, heterogeneous and interesting creed than has hitherto been described. When read in conjunction with recent work on Royalists and royalism during the 1640s, these essays constitute a quantum leap in our understanding of the lives, motivations and experiences of those who supported the Stuarts during the English Revolution. Yet they will also force us to rethink some of our assumptions about the opponents and enemies of the Royalists and, by so doing, provide us with a more rounded, and convincing, picture of the society in which they lived. It is to be hoped that in future years more and more graduate students will begin to study the Interregnum and that in so doing they will examine those remarkably neglected men and women who chose loyalty and royalty. Only then will it be possible to provide a modern, scholarly and convincing overview of the period.

II

The essays that follow give some sense of the scope of the Royalist experience during the 1650s, and between them they explore a number of themes that help to transform our understanding of the subject. This second section will briefly consider seven broad, interlocking themes which constantly re-emerge throughout the entire collection. We shall then suggest how these issues relate to a number of unresolved (and, in some cases, unasked) questions about royalism, before concluding with some suggestions as to the most fruitful directions for future research. The seven broad themes which emerge from these essays are: the idea that royalism during the 1650s was a 'broad church' with no monolithic ideology; the varying degrees to which Royalists conformed to the Interregnum regimes and reached an accommodation with them; the need to avoid privileging one particular group of Royalists at the expense of others; the value of exploring the literary and artistic dimensions of Royalist culture; the nature of Royalist allegiance and the complexity of loyalties to

Charles I and Charles II; the experiences of Royalists in exile on the continent and across the Atlantic; and, lastly, the relationship between Interregnum royalism and the Restoration of Charles II in 1660.

A number of the essays demonstrate that royalism in the 1650s was not so much a single, unitary phenomenon as a spectrum of different attitudes and beliefs. In Chapter 2, for example, Kenneth Fincham and Stephen Taylor argue that there were several shades of episcopalian royalism, ranging from hardliners such as Henry Hammond and Gilbert Sheldon to more flexible and pragmatic figures like Ralph Brownrigg and Thomas Fuller. This variegated pattern among the bishops was replicated in the parish clergy and the Royalist gentry. Similarly, Lloyd Bowen in Chapter 3 indicates the need for a definition of royalism that is broad enough to embrace many more than simply those who took up arms for the king. Among exiled Royalists, likewise, variety was the dominant characteristic, and Geoffrey Smith in Chapter 6 ably demonstrates the variety and fluidity of outlooks that could find a home under the Royalist umbrella.

A similar range of responses was evident in the extent to which Royalists were willing, or able, to reach an accommodation with the Interregnum regimes. Once again, the clergy were as diverse as the laity. Kenneth Fincham and Stephen Taylor reveal that most clergy were willing to accommodate themselves to varying degrees to political realities. Yet conformity was a complex and often protracted process that involved constant negotiation and interpretation. Those bishops who conformed did not represent one particular strand of churchmanship; rather, there was a spectrum of degrees of engagement with the post-episcopalian state church and the Interregnum regimes. Among both the episcopalian gentry and the parish clergy who were the recipients of their charitable relief we find a mixture of both conformists and nonconformists. Lay Royalists, such as John Evelyn, often combined public conformity with private nonconformity. It seems likely that many Royalists were able to reach an accommodation with the Interregnum regimes of the kind that Jan Broadway uncovers in Chapter 10 for the antiquarian William Dugdale, who adapted to the political realities of the times, thereby allowing him to continue his scholarly activities unmolested. Such co-existence was all the more feasible given that the republican regimes generally seem to have adopted a relaxed attitude towards those who did not present an overt or immediate political threat to them. This was true not only of Royalist peers, as D'Maris Coffman shows in the case of the Earl of Southampton in Chapter 12, but also of Royalist symbols and iconography, as Helen Pierce reveals in Chapter 4 in relation to the dissemination of images of Charles I during the early 1650s.

The emphasis upon diversity that emerges in these essays makes it all the more important to avoid excessive concentration on any one group of Royalists. It would be mistaken to assume that any particular sub-set of Royalists represents the 'true' or 'essential' Royalist experience. Just as we cannot regard the episcopalian hardliners as typical of the Royalist clergy as a whole, so we also need to widen our horizons beyond the social elite and to explore the little studied phenomenon of 'popular' royalism. Lloyd Bowen's chapter shows how much can be gleaned about Royalist attitudes among non-elite men and women by sensitive use of Upper Bench, assize and quarter sessions records. Bowen reveals that it was possible for comparatively humble individuals to articulate an oppositional discourse of royalism which was distinct from mere anti-Parliamentarianism. Bowen's chapter leads us into a world very different from that of the Royalist nobility and gentry: a world that is only beginning to receive the close scholarly attention that it deserves.

To grasp the full scope of royalism in this period also demands a willingness to examine as wide a range of different sources as possible, and a number of these essays argue that future research must involve more than the use of the well-mined papers of a small number of leading courtiers in exile: Hyde, Nicholas and Ormond. Historians will probably be receptive to this call, but, to judge from past form, they may well be much more sceptical about the need to embrace literary sources and methodologies. Yet two of these essays in particular reveal how rewarding an historicist reading of literary works can be. James Loxley shows in Chapter 8 how the difficulty of differentiating between person and office at the time of the trial and execution of Charles I produced a highly unstable politics of personhood in the years around 1649. This had a number of consequences, not least a preoccupation with disguise which is evident in plays such as John Tatham's *The Distracted State* (1650) and Cosmo Manuche's *The Just General* (1652). In Chapter 9 Marcus Nevitt offers us a provocative (and very convincing) reading of the 1655 edition of Shakespeare's *The Rape of Lucrece*. This edition of the popular narrative poem contained a fifteen-page continuation of Shakespeare's text by the Royalist writer John Quarles entitled *The Banishment of Tarquin: Or, the Reward of Lust*. Nevitt argues that Quarles's addition to the poem was consciously intended to downplay prevalent republican readings of Lucrece's rape by Tarquin as the key cause of that tyrant's expulsion from Rome, the end of the monarchy and the birth of the Roman republic. Instead, by presenting the text as a moral narrative about the punishment of Tarquin's licentiousness, Quarles sought to counter what had become a common anti-monarchical discourse of the 1640s and 1650s. Loxley's and Nevitt's readings of literary sources offer rich insights into the nature of Royalist strategies for coping with life under the republican regimes.

Helen Pierce's essay (Chapter 4) reveals the ambivalence of the Interregnum regimes towards the iconography of kingship in general, and the image of Charles I in particular. It seems that the regimes were not especially exercised by the fate of royal statues, works of art and coats of arms, except in 'serious times'. The regicides would obviously have preferred to have all such images speedily removed from all public spaces, but they often had more pressing political, administrative and military tasks to hand than trying to remove the royal coat of arms on public buildings or seizing pictures of Charles I or his son from bookshops or private dwellings. This administrative pragmatism, combined with the inevitable inefficiencies, indifference, inertia or incompetence of a variety of regulatory bodies including the army, the City authorities and the Company of Stationers, ensured that some contemporaries seem to have enjoyed much more latitude in the production and consumption of Royalist cultural material than has hitherto been suspected.[13] If Pierce's essay demonstrates the relative freedom with which images of the king could at times circulate, then Anthony Milton's essay (Chapter 5), intriguingly, reveals that it was not only the regicides who could be ambiguous about, or indifferent to, the iconography of the martyred king. Milton shows that Peter Heylyn, often regarded as among the most aggressive of Royalists, presented a sustained critique of Charles I's kingship and policies in his *Observations on the Historie of the Reign of King Charles* (1656). Heylyn's criticisms of Charles's shortcomings went right back to the failure of the Spanish Match, and the charge that Charles had 'vailed his crown' formed a leitmotif of Heylyn's analysis of his reign. In particular, by claiming that Charles had placed the pursuit of virtue and the protection of his own conscience above what was politically wise and necessary, Heylyn offered an implicit critique of the martyr cult that developed around Charles after the Regicide. Heylyn disliked the trend within Royalist writing after 1649 to praise Charles as irenic, moderate and willing to turn the other cheek; he even went so far as to contrast Charles's weakness in the face of Scottish rebellion with Cromwell's manly vigour against the Scots at Preston, Dunbar and Worcester. If a Royalist as committed as Heylyn was prepared to publish such an unflattering assessment of Charles I during the mid-1650s then clearly we need to be sensitive to the complexities and ambiguities that existed within Royalist allegiance.

A similar variety of outlook and experience is also evident in the three essays that examine Royalists abroad, whether on the continent or across the Atlantic. In Chapter 6, Geoffrey Smith argues that exiled Royalists did not conform to a series of discrete stereotypes, for example as courtiers or swordsmen, but frequently combined a range of circumstances and experiences within the same personality and career. He takes Daniel O'Neill – an anglicised Gaelic, protestant, Irish Cavalier – as a case study of an individual who resolutely defies simple categorisation. Similar complexities emerge in Chapter 7, by Ann Hughes and Julie Sanders, which draws out the prominence of women within the exiled community as intermediaries, patrons and activists. Figures such as Elizabeth of Bohemia and Mary of Orange stood at the centre of extensive epistolary networks that could be used for intelligence purposes. Hughes and Sanders also reveal the importance of place among exiled Royalists, not least in providing a setting for rituals and ceremonial displays that constituted acts of defiance towards the republican regimes. In examining Royalists abroad it is important to extend our horizons across the Atlantic, as Jason McElligott argues in Chapter 11. Six of the twenty-four British colonies in the New World rebelled against the regime that was established in England in 1649. Virginia seems to have been a particularly strong centre of royalism, and McElligott sets out his case for taking seriously a declaration abhorring the Regicide and pledging support for Charles II, ostensibly from that colony, that appeared in *The Man in the Moon* in January 1650. His chapter introduces us to a hitherto unknown network of Royalists associated with the book trade in Cromwellian London, and suggests that Royalist merchants in the City of London may have facilitated trans-Atlantic channels of communication which bypassed the exiled court on the continent. This is a potentially very fruitful area of future research, particularly as McElligott has focused on only one of the six colonies that rose for Charles II.

The final theme which emerges in these essays concerns the relationship between Interregnum royalism and the Restoration. These connections are addressed most directly in D'Maris Coffman's essay (Chapter 12), which traces the career of the Earl of Southampton, who, having lived in seclusion for most of the 1650s, perpetuated the excise that Parliament had established in 1643 once he became Lord Treasurer at the Restoration. Coffman analyses how Southampton made the excise work for Charles II, and demonstrates that there was thus continuity with the Interregnum regimes even though Southampton himself had refused to have anything to do with them. In other essays we can find similar links between the royalism of the 1650s and the Restoration. Lloyd Bowen's essay concludes by suggesting that popular attachment to the monarchy during the Interregnum laid the foundations for the popular monarchism and Toryism that emerged during the Restoration period. Similarly, Helen Pierce links the destruction of images of Cromwell and the reinstatement of royal arms at the Restoration back to the resilient attachment to the imagery of monarchy that had persisted throughout the 1650s. The study of Royalists and royalism during the Interregnum is therefore not a chronologically discrete story but rather one that has implications for our understanding of the period that followed it.

III

Although collectively the essays in this volume range very widely, they inevitably cannot cover every aspect of the Royalist experience. There is much that remains to be reconstructed about Royalist politics, religion and culture during this period, and the third and final section of this introduction will consider a number of questions that arise from these essays. These are problems that scholars working in this field may wish to address in the future. Firstly, there is not a single mention in these essays of Royalists retreating into a private world of retirement and seclusion among family and friends. This is surprising because the tropes of retreat, patient fortitude and self-imposed internal exile have dominated literary studies of Royalist writing, especially poetry, during the Interregnum. The disjunction between these essays and the work of distinguished scholars such as Earl Milner and Robert Wilcher is striking.[14] It may be a function of the fact that studies of Royalists and royalism are now moving beyond the small circle of well-connected writers who have hitherto constituted the canon of Royalist literary output. Or is the disjunction a result of the fact that we now have, and are continuing to develop, more sophisticated models of political activity and Royalist allegiance? It may well be true that the seemingly unproblematic word 'retirement' in fact conceals as wide a variety of behaviour and belief as 'royalism' itself.

Scholars may also wish to be clear as to exactly what is meant by the terms 'Royalist' and 'royalism'. In 2007, in the introduction to a volume of essays entitled *Royalists and Royalism during the English Civil Wars*, we suggested the need for a definition of royalism that was sufficiently flexible to do justice to the many different strands, complexities and ambiguities that existed within it. We asked whether it was time 'to move beyond *prescriptive* definitions of royalism – what people must have thought or believed in order to qualify for membership of the Royalist party – in favour of a descriptive definition which considers what actual Royalists thought, believed or argued'. We suggested that:

> When one considers the diverse men and women who sided with the King, the only acceptable definition of a Royalist is this: somebody who, by thought or deed, identified himself or herself as a Royalist and was accepted as such by other individuals who defined themselves as Royalists. These Royalists could (and did) hold a wide variety of political or theological opinions but they were united by a concern to see the Stuarts return to power on their own terms or, failing that, the best possible terms available.[15]

It should also be noted that in *Royalists and Royalism during the English Civil Wars* we argued against drawing a strict distinction between 'royalism' and 'loyalism' because the vast majority of those who adhered to Charles I seem to have used the terms as interchangeable synonyms. How useful are these definitions in the dramatically changed circumstances of the 1650s?

In the wake of the Regicide and the establishment of a regime in England which owed its survival to the power of the army to defeat and intimidate its enemies, can one really expect anything other than a small minority of Royalists to have courted trouble by identifying themselves as such? There were times when the Interregnum regimes were harsher against the Royalists than others; how should we deal with people for whom we have occasional surviving evidence of Royalist inclination or activity separated by long periods of inactivity? Can we really equate private, spoken opposition with public defiance or the organisation of armed plots during the successive military dictatorships of the 1650s? How should we navigate the long silences of royalism during the Interregnum? Can we chart the differences between what one might call significant and insignificant silences – times when people might have been silent because they had recanted their royalism, and times when they might have been silent because the balance of forces compelled them to bite their tongues and wait for better days? Furthermore, how can we tell when the silence of royalism during these years is merely a function of the weaknesses of the surviving sources?[16]

The essays in this book certainly demonstrate that royalism was a broad church encompassing a wide range of attitudes, beliefs and experiences, but how might this realisation affect the second part of our definition of a Royalist: somebody who defined herself or himself in this way and was accepted as such by other individuals who defined themselves as Royalists? To pose the question in a slightly different way: if mutual recognition of each other was the key to Royalist identity but that identity was itself complex, multifaceted, variegated and liable to change over time, what criteria did men and women consider to be essential in order to qualify as a Royalist, and what criteria – thoughts, words, beliefs or deeds – were considered desirable but not essential? What baggage (and how much of it) could one discard and yet still be considered a Royalist by contemporaries? Were there, as we suspect, discernible patterns to the choices made by groups of men and women: patterns that were influenced by contingent factors such as geographical location, social status and imperfect and entirely subjective assessments of the balance of political and military power? Lastly, how should we assess the third and final part of our definition of royalism: 'they were united by a concern to see the Stuarts return to power on their own terms or, failing that, the best possible terms available'? In the context of the military fiascos which culminated in the Battle of Worcester in 1651, and the spectacular ineptitude of the subsequent plots commissioned by small groups such as the Sealed Knot and Action Party, what are we to make of men and women who gradually, perhaps despite themselves, came to fear or despise any attempt to re-install the Stuarts on the British thrones by force of arms?[17] Some men and women evidently made a definitive break from royalism, but others seem to have moved temporarily away from the cause during particularly difficult periods before returning to their previous positions: the setbacks and reverses of 1655 seem to have caused many Royalists to lose their bearings momentarily and 'wobble' in their allegiance.[18] Some men and women may, in a general, abstract sense, or a purely emotional way, have wished for the return of the king beyond the seas, but it is not entirely clear that this cultural inclination or sensibility constitutes royalism. This falling-away from loyalty may mean that it is necessary, even if only for parts of the decade, to consider some people as royal*ish* or loyal*ish* rather than Royalist or Loyalist.

The second problem is that the main characteristic of royalism which the collection demonstrates is its extreme variability: it represented a spectrum of different beliefs and attitudes rather than a monolithic ideology. Although this is a valuable finding in itself, a careless reader (or reviewer) might form the impression that the subject has thereby lost coherence, and been turned into a ragbag of inchoate individual and factional experiences with little in common, about which correspondingly little can be said overall. It would be a pity if, in suggesting the complexity of the phenomenon under review, pointing out the problems with the simplistic model of 'absolutism' versus 'constitutionalism', and trying to look beyond the obsession with court factions which has so bedevilled studies of royalism, some readers form the mistaken impression that we are suggesting that the many hundreds of thousands of Royalists in Britain and Ireland during the 1650s had nothing in common. There evidently were things which bound these people together, and they clearly did find it possible to recognise each other, or, at the very least, recognise that other former subjects of the Crown were classified by the new regime as 'Royalists'. If nothing else, Royalists were bound together by the fact that their opponents viewed them as a separate group, but there was obviously much more to royalism than this: it would be unfortunate to fall back upon the hoary, rather simplistic notion of identity as being defined simply as being different from, or opposed to, some negative 'other'. We point out the nuances of the situation not to suggest that nothing can be done to elucidate the exact contours of the Royalist experience during the 1650s, but rather to put scholars on their guard about the intellectual rigour and sophistication with which they will need to tackle this problem over the coming years.

One of the most valuable aspects of the essays that follow is surely their willingness to consider new types of Royalists in a range of different social and geographical settings, not just the members of the exiled court or those actively engaged in conspiracy in England. This might well be extended further, not least by developing a sharper sense of regional diversity within Royalist studies. It would be useful to know how far the fate of individual Royalists depended on the sympathies of their neighbours, and to what extent their experiences varied between former Royalist and former Parliamentarian areas. We know that after 1660 the fate of Protestant nonconformists often depended on the zeal of local magistrates in enforcing the Clarendon Code; in an earlier era, much the same was true in determining whether Elizabethan and early Stuart Catholics fell foul of the laws against recusants. A similar sensitivity to regional variation would undoubtedly help to provide a more accurate impression of the Royalist experience during the 1650s in general, and during the rule of the Major-Generals from 1655 to 1657 in particular.

If regional studies draw us back to a methodology which was very much in vogue among students of Parliament and its armies in the 1970s and 1980s, how might the study of royalism in the 1650s benefit from the use of three methodologies that have developed rapidly over the past decade: Atlantic history, print-culture and gender history? Atlantic history is undoubtedly a fruitful area of research which opens up new perspectives on a variety of themes.[19] Yet, intriguingly, the examination of royalism in the American colonies reveals some of the shortcomings of Atlantic history as it is currently practised. In particular, it is clear that there has been a marked tendency among scholars to concentrate on Puritans, Parliamentarians and the New England colonies. The history of colonial America is, even now, too often presented as part of an on-going struggle for religious and political liberty that culminated in the revolution of 1776. The experience of Virginia and the other Royalist colonies in 1649 and 1650 may help to correct the distorting effects of this teleological, Whiggish 'high road to independence'. There was, as Brendan McConville has recently shown, nothing innately anti-monarchical about American culture in the two centuries before 1776, just as there was nothing inevitable or pre-ordained about the separation of the thirteen colonies from Britain even during the complex events which have subsequently been categorised as the American Revolution.[20] In other words, scholars of the English Revolution who focus solely on those in America who were sympathetic to the creation of a republic in 1649 risk creating a misleading picture of the society they purport to describe. They also risk falling into a Whiggish historical discourse which has not been acceptable in a British context for almost fifty years.

It was not so long ago that scholars of early modern Britain looked down on printed items in favour of manuscript sources. Print, it was often argued, was open to distortion and, if it was used at all, it was handled with evident disdain or distaste. Nowadays, such a view seems antediluvian. The past two decades have seen the publication of a number of important works on print-culture, and it is no great exaggeration to say that some of the most exciting work in the field of early modern British history and literary studies has been focused on this area.[21] By contrast, scholars of royalism have traditionally either ignored print-culture or confined themselves to the study of the *Eikon Basilike* and the mysterious, magical process by which it supposedly brought about the Restoration of the monarchy eleven years after it was first printed.[22] A number of essays in this volume use careful, nuanced readings of printed sources to shed new light on aspects of the Royalist experience, and are therefore extremely welcome additions to our understanding of the field. There is much that we do not yet know about Royalist print-culture, and research in this area will necessarily shed new light not merely on royalism itself, but on the role and function of print in society more generally. Such work may help to prise scholars away from Whiggish assumptions about print as an agent of social change, innovation and revolution.

This research will be greatly assisted by electronic platforms such as Early English Books Online (EEBO), but the easy availability of such material is not without its attendant problems. Its very accessibility can encourage a reliance on printed sources to the detriment of manuscript material, and this can cause distortions in the process of historical reconstruction. EEBO can create a beguiling impression of completeness when in fact printed items in this period were subject to a terrifyingly high, but unverifiable, rate of destruction. Nor was this destruction arbitrary: there appears to have been a relationship between price and survival rate, with more expensive items being significantly more likely to be preserved than cheaper ones. This in turn has direct implications for the nature and status of the surviving sources that scholars have available to them.[23]

It is important to stress that print does not necessarily give a 'true' or 'better' picture of royalism than other sources. It *can* empower us to ask new and different types of questions about the past, but the conceptualisation of print-culture by early-modernists has sometimes been simplistic and problematic. One might say that the study of print has sometimes resembled the characteristics of the physical pages it seeks to analyse: two-dimensional, flat and lacking depth. It has become too common for scholars to examine texts in isolation from the society in which they circulated: a process which can and does create a distorted, inaccurate account of the past. When one considers the methodological sophistication of scholars who work on manuscript records of court cases and legal interrogations, one can see that scholars interested in the study of print and print-culture need to think long and hard about developing tools which will allow them to calibrate, or filter out, the distortions that can be caused by both the injudicious use of printed texts themselves and the electronic platforms through which we increasingly access these texts.[24]

Another area of methodological innovation that is only belatedly being applied to royalism is gender history. Until very recently, one could have been forgiven for thinking that, apart from Queen Henrietta Maria, there were no female Royalists. We know much more about the role of women who were sympathetic to Parliament and the republic,[25] and it is therefore refreshing to see Ann Hughes and Julie Sanders undertaking research on Royalist women. Hughes and Sanders draw out the crucial role that women played as intermediaries, patrons and activists. This study is both important and innovative, but for some readers it may raise the question as to whether gender history in this context is merely a new way of 'doing' the history of the court and the Royalist elite. Can gender history illuminate the lives and experiences of less exalted Royalist women? If gender history becomes a sub-discipline of court history and is decoupled from the progressive agenda which motivated those who first developed the methodology, does it thereby lose its key strengths and importance? Some historians of popular politics may well feel that they, rather than gender historians, are the best qualified to recreate the lives and experiences of lowly female Royalists.

This last question leads us to an important point about a term used in a number of essays in this volume: 'popular' royalism. Some readers may wonder what exactly 'popular' signifies: a large percentage, perhaps a majority, of the general populace, or merely those at the bottom of the social hierarchy? Are the terms 'popular' and 'ordinary' – another term invoked in a number of essays in this book without any attempt to define its meaning – synonymous, as a number of authors seem to suggest? If 'popular politics' seems at times like a loose, vague and amorphous term, then perhaps it is necessary to understand that the concept of 'popular' politics was deliberately developed as a usefully loose, vague and amorphous idea by Communist parties throughout Europe during their 'Popular Front' strategy of the 1930s. The 'Popular Front' was designed to allow Communist parties to fight against fascism alongside a variety of middle-class and working-class groups which they had previously castigated as 'bourgeois reactionaries', 'petit-bourgeois dilettantes' or 'social fascists'. Communist Party cadres were encouraged not to think too hard about the contradictions, absurdities and obfuscations of 'popular' politics during the 1930s, but one may wonder whether, at the beginning of the twenty-first century, it is necessary to be much more systematic in defining the parameters of 'popular' politics. This may be particularly true in the context of the study of royalism during the English Revolution because there is a danger of erecting a simplistic dichotomy between 'elite' and 'popular', whereas much recent work on royalism has been at pains to argue against the use of dichotomous models in favour of a broader, richer and more colourful spectrum of gradations within royalism. Scholars need to think much more systematically about the range and diversity of positions and experiences which are subsumed within, and hidden by, the catch-all phrase 'popular royalism'.

Much further research is likewise needed on the extent to which Royalists were willing and able to reach some kind of accommodation with the republican regimes. One of the most interesting findings of this volume is the frequency with which such an accommodation was arrived at: we will encounter it in cases as different as many of the clergy, including Peter Heylyn, and the antiquarian William Dugdale. It appears to have been a very common and understandable strategy, and one that the Interregnum regimes were generally willing to accept and even encourage. It is important to try to get inside the mindset of Royalists during the 1650s, when they could not have known that the monarchy would be restored in 1660 and when the republic often appeared to be very firmly established. For many Royalists, to co-operate with the prevailing regime at such a time must have seemed to be the most – perhaps the only – sensible course of action. Yet how can one distinguish between co-operation, occasional, tactical collaboration and total capitulation? Did any Royalists make such distinctions at the time, or might it be argued that in so doing we in danger of inventing anachronistic and misleading categories?

Royalist correspondence in the year before the Restoration often reads rather like Lenin's lecture to young workers in the Zürich People's House in January 1917 when he observed that 'we of the older generation may not live to see the decisive battles of this coming revolution'.[26] Royalists in 1659 and early 1660 were often similarly pessimistic. Edward Hyde, for example, lamented in January 1659 that the Royalists had 'not yett founde that advantage by Cromwell's death as [they] reasonably hoped for'. If anything, they were 'the worse for it, and the lesse esteemed, people imagininge by the greate calme that hath followed, that the nacon is united, and that in truth the Kinge hath very few frends'.[27] The disastrous failure of Booth's Rebellion in August 1659 only seemed to confirm that a restoration of the monarchy was as far away as ever.[28]

That pessimism, when combined with the willingness of some to reach an accommodation with the London regimes, raises the question of the extent to which it was possible or necessary for some people to reinvent themselves as Royalists at the Restoration. If so many Royalists were willing to compromise, co-operate or collaborate with the Interregnum regimes, and felt pessimistic until a very late stage about the chances of a monarchical restoration, how far did they then have to adapt again when Charles II returned in 1660? Indeed, the stridency of the writings at the Restoration of men as different as John Crouch and Peter Heylyn may owe more than we have hitherto realised to their discomfort at the less than heroic paths they had followed during the 1650s. In this context, the traditional image of Royalists waiting patiently throughout the Interregnum for the tide to turn in their favour is obviously a fabrication which owes more to the changed politics of the early 1660s than to the realities of the 1650s.[29] This point raises one final intriguing, but unanswerable, problem: what might have happened to the broad, variegated and fractured identity of 'royalism' if the Rump or the army had somehow managed to hang on to power for another ten, twenty or fifty years?[30] In such circumstances, apart from a small number of die-hard zealots, would royalism have degenerated into nothing more than an occasional cultural pose or affectation? This question is an important reminder of the role of the contingent in shaping political allegiance and behaviour, and, in this regard, scholars of Royalist culture during the English Revolution might profit enormously from a familiarity with the historiography of Jacobitism in the eighteenth century. We might also learn much from the recent historiography of the sixteenth-century Reformation in England. This suggestion may sound outlandish to scholars who are uncomfortable working outside their own short period of chronological time, but the rich corpus of work on the English Reformation in effect traces the processes by which a series of contingent, piecemeal and potentially reversible reforms eventually brought about a fundamental shift in the innermost thoughts and religious identity of millions of Englishmen and women in the half-century or so after the 1534 Act of Supremacy.

The very diversity of Royalist experiences during the Interregnum ensured that when Charles II returned to England his followers were scattered along a wide spectrum of attitudes and beliefs. This must surely have had profound implications – more than has often been appreciated – for the nature of the Restoration Settlement and the politics of the 1660s. Several of the essays in this book conclude by looking ahead to the Restoration and connecting the Royalist experience during the Interregnum to the period that followed. Just as we cannot understand royalism in the 1650s other than in the context of the Civil Wars and the Regicide, so it is equally essential to understand its implications for the years after 1660. Near the beginning of this introduction we quoted Ronald Hutton's telling comment that 'the 1650s have always lacked an appeal for historians of both the preceding and succeeding ages, seeming to belong neither to one nor the other'.[31] We hope that the following essays will help to demonstrate that the 1650s, far from belonging to neither the preceding nor the succeeding ages, were in fact deeply connected to both, and that for none was this more profoundly true than those men and women who identified themselves as Royalists and longed for the return of the Stuarts to power. Their story, in all its rich variety, is the subject of this book.

NOTES

1 Paul H. Hardacre, *The Royalists during the Puritan Revolution* (The Hague, 1956).

2 C.H. Firth, 'The Royalists under the Protectorate', *EHR*, 52 (1937), pp. 634–48.

3 J.S. Morrill, *Seventeenth-Century Britain, 1603–1714* (Folkestone, 1980), p. 43.

4 David Underdown, *Royalist Conspiracy in England, 1649–1660* (New Haven, CT, 1960).

5 Morrill, *Seventeenth-Century Britain*, p. 43.

6 Underdown, *Royalist Conspiracy*, p. x.

7 For the conceptual and methodological problems associated with the use of the term 'radical' in the mid-seventeenth century see Glenn Burgess and Matthew Festenstein (eds), *English Radicalism, 1550–1850* (Cambridge, 2007), pp. 1–12, 62–81, 218–35, 313–31.

8 Geoffrey Smith, *The Cavaliers in Exile, 1640–1660* (Basingstoke, 2003).

9 Anthony Cotton, 'London newsbooks in the Civil War: their political attitudes and sources of information' (DPhil dissertation, University of Oxford, 1971), p. 33.

10 Ronald Hutton, review of Patrick Little (ed.), *The Cromwellian Protectorate* (Woodbridge, 2007), in *Cromwelliana*, 2nd series, 5 (2008), p. 110.

11 See, in particular, Little (ed.), *Cromwellian Protectorate*; and Patrick Little and David L. Smith, *Parliaments and Politics during the Cromwellian Protectorate* (Cambridge, 2007).

12 See Jason McElligott and David L. Smith (eds), *Royalists and Royalism during the English Civil Wars* (Cambridge, 2007), pp. 1–13; and Jason McElligott, *Royalism, Print and Censorship in Revolutionary England* (Woodbridge, 2007), pp. 1–20.

13 See also McElligott, *Royalism, Print and Censorship*, chapters 6–8.

14 Perhaps most fully in Earl Miner, *The Cavalier Mode from Jonson to Cotton* (Princeton, NJ, 1971), chapter 6; and Robert Wilcher, *The Writing of Royalism, 1628–1660* (Cambridge, 2001), chapter 12. See also Joshua Scodel, 'Alternative sites for literature', in David Loewenstein and Janel Mueller (eds), *The Cambridge History of Early Modern English Literature* (Cambridge, 2002), pp. 763–89.

15 McElligott and Smith (eds), *Royalists and Royalism*, pp. 1–12.

16 In the light of these questions, the editors would like to make clear that we believe that our definition of royalism is as useful for the 1650s as it is for the 1640s. We do, however, think that there is more scope for differentiating between royalism and loyalism in the 1650s.

17 John Crouch provides the obvious example of this process. See Jason McElligott, 'John Crouch: a Royalist journalist in Cromwellian England', *Media History*, 10:3 (2004), pp. 139–55.

18 Royalists as diverse as John Crouch, John Cleveland and Bruno Ryves came to terms with the Protector at this time. For Crouch see *ibid.* For Cleveland's petition to Oliver Cromwell see CUL, Add. MS 79, fols 24–6. For Bruno Ryves's correspondence with Cromwell see Donald F. McKenzie and Maureen Bell (eds), *A Chronology and Calendar of Documents Relating to the London Book Trade 1641–1700*, 3 vols (Oxford, 2005), vol. I, pp. 371, 375.

19 For an excellent overview of recent work in this area, see David Armitage and Michael J. Braddick (eds), *The British Atlantic World, 1500–1800* (Basingstoke, 2002).

20 Brendan McConville, *The King's Three Faces: The Rise and Fall of Royal America, 1688–1776* (Chapel Hill, NC, 2006).

21 See, for example, Adam Fox, *Oral and Literate Culture in England, 1500–1700* (Oxford, 2000); Joad Raymond, *The Invention of the Newspaper: English Newsbooks, 1641–49* (Oxford, 1996); Joad Raymond, *Pamphlets and Pamphleteering in Early-Modern Britain* (Cambridge, 2003); Mark Knights, *Representation and Misrepresentation in Later Stuart Britain: Partisanship and Political Culture* (Oxford, 2005); and William St Clair, *The Reading Nation in the Romantic Period* (Cambridge, 2004).

22 See, for example, Elizabeth Sauer, *'Paper-Contestations' and Textual Communities in England, 1640–1675* (Toronto, 2005), p. 71.

23 See Jason McElligott, 'The perils of print culture: Habermas, EEBO, and the I-generation' (forthcoming).

24 See Jason McElligott, 'Calibrating early-modern print culture' (forthcoming).

25 See, for example, Patricia Crawford, *Women and Religion in England, 1500–1720* (1993); Anne Laurence, *Women in England, 1500–1760: A Social History* (1994); and Anthony Fletcher, *Gender, Sex and Subordination in England, 1500–1800* (New Haven, CT, 1995).

26 *Collected Works of V.I. Lenin*, vol. XXIII (Moscow, 1964), pp. 236–53.

27 Bodl., Clarendon MS 59, fol. 417r (Hyde to [William Howard], 12 Jan. 1658/59).

28 On Booth's Rebellion, see Underdown, *Royalist Conspiracy*, pp. 254–85; and J.S. Morrill, *Cheshire, 1630–1660: County Government and Society during the English Revolution* (Oxford, 1974), pp. 300–25. For Hyde's pessimism in the months before the Restoration see *CHR*, vol. VI, pp. 163, 164.

29 The Royalist clergyman Anthony Sadler may be an illuminating case-study in this regard. His 1654 pamphlet *Inquisitio Anglicana* – which, incidentally, was printed and published by the strident Royalists John Grismond and Richard Royston – contains suitably humble petitions to 'his Highness The Lord Protector' and 'the high Court of Parliament' (sigs A2r, A3r). There was obviously no mention of this fact in Sadler's output immediately after the Restoration, which included the broadside *Maiestie Irradiant, Or The Splendor Display'd, of Our Soveraigne King Charles* and the quarto pamphlets *The Subjects Joy for The Kings Restoration* and the lengthy *The Loyall Mourner, Shewing the Murdering of King Charles the First*. Sadler even went so far as to claim that although *The Loyall Mourner* was published only in 1660 it had been written in the immediate aftermath of the Regicide. This may or may not have been true, but there seems little doubt that in 1660 Sadler was trying to erase any lingering memories of what he might have said and done during the mid-1650s.

30 It is arguable that the army and the Parliament might not have engaged in such suicidal internecine conflict during 1659 if they had actually feared the Royalists and believed for a moment that a Restoration was possible. Strange as it may seem, then, one could say that the Royalists were returned to power in 1660 precisely because they were so weak, ineffectual and unthreatening.

31 Ronald Hutton, review of Little (ed.), *The Cromwellian Protectorate*, p. 110.

Chapter 2

Episcopalian conformity and nonconformity 1646–60

Kenneth Fincham and Stephen Taylor

I

In 1655 Gibson Lucas, a Suffolk JP, chose to renounce his Presbyterian allegiance and be ordained by Bishop Joseph Hall, the former bishop of Norwich. Illegal episcopal ordinations were common enough in the 1650s, but Lucas's ordination is significant because we know that Hall was assisted in performing the ordination by Robert Cocke, minister of Deopham, and John Whitefoot, rector of Heigham, both conformists in the Cromwellian state church.[1] We can find other examples of such co-operation between an ousted bishop and conformist clergy in the period,[2] which raise a series of intriguing questions. Why did ministers such as Whitefoote and Cocke defy the law and assist Hall in the laying on of hands? How skin-deep was their conformity to the church of the Protectorate, and did they still owe Hall obedience as their diocesan? Were they in internal exile, serving their parishioners but praying for the restoration of the old order of episcopal government and a prayer book liturgy? Just what sort of episcopalians were they?

Such questions fit awkwardly with the dominant image of episcopalians during this period as hardline nonconformists.[3] By 1646, episcopalianism had been proscribed, with the abolition of bishops, the church courts and the Book of Common Prayer. Some episcopalians – John Cosin, George Morley, Richard Steward – followed the royal court abroad, where they were largely dependent on the charity of wealthy sympathisers. Those who remained in England refused to recognise the revolutionary regimes, especially after the execution of the king. Instead they survived, as Bishop Duppa put it, like the primitive Christians, as a persecuted church, 'in dens, and caves, and deserts'.[4] What this seems to have meant in practice is that they eked out an existence as tutors and chaplains in the houses of sympathetic gentry, or perhaps on revenues that had been saved from sequestration. However, episcopalianism did not remain frozen in aspic during these years. On the contrary, as Robert

Bosher and others have revealed, exile and persecution stimulated a dynamic movement, which reinvigorated episcopalianism and contributed not a little to the character of what later generations came to call Anglicanism. The apostolic status of bishops was defended against attacks from both Presbyterians and the Roman Catholic Church, while a number of writers, led by Henry Hammond, Jeremy Taylor and Richard Allestree, produced a body of popular, practical divinity that gave a distinctive shape to episcopalian piety in the Restoration and beyond. In these works we find the basis of a theological method that emphasised moderation and rationality, an abandonment of aggressive clericalism, and a more erastian outlook; all contributed to what one historian has described as the 'transformation of Anglicanism'.[5] But if it is possible to detect signs of growing theological moderation, the political position of these divines was uncompromisingly Royalist. For men in England like Gilbert Sheldon, Henry Hammond, Humphrey Henchman and the young William Sancroft, for those abroad like John Cosin and George Morley, and for those who acted as intermediaries like John Barwick and Richard Allestree, there could be no compromise with the regicides, with the 'usurper', as Cromwell was sometimes called, or with any of the regimes that came to power following the execution of Charles I. The only legitimate ruler of the country, and the head of the church, was his successor Charles II.

It has long been recognised that this is not the whole story. As John Spurr has noted, despite successive purges in the 1640s and 1650s perhaps three-quarters of all parochial ministers retained their benefices or were able to re-enter the ministry until removed by death or saved by the Restoration.[6] Most clergymen thus accommodated themselves, more or less willingly, to successive regimes. Some embraced the opportunities for further reform, but many remained episcopalians. Of these, some were, in Bosher's phrase, 'loyal "conformists"', who had a preference for 'the old Episcopacy' but felt able to participate fully in the religious life of the nation. Others were 'disaffected conformists', who observed the restrictions on Anglican worship only so far as they were compelled to do so.[7] As Spurr notes, 'the claim of the "sufferers" to embody the Church of England does not stand up to scrutiny'.[8] Even Bosher admits, albeit in a footnote, that 'it would be misleading ... to suggest that the history of the Church of England during the Interregnum can be written exclusively in terms of this minority'.[9] However, these insights have never been systematically explored. It is still tempting to dismiss those clergy who held on to their livings through successive changes of regime as timeservers, prepared to sacrifice whatever convictions they had to preserve their income or, perhaps, forced to do so by their responsibilities to a wife and children. Bosher makes it clear that the minority, the nonconformist hardliners, was the only group that mattered. Episcopalianism as a whole was disorganised, lacking leadership and solidarity. The void was filled by the hardliners, and therefore 'the study of Anglican policy can be confined ... to the views of this party'.[10]

It cannot be denied that there is something to be said for this perspective. First, episcopalian networks at the exiled court focused on the Sheldon–Hammond group in England and the wider networks of which they were the centre; in the eyes of the court that group was the leadership of *the* church in England. Second, Hammond was widely regarded as *the* leading episcopalian in scholarly debate during the 1650s; his views were key in the formulation of episcopalian doctrine. Third, many of the principal charitable benefactors were drawn from fairly uncompromising nonconformists. Fourth, the propaganda of the Commonwealth and Protectorate appeared to characterise all episcopalians as subversive, as malcontents, as Royalists – nowhere was this clearer than in Cromwell's proclamation of November 1655 prohibiting those 'sequestered, or ejected' from teaching in schools or serving as chaplains in gentry households. Finally, it was the hardliners, the 'sufferers', who emerged triumphant to lead the church after the Restoration. This is not to say that conformists were excluded after 1660; many, indeed, can be found even among the episcopate. But for over two decades the key voices in the formulation of the church's policy were Sheldon, Henchman, Morley and Sancroft.

At the same time, we should be conscious of how our understanding of Interregnum episcopalianism has been shaped by the accidents of source survival. Exceptionally rich sources have survived for the hardliners – principally the voluminous correspondence of Sheldon and Hammond, which is complemented by materials in the Clarendon manuscripts in the Bodleian and John Barwick's published letters. Even richer are the Sancroft papers, dispersed across various archives but principally to be found among the Tanner manuscripts in the Bodleian. The only extensive episcopal correspondence to have survived is that of Brian Duppa, the bishop closest to Sheldon and Hammond. By contrast, many other bishops have left almost no mark on the sources. In particular, there are no personal papers for Henry Tilson, Robert Maxwell and Robert Skinner, the three conformist bishops who were also most active in illegally ordaining clergy during these years. The first two are not even mentioned in the correspondence of the hardliners; Skinner receives only a couple of dismissive references.[11] As a result they have also been largely ignored by historians. In the *Oxford DNB* Skinner's ministry in the 1640s and 1650s receives only a paragraph, while Maxwell and Tilson do not even merit entries.

It should be emphasised at the outset that the purpose of this chapter is not to deny the significance of the nonconformist hardliners. The Sheldon-Hammond network played a key role in sustaining a strand of episcopalianism that was uncompromisingly Royalist, but was also adaptive enough to play a major part in the formation of Restoration Anglicanism. Rather, the prime aim of this chapter is to draw attention to the strength and vitality, and also some of the complexities, of episcopalian conformity, a strand of Interregnum religious belief and practice that has hitherto been neglected; nonconformity will be reconsidered through the prism of conformity. The first section of what follows will explore some of the ways in which episcopalians negotiated conformity in the years after the abolition of bishops and the execution of the king, revealing, *inter alia*, the often fine line that many of them trod between conformity and nonconformity. In the second section we shall, through a discussion of the evidence for episcopal ordination, reveal the extent of the practice and examine some of the meanings attached to it by the bishops and clergy involved, many of whom, despite their involvement in this act of nonconformity, conformed to the state church in the later 1640s and 1650s.

II

The principled nonconformity practised by figures such as Sheldon and Hammond was only one response to the 'broken times' of the later 1640s and the 1650s. Much more common were degrees of engagement with the post-episcopal state church and the successive regimes which sustained it, which drew episcopalians into a variety of roles and networks. It is clear that only a minority of clergy, certainly less than 25 per cent, were ejected from their parish livings in the 1640s and 1650s. The vast majority of those appointed before 1640 continued to serve in their benefices, and were joined by numerous sequestered ministers who were able to find re-employment in the church, as well as by most of those clandestinely ordained by bishops after the abolition of episcopacy in 1646.[12]

Why did so many clergy choose to conform? It is too easy to brand them as mere temporisers, vicars of Bray anxious to retain their status and their income, and here we should reflect on the sophisticated scholarship concerning conformity in the Tudor Reformation, which has demonstrated the complex pressures encouraging accommodation on a ministry facing religious upheaval, and the considerable space that existed between ejection and unfeigned compliance.[13] We should not lightly discount an episcopalian minister's sense of his obligation to his parishioners, his attachment to the powerful notion of service in a national church and his acceptance of the doctrinal orthodoxy of Presbyterianism, all of which encouraged conformity. Edward Rainbow, ejected master of Magdalene College, Cambridge, and future bishop of Carlisle, served in two parish livings in the 1650s, conscious of 'the generall duty which I owe to the Church of God, to which I am too great a debtor'.[14] Thomas Fuller wrote in 1654 that though he would have preferred to serve under episcopacy, he could accept the Presbyterian discipline as 'sound and perfect in all essentials necessarie to salvation', and therefore soldiered on in the parochial ministry.[15] In any case, outward conformity did not usually come at too high a price in the 1650s. The commission for 'triers' did act as gatekeepers to the parochial ministry, and the 'ejectors' could investigate accusations of flagrant nonconformity or misconduct, but the suppression of the church courts had ended the regular external scrutiny of parish religion. The formal oaths of conformity, such as the Engagement of 1650 recognising the legitimacy of the republic, were only fitfully imposed; and although the prayer book was officially proscribed, its replacement *The Directory for Public Worship* permitted a good deal of latitude in worship.

As a result, many serving clergy in the 1650s were able to combine loyalty to the old order with service in the new. Nathaniel Hardy had abandoned his Presbyterian views after hearing Hammond's defence of episcopacy at the Uxbridge negotiations in 1645, but retained a living in the City of London, was an active member in the Fourth Presbyterian Classis there between 1646 and 1651, and became a celebrated preacher of set-piece sermons in the 1650s. He was an enthusiastic supporter of the Restoration, and was rewarded with the deanery of Rochester.[16] The traditionalist instincts of some parochial clergy are well illustrated by the occasion in 1657 when John Beale attempted to introduce into Herefordshire a version of Richard Baxter's Worcestershire Association of moderately minded ministers, only to encounter a group of irredeemably episcopalian clergy

> Far infected with the old ulcer and soe wholly engaged to all the old formes that they must bee for all at once or for noe government or discipline at all: and these did soon become the overwhelming party ... the old episcopacy was their claime, as *jure divino*.

So influential was this group that Beale had to abandon, temporarily, his plans to create a Herefordshire Association.[17]

Among episcopalian conformists were several prominent bishops and theologians. Robert Skinner, bishop of Oxford, was sequestered from two livings but remained rector of Launton, Oxfordshire, and was the only bishop to retain a benefice throughout the 1640s and 1650s, which suggests that he may have cut a deal with the parliamentary authorities after the fall of Oxford in 1646.[18] His colleague Ralph Brownrigg, bishop of Exeter, turned down several offers of preferment in the 1650s, including the cure of the parish of St Gregory-by-St Paul's in London, a centre of prayer book worship, usually pleading ill-health, although he did spend much of the 1650s travelling regularly between Berkshire, London, Hertfordshire and Suffolk. However, in March 1659 Brownrigg agreed to become preacher at the Temple in London, perhaps sensing a turning of the tide following the death of Oliver Cromwell. It was to be a brief tenure, since Brownrigg died in December 1659, but there was time enough for him to receive financial support from the state, with a grant of £20 'for his releife' from the trustees for the maintenance of ministers.[19] Another conformist was Robert Sanderson, a distinguished casuist and future bishop of Lincoln, who lost his Regius Professorship at Oxford in 1648 and retired to his living of Boothby Pagnell in Lincolnshire. His experience in the 1650s shows how conformity was not an event so much as a protracted process, requiring constant negotiation and interpretation. Sanderson wrote publicly against the Engagement, although privately he made the case that under certain circumstances it was permissible to take the oath. A little later, in 1652, Sanderson advised a clergyman that he might put aside the prayer book in parish worship, while retaining its substance, so that 'the very same words and phrases' could be 'purposely transplaced, that it might appear not to be, and yet to be the same'. His opinion was widely circulated, and split noncon-formist episcopalians, finding supporters such as Duppa as well as opponents such as Hammond and Thorndike.[20] In 1653 Sanderson and others 'of the old stamp' were invited to join the combination lecture at nearby Grantham, an invitation which put the character of his own conformity under the spotlight. Sanderson's assent was necessary for the project to succeed, and while he did not wish to be blamed for blocking it, he was concerned at the scandal that his public association with Presbyterians and others might provoke. His intimate friend, Henry Hammond, saw not just scandal but real damage to episcopa-lianism. He wrote in alarm to Sheldon, noting that the lecture had not been authorised by the local bishop (who was still alive) and warning that Sander-son's participation would play into the hands of 'moderate reformable Pres-byterians' who were intent on perpetuating their own church government, as well as making schism harder, not easier, to solve. Under pressure, Sanderson agreed to decline the invitation.[21]

Other episcopalians were far bolder than Sanderson, and engaged in public or private dialogue with moderate Presbyterians and Independents. Brownrigg, as a renowned Calvinist, a former critic of Laudianism and a relation through marriage to John Pym, was a natural target for those inter-ested in pursuing Protestant unity. Early in 1652 Brownrigg agreed to attend a meeting with Presbyterians and Independents to explore common ground between them, and complained of 'our hypercriticall censurers' who made 'very scornful construction' of these discussions, a reference to Hammond and his circle, among others; but in the event, these talks quickly ran into the sands.[22] They were revived in 1654–55 by Richard Baxter, who had been in contact with Archbishop Ussher of Armagh, and the two had agreed (or so Baxter would later boast) within thirty minutes on the outline of a settlement, based on Ussher's model of reduced episcopacy which he had first devised in 1641. Baxter and Brownrigg exchanged letters, but negotiations stalled when Brownrigg objected to the proposal to deprive the bishop of a negative voice in ordination and excommunication, which in Brownrigg's view would make him 'a mere shadow'. From Baxter's perspective, things looked rather different: 'I found him [Brownrigg] too tenacious of the titular honours of the bishops ... [so] I wrote to him no more'.[23]

Another proponent of Protestant unity was John Gauden, whose career encapsulates many of the ideological complexities of the 1640s and 1650s. He had strong Puritan and Parliamentarian connections, as domestic chaplain to Robert Rich, second Earl of Warwick, the principal patron of godly clergy of Essex and a key opponent of Charles I. Through Warwick's influence Gauden acquired the rich deanery of Bocking in the early 1640s, and probably took the Solemn League and Covenant. But he was also a committed Royalist, protesting at the trial of Charles I and writing parts of *Eikon Basilike*, the king's political and religious meditations, for which he was rewarded with a bishopric at the Restoration.[24] The activities of the sects seem to have driven Gauden towards espousing a form of moderate episcopacy, influenced by Ussher's proposals of 1641, and in 1659 he preached Brownrigg's funeral sermon, holding him up as an exemplar of a 'primitive prelate'. Earlier, in 1656, Gauden had taken soundings from Presbyterians, Independents and episcopalians in London and Essex in the hope of achieving a 'fraternall harmony and union'. He found that 'the animosityes and distances of the episcopal and Presbyterian parties [have] much abated' and, via Nicholas Bernard, one of Cromwell's chaplains, had his findings forwarded to Secretary of State John Thurloe, no doubt to inform if not influence the Lord Protector himself.[25]

This was one of several forays by Gauden into the public arena. In 1653 he published a defence of tithes which was addressed to the members of the committee of the Barebone's Parliament which was reviewing the maintenance of the ministry. The following year he publicly urged MPs in the First Protectorate Parliament to reinstate marriage in church, which the Barebone's Parliament had abolished. In February 1656 he privately lobbied Cromwell to rescind his ban of November 1655 on sequestered ministers being employed as ministers, chaplains and schoolmasters. Archbishop Ussher came out of retirement to plead the same cause, but Cromwell was not to be moved.[26]

Other episcopalians also tried to influence Cromwell. Godfrey Goodman, bishop of Gloucester, dedicated his *Two great mysteries of the Christian religion* (1653) to 'his excellency, my Lord Oliv: Cromwell', and urged him to protect orthodox doctrine against Socinianism, filling the gap once supplied by bishops. Goodman rather spoiled his case, however, by drawing Cromwell's attention to the restoration of the font at St Margaret's, Westminster, which he hoped others would imitate, and praising the revival of the observation of holy days.[27] No less a figure than Peter Heylyn, the doyen among Laudian polemicists, wrote a manuscript foreword to Cromwell in his *Ecclesia Vindicata* (1657), in which he proposed the re-establishment of episcopacy as the best means to place civil peace on a sure foundation. Here was an attachment to episcopacy which, temporarily at least, outran Heylyn's royalism.[28]

The acceptance of office and involvement in public affairs should not conceal the nonconformity also practised by some of these episcopalians. Both Brownrigg and Skinner, as we shall see, ignored the ban on episcopal ordinations and regularly conferred orders; Brownrigg appears to have observed the prayer book, baptising and marrying according to its rites, while Skinner later claimed that he continued to confirm the young throughout the 1650s.[29] Both, in turn, provoked some sharp criticism from more hardline episcopalians. They were seen as impeding moves in 1659 to preserve the apostolic order of episcopacy by consecrating new bishops – possibly because such an act might jeopardise their position in the state church. John Barwick, ardent Royalist and episcopalian, condemned what he called Brownrigg's 'mistaken principle of peaceablenesse', while Edward Hyde noted in 1660 that the bishop's reputation had suffered for 'not being zealous enough for the church'.[30] There is an interesting difference, however, in the range of contacts that Skinner and Brownrigg maintained in the 1650s. Skinner seems to have cut his links, or had them severed, with the Hammond–Sheldon circle as well as with the Royalist court in exile; Brownrigg, on the other hand, was an intimate friend of William Sancroft, an unbending episcopalian, ousted from Cambridge University in 1651 for refusing the Engagement, and praised by John Cosin, writing in exile from Paris in 1657, for 'how firme and unmov'd you continue your owne standing in the midst of these great and violent stormes that are now raised against the church of England'. Brownrigg was no more successful than others who tried to entice Sancroft into chaplaincies or incumbencies in the church, but through Sancroft he developed close ties with a number of episcopalian nonconformists, among them the Gayer brothers of Stoke Poges, Buckinghamshire, and their household chaplain, George Davenport.[31]

The laity, too, could practise a rather similar mix of outward conformity and private nonconformity. John Evelyn is often, and rightly, cited as a devout episcopalian and Royalist. His father-in-law, Richard Browne, provided space in the early 1650s in his Parisian house for the chapel royal in exile, where Evelyn himself worshipped in 1650–52. The chapel retained an altar, to which celebrants bowed, and the prayer book was followed in all its detail. On his return to England in 1652 Evelyn became an active member of a London episcopalian fraternity which met first publicly in churches such as St Gregory-by-St Paul's and St Mary Magdalen, Milk Street and, increasingly after Cromwell's proclamation of 1655, in private houses. There the fraternity used the prayer book in worship, and heard sermons from ejected luminaries such as Jeremy Taylor and Peter Gunning, the latter preaching on such Laudian themes as the resistibility of divine grace and the propriety of imagery in churches. Taylor, indeed, became Evelyn's 'ghostly father', or spiritual adviser. In the privacy of his library at Sayes Court in Deptford, Evelyn had a local sequestered minister baptise his children, church his wife and administer holy communion to his family, all according to the Book of Common Prayer.[32]

There is another, perhaps less familiar, side to Evelyn's religious practices in the 1650s. To avoid being suspected as a Roman Catholic, he attended his local church at Deptford, which exposed him to the occasional uncomfortable service. In December 1653 he listened to 'a tradesman' and 'mechanic', the first 'phanatical preacher' he had experienced, and was not impressed with 'such truculent anabaptisticall stuff; so dangerous a crisis were things growne to'. In 1655 he heard a trooper preach, and also sat through a sermon from the chaplain to Admiral Pen, but was uncertain whether the preacher was even ordained. 'Into such times were we fallen' was Evelyn's later comment on this. Yet Evelyn's outward conformity had its spiritual benefits for a man hungry for edifying preaching. Many of the sermons at Deptford were delivered by the incumbent, Thomas Mallory, later to be ejected in 1660–62, whom Evelyn variously described as an Independent and a Presbyterian. He conceded, however, that Mallory 'ordinarily preachd sound doctrine and was a peaceable man' and kept detailed notes on his weekly sermons. Some of the visiting preachers impressed Evelyn, such as 'a very youth' who in January 1654 preached 'very well' on the necessity of regeneration, or 'Mr Pemberton', who gave 'an excellent discourse'. Moreover, Evelyn occasionally sought out celebrated preachers, such as Thomas Manton, 'the famous Presbyterian' at St Paul's, Covent Garden, who was also to be ousted in 1662.[33] For Evelyn, paradoxically, conformity in the 1650s was an opportunity for spiritual growth as well as a source of frustration and anguish.

Other episcopalian conformists found their local parish religion more to their taste, and did not have to resort so often to private services and sermons. One such was Anthony Blagrave of Bulmershe Court near Reading, whose diary for 1650–53 survives. John Spurr has given us a brief, sparkling account of Blagrave's traditional religious practices during these thoroughly untraditional times, but it is possible to investigate further Blagrave's experience and contacts.[34] He was a member of Sonning parish vestry, regularly attended church there, and rode into neighbouring Reading to hear godly sermons preached at the lecture and assizes. Crucially, the incumbent of Sonning was John Sexby, a survivor from the 1630s and a friend to Blagrave, and evidently also sympathetic to the old order. So like Evelyn, Blagrave had some rites performed at home, employing not a sequestered minister but Sexby, who conducted a baptism with godparents and the churching of his wife, both banned by *The Directory*, while his preparation sermons for holy communion may also have been privately preached at Bulmershe Court. Blagrave was also well acquainted with William Juxon, bishop of London, whose brother appears to have resided in the parish. The two went hunting together, and Juxon himself received communion at Sonning church in April 1651, which must have been according to the prayer book. In July 1652 Blagrave recorded that 'Dr Baker' preached in church – Dr Baker almost certainly being Samuel Baker, domestic chaplain to Juxon from the 1630s. Later that day 'my lord and his two chaplains' dined at Bulmershe Court, presumably a reference to Juxon, Baker and another chaplain. During the diary's brief span of three years, the incumbent John Sexby fell ill and the vestry, perhaps steered by Blagrave and like-minded episcopalians, invited a roster of visiting preachers, among them George Wilde, a leading light in Evelyn's London fraternity and once chaplain to Archbishop Laud; William Lloyd, future bishop of Coventry and Lichfield, who had been clandestinely ordained as a deacon by Bishop Skinner in 1648 and who worked as a private tutor in the area; and Richard Jaggard, John Grant and James Potter, all sequestered ministers.[35] Blagrave's and Evelyn's religious practices, in short, have points of similarity and difference. Both offered some outward conformity, but while Evelyn's nonconformist worship was covert, any sharp distinction between private nonconformity and public compliance does not apply to Blagrave, who could obtain congenial preaching, and quite probably traditional rites, within the confines of his parish church.

We have already touched on the overlapping networks of episcopalian conformists and nonconformists in the 1650s. Thus Bishop Brownrigg was drawn into the nonconformist circle of William Sancroft, and the conformist Robert Sanderson was in close contact with divines such as Hammond, Sheldon and Duppa, all of whom refused to serve in the state church.[36] This theme may be pursued further by examining charitable relief for sequestered or impoverished clergy. The operation, scale and significance of this charity have been overlooked by most historians, in large part because information about it is fragmentary, but it is possible to reconstruct something of its character and workings. Among the principal benefactors were episcopalian gentry such as Viscount Scudamore of Herefordshire, Sir Justinian Isham of Northamptonshire and Sir Robert Shirley of Leicestershire. In 1654 Shirley set up a trust for 'the good of the church' and on his death two years later bequeathed profits from impropriations and tithes to support 'orthodoxall and distressed clergie men'.[37] There were clerical benefactors too, including Bishop Godfrey Goodman and Bishop John Warner, the most munificent of all donors. Warner was the son of a London merchant and had the greatest private means among the pre-war bench of bishops, giving (on his own reckoning) £4,800 to sequestered clergy or their widows in the 1650s. Money was also raised by parishes, sometimes in response to printed appeals for support, such as that issued by Charles I's former servants in 1650.[38]

Nonconformist episcopalians bulk large in these charitable networks. The crucial figures were the intermediaries, usually nonconformists, who put donor and needy cleric in touch with each other. Scudamore used several such 'almoners', notably Jeremy Stephens, Timothy Thurscrosse and Henry Hammond, all sequestered ministers; Shirley chose Gilbert Sheldon and Hammond; while Isham often relied on his friend and correspondent Bishop Duppa of Salisbury. Sheldon, Duppa and Humphrey Henchman, future bishop of London, were solicitors to Warner on behalf of others.[39] Similarly, their prime task was to relieve ejected clergy and their dependents who were in financial difficulties, whether stationed at the royal court abroad, such as John Cosin and George Morley, or living penuriously in England. But donations were also directed to conformist ministers who were still serving in parishes but experiencing hardship through loss of one or more posts elsewhere. Among them were Henry Tilson, the elderly bishop of Elphin in Ireland, who retreated to Yorkshire, where he served the cure of Cumberworth near Huddersfield; and Anthony Farindon, who had lost a lectureship at Windsor and the vicarage of Bray, but acquired St Mary Magdalen, Milk Street, in London, which became a centre for prayer book worship.[40] Usually we can only identify the beneficiaries of this charity from their letters of thanks, such as those written by Tilson and Farindon, but in the case of Viscount Scudamore's charity there exist lists of recipients and the amounts they were given. As Ian Atherton has demonstrated, between 1652 and 1662 Scudamore paid out £1,650 to about eighty clergymen. While some were prominent figures such as Bishop Matthew Wren, a prisoner in the Tower of London throughout the 1640s and 1650s, many others were local, indeed Herefordshire, clergymen. Of the fifty who can be securely identified, at least thirteen were serving cures. They included William Higgs, minister of Little Birch, who received £80 in 1658, and four ministers who had lost their posts as vicars-choral on the suppression of Hereford Cathedral, to which Scudamore had been chief steward.[41] Conformist ministers were also active in helping to raise funds for sequestered clergymen. Nathaniel Hardy, incumbent of St Dionis Backchurch in London, organised a 'loyal lecture' to attract donations for suffering clergy, while John Evelyn recorded in 1658 that 'there is now a collection for persecuted and sequestered ministers of the Church of England, whereof divers [are now] in prison'.[42] This broad-bottomed endeavour to assist impoverished episcopalian clergy drew in both conformists and nonconformists alike, both as donors and as recipients.

III

While it is possible to point to the existence of a strand of episcopalian conformity in the years between 1646 and 1660, any assessment of its nature and extent is beset with difficulties. Many of the sources are fragmentary. One of the things that set episcopalians apart was a commitment to, or at least a belief in the desirability of, set liturgical forms, specifically the Book of Common

Prayer, and a hostility to extempore prayer. As has been seen, it was not difficult to find prayer book services during the 1650s, at least in London, and it
was not uncommon for ministers to make use of prayers derived from the
prayer book, even if it was inexpedient to use the liturgy. But we have little idea
of precisely how widespread these practices were.[43] A second characteristic
of episcopalianism was its assertion of the necessity for episcopal ordination
of ministers. As will become apparent, it has not hitherto been recognised
that the sources do survive for a systematic investigation of this practice. The
remainder of this chapter, therefore, will examine the extent of episcopal ordination in this period as a way of casting further light on the nature of episcopalian conformity.

Thanks to the memoirs of a number of Restoration divines, it has long
been well known that it was not difficult for those desirous of episcopalian
orders to find bishops who were prepared to ordain them clandestinely. The
extent and significance of this practice in the period between 1646 and 1660,
however, has been overlooked. The claim of Robert Skinner, bishop of Oxford,
for example, to have ordained between 400 and 500 men during these years
is sometimes treated with scepticism.[44] It is easy to see why. Skinner's claim
rests on his own testimony at a time when, in the early years of the Restoration, he was pushing his claims to further preferment. Neither his ordination
register nor his subscription book for this period survives; nor, indeed, does
that of any other bishop.[45] However, the details of many ordinations performed
after the abolition of episcopacy have survived in exhibit books, compiled by
many Restoration bishops and their officials during visitations in the 1660s
and 1670s. Although the significance of this material was noted in an article
in *Theology* in the 1940s and again by Evan Davies in an unjustly neglected
BLitt dissertation of 1972, only the collation of all the surviving exhibit books
in the Clergy of the Church of England Database 1540–1835 has made possible
the thorough examination of the evidence that they contain for the first time.[46]

The survival of exhibit books for the dioceses of England and Wales is far
from complete, and they present various problems of interpretation.[47] Nonetheless, they reveal a remarkable story, providing evidence of 559 clergymen
who received episcopal ordination between October 1646 and the restoration
of the monarchy in May 1660.[48] It is more helpful to think in terms of the
number of people ordained, rather than the number of ordinations, as the
normal practice was for a candidate to be made both deacon and priest on
the same day. The exigencies of the times provide an obvious explanation for
this wholesale departure from the canons, though it is worth noting, particularly in light of the prominence of Irish bishops among the ordainers, that it
was quite common in early seventeenth-century Ireland for both orders to be
conferred on the same day.[49] It is very difficult to know what proportion of the
total number of clergymen ordained between 1647 and 1660 is represented

by these 559 men. We do, however, have some points of comparison. The Restoration exhibit books also record details of men ordained before the Civil Wars and between the return of the monarchy in 1660 and the enforcement of the Act of Uniformity in August 1662. For both the earlier and later periods the complete ordination records of some bishops survive in their registers and subscription books. A comparison of all the surviving data for the three periods demonstrates that the 559 men represent no more than 16 per cent of all those ordained between 1646 and 1660. We can, therefore, be confident that around 3,500 clergymen were episcopally – and thus, also, clandestinely – ordained between the end of 1646 and May 1660.

Episcopal ordination, according to the Ordinal in the proscribed Book of Common Prayer, thus remained remarkably popular. So where was it taking place? Who was conducting the services? What meanings were attached to the rite by those who sought ordination? Around May 1650 John Evelyn wrote that Richard Browne's chapel in Paris was becoming the centre for episcopalian ordinations, 'there being so few Bishops left in England'.[50] Like many of Evelyn's comments about the state of episcopalianism during the Interregnum, this needs to be treated with some care; it is, in fact, highly misleading. Some ordinations took place in the English resident's chapel, but all the indications are that there were relatively few – firm evidence survives of only one, conducted by Thomas Sydserf, bishop of Galloway, on 5 June 1651.[51] Not one of the 559 ordinations recorded in the exhibit books took place in Paris. Ordination was a phenomenon not of the exiled church, but rather of the underground church. All but one of the 559 ordinations appear to have been conducted in England; the exception is one that took place in Dublin in 1659.[52]

It is clear, however, that, even among those bishops who remained in England through the Interregnum, some were far more committed than others to the continuance of an episcopally ordained ministry. A significant number of English and Welsh bishops, indeed, appear to have made no effort to confer orders after the abolition of episcopacy. That Matthew Wren should be among them is perhaps no surprise – he was, after all, incarcerated in the Tower of London throughout the period, though even in prison he may have ordained Richard Lee as priest on 9 July 1649.[53] What is more surprising is that neither of the two men who were to be elevated to the archbishoprics of York and Canterbury at the Restoration, William Juxon, bishop of London, and Accepted Frewen, bishop of Coventry and Lichfield, is recorded as ordaining anyone – Juxon lived in semi-retirement throughout this period and the whereabouts of Frewen are unknown.[54] Almost equally inactive were Warner of Rochester, Piers of Bath and Wells, Winniffe of Lincoln, and Ussher, who had been appointed to the vacant see of Carlisle in February 1642.[55]

In fact, a very small group of bishops was responsible for most of the ordinations that took place between 1646 and 1660 – nine ordained 94 per cent of the clergy about whom we have information – and, on the whole, it was a group who have not hitherto figured prominently in the story of the survival of episcopalianism during the Interregnum. Among the English bishops three men stand out – Joseph Hall of Norwich, Ralph Brownrigg of Exeter and Robert Skinner of Oxford – each of whom ordained about 10 per cent of ordinands. The other three of note were Duppa of Salisbury, Henry King of Chichester and Thomas Morton of Durham. Even more significant were three Irish bishops, who together ordained 52 per cent of men seeking episcopal orders in this period. Robert Maxwell, bishop of Kilmore, (not his notorious namesake John Maxwell, archbishop of Tuam), was responsible for about 10 per cent of the ordinations, while Henry Tilson, bishop of Elphin, ordained a further 8 per cent. The contribution of both Maxwell and Tilson was, arguably, even more significant than the raw figures suggest, since Maxwell returned to Ireland in 1654, and Tilson died in March of the following year. The figure who stands out, among the English as well as the Irish bishops, however, is Thomas Fulwar, bishop of Ardfert. If ordination is taken as a manifestation of activity, he was, by some distance, the most active bishop during the Interregnum, being alone responsible for 35 per cent of all the ordinations that took place. This suggests that Fulwar probably ordained close to 1,000 clergy during this period – that is, an average of some sixty per annum.

After 1646 the careers of this group of bishops followed different trajectories, highlighting the variety of patterns of engagement between episcopalianism, conformity and nonconformity. Most of Duppa's closest links were with the group of episcopalian nonconformists around Sheldon and Hammond; interestingly, and for reasons about which we can only speculate, he did not begin to ordain until 1655. Morton, King and Hall also seem to have kept the authorities of the Commonwealth and Protectorate at arm's length. But most of the others – Brownrigg, Skinner and Tilson – engaged in some way with the various regimes.[56] The ordinations conducted by these men were thus acts of guarded nonconformity in otherwise conformist careers. Fulwar's connections with the regime, if any, are unrecorded. We can infer from Restoration exhibit books that he spent most of his time in the East Midlands, although on at least two occasions, in the late summer of 1655 and the late spring of 1657, he undertook tours of the West Country, ordaining as he went.[57] It is implausible that the authorities were entirely ignorant of such activity, any more than the regular procession of young, educated men to visit Skinner in his parlour at Launton could have passed without notice. The public face of successive regimes may have remained resolutely hostile to episcopalianism; that was, after all, the message of Cromwell's proclamation of November 1655. Skinner may even have feared, as he later claimed, that he would have had 'my books, and my bed taken from me' had his activity been discovered.[58] But there is a strong circumstantial case that the Commonwealth and Protectorate were prepared to turn a blind eye to the fact that some bishops were continuing to exercise their episcopal functions. Might one go further? Might one suggest that Skinner had made some kind of deal with the regime, allowing him, tacitly or otherwise, to exercise some kind of primitive episcopal role in return for his acceptance of the *de facto* authority of the powers that be? This suggestion can be no more than speculation as far as any of the English bishops is concerned. But in Ireland the distinction between conformity and nonconformity becomes blurred to the point of invisibility. The Cromwellian regime, influenced perhaps by the desperate shortage of Protestant ministers, formally employed some of the Irish bishops as ministers of the gospel. In 1654 Maxwell and Henry Leslie, bishop of Down, were invited to return to Ireland, where they were granted government pensions of £120 per annum each.[59] There they joined John Leslie, bishop of Raphoe, who was already receiving payments from the government. But state employment did not put an end to their episcopal activity – all can be found conferring episcopalian orders on Irish clergy in the second half of the 1650s.[60]

If many of the ordinations of the years between 1646 and 1660 were performed by men, like Skinner, Maxwell and Tilson, who were, however tentatively, negotiating positions of episcopalian conformity, it is only to be expected that many of those ordained were also conformists. Some, it is true, found employment as chaplains and tutors in the houses of sympathetic gentry in the manner of Sheldon and Hammond. George Davenport, whom we have already met serving as chaplain to John Gayer at Stoke Poges, was ordained by Brownrigg in 1654, but did not accept a parochial cure until 1661.[61] Most, however, found some kind of living in the national church. A full proso-pographical study of the 526 clergymen who are known to have received ordi-nation at the hands of English and Irish bishops in this period remains to be done, but it is possible to trace a number of different trajectories which are suggestive of some of the varieties of episcopalian conformity. Those who, like Gibson Lucas, were old enough to have embarked on a clerical career before the Civil Wars but did not seek episcopal ordination until the 1650s appear to have been rare. Far more common were those, like John Witham, ordained by Fulwar in 1647, who then became rector of Mistley and Manningtree in the same year.[62] Ralph Garnons became rector of Tilbury following his ordination by Brownrigg in 1654.[63] Samuel Drake, having been ejected from his fellow-ship at St John's College, Cambridge, and then joined the royal army at the siege of Newark, was ordained in 1647 and then accepted the rectory of South Kirkby, Yorkshire, in 1650.[64] Many, however, sought out a bishop only after they had been serving a parish for a few years. William Mallowes had already been vicar of Webread, Suffolk, for two years at the time of his ordination in 1647.[65] Robert Townshend, who was instituted to the rectory of Radcliffe in Bucking-hamshire in 1649, was ordained by Skinner in 1651.[66] The full complexity of the relationship between episcopalianism and conformity, and the challenges that it presented to individuals, is suggested by two further examples. Henry Chamberlain is listed by Walker as a 'sufferer', having been ejected as a fellow of Oriel College, Oxford, in 1648. He did, eventually, obtain ordination from Skinner in April 1657. Before this, however, he had found employment as preacher and schoolmaster at Shellingford, Berkshire, and then, in 1656, was admitted by the triers as vicar of Haslingfield, Cambridgeshire.[67] The case of Matthew Bate is even more intriguing. As rector of Maids Moreton, Buckinghamshire, he transcribed the parish register book in which he described Parliament as 'wickedly rebelling against the best of princes' and recorded that, despite the order of the 'usurper Cromwell' that 'children aught not to be baptised, and marriages be by Justices of Peace ... it is here observed that not one in the parish complied with it, but christened the children in the church, and no persons bedded, before they were solemnly wedded in church'. But he had no problem serving as rector throughout the Protectorate, having been instituted no later than 1651, and it was not until 1655 that he presented himself to Skinner for ordination.[68]

Obtaining clandestine episcopal ordination was, therefore, clearly no barrier to preferment in the national church, but equally it was not the natural next step on the path to a sometimes comfortable career that it had been for many young graduates before the Civil War. Bishops were living, perhaps not in hiding, but certainly in retirement. It could sometimes be a challenge 'to find a Bishop to whom I might resort'.[69] Episcopacy was proscribed; ordination was an illegal act. Ceremonies were regularly conducted in private houses – by Bishop Joseph Hall of Norwich at Heigham outside the city, Bishop Henry Tilson of Elphin at Soothill in Yorkshire, Bishop Ralph Brownrigg at the house of Dr Thomas Buckenham in Bury St Edmunds and Bishop Robert Skinner of Oxford in the rectory at Launton.[70] In these circumstances seeking ordination was a significant ideological statement. The precise nature of that statement, however, is far from clear. Skinner, for example, claimed that throughout the period all those on whom he conferred orders 'subscribed to the Articles, and took the oath of allegiance'.[71] If this was the case, he was treading a particularly fine line between episcopalian conformity and Royalist nonconformity. Unfortunately, only one letters of orders issued by Skinner after the abolition of episcopacy survives and, while the ordination took place clandestinely within Skinner's house at Launton, little significance can be read into the fact that the candidate subscribed to the Oath of Allegiance as well as the canons, since it took place on 2 November 1648, before the death of the king.[72] After the execution of the king, practice varied.[73] Thomas Fulwar, bishop of Ardfert, explicitly recorded that ordinands had subscribed to the Articles of the Church of England, to which he added the vague phrase 'et omnia alia requisita praestantem'.[74] Brownrigg, by contrast, made no reference to any subscription, stating simply that the ordination had been conducted according to the custom and rite of the Church of England.[75] There were, of course, strong reasons for not recording on paper oaths that were made orally, and George Bull claimed that Skinner did not in fact issue letters of orders, instead sending them to those he had ordained at the Restoration.[76] But, while speculation is always dangerous, the evidence suggests that some bishops were prepared to salve the consciences of the ordinands – and perhaps also their own – by not insisting on the taking of the oath of allegiance. Bishops like Brownrigg and Fulwar represented a strand within Interregnum episcopalianism that was, in politics at least, pragmatic, flexible and accommodating. If it was Royalist, its royalism was of a very different temper from that of Sheldon, Hammond and the exiles.

As one might expect, there was often a great deal of soul-searching before men took the decision to seek episcopal ordination. The memoirs of Richard Kidder, the future bishop of Bath and Wells, offer an insight into the dilemma that must have faced many promising young graduates in the 1650s. As a fellow of Emmanuel College, Cambridge, he witnessed the 'frequent Ordinations ... in public Churches by Presbyters only'; he was exposed to the 'great disputes' between episcopal and Presbyterian divines; he received several invitations to take orders from the latter. Even so, as he recollected, he resisted 'the stream of that time' and chose to be ordained by a bishop before taking the college living of Stanground in Huntingdonshire.[77] George Bull's experiences highlight the combination of personal friendships and reading which probably brought many to episcopalianism. After he had been placed under the direction of the future dissenter William Thomas, the key relationship for Bull was his friendship with Thomas's son, Samuel, who, to borrow the father's phrase, 'corrupted' Bull by encouraging him to read Hooker, Hammond, Taylor, Grotius and Episcopius. Following his ordination he accepted first, in 1656, the living of St George, Bristol, and then, in 1658, the rectory of Siddington.[78] A few at least took both Presbyterian and episcopalian orders. Simon Patrick took Presbyterian orders from the London classis in April 1653 because 'he knew no better', but he was then convinced of their insufficiency by his reading of 'Dr Hammond upon Ignatius's Epistles, and Mr Thorndike's Primitive Government'.[79] This led him, through a college contact, to Bishop Hall's door at Heigham, where he was ordained in April 1654.[80] A similar combination of family and college networks is revealed strikingly by Edmund Ellis. First, his father's disapproval of his son's 'Fancy that the Presbyterian Ordination Qualify one to Preach' prompted the reflection and self-examination that led him to regard it as insufficient. Then his father came to Oxford, where Ellis resided as a fellow of Balliol College, and sent him to Skinner at Launton, accompanied by Clement Ellis, his 'Cousin German' and a fellow of Queens, who had already been ordained by Skinner and who then 'presented' him and 'some other of my acquaintance'. Shortly afterwards, Ellis succeeded his father in the rectory of East Allington, Devon.[81] However, as one further example will suggest, a degree of caution needs to be exercised before we accept as the norm this narrative of doubts about Presbyterianism leading to the embrace of the truth of episcopalianism. Memoirs written after the restoration of church and monarchy perhaps downplay too much the pragmatism and flexibility that characterised the attitude of many during the 1650s. Francis Mosley, for example, was ordained deacon and priest by Bishop Tilson on 27 October 1654, but then chose also to accept ordination from the Manchester classis on 10 January 1655.[82] He was not alone, and it is risky to assume that, in such troubled times, men such as him saw any fundamental incompatibility between the two acts.

IV

Four themes are worth highlighting by way of conclusion to this chapter. First, the link between episcopalianism and royalism was much less close than is often assumed, at least after 1649. This is certainly not to suggest that episcopalians did not welcome the restoration of Charles II in 1660. In the intervening years, however, the relationship between adherence to episcopalianism and loyalty to the Stuart monarchy was far more complex than the attitudes of men like Sheldon and Hammond would suggest. Not only did many people who had been episcopally ordained continue to serve in the English church through the later 1640s and 1650s and give assurances of their allegiance, or at least their peaceable conduct, to the Commonwealth and Protectorate, but also many of those who sought clerical office in the 1650s received episcopal ordination, even regarding it as necessary for the conduct of their ministry. This willingness to compromise and work with the powers that be is a neglected feature of episcopalian mentalities in the period.

Second, what is striking about the bishops who conformed, to a lesser or greater extent, was that they represented no single strand of churchmanship.[83] Brownrigg, as we have seen, was an old-style Calvinist, elevated to the episcopate by Charles I in 1641 in an attempt to conciliate the parliamentary opposition. Skinner and Tilson, by contrast, could be described as Laudians. In the 1630s Skinner was an advocate of Arminianism, appointed to the see of Bristol at the high-point of the personal rule in 1636, and played a leading role in the Convocation of 1640, imposing the controversial 'etcetera' oath on his diocese before the end of September.[84] Translated to the bishopric of Oxford at the end of 1641 just before the vote preventing bishops from attending the Lords, he was imprisoned in the Tower for four months. Tilson was an Englishman who served as vicar of Rochdale until in 1633, at the age of fifty-eight, he was asked by Thomas Wentworth to accompany him to Ireland as one of his chaplains. He appears to have become one of Wentworth's lieutenants in his efforts to reform the Irish church. Laud regarded Tilson as a 'honest man' and backed his promotion to the bishopric of Elphin in 1639.[85] Episcopalianism, in short, did not simply fragment along party lines in the 1640s and 1650s.

Third, the relationship between conformity and nonconformity within episcopalianism between 1646 and 1660 was complex and shifting. It is possible to point to a fracturing of connections. The absence of the leading ordainers – Fulwar, Maxwell, Tilson and especially Skinner – from the correspondence of Sheldon and Hammond is telling. But what does it reveal – the difficulties of maintaining contacts as the persecuted kept their heads down, or the deliberate severing of ties, because the task of maintaining the purity of the church required keeping one's distance from unsound brethren? In other cases, however, we see that conformists and nonconformists did not live in self-contained worlds – in the friendship between Brownrigg and Sancroft, in the charitable networks of Scudamore and Warner or in the group gathered to ordain Gibson Lucas in 1655. This should not surprise us, as individuals could not separate conformity and nonconformity in their own lives. Skinner may have been a conformist rector of Launton, signing testimonials as simply 'Rob. Skynner of Launton',[86] but every ordination and prayer book service that he performed was an act of nonconformity. Episcopalian laity, like John Evelyn, trod a similar path, seeking out clandestine prayer book services while also going to hear 'mechanic' preachers in their parish churches.

Finally, if we are to understand the impact of the Civil War and Interregnum on the Church of England and Anglicanism in the later seventeenth century, we need to move beyond a preoccupation with Sheldon, Hammond and the hardliners. There is no doubt that what might be described as the high churchmanship of Sheldon, Henchman, Morley, Fell and Sancroft, the men who dominated the leadership of the church during the Restoration, exercised a profound influence over the character of Anglicanism during these years and beyond. The high-water mark for the influence of this group came in the Tory reaction of 1681–86, with the restoration of altars, the persecution of dissenters, the prosecution of non-communicants and the condemnation of 'heterodox' works, before its eclipse under James II and defeat in 1688.[87] But there were also other networks which, as has been seen, helped in different ways to sustain episcopalianism during the dark days of the 1640s and 1650s and whose varying contributions to it during the Restoration and beyond have yet fully to be explored. On the episcopal bench in the 1660s, for example, were men like Hacket and Sanderson, who knew all about the pressures for conformity from their own parochial experience in the 1650s, who worked to build an inclusive church in the 1660s, and who tried to avoid divisive issues like the restoration of altars.[88] A very different group is represented by figures like Parker, Cartwright and Sprat, allies of Sheldon and Sancroft and commonly regarded as high churchmen in the reign of Charles II. But, as

M.J. Routh noted as long ago as 1833, their high churchmanship was of a very different stamp from that of Sancroft and the seven bishops. They were men who, to use Routh's words, were for active rather than passive obedience to the powers that be and they were prominent among the Anglican collaborators of James II in 1686–88.[89] They had also all been Interregnum conformists. Equally notable among the Interregnum conformists were men who came to be called low churchmen or latitudinarians, figures like Wilkins among the older generation and Stillingfleet and Tillotson among the younger. Such men appear to have imbibed very different lessons, pursuing a policy of 'moderation' in the church, campaigning for the comprehension of dissenters within it and maintaining friendly relations with Presbyterians like Richard Baxter.

NOTES

We are grateful to Alan Ford, Anthony Milton, Paul Vivash and Tim Wales for their help as we researched this chapter, to Ludmilla Jordanova for the opportunity to give an early version of it at the conference on 'Social Networks in Early Modern England' at New College, Oxford, on 18 September 2007, and to the participants in that conference for their comments. Some of the research on which this chapter draws was undertaken for the Clergy of the Church of England Database 1540–1835 Project. We are grateful to all who worked on that project and particularly our co-director, Professor Arthur Burns. See www.theclergydatabase.org.uk/about/personnel.html.

1 Bodl., Tanner MS 52, fol. 97. Cocke had been appointed in 1648 and Whitefoot in 1652: see J. and J.A. Venn, *Alumni Cantabrigienses Part 1*, 4 vols (Cambridge, 1922), vol. I, p. 362, vol. IV, pp. 390–1.

2 Bishop Skinner was assisted at ordinations by Thomas Lamplugh, as, very probably, was Bishop Brownrigg by his chaplain Seth Ward. Lamplugh was a fellow of Queen's College, Oxford, and a parish minister in the later 1650s; Ward was Savilian Professor of Astronomy at Oxford. S. Handley, 'Lamplugh, Thomas (*bap*. 1615, *d*. 1691)', *Oxford DNB*; W. Pope, *The Life of Seth Lord Bishop of Salisbury* (Oxford, 1961), p. 31.

3 R.S. Bosher, *The Making of the Restoration Settlement: The Influence of the Laudians 1649–1662* (1951), esp. chapters 1–2.

4 G. Isham (ed.), *The Correspondence of Bishop Brian Duppa and Sir Justinian Isham* (Northamptonshire Record Society, 17, 1955), p. 113.

5 J.W. Packer, *The Transformation of Anglicanism 1643–1660 with Special Reference to Henry Hammond* (Manchester, 1969).

6 J. Spurr, *The Restoration Church of England 1646–1689* (New Haven, CT, 1991), pp. 6–7.

7 Bosher, *Restoration Settlement*, pp. 27–8. The phrase 'the old Episcopacy' is quoted from Baxter. See also J. Maltby, 'Suffering and surviving: the Civil Wars, the Commonwealth and the formation of "Anglicanism", 1642–60', in C. Durston and J. Maltby (eds), *Religion in Revolutionary England* (Manchester, 2006), pp. 158–80.

8 Spurr, *Restoration Church*, p. 6.

9 Bosher, *Restoration Settlement*, p. 24 n. 2.

10 *Ibid.*, pp. 24–5.

11 *Ibid.*, pp. 100, 125 n. 2.

12 I.M. Green, 'The persecution of "scandalous" and "malignant" parish clergy during the English Civil War', *EHR*, 94 (1979), pp. 507–31; Spurr, *Restoration Church*, pp. 6–7; and see below, pp. 32–3.

13 Among much else, see P. Collinson, *The Elizabethan Puritan Movement* (1967); P. Lake, *Moderate Puritans and the Elizabethan Church* (Cambridge, 1982); M. Questier, *Catholicism and Community in Early Modern England* (Cambridge, 2006); E. Shagan, *Popular Politics and the English Reformation* (Cambridge, 2003); A. Walsham, *Church Papists: Catholicism, Conformity and Confessional Polemic in Early Modern England* (Woodbridge, 1999).

14 BL, Add. MS 4274, fol. 191r (12 Mar. 1660). Rainbow added that he feared political unrest and violence, and if this occurred 'I think I shall better serve in privacy'.

15 T. Fuller, *A Triple Reconciler* (1654), pp. 35–6.

16 A. Wood, *Athenae Oxonienses*, ed. P. Bliss, 4 vols (1813–20), vol. III, p. 396; C.E. Surman (ed.), *The Register-Booke of the Fourth Classis in the Province of London 1646–59* (Harleian Society, 82–3, 1953), p. 145.

17 N.H. Keeble and G.F. Nuttall (eds), *Calendar of the Correspondence of Richard Baxter*, 2 vols (Oxford, 1991), vol. I, p. 343.

18 A.G. Matthews, *Walker Revised* (Oxford, 1988), p. 12. Evidence relating to his compounding is unrevealing: TNA, PRO, SP 23/3/321, 117/711.

19 Bodl., Tanner MS 52, fols 14r, 178r; BL, Harleian MS 3783, fol. 226r; Lambeth Palace Library, COMM. 6a/9, p. 532.

20 BL, Harleian MS 6942, nos 28, 131; E. Vallance, 'Oaths, casuistry, and equivocation: Anglican responses to the Engagement controversy', *HJ*, 44 (2001), pp. 59–77; W. Jacobson (ed.), *The works of Robert Sanderson*, 6 vols (Oxford, 1854), vol. V, pp. 37–59; Bosher, *Restoration Settlement*, pp. 17–23.

21 BL, Harleian MS 6942, no. 77; Jacobson (ed.), *Works of Sanderson*, vol. VI, pp. 377–80.

22 H. Cary (ed.), *Memorials of the great civil war in England from 1646 to 1652*, 2 vols (1842), vol. II, pp. 397–8, 402, 415; BL, Harleian MS 6942, no. 113.

23 Keeble and Nuttall (eds), *Correspondence of Baxter*, vol. II. pp. 76, 78, 183–7, 225; R. Baxter, *The Grotian religion discovered* (1658), pp. 117–18 (where he claims that agreement with Ussher was reached in fifteen minutes); M. Sylvester (ed.), *Reliquiae Baxterianae* (1696), book I:1, pp. 172–9; G.R. Abernathy, 'Richard Baxter and the Cromwellian church', *HLQ*, 24 (1960–61), pp. 215–31.

24 F.F. Madan, *A New Bibliography of the Eikon Basilike of King Charles the First* (Oxford, 1950), pp. 126–33; J. McElligott, 'Roger Morrice and the reputation of the *Eikon Basilike* in the 1680s', *The Library*, 7th series, 6 (2005), pp. 119–32; R.A. Beddard, 'A reward for services rendered: Charles II and the Restoration bishopric of Worcester, 1660–1663', *Midland History*, 29 (2004), pp. 67–73. For the latest reading of *Eikon Basilike*, see S. Kelsey's essay in N. Tyacke (ed.), *The English Revolution c.1590–1720* (Manchester, 2007), pp. 150–68.

25 J. Gauden, *Hieraspistes: a defence by way of apology for the ministry and ministers of the Church of England* (1653), pp. 259–320; J. Gauden, *A sermon preached in the Temple-*

Chappel, at the funeral of ... Dr Brounrig, late lord bishop of Exceter (1660), p. 136; Bodl., Rawlinson MS A 44, fols 211–18, printed in T. Birch (ed.), *A collection of state papers of John Thurloe*, 7 vols (1742), vol. V, pp. 597–601.

26 J. Gauden, *The case of the ministers maintenance by tithes* (1653); A. Woolrych, *From Commonwealth to Protectorate* (Oxford, 1982), pp. 246–9; J. Gauden, *Christ at the wedding* (1654), pp. 1–2 and *passim*; *A declaration of his highness with the advice of the council, in order to the securing the peace of this commonwealth* (1655); J. G[auden], *A petitionary remonstrance, presented to O. P. Feb 4 1655* (1659), sig. E2r; Bodl., Tanner MS 52, fol. 105.

27 G. G[oodman], *The two great mysteries of Christian religion* (1653), sigs A2r–A3iv.

28 A. Milton, *Laudian and Royalist Polemic in Seventeenth-Century England: The Career and Writings of Peter Heylyn* (Manchester, 2007), pp. 162–9.

29 BL, Harleian MS 3783, fols 107r, 192, 194r, MS 3786, fol. 65r; Bodl., Tanner MS 48, fol. 25r, MS 52, fol. 111.

30 Matthews, *Walker Revised*, p. 12; Bodl., Clarendon State Papers MS 68, fol. 137, MS 69, fols 85v, 106; P. Barwick, *The life of the reverend Dr John Barwick* (1724), pp. 210, 218–19, 238–42, 488; Beddard, 'A reward', pp. 77–8.

31 S. Bendall, C. Brooke and P. Collinson, *A History of Emmanuel College, Cambridge* (Woodbridge, 1999), pp. 254–5; BL, Harleian MS 3783, fols 103r, 109r, 111r, 169r, 178r, 181, 192, 194; Bodl., Tanner MS 52, fols 12r, 83r, 142, 178r, 205, MS 56, fol. 163; Bodl., Rawlinson Letters 101, fols 62, 68–70.

32 K. Fincham and N. Tyacke, *Altars Restored: The Changing Face of English Religious Worship 1547–c.1700* (Oxford, 2007), pp. 288, 296–7; E.S. de Beer (ed.), *The Diary of John Evelyn*, 6 vols (Oxford, 1955), vol. III, pp. 17–245; BL, Add. MS 34702, fol. 219r; Bodl., Tanner MS 52, fol. 199.

33 de Beer (ed.), *Diary of John Evelyn*, vol. III, pp. 60, 80–1, 85, 91, 93, 142, 145, 147, 150, 184, 185, 212–13 and *passim*; BL, Add. MS 78364, fols 31r–2v, 33v, 34r, 35r–6v, 128r–40r, 142r–3r; A.G. Matthews, *Calamy Revised* (Oxford, 1988), pp. 335, 338; and the perceptive comments in J. Spurr, '"A sublime and noble service": John Evelyn and the Church of England', in F. Harris and M. Hunter (eds), *John Evelyn and his Milieu* (2003), pp. 150–4.

34 Bodl., Eng. Misc. MS e 118; Spurr, *Restoration Church*, pp. 1–2, 16–17.

35 Bodl., Eng. Misc. MS e 118, fols 17, 24v, 35v, 39r, 42v–3r, 52r, 53r, 63v, 68r, 70r, 78v, 79v, 86r, 89r, 89v, 89v–90r, 96r, and *passim*; Spurr, *Restoration Church*, p. 17; Matthews, *Walker Revised*, pp. 48–9, 70, 71, 219; A. Tindal Hart, *William Lloyd 1627–1717* (1952), pp. 14–16. The identification of 'Mr Jaggard' is tentative.

36 See above, p. 23; Jacobson (ed.), *Works of Sanderson*, vol. VI, pp. 314–17, 367, 377–80; Bodl., Tanner MS 52, fol. 41r.

37 I. Atherton, *Ambition and Failure in Stuart England: The Career of John, First Viscount Scudamore* (Manchester, 1999), pp. 65–8; Isham (ed.), *Correspondence*, pp. 14 n. 7, 89, 90, 206; E.P. Shirley, *Stemmata Shirleiana* (1873), pp. 155–8; V.D. Sutch, *Gilbert Sheldon* (The Hague, 1973), pp. 42–4. There were a host of minor lay donors, including Sancroft's former pupils John and Robert Gager, and Thankful Frewen, brother of Bishop Accepted Frewen: BL, Harleian MS 3783, fols 178r, 238r; Fincham and Tyacke, *Altars Restored*, p. 255.

38 G. Soden, *Godfrey Goodman, Bishop of Gloucester 1583–1656* (1953), p. 470; Bodl., Eng. Hist. MS b 205, fols 25v, 37r; Atherton, *Scudamore*, p. 67; BL, Harleian MS 3791, fol. 61r.

39 Atherton, *Scudamore*, p. 67; Shirley, *Shirleiana*, p. 158; Isham (ed.), *Correspondence*, pp. 89, 90, 206; Bodl., Tanner MS 52, fols 7, 211v; Bodl., Eng. Hist. MS b 205, fols 7r, 9r, 19.

40 C.L. Berry, 'Henry Tilson, bishop of Elphin', *Church Quarterly Review*, 132 (1941), pp. 59–60; Bodl., Eng. Hist. MS b 205, fol. 3r, Tanner MS 56, fol. 188; Matthews, *Walker Revised*, pp. 68–9.

41 TNA, PRO, C115/36/2206–38, 67/5879, 109/8877; the authoritative analysis of these lists is in I.J. Atherton, 'John 1st Viscount Scudamore (1601–71): a career at court and in the country, 1601–43' (PhD dissertation, University of Cambridge, 1993), pp. 455–80.

42 Wood, *Athenae Oxonienses*, vol. III, p. 896; de Beer (ed.), *Evelyn*, vol. III, pp. 213–14.

43 For the most recent discussion, see Maltby, 'Suffering and surviving', pp. 162–8.

44 V. Larminie, 'Skinner, Robert (1591–1670)', *Oxford DNB*.

45 As the bishops clearly maintained ordination records during this period, it is not clear why none survives. It may be that, in the absence of the diocesan administration, bishops' act books from this period were regarded as personal records which were never deposited in the diocesan registry following the Restoration.

46 E.H. Day, 'Ordinations under the Commonwealth', *Theology*, 44 (1942), pp. 341–6; S.L. Ollard, 'Commonwealth ordinations', *Theology*, 45 (1942), pp. 37–9; C.E. Davies, 'Robert Sanderson, Restoration bishop, his administration of the diocese of Lincoln, 1660–3', 2 vols (BLitt dissertation, University of Oxford, 1972). See also W.J. Sheils, *Restoration Exhibit Books and the Northern Clergy 1662–1664* (Borthwick Texts and Calendars: Records of the Northern Province, 13, York, 1987).

47 Relatively complete books survive for the dioceses of Bath and Wells, Exeter, Hereford, Lincoln, London, Norwich and the province of York, though those for Exeter and Hereford both date from the 1670s. More fragmentary documents for Chichester, Durham, Ely, Gloucester, Lichfield and Coventry, Peterborough and Salisbury. No exhibit books survive for the four Welsh dioceses. A discussion of these documents and the problems of interpreting the evidence they contain, as well as a fuller examination of episcopal ordinations between 1640 and 1660, will appear in another joint article, 'Vital statistics: episcopal ordinations and ordinands in England 1646–60', forthcoming.

48 These figures were collected from the evidence contained in the Clergy of the Church of England Database 1540–1835 in September 2009, www.theclergydatabase.org.uk.

49 We owe this point to Alan Ford. Such practices were not unknown in England: thus Thomas Dove, bishop of Peterborough (1601–30), often ordained candidates to the diaconate and priesthood on successive days, in contravention of canon 32 of 1604: K. Fincham, *Prelate as Pastor* (Oxford, 1990), p. 181. Canon 29 of the Irish canons of 1635 also prohibited the ordination of someone as deacon and priest on the same day. G. Bray (ed.), *The Anglican Canons 1529–1947* (Church of England Record Society, 6, Woodbridge, 1998), pp. 311, 500–1.

50 BL, Add. MS 78298, fol. 4, quoted in G. Darley, *John Evelyn: Living for Ingenuity* (New Haven, CT, 2006), p. 102.

51 de Beer (ed.), *Diary of John Evelyn*, vol. III, pp. 8–9. He ordained two candidates, Daniel Brevint and John Durel. Significantly, perhaps, both were natives of Jersey.

52 The exception is Simon Heath, who was ordained priest by Robert Maxwell in St John's, Dublin, on 20 Jan. 1659. In 1662 Heath was serving in the diocese of Chichester. West Sussex RO, Ep.1/19/11.

53 Lincolnshire Archives, L.C. V. On the evidence for Lee's ordination, see the comments in The Clergy of the Church of England database.

54 On Juxon, see Duppa's comments in Isham (ed.), *Correspondence*, pp. 144–5. Bosher notes that Frewen disappears 'into impenetrable obscurity' during the Interregnum: *Restoration Settlement*, p. 27.

55 Winniffe, who had ordained regularly right up to the abolition of episcopacy in 1646, died in 1654, followed by Ussher in 1656. Both Warner and Piers survived into the Restoration.

56 See above, pp. 25, 28.

57 www.theclergydatabase.org.uk; Fincham and Taylor, 'Vital statistics'.

58 Bodl., Tanner MS 48, fol. 25.

59 St John D. Seymour, *The Puritans in Ireland 1647–1661* (Oxford, 1912), p. 55. The government's position may have been easier – no formal ordinance to abolish the hierarchy of the Church of Ireland was issued, though in 1650 parliamentary commissioners were empowered to enforce the English ordinance abolishing the hierarchy and the Book of Common Prayer. Only in July 1659 did the reconvened Rump pass an Act giving Irish commissioners powers to enforce legislation 'now in force in England' in Ireland, including 'the abolishing of the Hirarchy and the Service book, comonly called the book of comon prayer'. T. Barnard, *Cromwellian Ireland: English Government and Reform in Ireland, 1649–1660* (Oxford, 1975), p. 97; C.H. Firth and R.S. Rait (eds), *Acts and Ordinances of the Interregnum 1642–1660*, 3 vols (1911), vol. II, pp. 1298–9.

60 The evidence for the activity of Maxwell and Leslie, along with William Baily, bishop of Confert, in ordaining clergy in Ireland in the 1650s comes from an exhibit book compiled by John Bramhall during his primary visitation of the archdiocese of Armagh in 1661. Public Record Office of Northern Ireland, DIO4/23/1/2. This material, since it relates to the church in Ireland, has not been included in the statistics discussed above, pp. 29–30.

61 BL, Harleian MS 3783, fol. 103r; Venn, *Alumni Cantabrigienses Part 1*, vol. II, p. 13.

62 Lucas was thirty-nine on his episcopal ordination in 1655: Venn, *Alumni Cantabrigienses Part 1*, vol. III, p. 112; Guildhall Library, MS 9537/16; TNA, PRO, E331 London/17. Witham was ordained on 17 June and instituted on 2 December.

63 CUL, EDR B/2/67; Venn, *Alumni Cantabrigienses Part 1*, vol. II, p. 197.

64 Venn, *Alumni Cantabrigienses Part 1*, vol. II, p. 64; Borthwick Institute for Archives, V.1667/Exh.Bk.

65 Herefordshire RO, HD5/2/23/1674; J. Foster, *Alumni Oxonienses*, 4 vols (Oxford, 1891–92), vol. III, p. 963.

66 Foster, *Alumni Oxonienses*, vol. IV, p. 1500; Lincolnshire Archives, L.C. V, fols 22–221.

67 Matthews, *Walker Revised*, p. 32; CUL, EDR B/2/58.

68 S.M. Mills, *Parish Church of St Edmund Maids Moreton* (n.d.), p. 14.

69 *The autobiography of Simon Patrick, bishop of Ely. Now first printed from the original manuscript* (Oxford, 1839), p. 23; A.E. Robinson (ed.), *The Life of Richard Kidder, D.D. Bishop of Bath and Wells Written by Himself* (Somerset Record Society, 37, 1924), p. 5.

70 Bodl., Charters Somerset MS 165A: letters of orders of Robert Collier, 2 Nov. 1648; *Autobiography of Patrick*, p. 24; Robinson (ed.), *Life of Kidder*, p. 6; Yorkshire Archaeological

Society, DD82: letters of orders of Timothy Wood, 11 Jan. 1648. Tilson may occasionally have ordained in Meltham church, near to Soothill. Berry, 'Tilson', p. 60.

71 Bodl., Tanner MS 48, fol. 25.

72 Bodl., Charters Somerset MS 165A.

73 The argument is necessarily tentative at this point, as very few letters of orders have survived. Practice appears to have varied somewhat even in the period between the abolition of episcopacy in 1646 and the execution of the king on 30 January 1649. The letters of orders issued by Tilson in January 1648 simply recorded that Wood had taken all the oaths required by the Church of England. Yorkshire Archaeological Society, DD82.

74 'and all other necessary requirements'. See Herefordshire RO, AL 19/18, fol. 181 (1656); Bristol RO, EP/A/12/4 (1659).

75 Bodl., Charters Camb. MS a. 1 (1656): 'secundum modum et ritum Ecclesiae Anglicanae'.

76 R. Nelson, *The life of Dr George Bull, late lord bishop of St David's* (2nd edn, 1714), p. 26. If true, this suggests that Skinner kept very careful records of his acts during the Interregnum which have not survived.

77 Robinson (ed.), *Life of Kidder*, p. 5.

78 Nelson, *Life of Bull*, pp. 22–4; R.D. Cornwall, 'Bull, George (1634–1710)', *Oxford DNB*.

79 H. Hammond, *An answer to the animadversions on the dissertations touching Ignatius's epistles, and the episcopacie in them asserted* (1654); H. Thorndike, *Two discourses the one of the primitive government of churches, the other of the service of God at the assemblies of the church*, 2nd edn (Cambridge, 1650).

80 *Autobiography of Patrick*, pp. 23–4; Bodl., Tanner MS 52, fol. 6.

81 Bodl., Walker MS c. 2, pp. 472–3, 495–6; Foster, *Alumni Oxonienses*, vol. II, p. 457.

82 Cheshire RO, EDV 2/8; Venn, *Alumni Cantabrigienses Part 1*, vol. III, p. 219; W.A. Shaw (ed.), *Minutes of the Manchester Presbyterian classis*, 3 vols (Chetham Society, 2nd series, 20, 22, 24, 1890–1), vol. II, p. 220. Mosley had been negotiating with the Presbyterian classis about his ordination since as early as May 1654. *Ibid.*, pp. 210–12, 218–20.

83 The same width of churchmanship is observable among those bishops who continued to ordain after 1646: from the staunch Calvinists Morton and Hall through the more moderate Calvinist King to the Laudian Duppa. Unfortunately we know too little about the careers of Fulwar and Maxwell to be able to comment on their churchmanship.

84 P. Lake, 'Joseph Hall, Robert Skinner and the rhetoric of moderation at the early Stuart court', in L.A. Ferrell and P. McCullough (eds), *The English Sermon Revised: Religion, Literature and History, 1600–1750* (Manchester, 2001), pp. 167–85; K. Fincham, 'Episcopal government 1603–1640', in K. Fincham (ed.), *The Early Stuart Church 1603–1642* (Basingstoke, 1993), pp. 81–2; Larminie, 'Skinner'.

85 W. Laud, *Works*, ed. J. Bliss and W. Scott, 7 vols (1847–60), vol. VII, pp. 147, 549. See also J. McCafferty, *The Reconstruction of the Church of Ireland: Bishop Bramhall and the Laudian Reforms 1633–1641* (Cambridge, 2007), p. 120.

86 Lambeth Palace Library, COMM. 3/7 (2 July 1658).

87 On altars, see K. Fincham, '"According to ancient custom": the return of altars in the Restoration Church of England', *TRHS*, 6th series, 13 (2003), pp. 29–54. On heterodox

books, see *The judgment and decree of the University of Oxford* (1683); R. Beddard, 'Tory Oxford', in N. Tyacke (ed.), *The History of the University of Oxford*, vol. IV: *Seventeenth-Century Oxford* (Oxford, 1997), pp. 891–8. On defeat in 1688, see M. Goldie, 'The political thought of the Anglican revolution', in R. Beddard (ed.), *The Revolutions of 1688* (Oxford, 1991), pp. 102–36.

88   Fincham and Tyacke, *Altars Restored*, pp. 307, 320, 323. Edmund Hickeringill recalled that Sanderson's nickname was 'the Presbyterian bishop': *The ceremony-monger* (1689), p. 2.

89   M.J. Routh (ed.), *Bishop Burnet's history of his own time*, 2nd edn, 6 vols (Oxford, 1833), vol. III, p. 145 note k; G.V. Bennett, 'The seven bishops: a reconsideration', in D. Baker (ed.), *Religious Motivation* (Studies in Church History, 25, Oxford, 1978), pp. 267–87.

Chapter 3

Seditious speech and popular royalism, 1649–60

Lloyd Bowen

I

Those Royalists of the Interregnum deemed worthy of scholarly attention have usually been the exiled aristocrats and courtiers on the continent, or the groups of discontented and conspiratorial gentry who remained in the British Isles. The notion that a more popular monarchism with its accompanying anti-Parliamentarianism could be found among men and women lower down the social order has never been given much credence.[1] This chapter uncovers a neglected reservoir of Royalist support among comparatively humble individuals in 1650s England. It does this by examining the words they spoke against the national government and its local agents, words which brought them to the attention of the courts because such language was interpreted as seditious, scandalous or traitorous. The topic of sedition and seditious words has recently received a good deal of attention, but this has focused very much on the periods before and after the Civil Wars, when it is understood largely as an anti-monarchical discourse.[2] This chapter looks to extend these methodologies and debates to the Interregnum, a period when seditiousness *was* monarchism.

The usual starting point for any discussion of Royalist resistance during the Interregnum is David Underdown's *Royalist Conspiracy in England, 1649–1660* (1960). Given the nature of his later work, however, it is surprising to read Underdown's sceptical and often rather scathing comments on the nature of popular royalism in the 1650s. Plebeian Royalists hardly feature in this volume beyond a faceless, formless mass activated and guided by their social betters. Hopeless and clueless canon-fodder in pitiful, disorganised and doomed adventures, the ordinary Loyalist is robbed of any kind of political agency or genuine conviction in Underdown's dissection of the high politics of Royalist plotting. Popular royalism is presented as outdated, childish, ill-formed, sentimental and unthinking. He describes the 'nostalgic' 'passive conservatism of

the unpolitical' and 'politically illiterate', who had a 'vague emotional attachment to the old order'.[3] This is royalism as reflex. He argues that there was a
'definite, though inarticulate, pro-monarchist sentiment smouldering beneath
the surface. Although powerless to express itself against the bared swords of
a triumphant Army, the very existence of this obstinate, unthinking attachment to the old order was a constant encouragement of conspiracy.' Underdown presents the ordinary Royalist as mute apart from futile 'drunken toasts
... seditious abuse ... [and] defiant gestures'.[4] This essay looks to place these
marginalised activities centre stage in an effort to revoice the Royalists and
explore their political culture and political language.

The general neglect of political conversation and seditious language in the
1640s and 1650s can be traced to the enormous interest in the explosion of
printed material and the development of a politically informed print-culture.
The novelty of this glut of political print and the wealth of evidence it provides
have caused a concomitant neglect of oral communication during the 1640s
and 1650s. We know a good deal about Parliamentarian, and to a lesser degree
Royalist, newsbooks and pamphlets, but there is a real paucity of work on the
way in which people discussed and interpreted the political transformations
of the mid-century. We are still at the stage of looking at production; reception has yet to be considered in any depth.[5] Partly as a result of this emphasis
on the printed word, Royalists are often portrayed as antipathetic to public
opinion and political discussion because they were allegedly much more wary
of the popular press than their opponents.[6] This may or may not have been
true for Charles I, Charles II and their aristocratic advisers, but it does not
necessarily hold for their more humble followers. Such individuals did not
support the monarchy mutely or curse themselves for having the temerity to
discuss their own political positions. In the existing secondary literature, the
vigorous (and often plebeian) discourses of popular monarchism and Toryism
are situated in a very different post-Restoration milieu, and are not seen to
have much in the way of antecedents from the Caroline or republican periods.

In its discussion of Royalist sedition, this essay explores the nature of
popular political discourse, which is to say the languages of criticism and the
vocabularies of association which helped bind politically like-minded individuals together and separate them off from their opponents. Recent work has
begun to explore such connections between the great constitutional, political
and military upheavals of the 1640s and 1650s and the ways in which these
were framed, discussed, criticised and dissected, frequently in scatological
and lewd terms, through popular print, manuscript verses and libels and
public exchange.[7] The modes of censure used by the non-elite Royalists were
distinct from the criticisms levelled at republican regimes by radicals such as
the Levellers, Quakers or Fifth Monarchists. Opposition to the Interregnum
governments did not fuse plebeian Royalists with disaffected radicals in a

lumpen mass of undifferentiated antagonists. For example, the anger directed against two Cheshire JPs by the husbandman James Browne of Newton and the wheelwright George Dawkin of Whitton in 1655 emerged from very different political and religious positions from those of Stuart sympathisers. They were brought before Chester's great sessions court for having described the justices as 'of the same generacon of people that put Christ to death & the same vengeance & plagues are upon you & shall bee upon you'.[8] This was the language of the Quakers.[9] Another Cheshire man who disturbed the authorities in 1655 was Hugh Bristoe, a husbandman of Over township. However, his seditious language was of a wholly different tenor from that of Browne and Dawkin. He was indicted before the same court for having said, while drunk, that 'Cromwell the traitor had like to have been taken to the devil in his coach but that he hanged upon oake bough at midsomer last'.[10] The ancillary charge against him of profaning the sabbath, presumably by drinking or gaming, along with the tenor of his speech, helps to identify these as Royalist words.

Having said this, it is often impossible to prove that those prosecuted for sedition were 'real' Royalists. Individuals could be impelled by a variety of political positions to rail against their governors in the 1650s. It would be too inflexible, however, to reduce the scope of Royalist words only to those who declared allegiance for the king while expressing opposition to the Interregnum authorities – a corollary of only seeing those who actively took up arms for the Stuarts as genuine Royalists. Although confident attribution of particular ideological positions cannot be made in all cases, especially where moderate Presbyterianism and royalism might overlap, a sensitivity to context and language allows for the identification of instances of Royalist sedition and resistance. The nuanced distinctions between the political speech of Royalists and a Royalist political language, and between royalism and anti-Parliamentarianism, cannot be pursued in any depth here, but this piece argues that there was a distinctive language of sub-gentry Royalist opposition in the 1650s – something Underdown has described as a 'half-submerged, vague, but unmistakably Royalist vocabulary'.[11] It would be difficult to understand the outburst of Ellen Bechett, wife of a Middlewich labourer, as anything other than 'Royalist', although we do not have any further details of her political affiliations. In July 1659 at Middlewich she swore at a local official, 'a curse of God goe with thee, thou art a Roundhead rogue'.[12]

This chapter aims to deal with 'popular' political sentiment, and the inverted commas alert us to methodological, historiographical and interpretative problems of dealing with non-elite politics. The concept of 'popular politics' is employed to distinguish the seditious utterances under consideration here from those of the social elites who have been the focus of most Royalist studies.[13] There is obviously a danger of insisting upon a binary distinction between 'elite' and 'popular' which is too gross and simplistic.[14] Both the prosperous merchant and the impoverished labourer were outside the traditional elite, but the distinctions between them were greater than those between the merchant and the gentleman. However, such a schema is an important first step in moving the focus away from the traditional preoccupation with elite royalism, and acts as a bridgehead for future micro-political studies which can better dissect the socio-politics of royalism further down the social order. Some suggestive results have emerged from this initial survey. It appears that it was the 'middling sort' – artisans, tradesmen and yeomen – who were most prominent in expressing seditious opinions during the Interregnum.[15] In a sample of thirty-three cases of Royalist seditious speech which came before the Middlesex and Westminster benches between 1649 and 1653 in which the social status of the offender is given, only three (9 per cent) involved gentlemen; cordwainers were the most visible group (15 per cent) followed by yeomen, butchers and innkeepers (9 per cent), and tailors and cutlers (6 per cent). Individual cases concerned a chandler, a clothier, a carpenter, a plasterer, a silk-weaver and a labourer. Four women (12 per cent) were accused of having spoken seditious words: one was a prostitute, one a labourer's wife, and two were widows. Although we might expect such an occupational profile in the London suburbs, the legal record of sedition in areas like Somerset, Wiltshire, Cheshire and Essex also shows a significant presence of artisans, tradesmen and yeomen. For example, in the twenty-eight cases of Royalist sedition considered by the Somerset quarter sessions between 1649 and 1660 where status can be ascertained, we encounter only one gentleman (3.5 per cent) but four yeomen (14 per cent). There is a significant presence from the county's clothing industry, with four weavers, two tailors, one clothier, one worsted comber, one dyer and a rag gatherer (36 per cent). The remainder includes two husbandmen, a plasterer, a labourer, a carpenter, a lime burner and the wives of an innkeeper and a miller. In the words of Buchanan Sharp, this is a 'decidedly plebeian' social snapshot, and the significant presence of tradesmen in these samples suggests that we may have to rethink our easy conception of the middling sort as the 'natural' supporters of Parliament.[16] It was the more prosperous, skilled and educated of those below the level of the gentry who were most vocal in criticising the Interregnum governments and their local representatives. It is difficult to add fine structure to the political complexion of the Royalists outside the gentry order – to distinguish between a prosperous innkeeper in London and a small alehouse keeper in the provinces, for example – but the forces pulling the category of 'popular politics' apart here can, I hope, be counterbalanced by the preponderance of artisans, tradesmen, yeomen and husbandmen speaking a similar political language.

There were articulate non-elite Royalists, and they were neither as exotic nor as rare as most accounts of mid-century politics would lead us to believe. These men and women were capable of articulating political ideas through their frequent discussions of the political landscape. These Royalists were not simply the creatures of the local gentry or an exiled court. They were individuals who had assimilated the ideals and traditions of monarchy, hierarchy and legitimacy, and who sought to articulate a sense of alienation, disaffection and downright resistance to the usurping authorities under which they found themselves living. These were men and women who were socially and politically conservative, or who had come to be so through the experience of what they perceived to be a Parliamentarian or republican tyranny.[17]

II

The law of seditious or treasonous words reached back to the treason statute of 1352, which made it a capital crime to 'compass or imagine' the death of the monarch. Tudor legislation had expanded this body of law, making it a treasonable offence to write or speak against royal policy.[18] The legal status of seditious words remained controversial, however, and in Pine's Case (1628) it was accepted that seditious speech could not constitute treason. It was thereafter accounted a misdemeanour punishable by imprisonment, fines, pillorying or being placed in the stocks.[19] However, the Commonwealth and Protectorate authorities nervously tried to protect their dubious legitimacy by passing several Acts and ordinances which redefined treason within a politicised and explicitly anti-Royalist framework. Within this body of legislation it was treasonous to speak out against the respective Interregnum governments, or to promote the interest of Charles I's line.[20] However, this draconian legislation seems to have been rarely invoked with respect to the vast majority of seditious utterances, even those supporting Charles II or denying the legitimacy of the republican regimes. These were proceeded against in common law courts as misdemeanours. Other legislation could bring politicised words within the compass of the law; for example, the protectoral ordinance of June 1654 against duels provided for the prosecution of individuals who used 'disgraceful, provoking words or gestures', which could include politicised epithets such as 'Roundhead' or 'traitor'.[21] Another important context here was the common law's growing competence in cases of defamation – something considered to be especially serious if this involved words against a public person, such as a local JP or constable, for, as Sir Edward Coke had observed, this 'concerns not only the breach of the peace but the scandal of the government'.[22] The words under consideration in this essay, then, were indictable in local courts or the Upper Bench because they were considered to threaten the state, they broke the peace, or they encouraged others to do so.[23]

This essay is based mainly upon the archive of prosecutions for seditious words which came before the Upper Bench (formerly King's Bench), the assizes of the northern circuit and the great sessions of Wales and Chester, and the surviving quarter sessions courts of Cheshire, Devon, Exeter, Essex, Norfolk, Norwich, Somerset and Wiltshire between 1649 and 1660, and also cases brought before the quarter sessions of Middlesex and Westminster between 1649 and 1653.[24] The varying nature and completeness of these archives mean that comparison between them is difficult. For example, the material from the northern assize circuit has survived largely in the form of informations, examinations and depositions rather than indictments, while the depositional material from Essex is highly deficient, and Somerset's indictment files are fragmentary. The material from the Middlesex and Westminster sessions is derived partly from the information included on recognisances, although use of indictments has also been made here.[25] The most plentiful material is to be found in the quarter session records of Cheshire, Middlesex, Somerset and Wiltshire and the assize records of the northern circuit, but few prosecutions made their way to the Upper Bench. It is important to note that the documents under consideration here were not concerned with fleshing out the circumstances in which seditious speech was used, but rather with the illegal words themselves. The state papers from the Interregnum do not contain the wealth of detailed reports and letters passed to the Privy Council in both the earlier and the later seventeenth century. The papers of Secretary John Thurloe do contain important material relating to seditious language, but this is often concerned with large-scale conspiracies as opposed to the more quotidian transactions of anti-governmental speech found in the tavern and the marketplace. In the indictments which provide a good deal of our knowledge of anti-government speech in the 1650s, then, the offending words have been wrenched from their context, the flesh torn from the bones of the illegal utterances at issue. What we have left are the words which the state wanted to hear. Sometimes this evidence can be augmented by pre-trial documentation, but even this was framed very much by the relevant discourses of the law, which omitted a good deal of extraneous detail that could bring to life the conversations and confrontations which produced the offending words.[26] This is a severe limitation to interpreting Royalist sedition, but there is also a positive aspect here in that the law was concerned with the *exact* words spoken, and we can be fairly confident that the tenor of the Royalists' political criticisms has survived.

III

One of the key constituencies which caused concern for the Interregnum authorities was the Royalist clergy. Underdown was disdainful of the inactive and ineffective Royalist ministers who had 'no stomach for conspiracy'.[27] Yet there is evidence that those who were disaffected were important disseminators of anti-republican speech, and that this helped to sustain and encourage like-minded figures in their communities. The Council of State was concerned enough about their influence to sponsor bills in Parliament in June 1649 and March 1650 against ministers' 'seditious and derogatory expressions, touching the Parliament and their proceedings', although little seems to have come of the initiatives.[28] One member of the Rump described the clergy in 1650 as 'the great incendiaries', whose congregations believed whatever they preached, even if it was to 'stir up the people to rebellion against the state'.[29] In April 1650 the Council of State wrote to Major Blackmore in Exeter that it was 'very sensible howe much the Commonwelth sufferd both in safety & reputation by the intemperate declamations and seditious invectives of some men in their pulpits'.[30] Marchamont Nedham believed that the republican government should wink at most examples of intemperate speech against the authorities, but his leniency did not run to the pulpits, where dissent was seen as dangerously corrosive to the state.[31]

One such target of the authorities was Richard Jaggard, minister of Lympne (Kent), who had been ejected in 1644, but who continued to preach against the Parliament and for the interest of the king.[32] Samuel Baxter, rector of Dibden (Hampshire), conformed to the stereotype of the Cavalier clergyman in articles produced against him around 1655. It was alleged that he taught parishioners how to drink for twenty-four hours without getting inebriated, but he was also accused of aspersing the Protector before his sermon, drinking a health to Charles II and saying that the world would never be well until the king had his own again.[33] In Drayton (Shropshire), the minister, one Mr Cooke, was accused in September 1649 of publicly supporting the Royalist cause. It was claimed that before his sermon he prayed for 'the delivery of all the nobell famelie in this kingdom that lives under the tiranicall government of the souldire that now rules over them' and for the 'reestablishing of the antient government of this kingdom'. When challenged that he presided over a malignant set of parishioners, he countered that he was honoured to be regarded as one of them, adding, 'what soe ever becumeth of their bodies and theire fortunes, it is my duty to be carfull of theire soules which shall be manifested by preaching loyelty to theire king'.[34] Cooke was a 'turncoat', a man who had sided with Parliament at the beginning of the conflict. He said his earlier support of Parliament had been misguided, for 'had I knowen of theire designe I would have seene the Parliament hanged be fore I would have bin of theire side'. His identification with the 'malignants' of his parish and his self-fashioning as a Royalist through his public speeches suggest how Royalists and royalism were products of particular moments and particular places. It also points to how Royalists were constructed through discourse, contingency, political language, gesture and associations: they were not simply the unwavering supporters of Charles I from the early 1640s.

Although only a tiny minority of the disaffected clergy were prosecuted for sedition, the government's concern about their continued destabilising presence suggests that we should not ignore their on-going influence. Although they occasionally appear in the legal record for having been charged with seditious words, more common was the Royalist language to be found emanating from their parishioners. We have plentiful evidence to confirm that comparatively humble individuals were commenting disapprovingly on the Interregnum regimes from a specifically Royalist standpoint after 'falling into some discourse' on the political situation or 'having some conference touching the times'.[35] Moments of upheaval or crisis intensified the discussion of controversial topics and produced more in the way of actionable language. The Regicide, the promulgation of the Engagement, the Battle of Worcester and the flight of Charles II, the fall of the Rump and the establishment of the Protectorate, were all key moments when voices of opposition and discontent became more audible in the political transcript. It is possible that this reflects a greater vigilance on the part of the authorities in rooting out such disaffection, but it seems likely that tensions in high politics produced discussion and opposition throughout the social spectrum.[36] Such a chronology of periodic peaks of Royalist seditious speech also reflects the traditional narrative of a greater degree of acclimatisation to the Protectorate compared with the Commonwealth, suggesting that Cromwell's policy of 'healing and settling' did have some degree of success in reconciling Royalist malcontents and critics to his rule.[37]

Prosecutions for seditious speech clustered particularly around the beginning of the Commonwealth, reflecting the widespread horror and revulsion of many at the execution of God's anointed, as well as the anger directed at the illegitimate rule of king-killers in the Rump Parliament.[38] Ralph Josselin reported in a diary entry of 4 February 1649 that Charles's execution was 'very much talked of, very many men of the weaker sort of Christians in divers places passionate concerning it'.[39] Passion and the desire for revenge for the Regicide were in evidence throughout a wide range of locales in the early Commonwealth. In December 1649, for example, Nicholas Wiltshire, a husbandman of North Petherton (Somerset), was accused of saying that 'they that did put the king to death were all rogues, & he did hope to see the confounding of them & theire throates cutt'.[40] This was echoed in Kirkby Mooreside (Yorkshire), where John Leeswood was accused of having said in March 1649 that the Commons were 'all traytors, and hee hoped to see them all cutt off ere longe'.[41]

Many ordinary men and women who were deeply shocked at the Regicide also expressed a definite, if unsophisticated, strain of 'constitutionalist' discourse in their hostile reflections on the fate of the king. One such conversation brought John Norris, a tailor of St Botolph's without Aldgate, before the Middlesex bench in April 1650. He was indicted for having said that Charles was 'illegally put to death' and that he hoped his persecutors would 'heereafter suffer for it, and that the power which they have is maintained only by the sword'.[42] Some key elements of Royalist discourse can be found here with the emphasis on the illegality of Charles's trial and execution, and, by extension, the illegitimacy of the entire republican state. There was also a clear sense that this had introduced tyrannous rule with no legal basis for the state's actions beside the might of the army. There was also the recurring Royalist trope of a desire to visit retribution on the guilty.

These accusations of illegitimacy and the interruption of lawful authority with the death of the king also provided disgruntled Royalists with a vocabulary for criticising local government and its officials. This flowed from a belief that authority and law had lapsed with the death of the sovereign, and, in the absence of a legitimate successor, all of the organs of the state were effectively acting *ultra vires*. As some of those taken with Penruddock averred at their trial at Exeter in April 1655, 'they had sworne ... to be true to the Kinge, and they at present [had] noe legall established government in this nacion'.[43] This position clashed with the republican case that Charles's treason against his subjects had seen him divested of his regal authority, which was relocated in the people.[44] Many Royalist sympathisers scoffed at such arguments, and attacked the legitimacy of local government through the reasoning of Royalist constitutionalism. John Lewys, a Norwich labourer, claimed in February 1650 that the legitimacy of the mayor, John Rayley, had lapsed with the Regicide. In a neat inversion of King James's 'No bishop, no king', he was reported to have said 'noe kinge, no maior ... for ought I know, master maior hath no power'.[45] John Shawe, a member of the Porters' Company, was accused in December 1652 of having said that the City of London had no power to make laws for the Company, 'their [i.e. the Company's] head being taken off', which was glossed by his accusers, 'meaning the kings head as they conceive'.[46] Cornelius Bell, a weaver of Messing (Essex), said in July 1651 that the state had no power to impress soldiers or punish anyone without a king.[47] This kind of critique was put rather more colourfully by a Somerset yeoman, John Dinham, who refused to acknowledge a warrant for his arrest in a plea of trespass in April 1654, saying 'he did not care a turd for the Lord Protector, not his warrant neither, for there is now noe proceedings in law'.[48]

In these attacks on the post-Regicide authorities there is little evidence of the evocation of the 'commonwealth' or the interests of the 'commons'. Such language had previously provided non-gentle orders with a fertile source for critical words against authority.[49] In the eyes of Royalist sympathisers, however, action in the interest of the commons and the radical programme of realising a functioning C/commonwealth had only produced a sea of blood, the social degeneration of authority and a headless, monstrous polity. It is not surprising that the tropes of 'commonwealth' discourse were not to be found in the mouths of more plebeian Royalists. Such terms had been appropriated by radical groups, and the claim to conduct politics in the interest of the common people had become tainted with the stain of potential social revolution. Even comparatively low-born supporters of the king shied away from horizontal associations with a collective commonality, and oriented their language towards the reestablishment of normative socio-political relationships within the state. This point about class and Royalist language will be developed further below.

Outbursts against local officials and justices are to be found throughout the early modern period. This has prompted some historians to dismiss such instances during the Interregnum as being of little consequence, a reflexive kind of denunciation with no political element: a 'simple, unselfconscious invective aimed at anyone in authority'.[50] However, the disparagement of local authority had clear political potential given the transformation in the complexion of local and central government after 1649, and such incidents need to be contextualised within their proper place and moment. This was an administrative apparatus which was no longer sanctioned by the mystical power of the monarch, and challenges to local authority were thus altered in their political meaning and rendered distinct from earlier invective against the king's officials. The denunciation of a justice, constable or tithingman might emerge simply from local struggles devoid of wider ideological contexts, but it also potentially encompassed challenges to the ruling order which could be articulated in explicitly Royalist terms. Such an instance was the comment of Thomas Butland, a Devonshire yeoman, who said in 1651 that 'there were none but scommes [scums] and runagate rogues that served the Parliament'.[51] In Westminster, William Reynolds, a victualler, was bound by a recognisance in October 1650 to answer the charge that he had said that 'the states were a companie of rogues [who should] ... kiss his arce', but also that he had connected his wider discontent to a local official, Richard Ingram, whom he called a 'rogue for servinge the state soe longe'.[52] John Sawyer, keeper of the Pope's Head tavern in London, tied the City's officials to their political masters in a case from October 1658. A known supporter of Charles II, Sawyer refused to admit constables to his house, where he was suspected of holding a meeting of disaffected persons. After the constables and some soldiers had forced an entry, he said to the guard, 'A turd for you and the power and authority you act by. I defy you all.'[53]

The chain of relationships which could tie the politics of the parish to that of the centre was also evident in August 1659 when Jasper Willis, a Cornish yeoman, found himself before the Upper Bench accused of having said that 'he did not care a fart for the Parliament, nor none of the Parliament, nor for any of the liberties of the said Parliament, nor for any justice of the peace, nor thou, constable'.[54] Such comments suggest the 'desacralisation' of the concatenary links in parliamentary authority in much the same way that earlier studies have suggested for seditious language both before and after the civil wars.[55] As David Cressy has argued with respect to the period 1640–42, the 'slighting of local authority enfeebled the body politic'; the body politic of the republic was seen by Royalist supporters from a range of social backgrounds as unlawful throughout its central and local members.[56]

The criticism of justices and local officials was particularly significant if they were parvenus who hailed from outside traditional ruling circles. The local face of the national revolution was often one which affronted established notions of hierarchy and rule, concepts which had been inculcated by many of the middling and common sort as well as their social superiors. In March 1651 John Swaine, a yeoman, was in conversation with Mary Helsall of Gawsworth (Cheshire) when he described Henry Bradshaw, a leading republican JP in the county and elder brother of John Bradshaw, Lord President of the Council of State, as a 'plowe chorle or plowe hogg', which is to say a man without rank who worked the land.[57] In the example of Thomas Butland given above, his reviling of Parliament's servants as 'scommes' provided a social as well as political commentary, suggesting they were the offscourings of society, the dross constituting the underclass. This element of class criticism is often unacknowledged in studies of royalism and popular politics more generally in the sixteenth and seventeenth centuries. Social historians have attuned our ears to the potent discourses of conflict which ranged the interests of the commons against those of the gentry and their social betters. However, we also need to realise that socially conservative sections among the lower and middling sorts could deploy a political language of class too, but this was one which invoked ideals of political hierarchy and social deference in the legitimate ordering of society. This was a political language which allowed for the criticism of social upstarts who had intruded themselves into the ruling order, and was deployed by comparatively humble individuals as well as the marginalised Royalist gentry.

William Price of Slebech (Pembrokeshire) was a man who could not sign his name to his examination, but he reacted sharply against the violation of the social hierarchies of politics in the 1650s. He was indicted before the local great sessions court in 1654 for saying that the Protector and those under his command were 'all rogues and tinkers'.[58] John Sawyer of Bishops Lydiard (Somerset) was discussing politics in a neighbour's house at the time of Charles II's attempted invasion in the summer of 1651, when he was reported to have said that 'since they have put the kinge to death, the gov[e]rn[o]rs of this kingdome are noe others then dishmakers, tinkers and coblers'.[59] The man with whom he was drinking was a fuller (one who beats cloth to clean and thicken it), which would suggest that Sawyer was of a similar social position. John Rodd of Chilton (Somerset) anticipated Sawyer's sentiments earlier the same year, claiming that 'there were none in the Parliament house but rogues, tinckers & pedlers'.[60] In Exeter, an innkeeper's wife derided one of the city constables as a 'mycannick fellow', adding that 'shee would not bee subiect to such constables'.[61] Richard Oliver, a gentleman of Aslacton (Norfolk), was representative of the affronted attitudes of more socially elevated Royalists in his critique of the Independent justice Edmund Burman. In October 1655 Oliver said that Burman was a 'pocke headed platery rascally fellow and that he [i.e. Oliver] kept better then he to wipe his shooes'.[62] He also focused on Burman's pretensions to sartorial declarations of status, mocking how he 'did runn about the country ... with his great roofe [ruff] about his neck'.[63]

This social critique of the intruded local and central government was succinctly conveyed in the ubiquitous Royalist reviling of their enemies as 'rogues' and 'knaves'. Although such terms were also used by Parliamentarians and republicans, they were rarely as common or as colourful as in the mouths of the Royalists. 'Rogue' carried the connotation of dishonesty and villainy, but it also suggested an individual who belonged to the underworld of vagrants and vagabonds. Similarly, while 'knave' implied a deceitful and unprincipled individual, it also insinuated that one was a servant or person of mean condition and low social standing. The 'knave' in a pack of playing cards was the lowest court card in a suit, and carried the picture of a soldier or servant.[64] One indictment brought before the Norwich quarter sessions in 1658, saw Thomas Browne, a worsted weaver, accused of having said that 'ther must be halfe a dozen knaves taken out of the packe of aldermen & the rest will be the better'. Browne had been before the city's mayoral court in 1655 for speaking against the Lord Protector and the Norwich authorities.[65] Terms like 'knave' in the Royalist speech of the Interregnum suggest a social critique carried within political messages about the illegitimacy of the government and the deep disquiet about the subversion of traditional order. Such language was not the preserve of the aristocracy and gentry, however, but was also used by politically conservative figures from the middling and lower strata of society.

Royalist opprobrium was not directed wholly, or even mostly, at local officials, however. The key targets for a good deal of the seditious speech which came to the attention of the authorities were the Rump Parliament, Cromwell, Fairfax, the army, Puritan ministers and local grandees. The Rump was derided as a company of low-born traitors and king-killers. Cromwell too was denounced as a murderer, a tyrant and a traitor who deserved hanging, after which he would roast in the fires of hell.[66] The political language of ordinary Royalists was often suffused with a desire for revenge and retribution, with graphic and violent threats often accompanying their derisive and profane words against the state. Richard Browne, a yeoman of Cleaburne (Westmorland), was accused in 1656 of having said that the Protector deserved to be beheaded or hanged, adding that if he could come 'privately' to Cromwell and his associates, 'God dame me body & soule if I would not cutt all their throates. And if I had them all in a hott burning oven, God confound mee if I would not sett upp the stone & burne them all to death.'[67] An indictment against Thomas Parsons of London recounted how he had vented his spleen against John Bradshaw, who he said should be hanged, drawn and quartered for 'iudginge & commandinge the kinge to dye'.[68] In these comments, we find respect for legal proceedings against the leaders of the Puritan revolution, with the attendant punishments of hanging (much more common than Browne's reference to beheading which was reserved for the aristocracy or, of course, royalty), alongside the extra-judicial violence which many wanted to see visited upon these traitors.

The modes of some of this imagined violence are worthy of comment. The retributive imagery employed by many Royalists like Richard Browne often focused on cutting the throats of the republican usurpers. This is noteworthy in that, in standard homicide cases, cutting the throat of one's adversary was far outside accepted practices of righteous male violence, which mainly resulted in mitigated punishments. Here, however, it clearly indicated the contempt in which Parliamentarians were held.[69] Not only were they not accorded the status of equal combatants, but they were effectively reduced to animals; cutting the throat was the usual method of slaughtering beasts (outside the more honourable hunt, of course). Cutting the throat was also a punishment meted out by the Turk, and perhaps also suggested that, for Royalists, traitors like Cromwell lay outside civil Christendom, and warranted the justice of the heathen whom so they resembled.[70]

The language of the Royalists was designed to exclude – to define and revile their enemies. However, it could also be a vehicle to draw others in and forge associations based on common political attitudes. This reflected the general use of political stereotypes which had divided the post-Civil War world into camps of 'us' and 'them', the 'Roundheads' and the 'Cavaliers'.[71] These badges carried a potential wealth of meanings in particular contexts and were important in constituting political group identities. To denounce someone as a 'roundheaded rogue' was to place her or him decisively outside one's own social and political spheres.[72] It was an act of self-definition as well as a means of defining the other. Aggressive assertions of Cavalier identities among comparatively humble people provide some striking examples of the ways in which the supposedly elitist political culture of royalism was appropriated and deployed by ordinary men.[73] In early 1650, for example, Humphrey Butler of Devizes (Somerset), a seller of cosmetics, was at the house of William Derrick at Wells when he drank the king's health and demanded 'all you that are cavelears com[e] alonge with me'.[74] Richard Collins of Barwick (Somerset), a miller, had an information sworn against him in August 1659 which claimed he had said that he 'was a cavaleer & he would be a cavaleer & the devil take all them that would not bee cavaleers'.[75] In Lewes (Sussex), Henry Woodcock was involved in an exchange with a Parliamentary opponent in January 1657 regarding the course of the Civil War and the respective fates of both parties. Railing against decimators, Cromwell and Puritans in general, Woodcock said that if he had as many lives as hairs on his head he would 'spend them all against such traytors and rebells as were against the cavaliers'.[76] Evidently the soubriquet of 'Cavalier', which is normally understood as a pejorative slander, was appropriated and used as a political signifier by some Royalist sympathisers.[77] It was a badge of loyalty, a symbol of suffering.

It is not coincidental that in the cases of Woodcock and Butler, the declarations of Cavalierism came in the context of drinking alcohol. In some ways drinking was itself a facet of the oppositional discourse of royalism as ranged against the stereotype of abstemious Roundheads. Drinking also potentially encompassed another important element in the construction of Royalist political associations and identities, however, through the practice of drinking healths and pledging allegiance to the king. As Angela McShane Jones has recently pointed out, drinking (and the attendant singing of ballads) became increasingly politicised in the Interregnum as the Puritan authorities sought to root out the political evils which emerged from an alehouse culture seen as dangerously Royalist.[78] She concentrates exclusively on ballad culture, but there is a considerable amount of evidence that the authorities were particularly concerned about the seditious toasting of the exiled king which went on when some men and women got their hands on a cup of ale. Such activity has usually been written off as sub-political, a further demonstration of the insignificance and impotence of royalism in the 1650s.[79] However, this is to miss the deeply political and oppositional nature of such acts.[80] This was not simply gesture politics, but rather a politics of gesture. It was also a means of political association and the public demonstration of allegiances akin to the taking of an oath as bystanders were asked to join in the pledge. As the Royalist newsbook *Mercurius Elencticus* remarked in January 1648, drinking the king's health had become an 'infallible symptom of malignancy', and it was a malignancy which many were proud to own publicly.[81] Through this activity, then, political links could be formed or re-affirmed and criticism of the state could be articulated.

At Cambridge's midsummer fair in July 1649, some 'freshmen' asked a group of older undergraduates, 'Gentlemen are you Royalists?' To demonstrate that they were, the group drank a health to Charles II and to the confusion of 'King Tom [Thomas Fairfax] ... and all his rogues'.[82] One of the group was expelled from the university for his actions. As Charles II's forces marched south to Worcester, an alehouse in Wilmslow (Cheshire) became a site for declaring allegiances and drawing political boundaries. Robert Newton, a wheelwright, grabbed a pot of ale and asked the other drinkers to pledge with him a toast to the king. A young husbandman in the company later deposed that Newton had also said that he hoped none of the Parliament's soldiers who were going to Worcester would return. Moreover, when Newton heard a report that the Cavaliers had assembled on Wilmslow Green, he said that 'hee would have given them a barrell of beere'.[83] He misjudged his audience, however, and found enemies rather than associates who not only refused to join his health (and thus drew an exclusionary political boundary of their own), but testified against him at the county's quarter sessions. A shoemaker from Youlgreave (Derbyshire) attested to similar activities in the north immediately after Cromwell's return from Scotland in September 1651. Hugh Sheldon, a lead miner, was drinking a health to King Charles II in an alehouse, where his companions had demonstrated their collective support by 'having all theire hatts throwen upon the flore'. Another miner, William Calton, said, 'God blesse King Charles & put of his hatt & said hee wold raigne ere long.'[84] The deferential gesture of doffing their hats, the communal participation in drinking and the seditious imagining of the king's return at the point of Cromwell's victory charged the atmosphere of this alehouse with a politics of resistance and defiance which cannot simply be dismissed as meaningless and empty.[85] We should also note here the conjunction of gesture with political words, something which is often lost in many of the bare descriptions of seditious words in the legal record, but which clearly formed vital contexts for, and accompaniments to, the articulation of Royalist opposition.

IV

How concerned were the Interregnum governments about such words? How significant, on a national scale, were the incidents recorded in the legal archive? Did the governments of the Interregnum feel threatened by these conversations? These questions are difficult to answer with any certainty, but the vigilance of the various regimes and their attention to potential sedition is revealing of their nervousness about popular anti-republican feeling. The several treason Acts and ordinances passed between 1649 and 1660 give some indication of the sensitivity of the several Interregnum governments to potential threats from within. The intelligence apparatuses of Secretary Thurloe and Thomas Scott were geared to rooting out potential subversion, and the atmosphere of surveillance was sometimes seen as oppressive indeed. Clement Walker described Scott's informers as 'swarming all over England as lice & frogs did in Egypt'.[86] In 1655 Henry Oxinden of Barnham (Kent) wrote to his wife that 'for public newes, men are afrayd to speke one to another, though freinds'.[87] The instructions to the Major-Generals warned them to 'keep a strict eye upon the conversation and carriage of all disaffected persons'.[88] The Interregnum authorities were clearly concerned with criticism. In April 1649, following reports that John Knight, a prominent Bristol merchant, had affronted the authority of Parliament by calling some individuals 'parliament dogs' and 'parliament rogues', the Council of State wrote to the city's mayor to warn him that 'the commonwealth cannot be preserved in peace if these attempts upon its authority be suffered to pass unpunished'.[89]

Yet there also seems to have been a degree of flexibility on the part of the central authorities and a sense that the fearsome intelligence machinery of the state, and the legislation which backed it up, were designed as much to deter as to punish. As Marchamont Nedham observed in 1649, 'it behoves states-men to know all things, but not to prosecute all things', for, he argued, exces-sive zeal would augment the numbers of recalcitrants, not diminish them. The laws should be 'as the bridle and the whip, to restrain disaffected persons ... But they are not to be put in execution except where absolute necessity requires; and then not in extremity neither.' Regarding 'opprobrious speeches against the government', he advised governors that 'such language as is not fit for them to heare, they must seem not to heare'.[90] It did not behove the republican governments to enquire too deeply into the political convictions of its citizens, for they knew that they would find a deep well of sullen resent-ment and outright antagonism.[91] A letter from the Council of State to the bailiffs and JPs of Ipswich in April 1649, concerning the seditious words of a surgeon, Henry Sherman, gives some suggestion of the reluctance to make martyrs of those who spoke intemperate words. Although the Council noted the seriousness of Sherman's speech (the subject is not specified), it asked the town's authorities to consider whether his 'high language' was 'spoken out of a habit of inveterate malice, or whether upon a surprise of passion and engagement in argument, as it seems by his answer'. Enquiry into the 'general course of his conversation' was necessary to ascertain the precise nature of his offence.[92] The Council was keen to discover whether his opinions were those of a determined opponent of the regime or simply an aberrant flare-up during a passionate argument. The latter could be studiously ignored, but the former demanded more determined punishment.

Local justices, too, appear to have discriminated between the seriousness of the sedition cases brought before them. Individuals who had been caught for the first time saying they 'did not care a fart for the justice' might be given a comparatively light fine or be bound over to keep the peace, while others who challenged the ruling order more directly, or who were known to be active Royalists and 'evilly affected' to the republic, were stung with swingeing fines.[93] Knowledge about the political trustworthiness and reliability of the individual was one component in the judicial response to individual cases of seditious and scandalous words. In a similar manner to the way in which the early modern bench distinguished between those it considered irredeemable criminals and those who were just recidivist malefactors, it often discriminated between the vocalising of opposition on the part of resolute and dangerous

Royalists and intemperate words spoken by otherwise reliable individuals in their cups.[94]

Despite the latitude in punishing some of those who uttered words against the state, it is clear that the various republican governments were concerned about oppositional language. In addition to the comments regarding the potentially complex nature of immoderate speech in the Council of State's letter to the Ipswich justices quoted above, for example, it also reflected that 'insurrections and commotions usually begin, and are fermented by, seditious language'.[95] That its worst nightmares of concerted and popular rebellion did not come to pass does not mean that the Royalist words under consideration here should be dismissed as insignificant. The evidence relating to Royalist speech from the 1650s should remind us that the outpouring of relief and support which greeted Charles II in May 1660 was not simply a politic and momentary alliance of diverse interests antipathetic to the republic.[96] Royalist sedition during the republic gives some indication of the bedrock of popular support which Charles II could call upon in parishes and towns throughout the kingdom. The roots of popular Toryism can, perhaps, be glimpsed in some of the declarations of Cavalierism and anti-Parliamentarianism which issued from the mouths of cutlers, cordwainers and cobblers under the republic.[97] It is impossible to be certain of the extent to which these cases of Royalist sedition represent the tip of a much larger constituency of anti-republican language which never came to the attention of the authorities, although one must suspect that this was the case. As one black-letter ballad put it on the eve of the Restoration, the Royalists would 'drink and pray no longer / For the King in mistical fashions, / But with trumpets sound / His health go round.'[98]

V

Seditious Royalist words did not threaten the state directly, for, as Underdown appreciated long ago, they never meshed with an effective body of armed resistance. However, the machinery of the state in the 1650s was in part shaped by the need to police the significant, and socially variegated, constituency of Royalist sympathisers. In giving voice and substance to what Underdown once described as the country's 'passive conservatism' during the 1650s, it is possible to reinvest Royalist language with agency and recognise its significance in shaping the structures which sought to control and suppress it. Such a project also has the potential to advance our understanding of the development of a politics of popular monarchism under Charles II. When Major-General John Desborough addressed the Commons at the first reading of the decimation bill on 7 January 1657, he said that he hoped those who had spoken against the government or drunk the king's health would be subject to decimation. Such actions, he continued, were 'the issues of their hearts. Out of the abundance of the heart the mouth speaks. How can you better distinguish them?'[99] His question remains relevant to Royalist studies, although few have sought to explore its ramifications for our interpretation and understanding of royalism as a potentially unstable and contingent political position. In the effort to refine our understanding of political allegiances *throughout* the period of the Civil Wars and Interregnum, it will be necessary to follow Desborough in paying greater attention to the conversations of non-elite men and women concerning the political and constitutional upheavals of the period. It was people's words, as well as their actions, that produced the kaleidoscope of fractured political communities of mid-seventeenth-century England and Wales; we should listen to them more closely.

NOTES

I would like to dedicate this piece to the memory of Dr James Thomas. He would not have been in the slightest bit interested in its subject matter, but would have been pleased that I had finally managed to get some swear words into my academic work. I am very grateful to Andy Wood and the editors for their comments and suggestions on this essay.

1 Although see Ian Gentles, *The English Revolution and the Wars in the Three Kingdoms, 1638–1652* (Harlow, 2007), pp. 130–5; Keith Lindley, 'London and popular freedom in the 1640s', in R.C. Richardson and G.M. Ridden (eds), *Freedom and the English Revolution* (Manchester, 1986), pp. 133–7; David Underdown, *Revel, Riot and Rebellion* (Oxford, 1985), pp. 242–6, 253–70.

2 For two examples from an extensive historiography, see Joel Samaha, 'Gleanings from local criminal-court records: sedition amongst the "inarticulate" in Elizabethan Essex', *Journal of Social History*, 8 (1975), pp. 61–79, and Buchanan Sharp, 'Popular political opinion in England, 1660–1685', *History of European Ideas*, 10 (1989), pp. 13–29. For the huge associated literature dealing with pre-Civil War news and popular verse, see Alastair Bellany, 'Railing rhymes revisited: libels, scandals and early Stuart politics', *History Compass*, 5 (2007), pp. 1–44, and the sources cited.

3 David Underdown, *Royalist Conspiracy in England, 1649–1660* (New Haven, CT, 1960), pp. 16, 255, 328.

4 *Ibid.*, p. 16. This echoes C.H. Firth, 'The Royalists under the Protectorate', *EHR*, 52 (1937), pp. 645–6.

5 Although see Dagmar Freist, *Governed by Opinion: Politics, Religion and the Dynamics of Communication in Stuart London, 1637–1645* (New York, 1997). Freist remarks on the lack of a study of seditious words in the Interregnum at p. 178 n. 4.

6 Joyce Lee Malcolm, *Caesar's Due: Loyalty and King Charles, 1642–1646* (1983); Jason Peacey, *Politicians and Pamphleteers: Propaganda during the English Civil Wars and Interregnum* (Aldershot, 2004), pp. 307–28; Jerome de Groot, *Royalist Identities* (Basingstoke, 2004), pp. 46–53. Cf. Jason McElligott, *Royalism, Print and Censorship in Revolutionary England* (Woodbridge, 2007).

7 Jason McElligott, 'The politics of sexual libel: Royalist propaganda in the 1640s', *HLQ*, 67 (2004), pp. 75–99; Mark Jenner, 'The roasting of the Rump: scatology and the body

politic in Restoration England', *P&P*, 177 (2002), pp. 84–102, and Angela McShane Jones's recent debate with Jenner in *P&P*, 196 (2007), pp. 253–86; David Underdown, *A Freeborn People* (Oxford, 1996); David Underdown, 'The language of popular politics in the English Revolution', in Alvin Vos (ed.), *Place and Displacement in the Renaissance* (Binghampton, 1995); James Grantham Turner, *Libertines and Radicals in Early Modern London: Sexuality, Politics, and Literary Culture, 1630–1685* (Cambridge, 2002), pp. 74–117.

8   TNA, PRO, CHES 24/131/1 (Oct. 1655).

9   For Browne as a Quaker, see Joseph Besse, *A Collection of the Sufferings of the People called Quakers* (1753), vol. I, pp. 102, 744.

10 TNA, PRO, CHES 24/131/1 (Oct. 1655).

11 Underdown, *Revel, Riot and Rebellion*, p. 267.

12 CCA, QJF 87/2/4/63.

13 Jason McElligott and David L. Smith (eds), *Royalists and Royalism during the English Civil Wars* (Cambridge, 2007), p. 14.

14 Tim Harris, *London Crowds in the Reign of Charles II* (Cambridge, 1987), pp. 15–22.

15 This agrees with the findings of Keith Lindley for London in the 1640s: 'London and popular freedom', p. 136.

16 Sharp, 'Political opinion in England', p. 14.

17 Robert Ashton, 'From Cavalier to Roundhead tyranny, 1642–9', in John Morrill (ed.), *Reactions to the English Civil War 1642–1649* (Basingstoke, 1982), pp. 185–207; McElligott, *Royalism, Print and Censorship*, chapters 2–4.

18 Adam Fox, 'Rumour, news and popular political opinion in Elizabethan and early Stuart England', *HJ*, 40 (1997), p. 599; John Bellamy, *The Tudor Law of Treason* (Trowbridge and Esher, 1979).

19 Harbottle Grimston, *The Reports of Sir George Croke* (1657), pp. 83–9; Roger B. Manning, 'The origin of the doctrine of sedition', *Albion*, 12 (1980), pp. 99–121.

20 *A&O*, vol. II, pp. 19, 120–1, 192–4, 831–5, 1038–40.

21 *Ibid.*, vol. II, pp. 937–9.

22 W.S. Holdsworth, 'Defamation in the sixteenth and seventeenth centuries', *Law Quarterly Review*, 40 (1924), pp. 302–15. See also Garthine Walker, *Crime, Gender and Social Order in Early Modern England* (Cambridge, 2003), pp. 213–15.

23 Freist, *Governed by Opinion*, p. 181.

24 The truncation of the Middlesex and Westminster sample was occasioned by the closure of the LMA during a crucial period of research.

25 On the Middlesex recognisances, see Bernard Capp, 'Republican reformation: family, community and the state in Interregnum Middlesex', in Helen Barry and Elizabeth Foyster (eds), *The Family in Early Modern England* (Cambridge, 2007), pp. 40–66.

26 Freist, *Governed by Opinion*, p. 182.

27 Underdown, *Royalist Conspiracy*, p. 183.

28 *CSPD 1649–50*, p. 199; *CSPD 1650*, pp. 58, 62, 68; *CJ*, vol. VI, p. 240.

29 John Fry, *The Clergy in their Colours* (1650), pp. 44–5.

30 TNA, PRO, SP 25/95, p. 71. See also *CSPD 1650*, pp. 390, 427, 442; *CJ*, vol. VI, pp. 501–2, 597.

31 Marchamont Nedham, *Certain Considerations Tendered ... to an Honourable Member of the Council of State* (1649), pp. 10–11. I am grateful to Jason McElligott for drawing my attention to this work.

32 *CSPD 1650*, pp. 17, 180; A.G. Matthews, *Walker Revised* (Oxford, 1948), p. 219.

33 Bodl., Rawlinson MS A26, p. 431.

34 BL, Stowe MS 184, fols 156, 158.

35 CCA, QJF 78/3/73; TNA, PRO, ASSI 45/5/2/87.

36 J.A. Sharpe, *Crime in Seventeenth-Century England: A County Study* (Cambridge, 1983), p. 82.

37 The classic account of this is David Underdown, 'Settlement in the counties, 1653–1658', in Gerald Aylmer (ed.), *The Interregnum: The Quest for Settlement, 1646–1660* (1972), pp. 165–82.

38 Stephen Roberts, one of the few historians to have given seditious words in the 1650s any serious consideration, notes that in Devon seditious words were more common under the Commonwealth than at any other time until at least 1670. *Recovery and Restoration in an English County: Devon Local Administration, 1646–1670* (Exeter, 1985), pp. 33–4.

39 Alan MacFarlane (ed.), *The Diary of Ralph Josselin, 1616–1683* (1976), p. 155.

40 Somerset RO, Q/SR/82/2/154. See also *ibid.*, Q/SR/81/87. His status as a husbandman is determined from *ibid.*, DD/AH/8/3/10.

41 TNA, PRO, ASSI 44/4 (unfoliated).

42 LMA, MJ/SR 1050 (352).

43 C.H. Firth (ed.), *The Clarke Papers*, vol. III (Camden Society, new series, 61, 1899), p. 36.

44 D. Alan Orr, 'The juristic foundation of Regicide', in Jason Peacey (ed.), *The Regicides and the Execution of Charles I* (Basingstoke, 2001), pp. 117–37.

45 Norfolk RO, NCR Case 11a/59 (Apr. 1650, no. 12).

46 LMA, CLA/047/LJ/01/0117.

47 Essex RO, Q/SBa 2/76; Q/SR 349/158; HMC, *Manuscripts of the Earl of Westmorland and Others* (1885), p. 511. Bell claimed he was merely reporting a conversation.

48 Somerset RO, Q/SR/89/47. This case eventually came before the Upper Bench: TNA, PRO, KB 9/862/147.

49 David Rollison, 'The specter of the commonalty: class struggle and the commonweal in England before the Atlantic world', *WMQ*, 63 (2006), pp. 221–52; Andy Wood, *The 1549 Rebellions and the Making of Early Modern England* (Cambridge, 2007). I am grateful to Andy Wood for letting me see portions of this work before publication.

50 Roberts, *Recovery and Restoration*, p. 33; John Morrill, *Cheshire, 1630–1660* (Oxford, 1974), pp. 255–6. Cf. David Cressy, *England on Edge* (Oxford, 2006), pp. 347–76.

51 Devon RO, Q/SB Box 55 (Easter 1651). Cf. *ibid.*, Q/SB Box 56 (Mich./Midsomer 1651): indictment of Mary Peter of Ashberton for having said 'that none but such rogues as hee [William Surrage, soapmaker] did serve the Parliament'.

52 LMA, MJ/SR 1059 (47), (184–5). For examples of such anti-Parliamentary language

during the Civil War, see J.C. Jeaffreson (ed.), *Middlesex County Records* (1886–92), vol. III, pp. 87–8, 94, 178.

53 *TSP*, vol. III, p. 573.

54 TNA, PRO, KB 9/884/187.

55 On 'desacralisation' in its monarchical context, see Robert Zaller, 'Breaking the vessels: the desacralization of monarchy in early modern England', *Sixteenth Century Journal*, 29 (1998), pp. 757–78.

56 Cressy, *England on Edge*, p. 362.

57 CCA, QJF 79/1/38. Swaine's yeoman status is derived from his will: CCA, Wills, John Swaine of Gawsworth (1683). See also CCA, QJF 79/1/78, where William Arderne, a gentleman, noted how Henry Bradshaw went about in 'soe plaine apparell' considering his 'eminency' in the country, and jokingly offered that he might be the king's elder brother.

58 National Library of Wales, Great Sessions 4/789/2/29. See also 4/789/2/27.

59 Somerset RO, Q/SR/83/1/85.

60 *Ibid.*, Q/SR/83/2/123; Q/SI/89/34–6.

61 Devon RO, ECA, QSOB 64, fol. 430v.

62 Another example of a Royalist claiming that a Parliamentarian agent was not sufficient to wipe his shoes can be found at LMA, MJ/SR 1115 (166).

63 Norfolk RO, C/C3/42. Cf. Essex RO, Q/SR 366/23; Q/SR 367/19. For Burman, see John Evans, *Seventeenth-Century Norwich* (Oxford, 1979), pp. 133, 182, 231, 233, 238; *A&O*, vol. I, p. 1240; *CJ*, vol. VII, p. 760; Norfolk RO, DUN 71; FEL 25, 546×6.

64 *OED*, http://dictionary.oed.com, s.v. 'rogue'; 'knave' (accessed Sept. 2007).

65 Norfolk RO, NCR Case 11a/68 (Apr. 1658, no. 4); NCR Case 16b/23, fol. 20v. See also Bodl., Wood 401(47): *A New Game at Cards* (1656); *The Royall and Delightfull Game of Picquet* (1656).

66 For example, Devon RO, QSOB 1/8, 13 Jan. 1652; QS/B Box 58 (Easter 1652); J.C. Atkinson (ed.), *North Riding Records. VI. Quarter Sessions Records* (1888), p. 18. I intend to discuss the treatment of Cromwell in popular Royalist discourse more fully in a future publication.

67 TNA, PRO, ASSI 45/5/5/6–7. He was found guilty and fined £10, later remitted to £5.

68 LMA, MJ/SR 1050 (353).

69 Walker, *Crime, Gender and Social Order*, pp. 33–48. I am grateful to Garthine Walker for discussing this point.

70 I owe this point to Jason McElligott.

71 Malcolm, *Caesar's Due*, pp. 149–64; de Groot, *Royalist Identities*, pp. 90–116. These categories were, of course, neither definite nor stable.

72 For example Devon RO, Q/SB Box 56 (Michaelmas/Midsomer 1651); TNA, PRO, SP 24/86, *Wray v. Abbey*.

73 Royalist women do not seem to have identified themselves as 'Cavaliers'.

74 Somerset RO, Q/SR/81/81.

75 *Ibid.*, Q/SR/97/63.

76 *TSP*, vol. V, p. 779.

77 Cf. Ian Roy, 'Royalist reputations: the Cavalier ideal and the reality', in McElligott and Smith (eds), *Royalists and Royalism*, pp. 89–111.

78 Angela McShane Jones, 'Roaring Royalists and ranting brewers: the politicisation of drink and drunkenness in political broadside ballads from 1640 to 1689', in Adam Smyth (ed.), *A Pleasing Sinne: Drink and Conviviality in Seventeenth-Century England* (Cambridge, 2004), pp. 72–5.

79 For example, Underdown, *Royalist Conspiracy*, pp. 16, 18, 73, 328, but see his later comments in *Revel, Riot and Rebellion*, pp. 268–70.

80 It was considered serious enough for a bill against the drinking of healths to be introduced in Parliament in November 1654. *CJ*, vol. VIII, p. 391; Firth (ed.), *Clarke Papers*, vol. III, p. 11.

81 *Mercurius Elencticus*, 10 (26 Jan.–2 Feb. 1648), p. 71.

82 CUL, Cambridge University Archives, Vice Chancellors' Court, I, 61, fols 74–5. I am grateful to Susan Sadler for this reference.

83 CCA, QJF 79/3/41. Although not given in the information, Newton's occupation can be ascertained from the 1661 administration bond after his death. CCA, Wills, admon., Robert Newton of Pownal Fee (1661).

84 Derbyshire RO, QSB 2/650. I am grateful to Andy Wood for giving me a copy of this document.

85 At an incident in Beverly (Yorkshire), in July 1651, a currier drank a health to Prince Charles 'King of the Scots', and pulled off the hat of a man who refused the join him, saying 'it was a health that deserved to be uncovered'. TNA, PRO, ASSI 45/4/1/13. See also LMA, MJ/SR 1030 (94); TNA, PRO, SP 19/6/91.

86 Clement Walker, *The Compleat History of Independencie* (1660), part III, p. 34.

87 BL, Add. MS 28,003, fol. 327.

88 W.C. Abbott (ed.), *The Writings and Speeches of Oliver Cromwell* (Cambridge, MA, 1937–47), vol. III, p. 844.

89 *CSPD 1649–50*, p. 84. For Knight, see B.D. Henning (ed.), *The History of Parliament: The House of Commons, 1660–1690* (London, 1983), vol. II, pp. 692–6.

90 Nedham, *Certain Considerations*, pp. 3–4, 8.

91 Rachel Weil, 'Thinking about allegiance in the English Civil War', *HWJ*, 61 (2006), pp. 189–90.

92 *CSPD 1649–50*, p. 79. Cf. the petition to the Somerset quarter sessions of William Davy, who, accused of seditious words, acknowledged by way of mitigation that 'some words may have been spoken in a passion'. Somerset RO, Q/SPET/1/136; Q/SR/89/55.

93 Roberts, *Recovery and Restoration*, pp. 33–4.

94 Cynthia Herrup, 'Law and morality in seventeenth-century England', *P&P*, 106 (1985), pp. 102–23.

95 *CSPD 1649–50*, p. 79.

96 Underdown, *Royalist Conspiracy*, p. 315; Harris, *London Crowds*, pp. 36–61.

97 Much more work has been done on the 1650s roots of Restoration Anglicanism, without a great deal of discussion of the concomitant political continuities: Robert S. Bosher, *The Making of the Restoration Settlement: The Influence of the Laudians, 1649–1662* (1957); John Spurr, *The Restoration Church of England, 1646–1689* (New Haven, CT, 1991); Judith Maltby, 'Suffering and surviving: the Civil Wars, the Commonwealth and the formation of "Anglicanism", 1642–60', in Christopher Durston and Judith Maltby (eds), *Religion in Revolutionary England* (Manchester, 2006), pp. 158–80. Harris, *London Crowds*, is something of an exception.

98 Bodl., Wood 416 (49): *The Cock-Crowing at the Approval of a Free-Parliament* (1660).

99 J.T. Rutt (ed.), *The Diary of Thomas Burton, esq* (1828), vol. I, p. 316. Cf. the information of George Evans of Blagdon, Somerset, who identified John Derrick and John Woodale as 'very malignant' by their 'discourse'. Somerset RO, Q/SR/83/1/95.

Chapter 4

———————◆———————

Artful Ambivalence? Picturing Charles I during the Interregnum

Helen Pierce

'Un-king-ship [was] proclaim'd, & his Majesties statues throwne downe at St. Paules Portico, & Exchange'.[1]

I

B etween 1650 and 1651, London citizens witnessed a spate of iconoclastic incidents, in which statues of the recently executed king were removed from the public spaces they had previously dominated. At St Paul's Cathedral, Charles's sculpted likeness was unceremoniously 'throwne downe', as John Evelyn noted in his diary. Orders were issued by the Council of State 'for the pulling down of the gilt image of the late Queen, and also of the King, the one in Queen Street, and the other at the upper end of the same street, towards Holborn', and for the removal of further statues of the king at Covent Garden and Greenwich.[2] The decapitation of Charles's statue at the entrance to the Old Exchange (itself now stripped of its own 'royal' status) was an event recorded in both private journals and public newsbooks: the head and sceptre of the statue were struck off, to be replaced by the inscription, 'Exit Tyrannus, Regum ultimus'.[3] Several weeks later, the damaged effigy was removed in its entirety, leaving only the bold and hostile lettering. According to a report of the event by the approving newsbook *Mercurius Politicus*, the inscription which remained was deemed 'not to be blotted out by all the Art under heaven'.[4]

In 1654 the entrepreneurial London print-seller Peter Stent issued a broadside advertisement detailing the substantial stock of engraved pictures available for purchase at his Newgate premises.[5] Stent's advertisement is the earliest known example of an English print-seller's stock list, and its content provides us with a rare insight into consumer tastes for the graphic arts during the Interregnum.[6] *A catalogue of plates and pictures that are printed and sould by Peter Stent* includes maps, sheets of signs and emblems, and copy books, as well as a small and eclectic assortment of moralising and humorous compositions. This list, however, is dominated by a large selection of that ubiquitous genre of early modern print, the portrait. Among the various likenesses which formed the basis of Stent's merchandise, images of 'His Excellency Ld. Cromwell' and 'The L.Gen: Cromwell' vied with a number of representations of the late king, many printed from ageing copper plates engraved several decades earlier, for the affections of the capital's print-buying public. In addition to visual representations of Charles I, there were family portraits featuring Queen Henrietta Maria and the royal offspring, and several more recently engraved sheets of 'K.Charles 2d of Scotland' included in Stent's detailed catalogue.

Although they did not quite amount to 'all the Art under heaven' as mentioned by *Mercurius Politicus*, the presence of these regal likenesses in Stent's self-promoting broadside suggests that the pictorial image of Charles I, together with the wider category of Caroline royal portraiture, was far from anathema within the burgeoning print market of 1650s London. Nor, given the broad range of engravings available to buy from Stent's shop, were such images the iconic preserve of embittered Royalist exiles. Indeed, when set against the earlier episodes of mutilation and destruction of royal statues, the inclusion of royal portraiture within this advertisement underlines the complex and problematic nature of the former monarch's image during the Interregnum.

While the range of visual representations of Charles I offered to a range of audiences across the seventeenth century has been the subject of a number of recent studies, the fate of the image of the late king during the period from Regicide to Restoration has been conspicuously overlooked.[7] Attention has turned to the broader influence of Caroline art upon republican portraiture and related imagery, a matter upon which scholarly opinion remains divided. Laura Lunger Knoppers has traced the development of the Cromwellian portrait as a deliberate revision and reworking of established images of kingship; conversely, the suggestion that the republican regime failed to construct for itself a viable alternative to the visual elements of monarchical rule, relying rather upon the straightforward duplication of familiar symbols and compositions, has been compellingly argued by Kevin Sharpe.[8] In what follows, the ambivalent status of Charles's visual presence during this period is explored, considering certain of the polemical, conventional and satirical representations of the late king and of kingship, made available to the public with relative openness in the years immediately following his execution. Certainly, the shaping of a new iconography of republican rule faced a significant obstacle in that continued visual presence, whether encountered in the guise of the martyr-king constructed by ardent Royalists or the more orthodox image delineated in conventional royal portraiture in both paint and print. It would be unrealistic to expect the new political regime of the Interregnum comprehensively to eradicate, and then re-write, the visual iconography of authority and rule in a matter of years; not surprisingly, certain symbols of royalty would remain firmly engrained in the cultural fabric of English life across the seventeenth century.[9] Yet the efforts of that regime and its supporters remained perceptively ambivalent, and at times uncertain, in their approaches to, and containment of, the late king's image. Furthermore, as the content of Peter Stent's print shop advertisement suggests, images of recent monarchs remained attractive to consumers during the Interregnum, with the iconography of royalty retaining a significant appeal. Although *Mercurius Politicus* might consider 'all the Art under heaven' to be of little threat to the aspirations of the republican government, the image of the king was to prove an enduring one.

II

Sean Kelsey has argued that England's new rulers were eager to establish a new visual identity of authority through the employment of artefacts specific to that regime, such as the arms of the Commonwealth and the parliamentary mace.[10] The removal of sculptural likenesses of Charles offered the republicans a further, important opportunity publicly to erase images of Stuart kingship which compromised this revised iconography of power and rule, and at times, that opportunity was taken. The decapitation of Charles's statue at the exchange and the removal of the same at St Paul's Cathedral were highly significant attacks upon the Caroline monarchy, given the considerable reverence associated with such effigies during the king's lifetime. In 1635 the innkeepers of Portsmouth had been admonished for obscuring with their signboards the bust of Charles designed by the French sculptor Hubert Le Sueur, which had been placed in the High Street, and the officers and soldiers of the town were instructed to remove their hats when passing it.[11] These subsequent, iconoclastic actions against similar artworks were a powerful demonstration of the new regime's authority. Yet even as the institution of monarchy was being described by the regicides as 'burdensome and dangerous to the liberty, safety and public interest of the people', the actual process of removing the visual reminders of that institution was proving at times tentative and difficult.[12] In January 1650 the issue of 'the taking down of the King's image and arms, in all places throughout this nation' was first raised by the Council of State, the official body which assumed responsibility for the fate of such monarchical symbols; eleven months later, the council felt it necessary 'to write to the Lord Mayor and Court of Aldermen of London, to take notice that in many churches and halls of companies in London, and other public meeting places, the arms and picture of the late King still remain, and require them to make strict inquiry in all those places, and cause all those arms and pictures to be taken down, and certify thereon'.[13] Despite such obligations, the matter of certain offending images remained unresolved, and was raised by the Council upon several further occasions. By February 1651 somewhat belated attention had turned to Whitehall and to the removal therein of all pictures and arms of the former king, 'whether they be in chambers or windows of chambers, or any other public or private place'.[14]

Certain of the Council of State's subsequent actions suggest that the fate of royal statues, pictures and arms was not considered to be a governmental priority. An order was initially given in October 1650, for example, that enquiry be made 'after the statue of the late King in Covent Garden, and that at Greenwich, both being cast in brass, and report in whose custody they are'.[15] The full-length bronze of Charles which had been installed at St Paul's Church in Covent Garden appears to have remained *in situ* despite its intended removal and that of similar artworks, with Cromwell's brother-in-law, John Disbrowe, being instructed 'to state the matter of fact touching the statue in the churchyard of Covent Garden, and to report' some five years later.[16] The outcome of that matter went unrecorded. St Paul's Cathedral was the site of a far more effective exercise in sculptural sabotage, with the statue of James I which stood on the western façade being pulled down together with that of his son. At the Old Exchange, however, despite the violent attack upon the statue of Charles at its entrance, particular measures were taken during the 1650s to maintain the series of effigies of former kings and queens of England which had been placed in the niches of the courtyard, with an order for their 'brushing washing and clensing' being issued in 1657.[17]

This curious mixture of action and apathy surrounding the destruction of sculpted representations of the former monarch reflected a wider reluctance within the visual arts actively to denigrate the Caroline iconography of kingship. Indeed, the decapitation of Charles's statue at the exchange and the 'throwing down' of the same at St Paul's represented unusual attacks in an English context, in both physical and symbolic terms, upon the king's visual presence. Pictorial critiques and lampoons of the monarchy were not unknown, but remained, even after Charles's death, the general preserve of foreign artists and designers. James I had been portrayed by Dutch cartoonists as a profligate spendthrift with prominently empty pockets, while in 1623 Simonds D'Ewes described in his diary an Italian satire concerning the journey of Charles and the Duke of Buckingham to Madrid to woo the Spanish Infanta, noting 'the picture at Rome, Twoe in a cage in splendid apparell resembling the Marquesse [Buckingham] and the Prince [of Wales], and an ancient man standing by, in a fooles coate resembling the King for letting them goe ...'.[18] Even the paper war which flared during the 1640s between Royalist and Parliamentarian polemicists was conspicuous for an absence of pictorial denigrations of the king. In a rare incident of 1642, an engraved sheet was brought before the House of Commons which represented Charles in a submissive pose at the feet of the governor of Hull, Sir John Hotham. The House acted quickly to censor this unacceptable image, immediately issuing the order that the engraving 'be burnt by the Hands of the common Hangman presently, in the Palace Yard; and the Vent or further Publishing of them strictly forbidden and prohibited. And that it shall be referred to the Committee for Printing, to inquire who was the Inventor, and who the Printer and Publisher, that they may be brought to condign Punishment."[19] Even in the wake of Charles's execution, any negative styling of his image by English artists remained markedly restricted. Engraved depictions of the Regicide, such as the broadside purchased by the London bibliophile and bookseller George Thomason in the spring of 1649, were products of the Dutch and German print markets, and contemporary painted accounts of the Whitehall execution scene, such as the anonymous work presently in the collection of the National Gallery of Scotland, were constructed from printed sources by continental artists.[20] No contemporary versions of this iconic composition by English artists or printmakers are known.[21] *The true manner of the Kings Tryal at Westminster-Hall* (see figure 4.1), an undated sheet of verses printed by Robert Ibbitson, is notable in that an execution scene is included in its bricolage of woodcut illustrations, yet in its appearance this cut is generic, rather than specific, to the events of January 1649. Although the same cut was used in several related publications, concerning the hangman Richard Brandon, Ibbitson also employed it as an illustration to *The Manner of the Beheading of Duke Hambleton, the Earle of Holland, and the Lord Capell*, while an identical scene adorns the title page of *A Great and Bloody Plot Discovered*, a 1660 pamphlet detailing the untimely deaths and executions of a number of 'actors and conspirators' in the Regicide.[22]

New pictorial representations of Charles I which appeared during the years immediately following the Regicide were predominantly the product of a Royalist programme of textual and visual material. This was a programme spearheaded by the publication in February 1649 of the *Eikon Basilike*, a collection of prayers and meditations ascribed to the former king. Running through thirty-five English editions during the first year of its publication alone, the *Eikon Basilike* cast Charles unequivocally in the role of royal martyr, a 'self'-fashioning firmly articulated by the persuasive imagery of its engraved frontispiece.[23] The work of the prolific English engraver William Marshall, it pictures Charles in a solitary meditation, gazing at a celestial crown while clasping a coronet of thorns, set against an emblematical backdrop of raging winds and waves which strike against a fixed and steady rock. This powerful portrait of the former king proved as ubiquitous as the text it accompanies: seven versions of the title page signed by Marshall are known, suggesting that serious wear was inflicted by the printing process upon each copper plate worked upon by the engraver. Five additional signed title pages by further engravers, along with a

Figure 4.1 *The True Manner of the Kings Tryal at Westminster-Hall* (c. 1649). Glasgow University Library, Department of Special Collections.

plethora of unsigned adaptations of Marshall's composition by both English and continental artists, attest to the potency of this image as part of the wider elevation of Charles from earthly ruler to divine martyr, a potency further reflected in the variety of single-sheet engravings, explanatory commentaries, needlework and embroideries which reproduce the iconic scene.[24]

It is not surprising, then, that the *Eikon Basilike*'s provocative and persuasive visual element prompted a number of negative responses from concerned commentators: 'The more such doggs bark against this Picture of King Charls, the more venoration will be given it', cautioned *The Man in the Moon*, while John Milton's *Eikonoklastes* derided what he termed the 'conceited portraiture' produced by Marshall, 'drawn out to the full measure of a Masking Scene, and sett there to catch fools and silly gazers ... the Picture sett in Front would Martyr him [Charles] and Saint him to befool the people ...'.[25] Such 'befooling' was echoed in observations of the subsequent state-sanctioned removal of civic statues of the former king; according to William Lilly, 'King Charles being Dead, and some foolish Citizens going a whoring after his Picture or Image, formerly set up in the old Exchange; the Parlament made bold to take it down ...'[26] Although the early publication history of the *Eikon Basilike* is one punctuated by episodes of censorship and intervention, this central tenet of Royalist ideology represented a publishing sensation which enabled many to either venerate or indeed attack a visual as well as textual portrait of the late king constructed with fiercely polemical intent. Furthermore, while written responses to the *Eikon Basilike* by its critics were forthcoming, the opportunity to oppose its visual elements through a corresponding pictorial rebuttal was not taken. The *Eikon Alethine* provides a rare example which hints at such a rejoinder, its title page prefaced by an engraved frontispiece depicting a curtain being drawn aside to reveal the shadowy figure of a priest, accompanied by verses which gesture towards the counterfeit nature of the king's authorship of the *Eikon Basilike*. Yet although the *Eikon Alethine* berates the reader who would 'judge of a man's Physiognomy by his Pourtracture rather then by his owne Face', no attempt is made to visually critique or lampoon the particular portrait of Charles through the medium of its own frontispiece.[27]

Intriguingly, a further engraved frontispiece picturing the late king was singled out for attention by the authorities almost immediately after its publication. On 31 May 1649 the London aldermen Isaac Pennington and Thomas Atkins were ordered by the Council of State 'to send for the author of the book called "The Papers which passed at Newcastle", examine him concerning the frontispiece, and proceed against him'.[28] The frontispiece to *The Papers Which Passed at New-Castle betwixt His Sacred Majestie and Mr Al: Henderson: Concerning the Change of Church-government*, which Pennington and Atkins were specifically charged with examining, features a full-length portrait of the monarch, again engraved and signed by William Marshall (figure 4.2). Beneath a blazing, cherub-borne banner proclaiming Charles as 'fidei defensor', the late king places a pair of dividers upon a globe, their needles resting upon Scotland. This representation of Charles provoked a swift reaction from the authorities: *The Papers Which Passed at New-Castle* had been entered into the Stationers' Register on 23 May 1649, and George Thomason's copy of the publication is annotated with the date of 29 May.[29] Just two days later, Pennington and Atkins were authorised to apprehend its author 'concerning the frontispiece'. Whether Richard Royston, the indefatigable Royalist publisher of both the *Eikon Basilike* and *The Papers Which Passed at New-Castle*, was questioned about the matter, is uncertain. By October 1649, however, Royston found his publishing activities somewhat curbed: having appeared before the Council of State, he was bound over for the sum of £500 to appear 'when required, and not to print or sell any unlicensed books or pamphlets in the meantime'.[30] Yet the objectionable nature of this particular aspect of *The Papers Which Passed at New-Castle* was to prove no obstacle to its further publication. In April 1651 an edition of *Certamen Religiosum*, an account of Charles I's religious opinions assembled by the clergyman and controversialist Thomas Bayly, was printed for Richard Royston and his fellow stationer William Lee; among its pages, William Marshall's engraving of Charles as 'fidei defensor' has been boldly inserted.[31] That same year, certain copies of *Reliquiae Sacrae Carolinae*, a collection of Charles's writings including the *Eikon Basilike*, were published with the same Marshall engraving inserted as a frontispiece. It also appeared in 1658, slightly reworked, prefacing John Gadbury's *Nativity of the Late King Charls*.[32] The Council of State's interest in a particular visual representation of the late king in 1649, and its ensuing appearance in several publications at several points during the 1650s, suggest a model of pictorial censorship and control closely mirroring the state's treatment of problematic texts in Cromwellian England. The practice of press censorship, as Jason McElligott has convincingly argued, was far from uniform, being based upon, and responded to, a number of external factors.[33] By April 1651 *Certamen Religiosum* was circulating in an entirely different context from *The Papers Which Passed at New-Castle* during 1649, and was subjected to very different controls, as the state turned its attentions away from the suppression of the largely moribund Royalist press to more pressing political and religious matters.

III

The publication and re-publication of Marshall's second representation of Charles I complemented the frontispiece in the *Eikon Basilike*. Yet despite their pervasiveness, such images were not the only visual representations of Charles in circulation during this period; nor was Charles's portrait the only pictorial rendering of kingship offered to English audiences of the 1650s. Peter

Figure 4.2 William Marshall, frontispiece to *The Papers Which Passed at New-Castle* (1649).
© Trustees of the British Museum.

Stent's open advertisement of more conventional portraits of Caroline royalty indicates that there was some measure of demand for this genre of print. Stent himself was regarded as a commercially adept individual at the head of a successful print-selling business. His decision on one occasion to refuse to pay the etcher Wenceslaus Hollar for a portrait plate of Thomas Hobbes, doubting its potential in terms of a profitable print, suggests a confident understanding of which subjects would provide an adequate financial return.[34] Stent's realisation that certain conventional aspects of a specifically Caroline royal iconography remained commercially viable during the Interregnum is underlined by a survey of pictorial material entered by the Stationers' Company member Richard Westbrooke into the Stationers' Register on 24 March 1656. Westbrooke entered a number of 'portratures cutt in copper plates', including 'The portrature of the late King Charles and his Queen and their children', 'the portrature of the late King Charles in his waistcoat' and 'Charles the 2nd, King of Scotland', together with 'The portrature of his highnes the Lord Protectour of England, Scotland and Ireland on horse backe'. Ten days later, Westbrooke registered a further selection of prints, listing engraved portraits of Charles on foot, on horseback and with Henrietta Maria, together with another portrait of Oliver Cromwell.[35] During periods of relative political calm, such publications appear to have been perceived as unthreatening, and thus unimportant to the authorities, again reflecting the peaks and troughs of the wider Cromwellian model of press censorship, containment and control.

Even more challenging representations of royalty, however, could be met with indecision. In October 1651 charges were brought against the engraver Robert Vaughan, then a resident of St Andrew's parish, Holborn, relating to a now-untraced portrait of the Scottish king. The primary concern of the bill of indictment was not the publication of a likeness of the young Charles, but, more particularly, the 'trayterous inscription' which accompanied it:

> Robert Vaughan of the said parish engraver made and engraved a certain picture of the sayd Charles Stuart son to the sayd Charles late King of England with the trayterous inscription ... following underneath the sayd picture in mettal advisedly maliciously and with a trayterous minde and intencion did ... engrave (to wit) 'Charles the Second (sonne to Charles I. The Martyr) King of England Scotland France and ... defendor of the faith &c. Nowe in the head of gallant and numerous army of the valliant and faithfull Scottes and the possession of the rest of his fathers Crownes with ... emblem of victory peace and mercy to restore to the Loyall their religion lawes and libertyes, To shew pitty and compassion to all the seduced and sorrowfull, retorning to their obedience, But to execut vengeance on the impenitent malitious and implacable murthers of his Royall Father.[36]

Despite the potentially provocative aspects of this portrait and its inscription, Vaughan declared himself to be not guilty of any crime, with a jury subsequently finding the same. This outcome again emphasises the often ambivalent nature of Interregnum audiences towards images of kingship; Vaughan's trial in October 1651 occurred in the wake of the Battle of Worcester, during a dangerous period for the state, and it is not surprising that his unambiguous call to arms and to Royalist intervention resulted in such charges. In this instance, however, the allegedly subversive element of the engraver's work, the 'trayterous inscription', was ultimately judged a matter with no need for further action. In contrast, portraits of Oliver Cromwell circulating in Paris in the summer of 1655 were judged to be unacceptable on account of certain verses attached to them, rather than their pictorial elements; according to Percy Church, an exile in the French capital, 'Cromwells picture hath bine here sold this long time, and of late with certaine verses underneath, which the other day occasioned an officer by order from ye Chancellor to sease them in shopps or elsewhere, which dune, ye verses taken away, the pictures were restored to ye howners.'[37] The majority of written accompaniments to printed portraits of royalty sought to assure rather than antagonise. In the cases of Stent's broadside advertisement, and in those engraved portraits which have been identified from the advertisement, as well as the list of printed images registered for Richard Westbrooke, this king is consistently referred to as the King of Scotland, *Caroli Scotorum,* with no claim, whether polemical or observational, made regarding an English throne.[38]

The visual lampoon was a form of critique to which Charles I had remained perceptively immune, during his lifetime and beyond. Such restraint, however, did not extend to the treatment of his son. Among the illustrated sheets acquired by George Thomason during the early 1650s are a number of unflattering representations of the younger Charles, seemingly provoked by his coronation at Scone in January 1651. By July of that year, Thomason and his fellow Londoners could purchase the satirical sheet *Old Sayings and Predictions Verified and fulfilled, Touching the young King of Scotland,* a caustic summary in both verse and prose of religious preferences north of the border, accompanied by the illustration of a Presbyterian minister holding Charles's nose to a grindstone, while 'Jockie' the Scot turns the wheel (see figure 4.3).[39] This composition represented a notable reversal of Stuart fortunes: during the 1620s, King James had himself been pictured as the aggressor in a now lost engraving playing on popular anti-Catholic sentiments, inflicting the same punishment upon the prostrate figure of the pope.[40] A further broadside, *A Mad Designe* (1651), imagines the Scottish king's flight to the continent following the events at Worcester in far less romantic terms than those found in narratives published at the Restoration. Seated upon a globe, Charles is pictured gloomily pondering his fate, shadowed by a motley collection of supporters, including Presbyterians, papists, 'Old Cavaliers' and 'two ridiculous Anticks, one with a Fiddle, and the other with a Torch', who erratically snake across the sheet.[41] Even orthodox representations of the future Charles

Figure 4.3 *Old Sayings and Predictions Verified and Fulfilled, Touching the Young King of Scotland* (1651). © Trustees of the British Museum.

The True Manner of the Crowning of Charles the Second King

of *Scotland*, on the First day of *January*, 1650. Together with a Defcription of his Life, and Throne; And a cleare view of his Court and Counfell.

82

Charles y 2. Crown'd King of Scotland Ian 1650.

The Manner of Crowning CHARLES the Second King of Scotland.

He Crown, Sword and Scepter, being brought to *Scoon*, by the Eftates of Parliament, their King fitting in his Chaire of State, and the Nobility, Barons and Burgeffes of Parliament about him, in the prefence Chamber.

The Marqueffe of *Argyle* made a Speech, advertifing the King, that the Parliament of *Scotland* were come to prefent his Majefty with the Crown, Sword, and Scepter; But the before he received it, he was to take an Oath, and fweare as his former predeceffors had done before him, which Oath was tendred to the King and he be fware to it as followeth.

The Oath fworn by CHARLES the Second, King of Scotland, at his Coronation, 1 Jan. 1650.

I Doe Promife and Vow in the prefence of the Eternall God, that I will maintaine the true Kirke of God, Religion, right Preaching, and adminiftration of the Sacraments, now Received and Preached within this Realme in purity.

And fhall abolifh and gain-ftand all falfe Religions and Sects contrary to the fame.

And fhall rule the people committed to my charge according to the will of God, and laudable Lawes and Conftitutions of the Realme; caufing Iuftice and Equity to be miniftred without partiality.

After this one of the Lords, uiz. the Marqueffe of *Argyle* and one of the Barons, and one of the Burgeffes, (which are three of the then Eftates of *Scotland*) held the Crowne, which they offered to the King; which they delivered to three Minifters of the Affembly or the

A Defcription of the Life and Vertue, &c.

This glittering Commet is not to be numbred amongft the fixed Starrs, his Crown carrieth no lufter, but what affumes a fained afpect to the pur-blind Jockyes, betwen *Fife* and *Orkney*, who deale with him, as their predeceffors did with their fimple ignorant King *Ethelme* the Second, whom they Crowned for reverence to the hate of *Freyng*, to carry the name of a King, but the Eftates governed him by a guard of Tutors, yet he himfelfe acts his defignes like *Natholum*, their thirtith King, who corrupting their Grandees with bags of faire promifes, obtained the Regall power.

This Artificiall Meteor, is only a Scottifh vapour, exhaled by French diftillation, and with clenfing thunder fhaken out of the Englifh horizon, fallen into the bofome of the Kirke of *Scotland*, and made their Baby in the Stoole of repentance, fwearing to once *Galum* did in the fame Thron. *So majoram conftilio acquiatorum.*

They having poured the oyle of the Presbytery upon him, and given him the Crown and Scepter to weare for them (though *Argyle* had not power to hold it right and eafily, on his difturbed and aking head) whilft they devide the rags of his tattered Throne between the Kirke and Cavaliers, whofe actings towards their new fooveraign, puts him into a worfe condition in the *Charles-Waine*, hey make him throw an honeft Englifh Carter that hath a Team of Horfes to put for him.

His unhappinefs in his fatall Progenitors, he may read in Capitalls, engraven even on the Throne he fits in, where is legible to his eyes, the œcumenicall difafters of the Family out of which he fprung, his Father was beheaded, H+ Grand Father (at fome Phifitians have delivered) poyfoned, His great Grand-Father, and fo on to feverall others before, fucceffively cut off, by difaftrous deaths.

And for himfelfe, His niger haire, and fwarthy complexion is a fifible hierogliffe of his gloomy manfions, in which he followes the fiction of his mothers councels and the Scots commands, refolved into politickes, as furioufly as his obftinate Father did the humor of his own will.

He hath defigned po; ularity from a child, and even in his tender years expreffed paffion againft his maidens,that difturbed thofe boys that came to play with him.

And he did-eften in the City of *London*, the metropolis of his fathers territoryes) to draw the peoples affections to be as fixed on him as on heir eyes, fcatter many handfulls of filver in fmal copfes, from feverall Windowes and Balconyes in Cheap-fide and other places, a-mongft the vulgar, and (as if he had Roman Royalty bred in his blogd) forced himfelfe to triumph in this liberality without any vifible change in his countenance. But the words of *Auguftine* continue the *Euemium* of charity: *Charitas eft amor rerum quas non nifi laborer amittuntur.*

In his fathers prefence, he feemed to admire his Throne, and before his mother, her Idols, yet to perfons popular, hee had many glances againft the Arch-Bifhop of *Canterbury* and others, whom the peoples difcontents ftruck at ; as if *Abfalom*-like, he chiefly ftudyed the preparation to his Fathers Kingdome.

But herein, he did but delude thofe pour dreamers, (as he doth now the Scotch Presbyters) who being rich onely whilft they fleep loofe all as foon as they awake, their dreames inrich them, but when they awake they are abundant of all, and reduced to their further poverty.

During the late bloody warres of his Fathers waging, againft the Parliament of *England*, he was either with him actually, or (in his abfence) carried on by the advice of *Digby*, *Carleton*, *Colepepor*, and of late by his Father appoynted for his abfolute Counfellors, and after his Fathers death, he wholly proftrated himfelfe to be fortune of his mothers and the Jefuites, and Popifh Priefts refolutions, as *Cadmus* did to the Monaftery of St. *Andrews*.

And after a foundation to act his defignes upon, which were laid with great confultations by power and policy to fubdue *England*, *Scotland*, and *Ireland* to his obedience which gave him fome fretting promifes (but on conclufion) at *Terfey*. His brother of *Orange* was thought to have more fublime wings to give influence to thofe cockatrife egges; who brooded fo effectually that the Treaty at *Breda* patched up a publicke agreement with *Scotland*, as wel an a private one with *Ireland* (though the Dutch Prince fo vefted his fpirits in it, that he foone dyed after) and *Charles Stewart* (upon his ill fuceffe again *England*) being forced to keep beyond *Fife*, and the Scots cooped up with him, they are like *Nilus* and the Jewes, (though averfe to each other) joyned in combination againft *England*. And in this fiery he hath fretched up the Crown of *Scotland*.

And with great difficulty hath he divide himfelfe to play his part that he may fit faft on that frozen Throne, To the Kirk he bequeaths his Tongue, to the Cavaliers his Armes, to the Englifh Courtiers his Back, and to the pure Malignants his Breft ; which makes me remember him that faid, *All the good Princes may be expected in arring.*

The Commonwealth of *Scotland* find fault with many inconfiftency pleafures of his youth, the Nobility cenfure his too much abafing both himfelf and them, the Kirke puritceh even his very thoughts, which they take upon them to divine and judge of ; and yet none deales fo plainly with him as the horfe befides-on, who gives warning by curvetting, that (being neither flatterer nor Courtier) hee will caft him to the ground, as wel an the pooreft Groome of his Stable ; and as for the common people (efpecially the women,) as wel an the Ladyes, though not with fo neat reception, they are daily and hourely folliciting, vifiting, or (at leaft) gazing upon him, fo that he may fry with King *Alphonfus*, that the Eftate of an *Affe*, is *better than predominion*,

And for the better advancement of their caufe, as pure Covenanters (they being a difembling people (from whence arifeth the proverb,*has falfe as a Scot*,) they fuffer him not truly to know the ftate affaires, deceitlvers not acknowledging the truth though never fo tranfparent, which made them before their coat at *Mufulborough*, to fit in confultation *what condition it was fit they fhould offer to the Englifh*, (*when in Scotland which they faid were flying away homeward*) *whether yes, no, quarter was to be allowed to any for their lives,*

---

the Kirk of *Scotland*, advertifing them that they were appointed by the Eftates in the Parliament of *Scotland*, to fee the Crowne and Dignity of the Realme of *Scotland*, prefented unto *Charles the Second* then prefent, the right Difcended Inheritor thereof. One of thefe Minifters made a Speech to the King, and an expreffe condition of his duty was laid down, before he received the Crown, and in anfwer to the fame he made this following Speech.

A Speech made by CHARLES the Second, King of Scotland at his Coronation on 1 January 1650.

I Will by Gods affiftance beftow my life for your Defence, wifhing to live no longer, then that I may fee this kingdome flourifh in happineffe.

Then the Scots King ftood upon a place where he might fhew himfelfe to the people and make proteftations of great love and affection to them, and the Crown being tendred to the King, by three Minifters of the Affembly, one of them fpake as followeth.

The Minifters Speech at the tendring of the Crown to the King.

SIR,

I Doe prefent unto you King Charles the Second, the right Defcended Inheritor, the Crown and Dignity of this Realm, (then turning his face towards the people, the Minifter faid further) Are ye not willing to have him for your king, and become fubject to him?

At which time the Crowne was held before the King three Minifters of the Affembly being prefent, then the King turned himfelf to be feen of the people, who cryed with a great noife, *God fave King Charles the Second.* And then he had the Crown put upon his head, by the Marqueffe of *Argyle*, and he took the Scepter in his hand, and the Sword he gave to a Lord of *Scotland* to bear it before him.

A

And now fince they have Crowned him, and made him *Generaliffimo*, to wear a Scepter, carry him on a hood-winke ar before, *Adafifry*, and the reft of the Englifh (in hopes to find their own fubfiftance in his fortune) pretend a great intereft and power in *England* to concurre with his defignes, by which they fqueeze fome favour from him (by the leave of the Kirk, upon the Presbyterian account) for imployment and maintenance in the interim. *Argyle* and the Scots they promife him greater things to be revealed to them, to be accomplifhed in the influence of St. *Patrick*, than any of their hobby horfes.

But the *Grandees* and *Papifts* tel him that it is moft conducing to make him great and glorious, to fatisfie the *Irifh*, and all other Romifh Catholickes in the three Nations, and fpeedily to difmiffe the two *Irifh* Lords *Ormond* and *Inchiquen*, with ample returns full of fatisfaction to the Affembly, that fo they being capable to reduce *Ireland*, they may,having accomplifht it, come over and go on helping to carry on the work *effective* in the three Nations.

But why doe the Papifts rage, and the Kirke imagine a vain thing the King of *Scotland* fet himfelf, and the Eftates take councel together, after fo great appeales, and fuch evident manifeftations of the Lords fo vifibly owning of his caufe againft them? He that fitteth in the heavens fhal laugh, the Lord fhal have them in derifion.

If fo many Emperours after *Pompey* the great, and *Cæfar*, could not but fall when the decree was gone out, if the Queen *Mary* of *Scotland*, if his own Father the late King , King *Charles* were both cut off with the Executioners hatchets, how can the Son thinke to efcape ? What are the great troublfe boaftings of *Englifh* Malignants the vaine hopes of *Irifh* Papifts, and the Royal Mofters in the North of *Scotland* for the South of *Fife* and *Sterling* they dare not attempt? forces even *Henry* the third (one of the Predeceffors of his mothers Family of *France*, was murdered wilfully by a little Mocke in the middeft of 40000 armed men.

FINIS.

Published by Authority. 1650.

London Printed by Robert Ibbitfon, 1652.

Figure 4.4 *The True Manner of the Crowning of King Charles the Second of Scotland* (1651).

II could be manipulated to derogatory effect. Prior to the publication of *A Mad Designe*, the name of its London printer, Robert Ibbitson, appeared on a deceptively conventional illustrated sheet, *The True Manner of the Crowning of Charles the Second King of Scotland* (figure 4.4).[42] A close reading of the letterpress which frames a likeness of the young king, in military garb and on horseback, reveals a barbed narrative undermining the aura of positive kingship which should arise from this image. In contrast to the aristocratic mien and chivalric prowess suggested by this conventional equestrian portrait of a noble sitter, the letterpress dwells on the melancholic possibilities of Charles's physiognomic appearance, and hints at less than gentlemanly aspects of his character. According to its text, his 'swarthy complexion is a visible heroglifix of his gloomy motions', while any chivalric prowess implied by his able horsemanship within the portrait is undercut by the observation that 'even in his tender years [he] expressed passions against his maidens, that disturbed those boys that came to play with him'.

IV

The printed images sold by Stent and Westbrooke were not the only medium through which examples of conventional royal portraiture could be accessed by Interregnum audiences. The sale of the former king's significant art collection presented the republican government with an important opportunity to raise funds, and a means by which to appease many of Charles's creditors; additionally, the act of dispersing and disposing of the royal pictures carried iconoclastic overtones, as further, conspicuous reminders of Caroline ascendancy and rule were erased. In common with the removal of certain of Charles's public statues, however, the aftermath of this purported episode of iconoclasm revealed somewhat ambivalent attitudes towards representations of the former king. According to Jerry Brotton, this sale of royal art was itself a revolutionary act, in terms, at least, of connoisseurship:

> In the space of just a few days in October 1651 almost 700 pictures were distributed among nearly 1,000 of Charles's creditors living in London's boroughs ... Ordinary Londoners could hold, examine, discuss, admire, buy and sell pictures and statues that, until then, had been destined exclusively for the pleasure and edification of the aristocracy.[43]

The fracturing of this important art collection, including a significant number of portraits of Charles I and his immediate family, chiefly by or from the studio of Anthony Van Dyck, introduced such works into a far more public domain than the courtly environs in which they had originally hung. These royal likenesses, in common with the rest of the collection, were bought or acquired by a wide range of individuals; their number included artists and art dealers, various creditors from the royal household, and London citizens such as John Bolton, the goldsmith from Foster Lane who purchased an equestrian canvas of Charles by Van Dyck for £40.[44] A further, significant group of buyers consisted of Parliamentarian officers and sympathisers. Colonel John Hutchinson, one of the signatories to Charles's death warrant, 'laid out about £2,000 in the choicest pieces of painting then set to sale, most of which were bought out of the King's goods ... [which] he brought down into the country, intending a very neat cabinet for them'.[45] Notably, certain members of the Council of State, the governmental body which assumed primary responsibility for the removal of images of Charles from both public and private locations, including John Lambert and Bulstrode Whitelocke, were keen to indulge in the acquisition of such artworks, and faced censure at the Restoration for their possession of the former king's pictures.[46] While motivations of an aesthetic kind are hinted at in John Hutchinson's assembly of royal artworks, financial reasons also ensured that certain works passed swiftly through a succession of owners with decidedly republican values, who evidently took greater pleasure in profiting from, rather than destroying, representations of Stuart kingship. Colonel William Webb, another parliamentary officer, was the cash purchaser of a number of iconic royal portraits by Van Dyck which were promptly sold on. These included *Charles I in Robes of State*, and *The King's Eldest Three Children*, acquired by Webb for £60 and subsequently offered to Monsieur de Bordeaux, London agent for Cardinal Mazarin, before passing into the hands of the painter Peter Lely.[47] Colonel Webb also purchased for £25 a portrait of the then Prince Charles as a youth in armour by the studio of Van Dyck.[48] A further, charming Van Dyckian interpretation of royal childhood, *The Five Children of Charles I*, was bought by a Captain Geere, and swiftly found its way to the London studio of the painter and occasional art dealer Emanuel de Critz.[49] The publication in 1651 of Balthazar Gerbier's *The None-such Charles His Character*, a caustic critique of the former monarch, saw Gerbier, who had previously acted as an art dealer for both Charles and the Duke of Buckingham, denounce his former employer's weakness for wasting money 'on old rotten pictures, on broken-nosed Marble'.[50] Several months earlier, Gerbier's own attention had turned to such excesses, with his purchase of an impressive equestrian portrait of the king by Van Dyck, which soon passed into the hands of a foreign purchaser; it now hangs in London's National Gallery.

It is difficult to estimate the further number of portraits of Caroline royalty which remained cloistered in aristocratic houses during the Interregnum, or the number of copies of key artworks being produced at that time; one can only speculate as to which compositions were included in the 'Abundance of Coppies of Ritrattos by Van dycke &c' encountered by the antiquary Richard Symonds in the house of a London painter in 1653.[51] What is certain is that the influence of Caroline portraiture upon Interregnum art was significant, as reflected by the Cromwellian portraitist Robert Walker's admission that 'if I could get better I would not do Vandikes'.[52]

The visual iconography of kingship was also openly referenced in artworks with their origins in less conventional commissions than those given to Walker and other 'court' artists, such as the portrait of Cromwell which was prominently placed in the courtyard of London's Old Exchange in May 1653. This curious incident saw 'a grave and wel-habited Gentleman' arrive at the exchange in a coach:

> and after he had walked a few turnes there, he went againe to his Coach, and from thence fetched a large picture of the General, and hung it up in open Exchange, so after a while departed & unknowne.[53]

The portrait of Cromwell deposited by the unknown gentleman was supplemented by a series of laudatory verses written beneath, calling upon the sitter to 'Ascende three thrones Great Captaine and Divine'. Public participation was also requested, with the painting's urban audience exhorted to

> ... kneele & pray
> To Oliver ye torch of zion starre of day
> Then shout O merchants, Citts, & Gentry sing
> Let all men bare heads cry God save the King.

This final phrase of 'God save the King' was set out in capital letters and finished in gold, enhancing the three crowns of the same colour which had been pictured above Cromwell's head.[54] Placed in 'open Exchange', and juxtaposed with the uncompromising inscription which had supplanted the mutilated statue of Charles, this visual call to Cromwell to assume a kingly role, some months prior to his acceptance of the title of Lord Protector, would have offered those who viewed it an ambiguous representation of quasi-kingship. The prominent inclusion in the composition of the three crowns, themselves referred to in lines which call additionally for 'robes, & gold ... Crownes & Scepters ...' to complete Cromwell's transition from leader to monarch, sits uneasily with the nearby condemnation of tyrannical kings. Yet the iconography of rule uppermost in this portrait, combined with its specific placement in the Old Exchange, framed by the courtyard's sculptural assembly of English monarchs, is made all the more potent by its referencing of established and familiar symbols of authority. Its persuasive visual and textual elements, addressing both Cromwell and the civic audience encountering his portrait at the exchange, acknowledge the powerful and pervasive nature of the royal image, and suggest that the adoption of the visual, symbolic elements of monarchical rule could only enhance Cromwell's political status.

Cromwell's own reported reaction to this painting is tantalisingly opaque:

after it had been gazed at for a long time it was taken downe and brought to the Major [i.e. Mayor]; but whether by order or no is not yet owned; his wisedom was pleased to bring it to the Generall, and told him, if he owned the doing of it, he would carry it there againe, otherwise he would dispose of it, as he should thinke fitt, his Excy smiled, and made merry with the major, saying, it was some odd fellow to make sport &c but such trifles as these were not to be considered these serious times, and so dismissed the major unsatisfied & the world unresolved.[55]

This alleged reluctance on the part of Cromwell to engage with this portrait reflects the general tendency of the Interregnum state to concern itself with transgressive texts and images during 'serious times', and to ignore or tolerate them during less contentious periods. His response can also be interpreted as part of a wider disinterest, rooted in Puritan ideologies or otherwise, in the visual arts. That an individual chose to incorporate a painting as a key element in a very public exercise in political persuasion, however, indicates that this disinterest was not the prevailing attitude in 1650s England. Indeed, pictorial representations of the future Lord Protector were considered by many, not least his detractors, to be more than mere 'trifles', and Cromwell's visual image was itself keenly contested and critiqued, in sharp contrast to the treatment of his predecessor. The delineation of a subservient Charles II in the 1651 broadside *Old Sayings and Predictions Verified and Fulfilled*, his nose being held to a grindstone by his Scottish aggressors, was a provocative yet relatively unusual exercise; Cromwell, however, was routinely cast by both his English and continental critics into a multitude of unflattering guises and situations, from the destructive tyrant pictured in Clement Walker's *Anarchia Anglicana*, through a bespectacled rustic, to the monstrous 'tail man' of numerous acerbic Dutch print satires.[56] This lack of deference towards Cromwell would extend in time to his son Richard, whose own inabilities as Lord Protector were lampooned in 1659 in a satirical woodcut depicting a curious hybrid of man and owl, known as 'His Highnesse Hoo. Hoo. Hoo. Protector of Lubberland'. The venom of this particular attack was reported to have been so acute that following its publication the young Cromwell anticipated attacks upon his person, and was 'confined to his chamber for fear of street baylieffes'.[57]

V

The difficult, if not impossible, task of thoroughly eradicating all visual representations of Charles I and his son appears to have faltered because the regimes of the 1650s always faced a range of far more pressing administrative, political and military tasks. The visual image of the late king remained largely uncontested, the result of a combination of governmental ambivalence and a broader cultural disinclination to denigrate the royal likeness, which persisted throughout the 1650s. In addition to an attitude of toleration, or at least indifference, towards symbols of monarchical rule during episodes of political calm, more immediate issues surrounding the Interregnum state took precedence over the removal of arms, portraits and statues on other occasions. The seemingly relaxed nature of the state at times enabled entrepreneurial stationers such as Stent to respond to a continued consumer interest in images of royal persons, ruling or otherwise, whether considered as objects of historical curiosity or continued reverence.

At the Restoration, the long-term roots of royal iconography and its sustained familiarity merged potently with public displays of affection for the reinstated Stuart monarchy. In contrast to the notable lack of urgency and, on occasion, a degree of reluctance, on the part of those charged during the Interregnum with the removal of images of Charles I and related royal iconography, such actions appear to have been undertaken with enthusiasm: one Michael Darby, painter to the Company of Mercers, erased the denigrating inscription at the Old Exchange, having 'freely volunteered to blot it out, engaging to do it before he slept, and accordingly performed it at a full Exchange time'.[58] Darby's actions were celebrated with a bonfire and cries of 'God bless King Charles the second!', and were commemorated with the publication of a rousing ballad, *An Exit to the Exit Tyrannus*.[59] Portraits of Cromwell and his wife were cast upon London fires, while in Boston in Lincolnshire similar conflagrations were accompanied by uninhibited expressions of festivity, as youths tore down and openly defecated on symbols of the republican regime; 'Such was there malice to the States armes in that towne', noted the Londoner Thomas Rugg sagely.[60] Rugg's commentary on life in the capital, as London adjusted to the return of a Stuart king, reveals the importance invested in the pictorial as a means of accentuating that return. Rugg recorded the reinstatement of signboards picturing the king's arms, which had been pulled down during the Interregnum, now 'sett up in more state than att the first', as well as the return of certain statues to public view. Such observations stress the strong cultural continuity of the monarchical, rather than republican, image of rule. As Rugg noted in his diary in 1660, 'Now in Westminster all statuters [*sic*] or figuers or inscriptions that was sett up either by the Protector, or in his dayes or before since these troubles, or any that was of the Protectors own effigis, or tokens or signes of him, was quit washed out and in the places of them as if they never had been.'[61]

NOTES

1 E.S. de Beer (ed.), *The Diary of John Evelyn*, 6 vols (Oxford, 1955), vol. II, p. 555.

2 *CSPD 1651*, p. 25; *CSPD 1650*, p. 389.

3 Commonplace book of Sir John Gibson, BL, Add. MS 37719, fol. 198v.

4 *Mercurius Politicus* (15–22 Aug. 1650), p. 162.

5 This advertisement is reproduced in Alexander Globe, *Peter Stent, London Printseller circa 1642–1665* (Vancouver, BC, 1985).

6 Stent appears to have been the only London print-seller using such advertisements during the 1650s: similar lists by contemporaries including Thomas Jenner and Robert Walton appeared after the Restoration. See Antony Griffiths, 'A check-list of catalogues of English print publishers c.1650–1830', *Print Quarterly*, 1 (1984), pp. 4–22.

7 Jane Roberts, *The King's Head: Charles I, King and Martyr* (1999); John Peacock, 'The visual image of Charles I', in Thomas N. Corns (ed.), *The Royal Image: Representations of Charles I* (Cambridge, 1999), pp. 176–239; David Howarth, *Images of Rule: Art and Politics in the English Renaissance, 1485–1649* (Basingstoke, 1997); Kevin M. Sharpe, '"So hard a text?" Images of Charles I, 1612–1700', *HJ*, 43 (2000), pp. 383–405.

8 Laura Lunger Knoppers, *Constructing Cromwell: Ceremony, Portrait and Print, 1645–1661* (Cambridge, 2000); Kevin M. Sharpe, '"An image-doting rabble": the failure of republican culture in seventeenth-century England', in Kevin M. Sharpe and Steven N. Zwicker (eds), *Refiguring Revolutions: Aesthetics and Politics from the English Revolution to the Romantic Revolution* (Berkeley, CA, 1998).

9 Sharpe, 'An image-doting rabble', pp. 41–2.

10 Sean Kelsey, *Inventing a Republic: The Political Culture of the English Commonwealth, 1649–1653* (Manchester, 1997).

11 Howarth, *Images of Rule*, p. 180.

12 *An Act For the Abolishing the Kingly Office in England, Ireland, and the Dominions Thereunto Belonging* (1649).

13 *CSPD 1649–50*, p. 481; *CSPD 1650*, p. 453.

14 *CSPD 1651*, p. 57.

15 *CSPD 1650*, p. 389.

16 *CSPD 1655*, p. 265.

17 *CSPD 1650*, p. 261; Katharine Gibson, 'The kingdom's marble chronicle: the embellishment of the first and second buildings, 1600 to 1690', in Ann Saunders (ed.), *The Royal Exchange* (1997), p. 344.

18 *CSPD 1611–18*, pp. 443, 600; Elisabeth Bourcier (ed.), *The Diary of Sir Simonds D'Ewes, 1622–1624: Journal d'un étudiant londonien sous le règne de Jacques Ier* (Paris, 1974), p. 142.

19 *CJ*, vol. II, p. 617.

20 BL, TT 669, fol. 12 [87]; Jonathan Brown and John Elliott (eds), *The Sale of the Century: Artistic Relations between Spain and Great Britain, 1604–1655* (New Haven, CT, 2002), p. 224.

21 Antony Griffiths, *The Print in Stuart Britain 1603–1689* (1998), p. 145; Kevin M. Sharpe, 'The royal image: an afterword', in Corns (ed.), *The Royal Image*, p. 294.

22 *The Manner of the Beheading of Duke Hambleton, the Earle of Holland, and the Lord Capell, in the Pallace Yard at Westminster* (n.d.); *A Great and Bloody Plot Discovered Against his Royal Majesty King Charles ... With the Beheading of One of the Grand Traytors* (1660).

23 Elizabeth Skerpan Wheeler, '*Eikon Basilike* and the rhetoric of self-representation', in Corns (ed.), *The Royal Image*, p. 122.

24 [William Somner], *The Frontispice* [sic] *of the Kings Book Opened. With a Poem Annexed* (n.p., 1650); J.L. Nevinson, 'English domestic embroidery patterns of the sixteenth and seventeenth centuries', *Walpole Society*, 28 (1939–40), p. 10; F.F. Madan, *A New Bibliography of the Eikon Basilike of King Charles the First* (1950), p. 187.

25 *The Man in the Moon* (7–14 Nov. 1649), p. 233; John Milton, *Eikonoklastes in Answer to a Book Intitl'd Eikon Basilike* (1650), sig. A4v.

26 William Lilly, *Monarchy or no Monarchy in England* (1651), pp. 118–19.

27 *Eikon Alethine. The Pourtraiture of Truths Most Sacred Majesty Truly Suffering, Though Not Solely* (1649), sig. A3.

28 *CSPD 1649–50*, p. 167.

29 *A Transcript of the Registers of the Worshipful Company of Stationers from 1640–1708*, ed. G.E.B. Eyre, 3 vols (1913), vol. I, p. 318; Thomason Tracts, BL, TT E.1243[3].

30 *CSPD 1649–50*, p. 524.

31 Thomas Bayly, *Certamen Religiosum, or, A Conference Between the Late King of England and the Late Lord Marquesse of Worcester Concerning Religion* (1651).

32 John Gadbury, *The Nativity of the Late King Charls* (1658); one of the BL's copies of this work, shelfmark 718.c.26, contains both the Marshall engraving and a small-scale portrait of Charles II.

33 Jason McElligott, *Royalism, Print and Censorship in Revolutionary England* (Woodbridge, 2007), chapter 8.

34 Globe, *Peter Stent*, p. 133.

35 *A Transcript of the Registers of the Worshipful Company of Stationers*, vol. II, pp. 41, 45.

36 *Middlesex County Records*, ed. John C. Jefferson, 4 vols (1886–92), vol. III, pp. 205–6; the ellipses indicate illegible parts of the document.

37 *NP*, vol. II, p. 352.

38 Globe, *Peter Stent*, p. 55.

39 BL, TT 669, fol. 16 [13].

40 Thomas Scott, *Boanerges. Or the Humble Supplication of the Ministers of Scotland, to the High Court of Pariament* [sic] *in England* (1624), p. 25.

41 BL, TT 669, fol. 16 [32].

42 *Ibid.*, fol. 15 [81].

43 Jerry Brotton, *The Sale of the Late King's Goods: Charles I and his Art Collection* (Basingstoke, 2006), pp. 258–9.

44 W.L.F. Nuttall, 'King Charles I's pictures and the Commonwealth sale', *Apollo* (Oct. 1965), p. 305.

45 Lucy Hutchinson, *Memoirs of the Life of Colonel Hutchinson*, ed. N.H. Keeble (1995), pp. 254–5.

46 Hilary Maddicott, 'A collection of the Interregnum period: Philip, Lord Lisle, and his purchases from the late king's goods, 1649–1660', *Journal of the History of Collections*, 11:1 (1999), p. 15.

47 Nuttall, 'King Charles I's pictures and the Commonwealth sale', p. 306; Susan Barnes et al., *Van Dyck: A Complete Catalogue of the Paintings* (New Haven, CT, 2003), p. 479.

48 Oliver Millar, *The Tudor, Stuart and Early Georgian Pictures in the Collection of Her Majesty the Queen*, 2 vols (1963), vol. I, p. 105.

49 Millar, *The Tudor, Stuart and Early Georgian Pictures*, vol. I, p. 99.

50 Balthasar Gerbier, *The None-such Charles His Character* (1651), p. 85.

51 Mary Beal, *A Study of Richard Symonds: His Italian Notebooks and their Relevance to Seventeenth-Century Painting Techniques* (New York, 1984), p. 303.

52 Quoted in Knoppers, *Constructing Cromwell*, p. 34.

53 Bodl., Clarendon MS 45, fol. 398.

54 *Ibid.*, fol. 399v. The BL holds a further manuscript copy of these verses, TT E.697[17].

55 Bodl., Clarendon MS 45, fol. 399v.

56 Clement Walker, *Anarchia Anglicana, or the History of Independency* (1649); H.C. Shelley, 'Cromwell in caricature', *The Connoisseur*, 15 (May–Aug. 1906), pp. 154–60; Elizabeth Staffell, 'The horrible tail-man and the Anglo-Dutch wars', *Journal of the Warburg and Courtauld Institutes*, 63 (2000), pp. 169–86.

57 Sheila O'Connell, *The Popular Print in England, 1550–1850* (1999), p. 168 n. 2.

58 *Mercurius Publicus* (16–23 Aug. 1660), p. 534.

59 Robert Latham and William Matthews (eds), *The Diary of Samuel Pepys*, 11 vols (1970–83), vol. I, p. 89; *An Exit to the Exit Tyrannus: or, Upon Erasing that Ignominius and Scandalous Motto* (n.p., 1660).

60 W.L. Sachse (ed.), *The Diurnal of Thomas Rugg, 1659–1661* (Camden Society, 3rd series, 91, 1961), pp. 90, 84.

61 *Ibid.*, pp. 109, 115–16.

Chapter 5

'Vailing his Crown': Royalist criticism of Charles I's kingship in the 1650s

Anthony Milton

I

The cult of the royal martyr Charles I undoubtedly acted as an important focus for Royalist beliefs, and quite properly it has loomed large in
accounts of Royalist thinking in the 1650s and beyond, especially with relation
to the book in which it received its most telling apotheosis, *Eikon Basilike*.[1]
The current orthodoxy regarding the changing image of Charles I presents
this cult as the end-point of a more ambiguous journey in Royalist perceptions of their monarch. At the beginning of the Civil War, Charles was still
regarded by many Royalists as a monarch who had implemented absolutist
policies: while royal propagandists like Henry Ferne complained that the king
had 'invaded some liberties granted to the subject upon agreement', even the
king's own pre-war declarations deplored recent policy excesses.[2] Awkward
memories of the Personal Rule meant that the personal image of Charles
did not figure largely in Royalist propaganda for much of the war. This situation was changed, however, by the capture and publication of the king's
private correspondence after the Battle of Naseby, and then (crucially) by the
king's imprisonment, which generated 'a major shift in the representation of
Charles'. It was only now, with Charles deprived of his power, that his personal
qualities could be brought to the fore – that he could be depicted as a family
man deprived of his rights, as prospective and then actual martyr. No longer
the absolutist monarch, Charles had been redeemed by his sufferings and loss
of power.[3] The implication in recent historiography has tended to be that the
martyr cult now superseded all previous Royalist attitudes towards Charles,
and that this image of Charles as more saint than king carried all before it in
subsequent years.

But were Royalist attitudes towards the royal martyr more mixed? Were
all Royalists satisfied with the image of a monarch redeemed by his loss of

power rather than his exercise of it? One remarkable book published in the 1650s seems to tell a rather different story. The anonymously published *Observations on the Historie of the Reign of King Charles* (1656) in fact manifests an outspoken rejection of the essence of the martyr cult – the praise of blameless royal suffering and forbearance – and in the process levels a series of devastating attacks upon Charles's practice of kingship. But this was no republican rant following in the footsteps of Milton's *Eikonoklastes*. Rather, it was written by Peter Heylyn, a man who had been a royal chaplain for many years, and had been an outspoken apologist for royal policies in the 1630s, in which capacity he had dedicated works to the very same King Charles (after whom he seems to have named one of his sons). He had also been the first editor of the Royalist newsbook *Mercurius Aulicus*, and was notoriously an upholder of firmly absolutist ideas.[4] This chapter will analyse the context in which Heylyn wrote his assault on Charles's style of kingship and the nature of his criticisms. It will then turn to the possible reasons why Heylyn's work has been completely misread in recent scholarship. It will be suggested that Heylyn's writings on Charles should prompt us to reconsider how at least some Royalists may have felt towards their executed monarch, and how dominant the martyr cult and its associations were in Royalist thought.

II

We will begin with the background to Heylyn's extraordinary publication. The *Observations* is notable as the first directly polemical piece of work that Peter Heylyn had written since the Civil War. In the intervening years Heylyn had compounded with the authorities, and he spent the early 1650s publishing works that seemed to shy away from overt confrontation with the political issues of the day: these were the *Cosmographie*, *Theologia Veterum* (a commentary on the Apostles' Creed) and his *Survey of France*.[5] In these years, while Heylyn had not entirely retired from public affairs, he was nevertheless not closely involved in the main Royalist clerical circles presided over by Henry Hammond and Gilbert Sheldon.[6] The *Observations* constituted a sudden return to outspoken argument and sustained commentary on political events. It was still in one sense a circumspect publication – unlike the three recent books mentioned above, the *Observations* was published anonymously, and Heylyn went to some trouble to protect his anonymity.[7] It is perhaps this anonymity which can partly explain his outspokenness in this volume, not least on the subject of Charles I himself. But why did Heylyn choose to publish the book at all?

The key lies in the volume which the *Observations* attacks. This is Hamon L'Estrange's *The Reign of King Charles* (1655). L'Estrange was, like Heylyn, a Royalist who had compounded, but he was not of Heylyn's stock. L'Estrange had dedicated his first book (an attack on Heylyn among others) to Parliament in 1641, and in August 1644 he had appealed to the Earl of Manchester for his support, 'having referred himself to a strict soliloquy and reconciled his opinion to the sense of the parliament'.[8] L'Estrange's *Reign of King Charles* offers a guardedly positive reading of Charles and his reign, with a balanced discussion of Charles's relations with Parliament, ship money and foreign policy. The Scots are depicted as cynically planning sedition for many years, and their Covenant is said to aim at the destruction of king and religion. L'Estrange condemns the Presbyterians' 'so principally occasioning our late sad distractions'.[9] There is much here that Heylyn would find to agree with – indeed, he would cite L'Estrange's work extensively in his later biography of Laud, *Cyprianus Anglicus*.[10] Even on religious matters L'Estrange's views sometimes corresponded with Heylyn's: he reflected that before Laud bishops had been negligent, criticised Archbishop Abbot's 'extraordinary remisnesse in not exacting strict conformity to the prescribed Orders of the Church in point of ceremony' and condemned Bishop Williams' reckless pursuit of popularity in endeavouring 'the supplanting of his Soveraign'.[11]

However, there was still a good deal in *The Reign of King Charles* that was unpalatable to Heylyn. While L'Estrange attempts to offer balanced assessments of Charles's policies in many areas, in religion he is much more critical, and admits in his preface that 'some will say I seem no friend to the Clergy'. When looking at the 1620s, L'Estrange adopts a firmly anti-Arminian line: he repeats Parliament's 1629 complaints of Arminianism, notes the dismay of 'the Orthodox party', describes Montagu's books as 'prejudiciall to the protestant cause' and remarks how his supporters created a fear of popery, though their popery was 'but part-boyled Popery, but Popery oblique'.[12] With regard to Archbishop Laud himself L'Estrange picks a careful path (although, as we will see, this care may reflect some very late revisions to the text). Laud is defended against charges of changing the coronation oath or favouring Roman Catholics, but while his basic policies are approved, it is added that he was 'a learned, pious and morally good man, but too full of fire', 'his zeal to order, that carried him thus far, transported him a little too far', he 'did a little out run authority', and he 'tampered indeed to introduce some ceremonies bordering upon superstition, disused by us, and abused by them [Roman Catholics]'.[13] The real problem, though, lay with Laud's subordinates, who tried to push forward their own ideas 'which came within a Mathematical line of Popery' and whose lives were also scandalous. Their exorbitances 'created a very great disgust against them', which aided the Presbyterians. It would also have been better, according to L'Estrange, if bishops had been less active in civil affairs: he does not flinch from using the term 'bishops' wars' for the campaigns against the Covenanters, and suggests that the bishops were behind the disastrous decision to dissolve the Short Parliament.[14] Laud was thus partly freed from blame by the fact that it was heaped upon subordinates, in the same way as Charles was partly exculpated by blaming his advisers, including Windebank, and the Attorney General, William Noy (who had been a personal friend of Heylyn's).[15]

There was of course nothing new in attacks upon the Laudian movement, and many of the Puritan assaults had been a great deal more savage. The key difference here was that L'Estrange was writing as a Royalist, and making his attack on Laudianism within a narrative that essentially offered a positive assessment of the king. Attacks from extreme Puritans were one thing – they could be ignored. But an attack on Laudianism from within royalism was a much greater threat to its orthodox credentials. L'Estrange complained in his response to the *Observations* that he and Heylyn were aware of each other even if they were not familiar acquaintances: 'the truth is, we have met in London at the same shop, I may safely say neer an hundred times; and ... not lesse then ten times, not only after the publication of my History, but after he had, to my knowledge, perused it, and before he had entred one line of his Observations into the Presse'.[16] For L'Estrange this demonstrated that Heylyn merely sought a quarrel, but from Heylyn's perspective it was their very proximity within contemporary royalism that necessitated his attack.[17]

There may have been a personal edge to these exchanges, too. Heylyn presumably considered himself to be included within L'Estrange's strictures on the extreme ideas of Laud's subordinates. L'Estrange had already written a pamphlet on the sabbath controversy (*Gods Sabbath before the Law, under the Law, and under the Gospel* (1641)) that was chiefly aimed at Heylyn's *History of the Sabbath*, although Heylyn's later comments imply that he was not aware of it.[18] It may also be relevant that L'Estrange had included much more outspoken and explicit attacks upon Laud and Heylyn in part of the initial printing of *The Reign of King Charles*. Rather than presenting the carefully balanced assessment of Laud which appeared in the published version, these initial sheets attacked Laud as being 'of a pragmatical and factious spirit, a bold Assertor of some dangerous and superstitious Tenets', and condemned the Book of Sports as 'a sacrilegious robbing of God' and a plot by Laud 'and his confederates' to force Puritan divines out of their livings. Heylyn is also the subject of a much more extended and offensive assault. L'Estrange explains how, arranging for an attack on Bishop Williams for his writing on the altar policy, the court bishops 'put out the work to their bold Champion Dr Heylyn, who thereupon undertakes the Bishop, and bungleth up a reply to him full of ignorance and virulence, so much the fiercer because he thought the Bishop not in the state of operating any thing considerably noxious to him. But the next lustre this Bishop became for a while illustrious, and then he did fawn upon and cringe to him, on whom he had formerly trampled, no man more.'[19]

Despite being printed, these sheets were not included in the published version. In suppressing them L'Estrange would seem to have been responding to adverse Royalist comment before publication: he remarks in his preface that his *Reign of King Charles* had been 'already by some reprobated for errors foreseen' 'even before it can speak, before it comes to the birth of edition, while it is yet in the womb of the Presse'.[20] Heylyn somehow managed to obtain these unpublished sheets (possibly because one of L'Estrange's publishers was the son of Heylyn's own publisher, Henry Seile), and quoted liberally from them in a book defending his *Observations* entitled *Extraneus Valupans* (1656). Heylyn claimed here that he had acquired the sheets only after he had heard that L'Estrange was planning an acerbic attack upon the *Observations*. It is at least possible, however, that Heylyn's decision to publish an attack on the *Reign of King Charles*, and the occasionally vehement nature of his criticisms, can partly be explained by the fact that he had already viewed the more inflammatory initial sheets, although he could not engage with them in the final text of the *Observations* because they had not been included in the published version of L'Estrange's book.[21]

Heylyn was an intensely polemical writer, which is what makes it so important to establish the context in which he chose to put pen to paper. Nevertheless, whatever his precise reasons for attacking L'Estrange's book, it must be stressed that Heylyn's *Observations* does not consist of a simple series of minor line-by-line corrections, nor for much of the time does the desire to disagree with L'Estrange introduce inconsistencies or incongruities into Heylyn's account, for all his outbreaks of petty point-scoring in correcting minor points of detail. In fact, Heylyn uses his engagement with L'Estrange's book partly as an excuse for him to deliver his own reflections on the period (and, as we shall see, in this it is comparable with his later *Bibliotheca Regia* of 1658 with its sometimes detailed annotations and reflections on documents). Heylyn states bluntly that the *Observations* can be read without a copy of L'Estrange's book to hand, just as 'the Disputations of Machiavell may be read with light and profit, without recourse unto the Decades of Titus Livius, whom he makes the Argument of his Discourses'.[22] Certainly, there are some extended discussions and commentaries in the book that are not direct corrections of passages in L'Estrange, but rather amplifications or alternative interpretations. In fact, Heylyn's comments are sustained by a specific argument concerning Charles and his government that is evident throughout the work.

In *The Reign of King Charles* L'Estrange had offered a guardedly positive view of Charles. In L'Estrange's eyes the king always meant well, and was often poised to secure agreement with Parliament. Charles seems to share his conviction that regular parliaments were a vital part of a healthy body politic. Thus in 1628 Charles called a parliament not merely to secure supply (L'Estrange explains) 'but also to give some better repose to his troubled spirit; for he felt no inward contentment, whilest he the Head, and his Subjects the Body, were at distance', and the king therefore resolved 'to frame and dispose himself to such obliging complacence and compliance, as might re-consolidate them by continuity of affection'. Similarly, L'Estrange opines that the Short Parliament would have succeeded if the king had made concessions over the prerogative and episcopacy, which would have gained the people's affection. On his account Charles was actually ready to make these concessions; therefore the dissolution of the Parliament must have been on the advice of ignorant episcopal councillors.[23] Evil councillors are to blame for disagreeable policy initiatives. The king in fact is always ready to make concessions which could have resolved the crisis: while some have seen his consent to the act against the dissolution of Parliament as a destruction of the regal interest, it could on the other hand be seen as a shrewd policy which gave the subject 'still further assurance of his clear intentions to the common-good'.[24] L'Estrange's picture of Charles's kingship is thus of a naturally mild-mannered man who wishes to work with his parliaments and win the affection of his people – he 'was of a genius, as not querulous, so if provoked, very placable'.[25] His downfall was due merely to evil councillors and malicious plotting.

It is this interpretation that Heylyn sets out to challenge in the *Observations*. He partly does this by a sustained critique of Charles's policies. Where L'Estrange is content to present a conspiracy against the Crown throughout the 1630s, Heylyn sees a conspiracy that only succeeded because of Charles's naivety and incompetence: 'who can save him' (Heylyn exclaims at one point) 'who neglects the meanes of his preservation?'[26] The whole work presents a sustained attack on Charles's performance as a monarch, dating right back to the collapse of the Spanish Match. The failure of this projected marriage of Charles (then Prince of Wales) with the Spanish Infanta, and the anti-Habsburg military campaign that followed it, was usually recounted as a fortunate escape for Charles and the country, but Heylyn instead presents the failure to secure the Spanish marriage as a great mistake by Charles, and the loss of a natural ally for the Stuarts. Heylyn stresses that it would have given the Crown the power to suppress the Puritans, 'that the ruine of Prince Charles might by this match have been prevented'. Charles then mismanaged all his parliaments in the 1620s, making damaging concessions. His failure to punish London for the tumults that led to the lynching of Buckingham's servant Dr John Lambe encouraged opposition by demonstrating 'that the King had rather patience enough to bear such indignities, than resolution to revenge them'.[27]

The king and his Council are seen as fatally mismanaging the Scottish prayer book crisis. Heylyn complains that L'Estrange 'omits the great oversights committed by the king and the Lords of that Councel, in the conduct and carriage of the businesse'. The initial riot would easily have been quashed 'had the King caused the chief Ring-leaders of this Tumult to be put to death'.[28]

Charles was particularly to blame for choosing the Marquess of Hamilton as his commissioner to the Covenanters 'against the opinion and advice of many of the Lords of that Kingdome', who when they warned Charles 'the King fatally carried on to his owne destruction, would not hearken to it'. Planning for the Scots campaign saw 'the King still going on in his fatall over-sights', and intending merely to overawe the Scots rather than to fight them. He then erred in disbanding his army, thereby encouraging opponents and frustrating the English gentry. Even the disastrous wording of the so-called 'etcetera oath' is blamed on Charles for rushing the Convocation to complete its work.[29]

Charles's errors multiply with the calling of the Long Parliament. Again, there are complaints of his high-minded naivety and lack of resolution, but increasingly the theme is one of betrayal: the king is depicted as spinelessly betraying his supporters and the cause of true religion. Charles's granting of the act of attainder against Strafford was of course a betrayal which the king had himself admitted, but Heylyn emphasises the king's broader responsibility for Strafford's fate. He had missed opportunities to save him, and by later publicising how the bridging appointments scheme had been offered to him as a means of saving Strafford's life 'he exposed himself to some disadvantages in the eyes of others, by giving them to understand at how cheap a rate (a rate which would have cost him nothing) he might have saved the life of such an able and deserving Minister'.[30] Charles's ill-judged speech to Parliament on 1 May 1641 not only hastened the earl's execution by enraging Parliament, but also greatly distressed Strafford by stressing that his misdemeanours were so great that he was not fit to serve even as a local constable.[31] Similarly, Charles's consent to the bill against the dissolution of Parliament was not just a fatal political error and act of folly, but was also an act of betrayal. This act 'put such an irrevocable power into the hands of his enemies, as was made use of afterwards not onely to His own destruction, but to the disinherison of His Children, *and the undoing of all those who adhered unto Him*'.[32] Among 'all those who adhered unto Him' Heylyn presumably included himself, and there may well be a sense of personal betrayal animating some of these remarks.

These were not mere corrections of political errors based on personal resentment, however. Heylyn also pursues a far more sustained critique of Charles that was encapsulated in the notion that the king had 'vailed his Crown'. Early on in the *Observations* Heylyn attaches particular importance to L'Estrange's report that, after he ended his speech at his first parliament, Charles 'vailed [i.e. doffed] his Crown, a thing rare in any of his Predecessours'. 'Vailing' (doffing or taking off) an item of head-dress could be seen in this period as a sign of respect or courtesy (as Charles presumably intended it), but could also be interpreted as a sign of submission. Certainly sixteenth- and seventeenth-century writers commonly used the term figuratively to indicate that someone had manifested submission, had yielded and/or had acknowledged their inferiority.[33] For Heylyn, this physical act of apparent submission by Charles to Parliament could also be used figuratively to describe Charles's continued abject self-abasement before this and future parliaments. He warned that the 'vailing' of the crown that L'Estrange recorded presaged

> those many *veilings of the Crown* in all the Parliaments that followed: For, first he *vailed his Crown* to this, in leaving Mountague in their hands, and his Bond uncancelled ... notwithstanding that he was his sworn Chaplain and Domestick Servant ... he *vailed his Crown* unto the next, when he permitted them ... to search his Signet Office ... he *vailed his Crown* unto the third, first in the way of preparation to it, releasing all the Gentlemen whom he had imprisoned ... next in the prosecution of it, when hearing that the Parliament had granted him some Subsidies, not a man dissenting, he could not restraine himself from weeping (which tendernesse of his was made good use of to his no small damage) ... and finally in the close thereof when He enacted the Petition of Right ... He vailed his Crowne unto all three, by suffering the House of Commons to set up a Committee for Religion ...[34]

In the rest of the *Observations*, 'vailing his Crown' becomes the leitmotif of Heylyn's analysis of Charles's misrule. Charles 'vails his Crowne' by releasing Eliot and Digges from prison. He 'vailed his Crown' to the Scots 'when having power to bring them under his command, he yeilded to the Pacification at Barwicke, not more unto his own dishonour than to their advantage', and vailed his crown by allowing the trial of Strafford, the triennial bill and the Act against the dissolution of Parliament.[35] The Dutch were encouraged to defy Charles by attacking the Spanish fleet in the Channel because they reasoned that Charles 'having vailed his Crown to the Scots and English, why might he not vaile it to them?' Charles's underwriting of his own name to a letter to the Lords pleading for Strafford's life 'was of as bad presage to him, as the vailing of his Crowne' to his first parliament, and led to the many other concessions successfully demanded from the king, 'incouraged by so strange a submission of himself to the Power and Courtesie of his People'.[36] Charles is also berated for having failed to keep up 'the Majesty of the Crown' by formal entries to London.[37]

This was an attack not just on Charles's pusillanimity, but also on the notion that it was in some way more honourable for him to exhibit a virtuous weakness than to act effectively. By implication this was an assault on the essential image of the royal martyr who had been guided by his conscience.[38] Indeed, Heylyn specifically condemns Charles's maxim 'that it was better to be deceived then to distrust', noting that this 'proved a plaine and easie way unto those calamities which afterwards were brought upon him'. Hence too Heylyn's complaint that the king 'had rather patience enough to bear such indignities, than resolution to revenge them'.[39] Heylyn attaches notable importance to Prynne's report that Charles wore white at his coronation:

> And this I look upon as an ill presage, that the King laying aside his Purple, and Robe of majesty, should cloathe himselfe in White, the Robe of Innocence; as if thereby it were foresignified that he would devest himselfe of that Regall Majesty which might and would have kept him safe from affront and scorn, to relie wholly on the innocence of a vertuous life, which did expose him finally to calamitous ruine.[40]

This was to depict the martyr cult's emphasis on conscience and virtue as the root of the calamities that had followed. This was not simply an attack on the rationale of the cult, but also an implicit assault on the text of *Eikon Basilike* itself.

In fact, implicit attacks upon the *Eikon Basilike* (the text of which Heylyn must have been very fully acquainted with) can be found in the *Observations*. For example, on Strafford's execution, Charles berates himself for his 'sinful compliance' in the shedding of Strafford's blood, but does not retract (or even mention) his condemnation of Strafford's 'misdemeanours' in his speech on 1 May (indeed he still reserves the right to criticise Strafford's government, reflecting that 'I cannot in My judgement approve all he did' and affirming that he would not have employed him again).[41] As we have seen, for Heylyn these criticisms were part and parcel of the king's betrayal of Strafford: these concessions to his enemies led naturally to the attainder. In the *Eikon Basilike* Charles stoutly defends his decision to grant the Act against the dissolution of Parliament, denies that he repented it and stresses his sincerity: 'although I may seem less a Politician to men, yet I need no secret distinctions or evasions before God'.[42] As we have seen, Heylyn condemned the same Act as securing not only Charles's own destruction, but also the undoing of all his supporters. The limited chronological overlap between L'Estrange's *Reign of King Charles* and the *Eikon Basilike* served to restrict the number of implicit attacks upon the latter in Heylyn's *Observations*, but in his other works Heylyn does not hesitate to take a very different line on Charles's attempted justifications of his behaviour.[43]

Even where Heylyn does not implicitly attack the *Eikon*, it is easy to see how he would have winced at many passages in it. Charles's prayer for God's help 'if not to conquer, yet at least to suffer'; or his expressed desire to remind himself that he is more a Christian than a king, and that where a king is tempted to take revenge a Christian forgives; or the king's reflection that the Nineteen Propositions did him an honour 'to put Me in the giving part, which is more princely and divine' would all have infuriated Heylyn.[44] In the *Eikon Basilike* military defeat simply serves as a salve for the king's conscience: his opponents' seizure of magazines, forts, navy and militia testifies to his innocency in provoking the war, leaving only prayers and tears, which serve if not to conquer as a soldier, yet to suffer as a martyr. The seizure of them, Charles reflects, 'is best for me', as it teaches him to trust only in God.[45] The general thrust of the *Eikon Basilike* encapsulates Heylyn's complaint that Charles put his own search for virtue before his duties as a king. Charles writes that a Christian king must prefer the peace of his conscience before the preservation of his kingdoms, that he would rather suffer the greatest injuries than sin against his conscience, and that it was better to die with 'enjoying this Empire of My Soul' than to live with the title of a king but without the use of his conscience.[46]

This is not to suggest that Heylyn simply sought to champion *realpolitik* over the dictates of conscience. He had certainly read Machiavelli, and (as we have seen) conceived of his *Observations* partly as a series of historical reflections similar in style to Machiavelli's *Discourses on Livy*.[47] But in this case he was more convinced that the king had indulged in a poorly instructed conscience. As a king, Charles should have been compelled by his conscience to act in the authoritarian manner that would have best preserved the lives and fortunes of his people – the dictates of conscience and the preservation of his kingdoms should not have pointed him in two different directions. But he had also directly violated his conscience in ways that the *Eikon* did not choose to identify. He was capable of cynical statecraft, but only of an incompetent sort, in consistently betraying his friends and supporters in attempting to placate his enemies. An early example was his attempt to appease Parliament by calling in Richard Montagu's *Appello Caesarem*, leaving Heylyn to the pious lament that 'it never falleth out well with Christian Princes, when they make Religion bend to Policy, and so it hapned to this king'.[48] If this did not directly suggest that Charles's fate reflected God's judgement upon him for his inconstant support for Laudianism, then it came very close.

After all this, there is a certain amount of irony in the fact that Heylyn charged L'Estrange with disloyalty for his criticisms of Charles. L'Estrange, not surprisingly, responded by accusing Heylyn of much more obvious attacks. He commented that Heylyn's book might more correctly have been entitled 'Observations against King Charles, than Observations upon his History'.[49] (Thomas Fuller also chipped in soon afterwards with the observation that Heylyn had 'so saucily and unsubject-like counted how often King Charles waved his Crown', and made pointed remarks about how some 'high Royalists' had written of the king 'in a base and disparaging language'.)[50] In reply to L'Estrange, Heylyn defended his own criticisms as simply being examples of a historian noting 'errors in conduct of affairs' and failings in 'the Arts of King-craft', and in return accused L'Estrange of consistently attacking Charles in the unpublished sheets of the *Reign of King Charles*. He claimed to quote L'Estrange's description of Charles as 'a man that was within the incidence of frailty' and how 'swayed by supine and implicit faith, in the either wisdom or integrity of those who seemed to advise him, he was precipitated upon designs which could promise nothing but confusion'. In the same unpublished sheets

L'Estrange had also accused Charles of letting corruption flourish at court and of indulging recusants, and had complained that 'he miscarried in his regal Ministration, by departing to arbitrary power'.[51] Both authors clearly had strong reservations about Charles as a ruler – his weakness leading him either into absolutism or into a yielding passivity – however much they felt compelled publicly to deny having attacked the royal martyr.

III

It is remarkable that the current principal historian of the martyr cult has provided a very different description of the exchanges between Heylyn and L'Estrange from the one provided above. Heylyn's aim in the *Observations* (he claims) 'was to defend the image of the innocent and saintly Charles constructed by the Royalist eulogists and preachers and to refute any suggestion that he bore any responsibility for the events of the 1640s and his own defeat'. Yet, as we have seen, Heylyn's aim would appear to have been precisely the opposite.[52] The same historian has claimed that Heylyn made his attacks on L'Estrange and the Royalist historian William Sanderson because they were 'not sufficiently hagiographic', and remarks that 'it was Heylyn's full-blooded Royalist Anglican view of the innocent and saintly martyr which was to dominate as the only officially sanctioned version'.[53]

Why should Heylyn have been so misread? It is partly, perhaps, a matter of assumption. Since Heylyn is known to have been an outspoken defender of royal absolutism, it is assumed that he must also have been an uncritical admirer of the royal martyr. Perhaps, too, Heylyn's authorship of the supposedly hagiographic *A Short View of the Life and Reign of King Charles* (1658) has been taken to typify his attitude – indeed, it has been suggested that in this work Heylyn 'obviously saw himself as the defender of cult orthodoxy'.[54] But if the *Short View* is read in the light of the *Observations* rather than the other way round, then a rather different interpretation of even this text is possible.

The *Short View* appeared as an introduction to one edition of Richard Royston's collection of Charles's works entitled *Reliquiae Sacrae Carolinae*; it was also published separately under its own title page.[55] While the *Short View* obviously offers a favourable account of Charles's life, it is not a simple hagiography. In fact it offers a restrained political history of the king's life and times. It is true that there are two purple passages which reflect standard Royalist hyperbole, and two brief parallels with the suffering of Christ.[56] But these are the only examples of such language in over 160 pages of text. By contrast, the account of Charles's trial and execution is relatively brief and perfunctory, and does not compare with the elaborate account that Heylyn wrote of the execution of Laud in the 1640s.[57] This was emphatically not a contribution to the martyrological tradition – it concludes not with a quotation from the

Bible, but with one from Tacitus's life of Julius Agrippa. It is a ruler who is being commemorated, not a saint or martyr.[58] Charles is also presented as a ruler who made mistakes, and again Heylyn's criticisms are directed at errors of weakness, compliance and inconstancy. The text revisits a number of the royal errors that Heylyn had first rehearsed in the *Observations*. It is suggested that in his alliance with Parliament for a war to regain the Palatinate, Charles followed Buckingham's emotionalism, and his desire to please the House of Commons, rather than the interests of the Crown. If Charles had made peace with Spain after the initial failure of the fleet then he could have avoided further problems with parliaments and the rupture with France. He is shown as departing with all his powers and prerogatives in the early 1640s, and then as having missed an early chance to win the Civil War.[59] Heylyn also notes how in the Second Civil War Charles was still meditating on God's displeasure as a judgement for his earlier mistakes, and quotes in italics the section of *Eikon Basilike* where Charles confessed that 'worldly wisdome' had led him to permit improper divine worship to be set up in Scotland and to allow the bishops of England to be injured.[60] Heylyn presumably felt that Charles merited this self-reproof.

The *Short View* may thus be very different in tone to the *Observations*, but nevertheless the blunt criticisms in the earlier work provide at least part of the explanation for what is a very restrained account that manifests little enthusiasm for martyrological tropes. If this made the *Short View* seem rather out of place in the *Reliquiae* volume, it would seem that Heylyn thought this too. In the following year he published his own annotated collection of Charles's works entitled *Bibliotheca Regia*. Not the least remarkable thing about this book is its explicit attack on the *Reliquiae Sacrae Carolinae*.[61] In condemning this volume (which included a reprint of *Eikon Basilike*) Heylyn attacked the whole shift in Royalist writing towards an emphasis on Charles's personal qualities. The *Reliquiae*, he complained, 'did rather represent his Majesty in his Personal, than his Political capacities, and rather shewed his great abilities, as a private man, digesting his sad and solitary thoughts into Meditations, and mannaging disputes with particular men; than acting as a Free Monarch, and a Powerful Prince'. Even 'for the civil part', the *Reliquiae* 'speaks him in a time of trouble and disadvantage, necessitated to comply with a potent faction, awed by the Armies of his own Subjects, or under such Restraints as render him not so much the Master of himself, as a servant to others'. Heylyn was manifestly not interested in the martyrological tradition, and in *Bibliotheca Regia* he presented his own collection of Charles's works that concentrated more on his time in power, in the pre-war period. Even here, however, his treatment of Charles's kingship was not without its pointed criticisms, especially of his Scottish policy.[62] Heylyn is emphatic that it was the king's lack of consistency that encouraged Puritans in England and Scotland to demand concessions which Charles in turn yielded too easily, so that the king 'did but accelerate his own fall'.[63] In his preface Heylyn states baldly that Charles's behaviour in England and Scotland offered a warning example to other princes and supreme magistrates 'not to engage themselves in any action of concernment, but what they are both able and resolved to go through with. The doing of such work by halves, overthrows the whole.'[64] Heylyn may not have used the term 'vailing his Crown' in the *Short View* and *Bibliotheca Regia*, but these are manifestly the works of the author of the *Observations*. Just like the *Short View*, the *Bibliotheca Regia* has been interpreted by scholars as a simple work of Royalist hagiography, on the basis (apparently) of the emphatically Royalist iconography that is displayed on its frontispieces.[65]

This would all seem to suggest that historians need to exercise more care in their reading of apparently hagiographical writing about Charles. Even Heylyn, as we have seen, felt required to make the occasional gesture towards the martyrological tradition in the *Short View*. But if some of the tropes of the martyr cult had become standardised in Royalist writing, this need not mean that the authors who used them necessarily accepted the whole ideological baggage that is assumed to have gone with it. Similarly, the sermons of 30 January may seem to advocate a remarkably consistent set of martyrological assumptions and a coherent political ideology, but this may reflect the fact that they constituted a distinctive and limited genre of address and publication, rather than that they represent the key to an unchanging, monochrome Royalist perception of Charles I. Here it is useful to recall the 1658 edition of the *Reliquiae* that included both *Eikon Basilike* and Heylyn's *Short View*. Wheeler has stressed that as *Eikon Basilike* had no single author and no single authorised version, its authorship should be seen as 'collective, collaborative and participatory'.[66] Certainly, the edition that was accompanied by Heylyn's *Short View* carried its own potential gloss – the reader was being offered a range of ways of thinking about the king. After the Restoration, the new edition of the works of Charles – *Basilika* (1662) – substituted a different life of Charles, this one written by Richard Perrinchief. While lifting a good deal of Heylyn's text, Perrinchief presented yet another picture of Charles, this time as an inspired military commander. Despite the occasional martyrological trope (and a passing suggestion that the reported cures affected by handkerchiefs dipped in the royal martyr's blood were genuine) and an extended contemplation of the king's personal qualities at the end, Perrinchief's desire to present Charles as a heroic military leader (albeit one keen to avert bloodshed) still represented an uneasy coupling with the passive, pusillanimous monarch of the *Eikon Basilike* which followed in the same volume.[67]

IV

Was Heylyn unique as a Royalist in being unimpressed by the image of Charles as the pacific, persecuted man of conscience, made victorious by his sufferings? There were certainly other Royalists in the 1640s who deplored the king's many concessions, and saw them as evidence of unkingly weakness rather than of a generous and saintly yielding to unscrupulous enemies. Griffith Williams, bishop of Ossory, observed pointedly in a publication of 1644 that some princes gave away their rights 'to the prejudice of themselves and their posterity' out of 'their Princely clemency and facility, to gaine the more love and affection ... from their Subjects'. Charles's signing of the Act against the dissolution of Parliament showed the king 'no better then merely cheated by the faction of the Parliament', although he 'ought to have been as wise to prevent them, as they were subtle to circumvent him'. The king in fact had no right to make such a grant, which was 'contradictory to Gods will'. Indeed, Williams argued that the king's many concessions and promises – including specifically the Act excluding the bishops from Parliament – were more than he needed to or should have granted, 'being to the dishonor of God, and the prejudice of his Church'. Williams expressed the hope that Charles would not be offended by what he had written, but if the king was indeed offended, he declared, 'I had rather suffer the anger of any mortall man, then endure the wrath of the great God'.[68] These were complaints published in Royalist Oxford at the height of the Civil War, and it seems unlikely that such attitudes merely disappeared with the emergence of the cult of the royal martyr, which encapsulated this sense of Charles's pusillanimity. Sean Kelsey has also suggested more recently that, in the last hectic weeks of the king's negotiations at Newport in 1648, as concession followed concession, there may well have been some Royalists keen to see a swift royal martyrdom so that Charles could be replaced by a son who could negotiate from a stronger position.[69]

By the 1650s Royalists of an absolutist persuasion (of whom Hobbes is only the most obvious example) could easily have found Oliver Cromwell a more attractive proposition as a leader than the apparently spineless, prevaricating and martyrdom-obsessed Charles, happy to sacrifice his kingdom to save his conscience. Indeed, Heylyn himself appears to have made approaches to Cromwell when Royalist fortunes were at their nadir (and his *Observations* include some notably positive remarks about the Lord Protector).[70] Even when Heylyn writes at his most exuberantly absolutist he still persists in making implicit criticisms of the royal martyr. Replying to Harrington, and emphasising the need for kings to have a standing army, he still noted that a people would force a generous king to give away royalty itself, while his reflection that there was no infirmity or insufficiency in monarchy until the reins of government were let loose by folly, supposedly reflecting on Sparta, had a very obvious (and surely conscious) application to Charles I.[71]

Historians' discussions of opposition to *Eikon Basilike* and the royal martyrological cult have always tended to focus on the attacks made by the doughtiest opponents of the Royalist cause, with their innate hostility towards ideas of sacred kingship, set prayers and idolatry.[72] But there is an obvious need to move beyond a simple model of Royalist martyrology versus republican anti-martyrology, and to make space in the history of representations of Charles for *Royalist* critiques of the martyr cult. When radicals accused Charles of Machiavellianism, Heylyn must have felt that this was wishful thinking.[73] The extraordinary number of editions of *Eikon Basilike* has led historians to focus exclusively on the reasons why the book was an ideal vehicle for sustaining Royalists' morale and self-identity. But we may need to allow for the fact that for some Royalists of the time the message of *Eikon Basilike* may have been ambiguous, while for others it was deeply frustrating, even abhorrent. Rather than nursing their sense of identity, for some Royalists the *Eikon Basilike* instead may have seemed to explain and encapsulate why the Royalists had lost. Doubtless, few Royalists would have dared to express such concerns directly in print in the manner in which Heylyn did. But ultimately it is immaterial if we are unable to uncover any more books that can match the outspokenness of Heylyn's *Observations*. The ultimate value of Heylyn's *Observations* is that it enables us to detect the ambiguities, omissions and reservations in his other works. And it is important to remember here that Heylyn's *Short View* and *Bibliotheca Regia* were published within the heart of the Royalist movement, by publishers and booksellers who had nurtured and to some extent initiated the martyrological tradition.[74] If such fundamental misgivings about the cult of the royal martyr were felt by a figure such as Heylyn, and can be detected even in his prominent works commemorating Charles, then it is at least possible that *implicit* disagreements with the martyr cult may still lie unobserved in other Royalist writings of this period, awaiting discovery.

NOTES

I am grateful to the editors for their comments on an earlier draft of this chapter.

1 For example, R. Wilcher, *The Writing of Royalism, 1628–1660* (Cambridge, 2001); S.N. Zwicker, *Lines of Authority: Politics and English Literary Culture, 1649–1689* (1993), pp. 37–59; A. Lacey, *The Cult of King Charles the Martyr* (Woodbridge, 2003); Lois Potter, *Secret Rites and Secret Writing: Royalist Literature, 1641–1660* (Cambridge, 1989).

2 J. Sanderson, *'But the people's creatures': The Philosophical Basis of the English Civil War* (Manchester, 1989), pp. 39–40, 192.

3 J. Raymond, 'Popular representations of Charles I', in Thomas N. Corns (ed.), *The Royal*

Image: Representations of Charles I (Cambridge, 1999), pp. 60–2; Kevin M. Sharpe, '"So hard a text"? Images of Charles I, 1612–1700', *HJ*, 43 (2000), p. 391.

4   A. Milton, *Laudian and Royalist Polemic in Seventeenth-Century England: The Career and Writings of Peter Heylyn* (Manchester, 2007), pp. 29–31, 53–63, 122–5, 224–5.

5   In fact these works did engage with contemporary issues: see *ibid.*, pp. 152–62.

6   *Ibid.*, pp. 146–52.

7   See Peter Heylyn, *Extraneus valupans* (1656), *passim*; Milton, *Laudian*, p. 177.

8   W.A. Shaw, 'L'Estrange, Hamon (1605–1660)', rev. S. Kelsey, *Oxford DNB*.

9   Hamon L'Estrange, *The Reign of King Charles* (1656), sig. A2v, pp. 133, 138, 149.

10 E.g. Peter Heylyn, *Cyprianus Anglicus* (1668), pp. 152, 156, 165, 168, 195, 251.

11 L'Estrange, *Reign*, pp. 127, 137, 145.

12 *Ibid.*, sig. A1v, pp. 96, 110.

13 *Ibid.*, pp. 20, 137, 138, 174, 182, 184.

14 *Ibid.*, pp. 138, 186.

15 *Ibid.*, pp. 131–2. For Noy's friendship with Heylyn see Milton, *Laudian*, p. 43.

16 According to the book's title page, one of those involved in the publication of L'Estrange's work was 'Henry Seile the younger'. Seile's father had been Heylyn's principal publisher for many years. It was presumably in the elder Seile's shop that the meetings of Heylyn and L'Estrange had taken place.

17 Hamon L'Estrange, *The Observator Observed: or Animadversions upon the Observations on the History of King Charles* (1656), p. 45.

18 Heylyn mocks the pamphlet's obscurity, saying that it was 'either so short lived, or made so little noise abroad, that it was not heard of' (Heylyn, *Extraneus*, p. 129).

19 *Ibid.*, pp. 22–3, 25, 112–13.

20 L'Estrange, *Reign*, sigs A2v–A3r.

21 Heylyn, *Extraneus*, sigs A3v–A4r, A7v. For other remarks regarding the unpublished sheets see *ibid.*, pp. 9–11, 14–15, 19, 26. Neither L'Estrange nor any other of Heylyn's many combatants ever sought to suggest that Heylyn's account of the contents of these unpublished sheets was not accurate.

22 Peter Heylyn, *Observations on the Historie of the Reign of King Charles* (1656), sig. A4r–v.

23 L'Estrange, *Reign*, pp. 74, 183, 184, 202.

24 *Ibid.*, p. 259.

25 *Ibid.*, p. 165.

26 Heylyn, *Observations*, p. 105.

27 *Ibid.*, pp. 8–9, 146.

28 *Ibid.*, p. 145.

29 *Ibid.*, pp. 147–8, 156–7, 160–1, 191.

30 *Ibid.*, pp. 227–8.

31 *Ibid.*, pp. 232–3.

32 *Ibid.*, p. 243 (my italics). Heylyn is left unable to say 'by what private perswasions and secret practises He [Charles] was drawn to that, which proved so prejudiciall to Him, that it made Him presently grow lesse in the eyes of his people' (p. 244).

33 *OED* (1989), vol. XIX, p. 399.

34 Heylyn, *Observations*, pp. 28–30; L'Estrange, *Reign*, p.11.

35 Heylyn, *Observations*, pp. 31–2, 48.

36 *Ibid.*, pp. 166, 247–8.

37 *Ibid.*, pp. 108–9.

38 For the importance that Charles attached to his conscience in his overall political vision see K. Sharpe, *Remapping Early Modern England* (Cambridge, 2000), pp. 177–95; R. Cust, *Charles I: A Political Life* (2005), pp. 17–19.

39 Heylyn, *Observations*, pp. 105–6, 146.

40 *Ibid.*, p. 29.

41 *Eikon Basilike*, pp. 5–6, 8. All quotations from the *Eikon Basilike* are taken from the edition published in *Reliquiae Sacrae Carolinae* (1658).

42 *Eikon Basilike*, pp. 24–5, 27.

43 For example in the *Eikon Basilike* Charles justifies his consent to the bishops' exclusion bill on the grounds that the bishops themselves had consented to this as a temporary concession (p. 53). Heylyn instead claimed that Charles's consent had been extorted from him in a manner that made the Act illegal: *The Stumbling Block of Disobedience and Rebellion* (1658), pp. 215, 307. See also Griffith Williams, *Jura majestatis* (Oxford, 1644).

44 *Eikon Basilike*, pp. 42, 63, 67.

45 *Ibid.*, pp. 58–60.

46 *Ibid.*, pp. 8, 10, 31, 34, 35.

47 Heylyn, *Observations*, sig. A4r–v, p. 208.

48 *Ibid.*, p. 70.

49 L'Estrange, *The Observator Observed*, sig. A2r.

50 Peter Heylyn, *Certamen epistolare* (1659), p. 326.

51 Heylyn, *Extraneus*, pp. 6–8, 9–11, 12. Note also the attack on James's Spanish policy in the unpublished sheets (pp. 14–15). An intriguing example of Heylyn and L'Estrange both agreeing and disagreeing in their perceptions of Charles can be seen in L'Estrange's emphasis on the significance of Charles giving up some of his powers in the 1620s. His remark that by the Petition of Right 'never Arbitrary power since Monarchy first founded did so ... vaile its Scepter; never did the prerogative descend so much from perch to popular lure, as by that Concession' was approvingly quoted in full by Heylyn (*Observations*, p. 31), yet L'Estrange had intended this remark to indicate Charles's moderation and good faith towards Parliament, rather than to deplore Charles's weakness.

52 Lacey, *Cult*, p. 69.

53 *Ibid.*, pp. 69–70.

54 *Ibid.*, p. 70.

55 Heylyn's involvement in the *Reliquiae* project seems to have sprung from the fact that his main undertaker, Henry Seile, seems himself to have become active in it: J.H. Walker, 'A

descriptive bibliography of the early printed works of Peter Heylyn' (PhD dissertation, University of Birmingham, 1978), pp. 402–3. It is notable that Seile and Royston also collaborated in the publishing of Heylyn's *Examen historicum* the following year. On Royston's career as a wealthy and committed publisher of subversive Royalist material see J. McElligott, *Royalism, Print and Censorship in Revolutionary England* (Woodbridge, 2007), pp. 144–7.

56 Thus a remark of stoical patience made by Charles when standing in the rain is described as 'a speech so heavenly and Divine, that it is hardly to be paralell'd by any of the men of god in all the Scripture'; when Charles is sold by the Scots there is the inevitable comparison with Christ; a soldier who spits in his face receives 'Divine vengeance' shortly afterwards; and at his execution the king exchanges his 'Crown of Thorns' for 'an immarcessible crown of Glory'. He is saluted as 'the meekest of Men and the best of Princes' (Peter Heylyn, *A Short View of the Life and Reign of King Charles* (1658), pp. 107, 133–4, 149, 152, 161).

57 *Ibid.*, pp. 148–53.

58 *Ibid.*, p. 163. The title page also bears a quotation from Tacitus.

59 *Ibid.*, pp. 32, 42, 83–5, 109–10.

60 *Ibid.*, pp. 113–14, 141–3.

61 This is particularly striking because Seile, who published *Bibliotheca Regia*, would also seem to have been involved in the 1658 edition of *Reliquiae* in which Heylyn's *Short View* had appeared. See above, n. 55 and F.F. Madan, *A New Bibliography of the Eikon Basilike of King Charles the First* (1950), pp. 77–8, 174.

62 For example, Peter Heylyn, *Bibliotheca Regia*, sig. **1r–v, pp. 169, 171–2.

63 *Ibid.*, sigs **1r–v, **3r.

64 *Ibid.*, sig.**1v.

65 Potter, *Secret Rites*, pp. 198–202.

66 Elizabeth Skerpan Wheeler, '*Eikon Basilike* and the rhetoric of self-representation', in Corns (ed.), *The Royal Image*, p. 135.

67 *ΒΑΣΙΛΙΚΑ. The Works of Charles I with his Life and Martyrdome*, 2 vols (1662), 'The Life of Charles I', esp. pp. 92–3, 96–116.

68 Griffith Williams, *Jura Majestatis* (Oxford, 1644), pp. 148, 156, 164, 165r, 166r, 187.

69 S. Kelsey, '"A No-King, or a New": Royalists and the succession, 1648–1649', in Jason McElligott and David L. Smith (eds), *Royalists and Royalism during the English Civil Wars* (Cambridge, 2007), pp. 192–213.

70 Milton, *Laudian*, pp. 162–6, 168–70; Heylyn, *Observations*, pp. 94–5, 205.

71 Peter Heylyn, *Certamen Epistolare* (1659), pp. 236, 244–5, 247.

72 See Corns (ed.), *The Royal Image* – notably D. Loewenstein, 'The king among the radicals: godly republicans, Levellers, Diggers, and Fifth Monarchists' (pp. 96–121) and S. Achinstein, 'Milton and King Charles' (pp. 141–61).

73 Loewenstein, 'The king among the radicals', p. 97.

74 See above, nn. 55, 62. It is also notable that Seile and Royston collaborated in the publication of John Arnway's extravagant salute to the royal martyr *The Tablet* (1661).

Chapter 6

Royalists in exile: the experience of Daniel O'Neill

Geoffrey Smith

I

S ome time after the Restoration, John Aubrey claimed to have heard the poet Edmund Waller say 'that the Lord Marquis of Newcastle was a great Patron to Dr Gassendi, and M. DesCartes, as well as Mr Hobbes, and that he hath dined with them all three at the Marquis's Table at Paris'.[1] Waller's recollections of exile, discussing learned questions of philosophy and science with Pierre Gassendi, René Descartes and Thomas Hobbes at the hospitable table provided by William Cavendish, make a stark contrast with the experiences of other exiled Royalists who found themselves in Paris after the defeat of the armies of Charles I in the Civil Wars. For example, in October 1658 Percy Church, a member of the household of Queen Henrietta Maria, wrote to Sir Edward Hyde, Charles II's principal adviser during the years of exile, that the Northumbrian Cavalier Colonel Thomas Carnaby was 'in danger to perishe for want of bread and cloathing, being destitute of friends in this place'. Hyde was able to despatch some money from Brussels to relieve Carnaby's situation, for as Church explained, he had done his 'uttermost to keep him alive with victuals but to cloathe him my credit cannot doe it', his condition being so desperate that he might soon have 'to begg from door to door'.[2] So, although emigration provided for some Royalists the opportunity for stimulating contacts with distinguished European scholars, writers, artists and scientists, for others life in exile was a relentlessly grim and unpleasant ordeal, a constant nagging struggle to survive in miserable circumstances. Sir Edward Hyde's correspondence with fellow exiled Royalists provides a sharp contrast to Waller's picture of cultivated Royalists discussing the finer points of philosophy and science with distinguished continental scholars at an elegant dinner generously provided by an aristocratic host.

While Hyde was living in Paris during the early 1650s, he corresponded regularly with the king's Secretary of State, Sir Edward Nicholas, who remained at The Hague. The two old friends tried to cap each other's accounts of their 'miserable and necessitous condition', with constant references to their 'beggarly state' and to the possibility, expressed by Nicholas, that his wife and children 'may starve, for aught I know, within these three months'. In December 1652, in the depths of a Parisian winter, Hyde complained that he was so cold that he was 'scarce able to hold my pen and have not three Sous in the world to buy a faggot'.[3] It is not difficult to find in the correspondence of Royalist refugees plenty of evidence that exile could be a grim, bleak and melancholy experience.

On the one hand, the cultural life of Royalists in exile can be viewed as a rich subject deserving of more study. As Paul Hardacre pointed out in a pioneering article over fifty years ago, 'in some cases exiles found new opportunities for scholarship and research'.[4] On the other hand, studies that have focused on the peregrinations of the exiled court and the fortunes of Charles II have presented the Royalist emigration as an overwhelmingly negative experience, stressing 'the constant nagging disadvantages of exile: the poverty, the uncertainty and the endless, sterile faction-fighting'.[5] A Royalist's experience of exile therefore could vary widely, and could swing between the two polar extremes of the enjoyment of scholarly discussions in convivial and comfortable surroundings and the real fear of death from starvation in miserable circumstances. Nothing illustrates more clearly the range of situations and experiences that an exiled Royalist could encounter than the career of the Irish Cavalier Daniel O'Neill.

Few if any Royalists had more exposure to the varied aspects of life in exile than Daniel O'Neill. Between June 1641 and April 1658 O'Neill went into exile on at least nine separate occasions and in a wide variety of circumstances.[6] During his years in exile he lived, and travelled widely, in France, the Low Countries, Spain and some of the German Rhineland principalities. His periods of foreign residence were interspersed with journeys on 'the king's business' to, and flights or expulsions from, Ireland, England and Scotland. During his years of banishment he became all too familiar with the different hardships that afflicted the exiled Royalists, in particular the constant shortage of money. In June 1654 he complained to his friend Colonel William Ashburnham that he had run out of money: 'his credit and bank ... exhausted'. Yet at the same time O'Neill was notorious for his ability to live well in the different Stuart courts where he was a prominent presence. In February 1656 Nicholas confided to his friend the Cornish Royalist Joseph Jane that O'Neill had no intention of leaving the hospitable court of Mary of Orange at The Hague to join the king 'whatever he says to you, for he finds great ease in here at a good table, and no expense to him'.[7]

The combined influences of Daniel O'Neill's unusual background, the wide range of his activities and his varied talents made him well suited not only to survive the rigours of exile but even to exploit their possibilities in order to advance his own career and prospects. O'Neill's background and early years were determining influences in his career. A Gaelic Irishman, he was connected to many of the old ruling families of Ulster. Through his mother he was descended from the 'Great O'Neill', Hugh, second Earl of Tyrone, the leader of the Ulster rebellion against English rule. He was also related to that controversial figure Randall Macdonnell, Marquess of Antrim.[8] In the years before the Civil War these connections did not inspire confidence from the Lord Deputy, Thomas Wentworth, who assumed, totally incorrectly as events turned out, that Daniel O'Neill would take after his father, Con, the lord of Upper Clandeboy in County Down, who in 1601 had joined Tyrone's rebellion. Con O'Neill's rash action, followed by his irresponsibility and general feckless-ness in dealing with the political and financial consequences, combined to cause the loss of a great landed inheritance in Ulster, leaving young Daniel to be made a ward of chancery and raised in England as a Protestant.[9]

Left to live by his wits, he was in this respect well supplied, as, according to Clarendon, he 'was in subtlety and understanding much superior to the whole nation of the old Irish'. With an insignificant income and, in English eyes at any rate, a dubious ancestry, O'Neill saw his career and his fortune in the court and in the camp.[10] Military service first as a volunteer in the Nether-lands in the 1630s, then in the Bishops' Wars, where O'Neill was one of the few to distinguish himself at the disastrous Battle of Newburn, was followed by active involvement in the army plots before taking the field as a cavalry officer in several campaigns during the English Civil War.[11]

Despite his extensive military experience, O'Neill was more than just another Cavalier swordsman. His employment as 'the fittest person to steer' the erratic Marquess of Antrim on a mission to Ireland early in 1644 was rewarded with the long-sought-after position of a groom of the bedchamber to Charles I, an appointment that was principally the result of a prolonged lobbying campaign by O'Neill's friend Lord Digby.[12] It was during these two missions to Ireland, in 1644 and again in 1645, on increasingly desperate attempts to obtain Irish troops to sustain the faltering Royalist war effort in England, that O'Neill confirmed a strong and lasting friendship with the king's Lord Lieutenant, James Butler, Marquess of Ormond. When the Commonwealth was established in 1649 O'Neill was still in Ireland, acting on Ormond's behalf in long and frustrating diplomatic attempts to persuade his 'superstitious old uncle', Owen Roe O'Neill, to combine his Ulster army with Ormond's Royalist forces.[13]

With the collapse of Royalist and Irish resistance to the Cromwellian inva-sion, O'Neill once again was compelled to go into exile. He arrived in May 1650 at The Hague, where, abandoning his original project of taking a company of Irish soldiers into Spanish service, he made the momentous decision, as far as his future was concerned, to join Charles II's expedition to Scotland, with whose Covenanter regime the king had concluded an alliance characterised on both sides by misgivings and insincerity.¹⁴ As one of the most notorious Cavaliers among the 'malignant and profane persons' whose presence about the young king so horrified the Covenanters, O'Neill was promptly arrested, interrogated and then banished upon pain of death if he returned to Scotland without official permission.¹⁵ By September he was back at The Hague, but not for long. In October he reported to Lady Ormond the news of Charles's coronation as King of Scots, observing that the king was now held 'in much more esteem and authority than hitherto', and so, it was hoped, was in a position to protect his loyal friends. Treating with fine contempt the Covenanters' threatened penalties, he returned to Scotland early in 1651 and joined the king at Stirling, in time to take part in the invasion of England that culminated in the Battle of Worcester. Unlike most of the Royalist officers who survived the battle, the endlessly resourceful O'Neill eluded capture and escaped once more back into exile. From The Hague Nicholas wrote to Ormond on 12 November to report that 'Dan O'Neill ... [came] the last week to this place safe out of England'.¹⁶

II

By this time O'Neill had been intensely involved for over ten years in a wide range of activities in support of the Stuart cause. As a soldier, a courtier, a diplomat, a courier and a conspirator he had been constantly employed on one mission, plot or campaign after another, in all three Stuart kingdoms as well as in France and the Netherlands. But by October 1651, when O'Neill, once again a fugitive, escaped back into exile, the Royalist cause seemed to be in ruins. As a notorious delinquent, O'Neill now faced an indefinite period in exile, and this was exactly at a time when, as Nicholas wrote to Hyde from The Hague on 21 October 1651, 'there are an abundance of Royalists gone for England from these parts and many more are going, as having little hopes left them'.¹⁷

Yet in many ways O'Neill was peculiarly well suited to cope with, and even profit from, his apparently depressing circumstances. His continued physical survival supports the accuracy of Clarendon's opinion of his resourcefulness, his 'subtlety and understanding'. In his double-edged character assessment in *The History of the Rebellion* Clarendon acknowledged O'Neill's 'natural insinuation and address' which made him acceptable in the best company, his skill as 'a great discerner of men's natures and humours', his 'notorious' courage and capacity for 'indefatigable' industry. Yet Clarendon suggested that the exercise of these talents was essentially motivated by O'Neill's desire to further 'his particular interest', as 'his inclinations were naturally to ease and luxury'.

Daniel O'Neill was clearly a complex figure, well deserving of the distinctive nickname 'Infallible Subtle', to which Clarendon made indirect reference when he praised the Irishman's subtlety.[18]

So, although by the end of 1651 he was a penniless fugitive, disqualified by his notoriety from joining the flow of disillusioned exiles back to England to make their peace with the Commonwealth, O'Neill's future prospects were by no means totally depressing. To a landless Irish swordsman, with no significant English political or family interest, exile offered prospects for advancement that would not have existed in other more 'normal' circumstances. By this stage of his career O'Neill had constructed an extensive if fragile network of patrons and friends, many of whom were also émigrés. His first priority, if he was to cope successfully with the rigours of exile while also putting himself in a position to be suitably rewarded if the king ever came into his own again, was to become a trusted intimate of Charles II. Unlike O'Neill, the other five surviving grooms of the king's bedchamber were all English. With the exception of Colonel Thomas Blague, they all had long-standing court connections, and at this time Charles would have known them much better than he did O'Neill. Three of them had accompanied the Prince of Wales into exile in 1646, first in Jersey and then on to France and Holland, at a time when O'Neill was still in Ireland with Ormond.[19] It was therefore very much in O'Neill's 'particular interest', when he arrived in Holland from Ireland back in May 1650, to join immediately Charles's following of loyal attendants on the expedition to Scotland. This need to establish a close relationship with Charles also helps to explain why O'Neill, after his expulsion from Scotland in August, did not remain at The Hague to enjoy the comforts of Mary of Orange's household. Instead, he took the considerable risk of returning to Scotland early in 1651 to join the king at Stirling.[20] Although O'Neill's natural inclinations may have been to 'ease and luxury', as Clarendon claimed, he was prepared to display 'indefatigable' industry and 'notorious' courage when these qualities were required, either by the demands of loyalty to the Stuart cause or by his 'particular interest'. To O'Neill these two elements may have been inseparable.

It was during the expedition to Scotland and the Worcester campaign that O'Neill earned his passage into the king's inner circle of friends and advisers. Within a couple of weeks of his arrival at The Hague after his escape from Worcester he once again abandoned the comforts of Mary of Orange's household and, accompanied by his fellow Irishman Lord Taaffe, headed for Paris, where a small court was assembling around the king.[21] His presence was clearly welcome, and in October 1653 a sceptical Nicholas, still stubbornly entrenched at The Hague, was assured by Hyde that 'the King has a good opinion of Dan. O'Neill'.[22] As we shall see, Charles came increasingly to depend on O'Neill's resourcefulness and varied talents, although O'Neill saw these attributes as being exercised on a much broader field than the impoverished and quarrelsome little court in exile. Although confirmed in his position as a groom of the bedchamber, he was not content to be merely a courtier, dependent on the irregularly paid allowances to official placeholders in the royal household. For O'Neill was also well known in the other Stuart courts in France and Holland. His acquaintance with Queen Henrietta Maria, whose household during the 1650s moved between the palaces of the Louvre and St Germain, went back to his involvement in the army plots of 1641; with Elizabeth of Bohemia at The Hague it went back even further, to his military service under Prince Frederick Henry of Orange in the late 1630s.[23] But the Stuart court whose appeal for O'Neill rivalled that of Charles II's was that of the king's sister, Mary, the Princess Royal and widow of William II of Orange.

It is not known exactly when O'Neill established his close friendship with Mary and with two of her most trusted friends and advisers, the superintendent of her household, the experienced Dutch diplomat Jan (Jehan) Polyander van den Kerckhoven, Lord of Heenvliet, and his wife Katherine, Lady Stanhope, governess to the princess. As a young officer who was often around Whitehall in the spring of 1641, he may have witnessed the reception of the young William of Orange and his betrothal to the even younger Princess Royal. As an ambassador of the States General, Heenvliet played a prominent part in the marriage negotiations, and it was at this time that he married, somewhat controversially, Katherine Stanhope, a recently widowed and prominent lady of the court. Katherine Stanhope was to become Mary's most intimate friend and eventually would take Daniel O'Neill as her third husband.[24]

Mary remained closely dependent on the support and advice of the Heenvliets, who moved quickly to fill the gap left by the sudden and premature death of William II early in November 1650. 'The great governors here in the Princess Royal's family and business are the Lady Stanhope and her husband', reported Nicholas to Lord Hatton on 20 November, adding, 'and the great men with them are Lord Percy and Dan. O'Neill'.[25] As the influence of the Heenvliets was regarded with some suspicion in Royalist émigré circles, O'Neill's apparently privileged position in Mary's household was also sometimes criticised, while the exact nature of his relationship with 'his shee friend' Katherine Stanhope was a constant source of occasionally scurrilous speculation among the exiles. On 20 October 1654 Lord Hatton, who loved to disseminate gossip among the Royalist exile community, the more malicious the better, informed Nicholas that Lord Percy, a prominent courtier in the circle around the queen at the Louvre, as well as criticising Ormond and Hyde, was spreading 'scurrilous stuff of Dan O'Neill and Lady Stanhope'.[26]

Contrary to émigré gossip, O'Neill was not just a penniless refugee Cavalier sponging on the good nature of Mary of Orange and the affections of Katherine Stanhope. He was also a courtier with a high opinion of his own diplomatic skills, an opinion shared at times by such diverse Royalist leaders as Hyde, Ormond and Digby.[27] In early modern courts, the courtier's 'most profitable business was brokerage', in other words, acting as an intermediary in the distribution of grants, offices and favours between patrons and clients.[28] There is plenty of evidence in O'Neill's activities to support this viewpoint. In wartime Oxford, as a newly appointed groom of the bedchamber, he acted for patrons like Digby and Ormond in this role, and he was still performing the same function in the post-Restoration court, receiving petitions asking him 'to influence the king' and acting as an intermediary between Charles and ministers like Henry Bennet, Earl of Arlington, at Whitehall and Ormond in Ireland.[29] His privileged position in the household of Mary of Orange placed him in a similarly strategic position to influence the sometimes tense and delicate relations between the two Stuart courts.

It is clear that O'Neill enjoyed not only the trust of the king and Ormond but also, which is rather more surprising, that of Hyde himself. His membership of a family with a long record of rebellion against the Crown, his involvement in the army plots and his friendship both with courtier swordsmen like Harry Wilmot and William Ashburnham and with controversial figures like Digby and Antrim made him a suspect figure to some prominent émigrés, Nicholas for example, but not apparently to Hyde. Although not naturally well disposed to Gaelic Irishmen, especially those whose lineage was well stocked with Catholic rebels, he clearly made an exception of Daniel O'Neill, whom in his *Life* he acknowledged as having 'for many years lived in very good correspondence with the chancellor'.[30] On 28 November 1653 Hyde defended O'Neill to Nicholas, claiming that 'you will find him ingenious and reasonable in all things, and he is honest and kind to the Marquis of Ormond and me, and sufficiently odious to Jermyn and c.', a reference to Lord Jermyn, one of the so-called 'Louvrians', a loosely defined collection of courtiers who looked to Henrietta Maria for leadership but whose only common policy was hostility to the influence of Hyde and Ormond over Charles II.[31] Hyde maintained that O'Neill could not 'be corrupted or outwitted', and so the Irishman was employed to heal differences between the two courts, as he 'was very acceptable in the court of the princess royal, and to those persons who had the greatest influence upon her councils and affections', in other words the Heenvliets. O'Neill was required to defend Hyde against the false charge of disrespect to Mary, and to 'assure Lady Stanhope and Heenvliet of the King's friendship for them'. His 'good offices' were so successful that Mary found a place for Hyde's daughter Anne among her ladies in waiting and a rent-free house in Breda for Lady Hyde and her other children.[32]

O'Neill's activities were not confined to easing tensions between the two Stuart courts. He was also drawn into the wider spheres of Royalist diplomacy. For example, in the early months of 1656, when the nomadic royal court was based in Cologne, secret negotiations were under way with the Spanish authorities that resulted in a Royalist alliance with Spain and the transfer of Charles's household to Bruges in the Spanish Netherlands. In January 1656 O'Neill left The Hague with Mary, who was on a journey to Paris, but he never crossed the French border. Instead, accompanied by Heenvliet, he left the princess's party at Valenciennes. Joseph Jane, Nicholas's principal correspondent at The Hague, reported that 'Mr O'Neill went hence with the Pr[incess] R[oyal], but I believe he returns with Mr Heenvliet, his principal business being to meet with my Lord of Ormond' (Ormond was involved in negotiations with the Spanish authorities in Flanders).[33] These secret quasi-diplomatic activities annoyed Nicholas. 'Is Mr. O'Neill there now at The Hague', enquired the Secretary from Cologne anxiously, replying on 4 March to Jane's letter. 'For there is a report that he is gone into Flanders, which I cannot believe [it was true], though he is more of the secret council than I am, being a great confidant of Hyde's. I wish he may prove worthy of the trust imposed in him,' added Nicholas querulously, 'but it's no wisdom to make those who are not sworn to be secret privy to the secrets of state.'[34] He advised Jane not to be swayed by O'Neill's 'natural insinuation and address', warning him that 'you will find he is like his name, subtle'.[35]

The Secretary's fears that O'Neill was helping to direct the policies of the exiled court were justified. Hyde himself acknowledged as early as 29 March 1652, about three months after O'Neill's arrival in Paris from The Hague, that he had organised a meeting with Ormond, Digby and 'Dan O'Neile' to discuss the management of the king's affairs in France. Almost two years later, on 27 November 1654, by which time the court was established at Cologne, Mary of Orange's chamberlain, the Scottish Royalist Sir Alexander Hume, informed the doubtless irritated Secretary that he was 'not a little amazed to hear that Secretary Nicholas is so much a stranger to all advertisements that come from our court, that correspondence being wholly managed by Dan. O'Neill and Mr Chancellor'.[36]

Close involvement in court affairs, whether at The Hague, Paris, Cologne, Bruges or Brussels; participation in the intrigues and lobbying of different factions; maintaining good relations with a complex and extensive network of patrons and friends: these activities were only a part of O'Neill's experience of exile. Yet taken together, and combined with his natural resourcefulness, they enabled him to cope effectively and even with some relish with the numerous difficulties and problems that constantly beset the 'crowd of fugitives' who gathered around Charles II's nomadic court.[37] His talents were employed not only to make his own life in exile more comfortable but also to benefit some of his fellow émigrés. There are many examples of the king's advisers resorting to O'Neill to deal with an extraordinarily wide range of requests and problems. When the court moved from Cologne to the Spanish Netherlands in the spring of 1656, Hyde wrote to Ormond asking him to 'remind O'Neale to make a good provision of sherry and to send a hogshead of pippins' to the royal household at Bruges, while Charles requested the Irishman's advice on the best route for the transport of his goods. Whether it was providing a suitable campaigning tent for Ormond or furnishings for his lodgings, sending to the court a consignment of bottles allegedly of 'the wine de Bone' or employing his famous subtlety to settle a dispute with Hyde's landlady, the range of O'Neill's activities represented a dramatic expansion of the accepted responsibilities of a groom of the bedchamber.[38] Clearly idleness, one of the vices traditionally associated with an exile's life, was not one of his weaknesses. On the contrary, O'Neill's industry and enterprise on their behalf served only to increase the regard in which the king and his principal advisers held someone whom Hyde acknowledged to Ormond in June 1657 as being 'a sharp-sighted fellow, and sees as far before him as an ordinary almanack'. Both the range and the frequently personal nature of O'Neill's useful activities served to establish an unusually close and informal quality to his relationship with his patrons. 'You may, upon occasion, send that fool O'Neale to me', wrote Hyde to Ormond from Cologne in April 1656: language that suggests that, although the chancellor sometimes considered the Irishman's behaviour frivolous or extravagant, he needed him and even liked him.[39] In the middle of packing to leave for Bruges, he obviously had found another task for him.

Charles's respect for O'Neill's abilities as a 'fixer' is well illustrated by the king's resort to the Irishman to deal with the problems caused by the deplorable behaviour of the unfortunate Lucy Walter. The trials and tribulations of Lucy Walter have been examined by a number of historians, with considerable debate over whether she was more sinned against than sinning; the evidence would seem to support the latter opinion.[40] Until her death in 1658, Lucy Walter's scandalous behaviour, in being passed from one Royalist émigré 'protector' to another while she neglected her young son by Charles, led to a series of attempts by different agents both to compel the mother to lead a less disorderly life and to remove her son from her custody. O'Neill acknowledged receiving the king's 'commands concerning Mrs Barlow', as Lucy Walter was commonly known, early in 1656 when he was, as was often the case, at The Hague, but on this occasion he failed to carry them out. Little James, the future Duke of Monmouth, remained with his mother, while she continued to generate scandal. O'Neill expressed his concern to Charles at 'the prejudice her being here does your majesty; for every idle action of hers brings your majesty upon the stage', but he achieved little to improve this situation. Although he was able to use his influence with Heenvliet to persuade the Dutch authorities not to have Lucy Walter 'banished this town and country for an infamous person, and by sound of drum', essentially his advice was to force Charles's ex-mistress to behave more modestly and discreetly by cutting off her supply of money from past or present lovers. 'The only way (to make her behave) is to necessitate her.'[41] But O'Neill soon left the Lucy Walter problem to be dealt with by other agents. For during the early months of 1656 the king's conclusion of a Spanish alliance, the consequent removal of the court from Cologne to Bruges and the revival of Royalist conspiracy all were of more moment to O'Neill than the 'infamous manner' of behaviour of a discarded royal mistress.[42]

Unlike a number of exiled Royalists, O'Neill did not take advantage of the opportunities for study and scholarship that his circumstances provided. Despite his periods of residence in Paris and The Hague, dinners with philosophers and poets like Descartes, Hobbes and Waller did not feature among his activities. He certainly knew Abraham Cowley, Jermyn's secretary in Paris in the early 1650s, whom he disparaged as an untrustworthy lackey of the so-called 'Louvrian' faction, 'a poet and a malicious enemy of yours'.[43] He was also familiar with the popular verse of Sir John Mennes, from which he quoted in the middle of a long and unjustifiably optimistic – as events turned out – letter to the king, written in London on the eve of the outbreak of the Royalist insurrection in March 1655:

> If this day thrive, we'll ride in Coaches;
> If not, bonnes noches.

Unlike Cowley, Mennes was an old friend, a comrade in arms from the Civil Wars, and famously convivial company.[44]

Nor was O'Neill among those unfortunate Royalist refugees who were overwhelmed by their poverty, existing on the edge of starvation in miserable lodgings. With his unquenchably optimistic outlook, he successfully escaped this bleak and melancholy but all too common feature of the exiled Royalist's existence.

Although, as one of Charles's grooms of the bedchamber, he was at the centre of the royal household, he also seems largely to have avoided the sterile quarrels and pointless feuds of idle and embittered courtiers that have done so much to create a negative picture of the behaviour of the king's entourage.[45] Certainly, as a loyal client of Ormond and Hyde, O'Neill was involved in the personal and factional disputes that divided the exiles, as is illustrated by his hostile references to Cowley whom he clearly and correctly regarded as attached to the so-called 'Louvrian' faction.[46] Also, while in exile O'Neill fought one duel, in Paris in October 1647, in which he acted as a second for Digby in a duel with Harry Wilmot, two of his personal friends.[47] His efforts to prevent the encounter were on this occasion unsuccessful. In his long and lively account of the duel to Ormond it is clear that O'Neill regarded the whole occasion as pointless and even ridiculous. His opponent, for this was one of those free-for-all affairs in which seconds also took part, was the notoriously quarrelsome Lord Wentworth, 'who had first profess'd one to another we had rather have met at a bottle'.[48] Although O'Neill's physical courage could not be questioned, at least on this occasion he would rather have drunk than fought.

III

Clearly the 'Infallible Subtle' Daniel O'Neill is too complex a figure to define as merely a courtier or a soldier. There is a temptation to categorise the exiled Royalists: the impoverished fugitive huddled in miserable lodgings, hiding from creditors and with not enough for himself or his family to eat; the eager book collector and student of philosophy, literature, history or theology, engaging enthusiastically with the newest developments in European scholarship; the swaggering swordsman wallowing in the varied attractions of wine, women and song in a desperate attempt to wipe out the frustration and bitterness of military defeat; the scheming courtier, endlessly obsessed with sterile factional intrigues; and the withdrawn recluse, retreating fatalistically into private study and contemplation while waiting patiently for the divine plan to reveal itself. Realistically, it is not reasonable to depict the exiled Royalists as a set of discrete stereotypes. The members of Charles II's exiled court were too diverse a collection of individuals, and the stereotypes constantly overlap. Colonel Sir Samuel Tuke, for example, was a notorious duellist who was also a playwright. Thomas Ross was actively engaged in Royalist conspiracy and made several dangerous journeys to England, but when he returned to the continent he resumed work on his massive history of the Punic Wars.[49] It is inadvisable to make facile generalisations about Charles II's companions in exile.

The behaviour of O'Neill's great friend and patron Ormond illustrates both the diversity and the complexity of the responses to exile among Charles II's followers. Ormond, who first settled in Caen after his withdrawal from Ireland in December 1650, wrote a reflective letter to Nicholas soon after hearing the devastating news of the Royalist defeat at Worcester. With all attempts at 'the recovery of the royal interest' having failed, he regarded further military action as pointless and useless. Rather, it was now time to wait patiently either for the Commonwealth to collapse through its own internal divisions or for the unlikely event of a crusade by the princes of Europe, they having at last come to recognise 'the English Rebels as a common enemy even before the Turk'. Ormond saw the failure of all the Royalists' enterprises and the consequent disastrous condition of the 'royal interest' as 'a command [from God] to stand still and see the salvation He will work for us'.[50] This is an excellent statement of the passive and resigned viewpoint accepted by many Royalists, both in England and in exile: the policy of waiting patiently for God's plan to reveal itself; and in the meantime for the king 'to lie still, and expect further events'.[51] But, not surprisingly, Ormond rejected his own advice; he did not spend the next nine years waiting patiently for this divine revelation to unfold. On the contrary, he became actively involved in a range of plans and projects to put Charles II back on the throne, plans that involved military action, invasions by Spanish troops and risings by Cavaliers. He even went to the extent of making a personal and highly dangerous visit to London early in 1658 to assess the prospects for a successful Royalist insurrection. And on this dangerous mission he took Daniel O'Neill with him, for the other great area of activity during O'Neill's years in exile was the organisation of a Royalist rising to overthrow the Protectorate.

IV

An examination of O'Neill's role in the organisation of Royalist conspiracy illuminates significant aspects of the culture of the émigré community in which he moved. The divisions in the Royalist high command in wartime Oxford, the 'discomposures, jealousies and disgusts' so lamented by Clarendon, continued to bedevil the exiled court, but were now widened and intensified by the bitterness and frustration of defeat and banishment, the replacement of the enjoyment of power and influence by the miseries of poverty and separation from family and friends.[52] The letters of exiles with a taste for gossip, like Hatton and Nicholas, refer frequently to a court torn by 'the divisions and quarrels of Fraiser and Wentworth, Fraiser and Newburgh, Wentworth and Fleming, Newburgh and Taaffe'.[53] The attempts to establish lines of communication between the exiled court and the king's (supposedly) active supporters in England, with the long-term objective of carrying out a successful rising to overthrow the Protectorate, were frequently hampered by these divisions and quarrels. With fluctuating success, the king's chief counsellors – Ormond, Hyde and Nicholas – attempted to create and run an intelligence-gathering system and to direct the various secret committees authorised to organise conspiracy. Not only did their agents have to cope with the normal hazards of seventeenth-century travel while also evading the vigilance of the Protectorate's counter-intelligence system directed by the extremely efficient John Thurloe, but they were frequently in competition with other networks controlled, if that is not too strong a word, by other prominent Royalists.[54]

O'Neill made three clandestine journeys to England during the eight and a half years between his escape from Worcester and his return in the entourage of the restored Charles II. The first visit, beginning late in 1652 and lasting for about three months, was in many ways the most surprising. It seems to have been a purely private intelligence-gathering mission at a time when the Stuart cause still lay in ruins, apparently crushed by a long series of fresh disasters: the suppressing of Royalist conspiracies in England, the 'fatal overthrow at Worcester', the Commonwealth's conquest of Ireland and Scotland and the mopping-up of the last Royalist outposts, Jersey and the Isle of Man.[55] The

Sealed Knot, the secret committee with the task of organising a Royalist rising, would not be created for another year.[56] 'There is no talk of Presbyterian nor Royalist at present', was O'Neill's uncharacteristically gloomy assessment in the report, entitled 'a brief Relation of the Affaires of England as they stand at present', presented to Hyde on his return to Paris in March 1653. In fact, the report is much more concerned with the rivalries of the two factions led by Cromwell and Harrison in the army, and with relations between the army and the shortly to be expelled Rump Parliament, than it is with the condition of the Royalists.[57] It is also significant that O'Neill presented his report not to Ormond, his principal patron and someone for whom he had a strong and lasting friendship, but to Hyde, who against considerable opposition was establishing himself during 1653 as the king's principal counsellor. This may be another example of why O'Neill acquired the nickname 'Infallible Subtle'. Although he certainly remained a prominent member of Ormond's clientage network, he was now establishing himself in Hyde's as well.

O'Neill's other two missions were connected with ambitious Royalist designs to overthrow the Cromwellian Protectorate. He was at the heart of the planning of the rising that broke out in March 1655, hiding in London and co-operating with his old comrade in arms and fellow exile Henry Wilmot, now Earl of Rochester, who was entrusted with the overall military command of whatever Royalist forces could be raised.[58] His letters to the king from London on the surface purport to be from a Mr Bryans describing his attempts to reach agreements with the creditors of a debtor, Mr Jackson, who has fled the country. The reports reveal O'Neill's energy, the range of his contacts and his irrepressible (and, in the circumstances, unjustifiable) optimism, as he recounts how he originally despaired of success as he found 'all your accounts and business in such disorder by the absence of some of your friends and the restraint of others', but soon changed his mind after speaking 'with half a score, who [agreed] with great cheerfulness to take 2sh in the pound rather than that you should continue a banished man'.[59] Following personal approaches to creditors, in other words to the potential leaders of risings in the counties, and the employment of friends of Mr Jackson (Charles II) like Mr Ambrose (in fact, the Royalist agent Major Nicholas Armorer), O'Neill optimistically concluded that 'all your creditors [had been brought] to such a composition as we hope will not displease you'.[60] This optimism was not justified. After the government's swift suppression of Penruddock's rising in March, O'Neill was once again compelled to flee across the Channel. His destination, also once again, was the hospitable household of Mary of Orange at The Hague, from where Hyde wrote to Charles on 24 April that 'O'Neale is safe in this town by his usual good luck in avoiding being hanged'.[61]

The Royalists took some time to recover from the suppression of Penruddock's rising and the consequent increased government surveillance and reprisals. It was not until early in 1658 that O'Neill returned to London as a companion of Ormond on the marquess's dangerous and inadequately concealed visit to assess the chances of success of another planned insurrection. When, after only a few days in London, Ormond withdrew hastily to the continent before Thurloe's agents could locate him, O'Neill remained behind for some weeks, negotiating with a motley collection of understandably nervous conspirators, some of whom claimed to be impatient for action while others needed to be persuaded. Unjustifiably over-confident, O'Neill claimed in his reports to Hyde that 'the game never was fairer', while the Protectorate regime never had 'fewer friends'.[62] Without Ormond's restraining influence, he was in his element – 'full of negotiations and had set many treaties on foot', according to Hyde – while the planned insurrection disintegrated around him in a welter of arrests.[63] Understandably, Hyde was concerned for O'Neill's safety and worried that 'he may not have proved too active' in promises and commitments. It was only after repeated orders from the chancellor that O'Neill reluctantly agreed to return 'from whence we came', in other words, back into exile, 'whither I shall go with the same unwillingness I would to Tyburn'.[64]

O'Neill's involvement in Royalist conspiracy not only adds another dimension to his career in exile but also illustrates some significant features of the whole émigré experience. O'Neill, ever since his participation in the army plots in 1641, was clearly at home in this cloak-and-dagger world of false names and identities, clandestine journeys and secret meetings, letters in code and safe houses.[65] To his already extensive and varied network of friends, contacts, clients and patrons he could now add some of the more prominent conspirators, like the members of the Sealed Knot and Lord Mordaunt, and the most resourceful and trusted of the Royalist agents. Two who feature prominently in the reports he sent from London in March 1655 and in the early months of 1658 are one of Ormond's officers from the Irish Wars, Colonel John Stephens, and the Northumbrian Cavalier Major Nicholas Armorer. In particular, O'Neill clearly developed a high opinion of Armorer, whose daring and record of narrow escapes equalled his own, and who accompanied him on his two journeys to England in 1655 and 1658.[66]

Royalist espionage and intelligence-gathering and the planning of insurrections to overthrow the Protectorate regime and bring back the king were not only the concern of experienced agents and conspirators like O'Neill and Armorer. These plots and projects also drew in the leaders of the Royalist party in exile, in particular Hyde, Ormond and Nicholas. Their correspondence contains countless letters – intelligence reports, instructions, commissions, appeals for money or support, cipher keys, and so on – to and from men, and sometimes women, engaged in Royalist conspiracy.[67] Also, given the bitterness and strength of the personal antagonisms that constantly fractured the exiled court, it is not surprising that other prominent émigrés, men like Lord Gerard and Sir Marmaduke Langdale, jealous of the predominance in the royal counsels of Hyde, Ormond and Nicholas, also sometimes organised their own rival networks of agents and conspirators.[68] According to the courtier and part-time conspirator Thomas Ross, writing to Nicholas on 21 April 1658, these personal rivalries and disputes largely explain the failure of the plans for a rising to break out in the early months of that year, as some otherwise committed Royalists were 'extremely troubled that the King was forced to put so weighty an affair into the hands of one so odious to them as O'Neale'.[69] It is easy to understand that O'Neill could seem 'odious' to the notoriously cautious 'wary gentlemen' of the Sealed Knot, to Royalists and previously uncommitted Presbyterians and 'neutrals' who were uneasy about risking their necks and their estates in yet another rising that was doomed to fail, or to those plotters who looked for directions from leaders who were no friends of the chancellor and his clients.[70] An Irishman, but without Ormond's immense prestige and status, a swordsman and hanger-on around courts, with no landed interest in England, O'Neill, for all his energy and resourcefulness, was probably not the man to organise the insurrection that would overthrow Oliver Cromwell.

Despite the lack of success, the organisation of plots and risings remained a significant part of the life of exiled Royalists. It was a world in which Daniel O'Neill felt at home, and to which his associates and patrons, whatever their rank and position, and despite any natural disdain they might have had for its more murky and unpleasant aspects, also had to become acclimatised. As Alan Marshall has pointed out, the exiles 'had suffered, fought and plotted their way through the 1650s and [after the Restoration] Charles and his key ministers brought all these experiences into government with them'.[71] In fact, O'Neill's serious involvement with conspiracy ended with his return into exile in the spring of 1658. There were no more secret journeys to England to be followed by hasty flights back across the Channel, but his travels were not yet over. The suppression of the next serious Royalist attempt to overthrow the Commonwealth by force, Sir George Booth's rising in August 1659, left Charles II, accompanied by a few companions including Ormond, O'Neill and Digby (now Earl of Bristol), stranded on the coast of Brittany at St Malo. They were waiting for the summons, which never came, to join the Royalist insurgents.[72] On learning that the insurrection had been crushed, Charles resolved instead to attend the Franco-Spanish peace negotiations at Fuenterrabia on the Pyrenees frontier. During both the journey to Fuenterrabia and Charles's fruitless attempts to obtain aid from either the French or Spanish crowns that followed, O'Neill was in his element. The incognito journey through France, which was still an ally of the English Commonwealth, was leisurely and informal. O'Neill, in the company only of Charles and his old friends Ormond and Bristol, plus a couple of servants, naturally had the responsibility 'to take care that they always fared well in their lodging, for which province', Clarendon added somewhat waspishly, 'no man was fitter'.[73]

O'Neill's responsibilities were not confined to reaching satisfactory agreements with innkeepers and ensuring the supply of adequate food and drinkable wine; his diplomatic skills were also required. The leisurely journey through southern France by Charles and his cheerful party meant that when they finally arrived in Spain in October there was some confusion as to where the peace conference was actually taking place, whether in fact it was still in progress at all and how the titular king of England would be received by the French and Spanish ministers, Cardinal Mazarin and Don Luis de Haro. Once again, it was left to Ormond and O'Neill, travelling hastily between one Spanish town and another, to sort these matters out and to make sure that when Charles eventually arrived at Fuenterrabia he received an appropriately courteous and dignified reception from the Spanish minister.[74] That was about all the king did receive, and the news, brought by Nicholas Armorer, that General Lambert had expelled the restored Rump in a military coup, soon brought Charles and his followers through France and back to Brussels.[75] For O'Neill one result of a politically fruitless – but probably personally quite enjoyable – expedition was the opportunity it gave him to strengthen his friendship with Henry Bennet, the king's ambassador to Spain, a friendship that was to become increasingly important to both men after the Restoration.[76]

In a letter to Hyde written on his return journey, O'Neill referred to the 'long, dangerous and expensive journeys' he had made on the king's business.[77] This is an appropriate summary of O'Neill's whole adult lifetime as a courtier, courier, soldier, diplomat, conspirator, royal companion and general fixer in the service of both Charles II and his father. When, less than six months later, the Stuart monarchy was restored, generous rewards, but surprisingly not a title, were piled on O'Neill by a grateful ruler. Pensions, land grants, monopolies, sinecures and offices, both in England and Ireland, combined to make 'the great O'Neale', as Pepys called him, with a knowing reference to his famous great uncle the second Earl of Tyrone, one of the richest men in the Stuart kingdoms.[78] It is inconceivable that O'Neill would have been so well rewarded after the Restoration if ten years earlier he had not joined and then, defying his official banishment, rejoined Charles II in Scotland. During the long years of exile he managed to make himself indispensable in many areas to the king, to other members of the Stuart family and to several of the most influential royal advisers. Exile was the making of Daniel O'Neill.

The new 'great O'Neale' had fewer than four years in which to enjoy the rewards of his services. Shortly after the Restoration he finally married, as her third husband, the recently widowed Katherine Stanhope. Together they rebuilt the Elizabethan mansion Belsize House in Hampstead, at 'vast expense' according to John Evelyn.[79] Despite land grants and membership of the Irish

Parliament, O'Neill seems never to have returned to Ireland after the Restoration and did not attempt to rebuild the lost family estates in Ulster. For all his 'long, dangerous and expensive journeys', his policy, as it had always been, was to remain as close as possible to the monarch. So it was appropriate for a groom of the bedchamber to both Charles I and Charles II that he died in his Whitehall lodgings on 24 October 1664. That same night Charles II reported his death in a letter to his sister, the Duchess of Orleans: 'Poor Oneale died this afternoon of an ulcer in his guts; he was as honest a man who ever lived; I am sure I have lost a very good servant by it.'[80]

V

O'Neill represents an activist strand in royalism, which was not reflective or philosophical and had no serious consideration of religious issues or political theories to strengthen it. Raised a Protestant but with many family and personal links to Catholics, O'Neill in exile moved easily back and forth between the two confessions, as easily as he did between Irishmen and Englishmen in the exiled court, or between old Cavaliers and Presbyterian ex-Parliamentarians in his negotiations with active and potential Royalist conspirators.[81] Naturally tolerant, and equally at home in the different cultures of different courts, he could deal with a Spanish grandee in Brussels or Fuenterrabia as easily as he could with the Calvinist Heenvliet in The Hague. O'Neill could also slip easily between the elegant and formal world of courts, on familiar terms with princes and aristocrats, and the dark and dangerous back streets of London, one step ahead of the informers and the agents of Thurloe.

An important consequence of this varied experience of exile was the breakdown in traditional habits of deference and formality. Like Ormond and Hyde on occasion, O'Neill was quite prepared to criticise Charles II directly. 'I beseech your majestie', wrote an exasperated O'Neill to the king on one occasion in 1655, 'when you change your opinion in those things which you command your servants that you will be pleased to have them acquainted with it.'[82] This frankness went with a disregard for traditional deference in his relations with his patrons. He concluded a long report to Charles, written in London in March 1655 on the eve of the Royalist rising, with the comment, 'if the fat fellow be with you, I hope he will not complain I write short letters'.[83] Disrespectful references to the chancellor's girth illustrate O'Neill's capacity to be cheerful and good-humoured, however dangerous or unpleasant his circumstances.

Even though it was not supported by deep or considered political beliefs, O'Neill's royalism, from the Battle of Newburn in 1640 to his death in Whitehall Palace twenty-four years later, never wavered. It has recently been suggested that 'shifts in allegiance were much more common than has hitherto been realized', that political allegiance was not an 'unchanging and unchangeable entity'.[84] This was not the case with Daniel O'Neill. In a letter to Ormond, written in Oxford on 12 April 1645, he revealed quite clearly that he expected Parliament, with its far greater resources in 'numbers of men, money and all materials', to win the Civil War, yet he had no thought of surrender or of trying to make terms, claiming that the Royalists 'have a just cause, and the resolution of desperate lovers to defend it to the last of our party'.[85] Although he referred to the justice of the Royalist cause, essentially he saw the conflict in personal human terms, and not as one between opposing theories or principles. Having lost the family's Ulster inheritance, O'Neill saw no future for himself as an Irish magnate, a Clanricard or Castlehaven; his future prospects depended on personal service to the monarch, which was the essential element in his royalism. So when the armies of Charles I were defeated, O'Neill remained committed in exile to continue the struggle by whatever means were available, from diplomacy and foreign alliances to conspiracy and the planning of insurrections and invasions. His allegiance to the Royalist cause shaped this response, but so did what Clarendon called 'his particular interest, which he was never without'.[86] There was no withdrawal into the world of books or any display of patient resignation from Daniel O'Neill, or from the many other Royalists who thought and acted as he did, whether we consider a grandee like Ormond (whatever he sometimes said) or a cloak-and-dagger agent like Nicholas Armorer. Their world was one of 'long, dangerous and expensive journeys', of plots and intrigues, spies and traitors, elements that were to continue to be prominent features of the reign of Charles II.[87]

NOTES

1 Oliver Lawson Dick (ed.), *Aubrey's Brief Lives* (1962), p. 360.

2 Bodl., Clarendon MS 57, fols 56–7, 93–4.

3 For examples see *CSP*, vol. III, pp. 73, 124, 126, 174, 237; *NP*, vol. I, p. 238; vol. II, pp. 11, 12, 14.

4 P.H. Hardacre, 'The Royalists in exile during the Puritan revolution, 1642–1660', *HLQ*, 16 (1952), p. 361.

5 John Miller, *James II: A Study in Kingship* (1989), p. 5.

6 *CSPD 1641–43*, pp. 14, 21, 27; *CClSP*, vol. IV, pp. 28, 44, 46.

7 Bodl., Rawlinson MS A15, fols 67–9; *CSPD 1655–56*, p. 159.

8 Donal Cregan, 'An Irish Cavalier: Daniel O'Neill', *Studia Hibernica*, 3 (1963), pp. 64–72, 77; J.I. Casway, 'O'Neill, Daniel (*c.*1612–1664)', *Oxford DNB*.

9 Cregan, 'An Irish Cavalier', pp. 63–8.

10 *CHR*, vol. III, p. 513.

11 Casway, 'O'Neill, Daniel'; Cregan, 'An Irish Cavalier', pp. 79–100; Donal Cregan, 'Daniel O'Neill in the Civil Wars, 1642–51', *Studia Hibernica*, 4 (1964), pp. 104–30.

12 *CHR*, vol. III, pp. 513–15; Thomas Carte, *The Life of James Duke of Ormond*, 6 vols (Oxford, 1851), vol. VI, p. 32. See also Jane Ohlmeyer, *Civil War and Restoration in the Three Stuart Kingdoms: The Career of Randal MacDonnell, Marquis of Antrim, 1609–1683* (Cambridge, 1993), pp. 131–4.

13 J.T. Gilbert (ed.), *A Contemporary History of Affairs in Ireland from 1641 to 1652*, 3 vols (1879), vol. I, pp. 569–602, 649–710, *passim*; vol. II, pp. 237, 240, 294, 297, 344–5; Richard Bagwell, *Ireland under the Stuarts and during the Interregnum*, 2 vols (1909), vol. II, pp. 61, 69, 126, 149.

14 Thomas Carte (ed.), *A Collection of Original Letters and Papers, concerning the Affairs of England … 1641–1660, Found among the Duke of Ormond's Papers*, 2 vols (1739), vol. I, pp. 384–8; Sir Arthur Bryant (ed.), *The Letters, Speeches and Declarations of King Charles II* (1968), p. 17; Ronald Hutton, *Charles II, King of England, Scotland and Ireland* (Oxford, 1989), pp. 45–8.

15 Carte (ed.), *Letters and Papers*, vol. I, pp. 384–8; *CClSP*, vol. II, pp. 69, 74; *CHR*, vol. V, pp. 133–4.

16 Carte (ed.), *Letters and Papers*, vol. I, pp. 388–90; vol. II, pp. 31–3; HMC, *Manuscripts of the Marquess of Ormonde*, new series, vol. I (1902), p. 230.

17 See for example *CSP*, vol. III, p. 268; *NP*, vol. I, p. 278.

18 *CHR*, vol. III, p. 513. For Hyde's use of the nickname in correspondence with O'Neill see Bodl., Clarendon MS 46, fol. 361: Hyde to O'Neill, Paris, 31 Oct. 1653. It comes as no surprise to learn that O'Neill also had another nickname, 'Principe Barbaro', apparently used only in correspondence with Ormond. See Carte (ed.), *Letters and Papers*, vol. II, p. 32.

19 HMC, *Pepys Manuscripts* (1911), pp. 244–5; Geoffrey Smith, *The Cavaliers in Exile, 1640–1660* (Basingstoke, 2003), pp. 18–20, 31, 48, 155.

20 *NP*, vol. I, p. 203; Carte (ed.), *Letters and Papers*, vol. II, pp. 31–2.

21 Bodl., Clarendon MS 49, fol. 107; *NP*, vol. I, p. 278; *TSP*, vol. VII, p. 271; HMC, *Manuscripts of the Marquess of Ormonde*, new series, vol. I, p. 230.

22 *CClSP*, vol. II, p. 262.

23 *CHR*, vol. III, pp. 513–15; M.A.E. Green, *Lives of the Princesses of England*, 6 vols (1850–55), vol. V, p. 511; *CSPD 1641–3*, p. 27.

24 Donal Cregan, 'An Irish Cavalier: Daniel O'Neill in exile and Restoration, 1651–64', *Studia Hibernica*, 5 (1965), pp. 46–7. For Katherine (sometimes Catherine) Stanhope see Sarah Poynting, 'Stanhope, Katherine, *suo jure* Countess of Chesterfield, and Lady Stanhope (*bap.* 1609, *d.* 1667)', *Oxford DNB*.

25 *NP*, vol. I, p. 203.

26 *CSP*, vol. III, pp. 200–1, 204, 207, 212; *CClSP*, vol. II, p. 262; *NP*, vol. I, p. 204; vol. II, p. 111; vol. III, p. 6.

27 Carte, *Life of Ormond*, vol. VI, pp. 21, 149; Gilbert (ed.), *Contemporary History*, vol. II, pp. 237, 251 and *passim*; *CSP*, vol. III, pp. 200–1.

28 Antoni Maczak, 'From aristocratic household to princely court', in Ronald G. Asch and

Adolf M. Birke (eds), *Princes, Patronage and the Nobility: the Court at the Beginning of the Modern Age* (Oxford, 1991), pp. 17, 319–21. See also Alan Marshall, *The Age of Faction: Court Politics, 1660–1702* (Manchester, 1999), pp. 36–9.

29 For an example of O'Neill acting as intermediary between Ormond and Digby over an Irish appointment in 1644 see Carte, *Life of Ormond*, vol. VI, pp. 165–6. For examples of his brokerage activities after the Restoration see Bodl., Carte MS 32, fols 346–7; *CSPD 1660–61*, p. 80.

30 Edward Hyde, First Earl of Clarendon, *The Life of Edward, Earl of Clarendon*, 3 vols (Oxford, 1827), vol. I, pp. 301–2.

31 *CSP*, vol. III, p. 200.

32 *Ibid.*, vol. III, p. 201; *CClSP*, vol. III, p. 86; Clarendon, *Life*, vol. I, pp. 301–2; Cregan, 'O'Neill in exile and Restoration', pp. 47–9, 50; Poynting, 'Stanhope, Katherine'.

33 *NP*, vol. III, pp. 255–7, 268.

34 *CSPD 1655–56*, p. 209.

35 *CHR*, vol. III, p. 513; *CSPD 1655–56*, p. 159.

36 *CClSP*, vol. II, p. 127; *NP*, vol. II, p. 141.

37 The expression is used by J. Oldmixon in *The History of England during the Reigns of the Royal House of Stuart* (1730), p. 72.

38 *CSP*, vol. III, p. 296; *CClSP*, vol. III, pp. 112, 304, 379; Smith, *Cavaliers in Exile*, p. 135; Cregan, 'O'Neill in exile and Restoration', p. 43.

39 *CClSP*, vol. III, pp. 114, 318.

40 See for example Antonia Fraser, *King Charles II* (1979), pp. 154–5; Hutton, *Charles II*, pp. 125–6; Hester W. Chapman, *The Tragedy of Charles II in the Years 1630–1660* (1964), pp. 26, 308–9, 328–35. Involvement in the sordid affairs of Lucy Walter has not been good for O'Neill's posthumous reputation. Hester Chapman refers to him as 'an extremely shady individual' (*ibid.*, p. 262), while Brian Masters, in *The Mistresses of Charles II* (1997), considers him to have been 'a scoundrel' (p. 33).

41 *TSP*, vol. I, pp. 683–4.

42 *Ibid.*, vol. I, p. 684; Hutton, *Charles II*, pp. 125–6.

43 *NP*, vol. II, p. 219.

44 *Ibid.*, vol. II, p. 220. For Mennes see Timothy Raylor, *Cavaliers, Clubs and Literary Culture: Sir John Mennes, James Smith and the Order of the Fancy* (Newark, DE, 1994), esp. pp. 180–1, 198–202.

45 *TSP*, vol. V, pp. 645–6. For a discussion of the moral tone of the exiled court in Flanders see Hutton, *Charles II*, pp. 122–4.

46 The extent of the existence and the importance of the role of factions among the exiled Royalists remains an on-going if sometimes rather sterile subject of controversy. See Smith, *Cavaliers in Exile*, pp. 115–17; Jason McElligott and David L. Smith (eds), *Royalists and Royalism during the English Civil Wars* (Cambridge, 2007), p. 9.

47 Gilbert (ed.), *Contemporary History*, vol. I, p. 597.

48 Carte (ed.), *Letters and Papers*, vol. I, pp. 154–9.

49 For Wentworth, Tuke and Ross see *Oxford DNB*.

50 *NP*, vol. I, p. 276: Ormond to Nicholas, Caen, 19 Oct. 1651.

51 Quoted in David Underdown, *Royalist Conspiracy in England, 1649–1660* (New Haven, CT, 1960), p. 56.

52 *CHR*, vol. III, pp. 520–1; Smith, *Cavaliers in Exile*, pp. 117–25.

53 *NP*, vol. II, pp. 156–7.

54 The definitive study of Royalist conspiracy is Underdown's *Royalist Conspiracy*, but see also Philip Aubrey, *Mr Secretary Thurloe: Cromwell's Secretary of State, 1652–1660* (1990), pp. 94–128.

55 'Fatal overthrow at Worcester': Ralph, Lord Hopton, to Nicholas, 4 Oct. 1651, quoted in F.T.R. Edgar, *Sir Ralph Hopton* (Oxford, 1968), p. 196.

56 Underdown, *Royalist Conspiracy*, pp. 73–7.

57 O'Neill's 'brief Relation', with commentary by C.H. Firth, is printed in the *EHR*, 8 (1893), pp. 529–32.

58 For a detailed account of the March 1655 rising see Underdown, *Royalist Conspiracy*, pp. 127–58.

59 *NP*, vol. II, pp. 217–23. Normally Royalist agents and conspirators employed numerical ciphers. See Underdown, *Royalist Conspiracy*, pp. 341–9. O'Neill's employment of the cover of a report to a debtor wishing to compound for his debts is unusual, but this kind of communication would have appealed to someone like O'Neill as it was much quicker both to compose and to decipher.

60 *NP*, vol. II, p. 217–23.

61 HMC, *Manuscripts of the Marquess of Ormonde*, new series, vol. I, p. 318.

62 For O'Neill's reports from London in 1658 see Bodl., Clarendon MS 57, fols 129–30, 263, 303.

63 Carte (ed.), *Letters and Papers*, vol. II, p. 132. For the Royalist rising planned for early 1658 see Underdown, *Royalist Conspiracy*, pp. 208–29.

64 Bodl., Clarendon MS 57, fol. 129. The 'we' is a reference to his companion, Nicholas Armorer.

65 After the Restoration both John Kay and Mrs Carter claimed to have hidden in their houses and lent money to O'Neill and other Royalist agents. *CSPD 1665–6*, p. 128; *1666–7*, p. 25.

66 *CClSP*, vol. IV, pp. 12, 18, 20, 23, 25, 34, 36, 39; *NP*, vol. II, p. 218. For Armorer see G. Smith, 'Armorer, Nicholas (*c.* 1620–1686)', *Oxford DNB*.

67 For examples see BL, Egerton MS 2550, *passim* for a large collection of Nicholas's cipher keys with various Royalist agents and conspirators. In October 1655 Charles expressed his gratitude to Mrs Ross, the wife of the courtier and part-time agent Thomas Ross, who was going into England on behalf of her kinsman and fellow exile, the Scottish Royalist Sir William Keith, 'who cannot safely make the journey'. *CClSP*, vol. III, p. 62.

68 HMC, *Manuscripts in Various Collections*, vol. II (1903), pp. 351, 353, 355; *CClSP*, vol. II, pp. 149, 323; vol. III, pp. 100, 224; Underdown, *Royalist Conspiracy*, pp. 98–102, 139, 157–8, 206–8.

69 *CSPD 1657–58*, p. 372.

70 For O'Neill's negotiations with the Sealed Knot and discussion of the Knot's 'wariness', see Underdown, *Royalist Conspiracy*, pp. 219–20, 234–5, 322–3.

71 Alan Marshall, *Intelligence and Espionage in the Reign of Charles II* (Cambridge, 1994), p. 8.

72 *CHR*, vol. VI, pp. 117–22; F.J. Routledge, *England and the Treaty of the Pyrenees* (Liverpool, 1953), pp. 56–65. For Booth's rising see Underdown, *Royalist Conspiracy*, pp. 254–85.

73 *CHR*, vol. VI, p. 130.

74 *Ibid.*, vol. XVII, pp. 66, 68–72; *CSP*, vol. III, pp. 597–8; *CClSP*, vol. IV, pp. 416, 418, 419; Routledge, *England and the Treaty of the Pyrenees*, pp. 71–5, 94, 117.

75 Bodl., Clarendon MS 66, fols 95, 147; Smith, *Cavaliers in Exile*, pp. 163–4.

76 Routledge, *England and the Treaty of the Pyrenees*, pp. 87–8; Clarendon, *Life*, vol. II, p. 99; Smith, *Cavaliers in Exile*, pp. 163–4.

77 Bodl., Clarendon MS 67, fols 191–2.

78 Cregan, 'O'Neill in exile and Restoration', pp. 64–70; Casway, 'O'Neill, Daniel'; Robert Latham and William Matthews (eds), *The Diary of Samuel Pepys*, 11 vols (1970), vol. V, p. 304.

79 Cregan, 'O'Neill in exile and Restoration', pp. 66–7; Poynting, 'Stanhope, Katherine'; E.S. de Beer (ed.), *The Diary of John Evelyn*, 6 vols (Oxford, 1955), vol. IV, pp. 91–2.

80 Bryant (ed.), *Speeches and Declarations of Charles II*, p. 168; *CSPD 1664*, p. 43.

81 See T.C. Barnard, 'The Protestant interest, 1641–1660', in Jane Ohlmeyer (ed.), *Ireland from Independence to Occupation, 1641–1660* (Cambridge, 1995), p. 226. For O'Neill's approaches to the Parliamentarians Fairfax and Lord Willoughby of Parham in March 1655 see *NP*, vol. II, pp. 217–18.

82 *TSP*, vol. I, p. 682.

83 *NP*, vol. II, p. 221.

84 McElligott and Smith (eds), *Royalists and Royalism*, p. 15; Jason McElligott, *Royalism, Print and Censorship in Revolutionary England* (Woodbridge, 2007), chapter 4.

85 Carte, *Life of Ormond*, vol. VI, pp. 276–7.

86 *CHR*, vol. VI, p. 513.

87 For discussion of the view that 'the century or so following the restoration was the great era of conspiratorial fears and imagined intrigues', see Mark Knights, 'Faults on both sides: the conspiracies of party politics under the later Stuarts', in Barry Coward and Julian Swann (eds), *Conspiracy and Conspiracy Theory in Early Modern Europe* (Aldershot, 2004), pp. 153–72.

Chapter 7

Gender, geography and exile: Royalists and the Low Countries in the 1650s

Ann Hughes and Julie Sanders

I

On 19 January 1651 the leading newsbook of the English republic, *Mercurius Politicus*, reported from The Hague on the baptism of the young William of Orange, son of the recently deceased William II, and Mary Stuart, daughter of Charles I:

> The young Prince was christened last Saturday in great State & was named Willielmus Frederic Henricus. There accompanied him at least 30 Coaches with six horses, all covered with mourning, the States General, States of Holland, States of Utrecht, of Zealand, the Townes of Delft, Leyden, and Amsterdam were his Godfathers; the Queen of Bohemia and the Princess Dowager, were his Godmothers.[1]

The baptism reflected divisions within the prince's immediate family, as well as conflicts between the princely ambitions of the house of Orange and the republican commitment of the towns of Holland, the most powerful of the provinces which had won independence from Spain after an eighty-year struggle.[2] William II's plans to renew the war with Spain and to challenge the English Commonwealth inaugurated a bitter struggle with the towns of Holland in the summer of 1650, which was defused only with the prince's death. The prominence of the states and towns in the baptism ceremony represented a resurgence of urban republicanism, and was followed by the refusal to elect the baby prince or any other Orange representative as stadholder (a sort of provincial governor) in the major provinces of the Netherlands. The baby's elaborate clothing in black and white, bedecked with ermine fur, 'king like', met with much disapproval. Mary had wanted the baby to be named 'Carel William' for her martyred father, but his grandmother, the Princess Dowager Amalia van Solms, widow of the stadholder Frederick Henry, feared provoking the new English regime and insisted on the more cautious William.[3] This disagreement was the harbinger of years of jockeying for power within the Orange family over the guardianship and education of the young prince. Consequently the balance of power within the Netherlands, and indeed within the house of Orange, was of immediate relevance to the fortunes of the Stuarts and in turn to the recently established English republic because Mary's capacity to help English Royalists was determined by her status within her marital family, and by the fortunes of the Orangists within the United Provinces.[4]

Our aim in working together as a historian and a literary scholar has been to examine Royalist exile in the Low Countries (the United Provinces and the Spanish Netherlands) in the later 1640s and 1650s through the prism of gender, discussing the experiences of women and the disruptive impact of exile on familial authority and relationships.[5] In this chapter our themes are gender and place, both of which require attention to interrelationships and connections. Displacement and exile highlighted the importance of female agency in maintaining networks in unfamiliar contexts and a variety of spaces. As Geoffrey Smith has emphasised, 'There is an enormous difference between exile as it was experienced in the royal court in Bruges or Brussels, in army camps and garrisons in Flanders, in modest family lodgings in Paris or Rotterdam, or in quiet communities of émigrés in Caen or Blois'.[6] Encounters with host communities, themselves divided and subject to change, took place in the United Provinces and the Spanish Netherlands alongside tense accommodations between Royalists and a range of longer-standing expatriate communities of English and Scots, intellectuals, traders, soldiers and religious dissidents. Here we suggest how the distinct characters of different places in the Low Countries, The Hague, Middelburg, Breda and Antwerp helped to structure Royalist interactions, particularly those where women played a prominent role. William's baptism introduces many of our detailed concerns: the inescapable connections between the fortunes of Royalist exiles and the tangled (often family) politics of continental states, the importance of ceremony as a mode of defiance for the politically marginalised and the various ways in which ceremony and display might play out before hostile as well as sympathetic audiences.[7]

These 'real' places of the Low Countries were not far distant by road or boat, but their cultural, religious and political geographies differed significantly. Royalists were displaced from 'home', and from previous centres of influence and identity, even while they were precisely located in these distinct spaces. Consequently imagined and remembered places, whether home or abroad, were an important element in Royalist culture, and the maintaining of connections between dispersed friends and family through journeys, letter-writing, cultural and ritual exchange was a crucial element in Royalist practice. Recent scholarship has shown how theatrical forms might be deployed to proclaim defiant allegiances despite the traumatic dislocations of exile and defeat,[8] and here we look at other forms of display, baptisms, garter ceremonies and political demonstrations. Everywhere we will find women prominent as intermediaries, patrons and activists.

II

In 1655 the Dutch poet and official Constantijn Huygens wrote to an old friend Lady Mary Stafford, the widow of Sir Robert Killigrew, who was considering whether to join her son, the playwright Thomas Killigrew, in the Netherlands. He urged her to come to The Hague rather than Maastricht as Thomas had suggested. Maastricht was:

> In an excellent aire indeed, but as far from the Queen of Bohemia as the Haghe from thence, and no such conversation there, nor such pictures, nor such performes, nor such musicke as we are able to afford you here. To be short Madam, if your Ladyship doe us the honour to passe the seas, we will endeavour to make you passe your time in such a manner, that the good old days of Lothbury howse will sometimes come backe into your memory.[9]

Huygens, a diplomat and latterly secretary to successive Princes of Orange as well as a distinguished poet and musician, and a central figure in European intellectual networks, was a vital mediator between English exiles and courtly, intellectual and political culture in the Netherlands. Contacts made on diplomatic missions to England in the 1620s endured throughout his life; at Sir Robert Killigrew's Lothbury home he had met Francis Bacon and John Donne (whose poems he translated into Dutch).[10] While attempting to find a compromise over Orange divisions, Huygens was concerned to speak with 'Seigneurs Anglois' to reassure them that the honour of the daughter of 'leur Grand Roi defunct' was not affronted by proposals to associate Amalia and her son-in-law the Elector of Brandenburg in the guardianship of the prince. The formal, almost neutral language used to describe the martyr king perhaps suggests the compromises in political language required in the republican Netherlands.[11] For Huygens, The Hague was an intimate, cultured space, a complex, crowded arena in which different interests in Dutch, English and European politics jostled for supremacy before sophisticated audiences.[12] Despite having a population of some 20,000 by 1650, The Hague was, in jurisdictional terms, a village, without the legal privileges and political structure of other Dutch cities, deliberately maintained as a neutral place in which other powers operated rather than a political entity in its own right. As the seat of Dutch government it hosted rival diplomats from all over Europe, including Spanish representatives after the final conclusion of the eighty-year war in 1648. It was the headquarters of the States of Holland from 1577, and of the States General of the United Provinces from 1588, republican bodies matched by the increasingly elaborate court of the Orange stadholders.[13] The apparently straightforward sending of condolences on the Regicide to Henrietta Maria in Paris involved multiple messages from The Hague. As Lord Hatton in Paris reported to Sir Edward Nicholas in Caen, there was 'an envoyee from the Prince of Orange, another from the Princess Dowager, another from the Queene of Bohemia, another from the Princess Royal', besides a deputation from the States General.[14] By the 1650s three (widowed) female-headed courts existed in sometimes uneasy proximity here; Frederick William's widow Amalia and her daughter-in-law Mary Stuart were bitter rivals for much of the decade; while another Stuart widow and exile, Elizabeth of Bohemia, the sister of Charles I, was fond of her niece Mary, but had a more difficult relationship with Amalia, who had been her lady in waiting.[15]

For exiled Royalists the female-headed courts of Elizabeth of Bohemia and Mary Stuart were vital resources for intrigue, information, patronage and entertainment. Despite the difficulties faced by both Stuart women, they nonetheless had a solidity most exiles lacked. Mary's dual Orange and Stuart status ensured much freedom of action even as she professed her loyalty and obedience to her brother, the exiled Charles II. Mary's stubbornness over her son's guardianship and the consequent fragmentation of the Orange cause made it more difficult for Charles to obtain any support in the Netherlands, and Mary's reluctance to dispense patronage to Dutch politicians who might be sympathetic to the king was a further irritation. The peripatetic and cash-strapped Charles had no means of coercing his sister.[16] Nonetheless, many Royalists did find employment with Mary, and the benefits of financial security and of close informal relationships were often greater for wives, daughters and sisters than for leading male politicians, with some interesting implications for family relations. Edward Hyde's sister-in-law Barbara Aylesbury and, later, his daughter Anne both served in Mary's household; Anne and Edward Nicholas's daughter Susan were both intimates of the Queen of Bohemia.[17] Mary's principal female confidante was Katherine, Lady Stanhope, who had been her governess since 1642, and who had married in 1641, as her second husband, the Dutch diplomat Jehan van der Kerckhoven, Lord of Heenvliet, an active promoter of the Stuart–Orange match.[18] Heenvliet was superintendent of Mary's household, and anxiety about the influence of Stanhope and her husband over the princess was a persistent focus for Royalist disquiet at Mary's autonomy. Sir Edward Nicholas was consistently hostile towards Stanhope in his correspondence while Hyde was more sympathetic.[19] Stanhope's Dutch marriage and her influence over Mary suggest the ways in which women might be empowered by the specific context of exile and male displacement. She was the subject of an English poem by Huygens which hints further at the richness of Anglo-Dutch links: 'Brave Henrie Wottons Neece, perfect model of Grace / Full place of honour and full honour of your

place'.[20] Long-standing enthusiasm for English culture was evoked in identifying Stanhope with her paternal family and strengthened political ties in the
1640s and 1650s as both Stanhope and Huygens sought to serve the divided
house of Orange.

Elizabeth of Bohemia had been in The Hague since the 1620s, when she and
her husband, the Elector Palatine, had been driven from the Palatinate as well
as from their adopted kingdom of Bohemia. Since her husband's death in 1632
she had struggled to maintain a large family and by the 1650s was massively in
debt. By the 1650s, with her children grown up, her formal authority over her
family had ceased. Her eldest surviving son, Charles Louis, had been restored
to part of his Palatine inheritance at the Treaty of Westphalia, but his Parliamentarian stance in the English Civil War strained relationships with the
rest of his family, and there was little prospect of any invitation for Elizabeth
to return to Heidelberg. The Royalist defeat in England and the stopping of
Elizabeth's pension were disastrous for her finances. Elizabeth made undigni-
fied and unavailing attempts to persuade the Dutch to include demands for
recompense in their negotiations of an alliance with England, petitioning the
States General, 'High and Mighty Lords, our very dear and very good friends',
on 29 May 1651 that they include an article in the projected treaty for payment
of £10,000 of pension arrears so that 'our creditors and furnishers who are
your subjects and fellow-citizens, may find their satisfaction therein'. The
States General did pass her request on, but it was contemptuously rebuffed
by the English ambassadors at The Hague: 'we cannot but think it enough
for us to say that when the queen of Bohemia thinks fit to make any address
to the parliament of the commonwealth of England, for anything she hath in
demand from them, it will be then time enough for her to expect an answer
thereunto'. The grants from her father and brother had never been ratified
by Parliament, so the Commonwealth was not bound in 'law or equity' to pay
them. They noted that 'she hath no reason to expect any thing from the parliament of grace and favour ... because the queen, by herself and all her relations,
hath opposed to her power the commonwealth of England, and upon all occasions expressed the greatest enmity therunto'. Her description of the late king
as 'Charles the First' did not impress the English, for it 'implies that there is a
second Charles king of England; against which expression in the name of the
commonwealth of England we do protest, no person whatsoever having any
right or title to be king of England'.[21]

Elizabeth nonetheless retained her status as the senior member of the
British royal family in The Hague, and her roles illuminate the social and
political character of the place. She had been in The Hague since April 1621,
knew everyone in this large village and was acquainted with most of the crucial
figures in German and northern European politics. Her mother-in-law was a
daughter of William the Silent and hence the half-sister of the stadholders

Maurice and Frederick Henry. Her son, Charles Louis, was part of the politics of the empire, while the Elector of Brandenburg, who was married to a daughter of Frederick and Amalia and was a guardian of the young Prince William, was her nephew by marriage. Elizabeth was at the heart of the hectic sociability in The Hague courts. She passed on to Sir Edward Nicholas news of Charles's escape after the defeat at Worcester following 'an express from France' to the Princess Royal, while Nicholas witnessed directly the 'uncomely carriage' of the Dowager Princess Amalia to the Princess Mary when he happened to be present 'at their accidental meeting at the Queen of Bohemia's'.[22] Misunderstandings could easily arise at The Hague through a collision between plans formulated at a distance and intrigues carried on by people who, in this crowded place, had too much direct contact. When a marriage was mooted in Royalist circles, Sir Alexander Hume, Mary's Chamberlain, proposed that it be suggested to Mary by King Charles II, but, as Elizabeth reported to Nicholas, Hume told his 'cousin german the Elector of Brandenbourg', who 'can conceal nothing from the Princess Dowagere of Orange', who in turn 'in her usual charity to the Princesse Royal hath done all she can to make it public'.[23]

Much of Elizabeth's contribution to the Royalist cause in the 1650s involved circulation of precious information in person or by letter. The importance of Elizabeth's European information networks has been stressed by Nadine Akkerman for the 1630s, and her ebullient letters continued to bolster morale and foster connections after 1649.[24] The Hague was ideally placed both for discovering material, and for passing it on. The regular letters sent by Sir Edward Nicholas in The Hague to Sir Edward Walker, who was living in the Countess of Arundel's house in Amsterdam, depended largely on Elizabeth's intelligence networks. In February 1653, for example, Nicholas could not send news of the countess's son Lord Stafford as the Queen of Bohemia had not received her usual weekly letters from the diet of Ratisbon.[25] Elizabeth's access to gossip and news became even more important when Royalist exiles were dispersed following the end of the Anglo-Dutch War (when the 1654 treaty required the Dutch republican authorities to promise to cease any help for the Stuarts and to continue to exclude the house of Orange from office in the Netherlands) and the alliance between France and the English republic which forced Charles and his brothers to leave Paris. Sir Edward Nicholas left The Hague in July 1654 to follow the king to the Rhineland, but was consoled by regular letters of entertainment and instruction from Elizabeth. Her subjects ranged from the exploits of her dog – 'Apollo with leaping into my lapp has made this blott' – to serious political and diplomatic developments in England, the United Provinces and the rest of Europe. She passed on the news that her chaplain George Morley received from England and her own (erroneous) intelligence on 29 September 1654 of Cromwell's dissolution of his first

Parliament: 'it was confirmed to me the last night by one of the States Generall ... but it was so late that I could not heare of the particulars'. A few weeks later she reported that 'The K[ing] of Poland is in Silesia, hunts and passeth his time with little care of anie thing else, this I have from his own resident.'[26] Elizabeth's correspondence with the peripatetic King Charles II drew on the resources of The Hague and on all her diplomatic networks. In August 1653, for example, Charles II wrote to her asking her to pass on letters to the Queen of Sweden and the King of Denmark through their ambassadors in The Hague.[27] In December 1655 Elizabeth reported on contacts in Germany, and in the following February she assured Charles, 'I give your majestie humble thankes, that you are so well pleas'd with my smale service concerning the landgrave of Hesse: it is but my dutie; I am onlie sorie I ame in so unfortunat a condition, that I cannot doe your majestie no greater service.'[28] It is not surprising that in January 1656, in the absence of Mary, who was on her way to France, the Norwegian diplomat Hannibal Sested urged Charles II to write only to Elizabeth and not to Amalia or Count William.[29]

Elizabeth also featured prominently in the rituals and displays through which beleaguered Royalist exiles sought to win support and defy the English republic. As Charles II had few material ways of rewarding prominent followers or potential foreign supporters, the courtly, chivalric trappings of the Order of the Garter became more significant than before. Henry, Duke of Gloucester, was installed as a knight of the Garter in March 1653, shortly after his release from prison in England, at the same time as Henry, Prince of Tarente, a close friend of Elizabeth's and a military commander in the service of the States General. The infant Prince William joined them the following month.[30] The most pains, however, were taken over the offer of a garter to Elector Frederick William of Brandenburg, in the hopes that the honour would encourage him to rally support for Charles at the Imperial Diet at Ratisbon, and to use his status as a co-guardian of the young Prince William to act as an honest broker in the conflicts between Mary and Amalia. The George and Garter were to be sent via Antwerp with the king's instructions to Elizabeth, who was to pass them on to Sir Edward Walker (Garter king of arms) for presentation. It may be that the prickly Walker felt excluded from full participation in these arrangements, for the Clarendon State Papers include a vindication of his right to deliver the insignia of the garter to foreign princes.[31] Although Frederick William wrote warmly to thank Charles, the honour did not win his enduring support. Elizabeth reported indignantly to Charles in January 1656 that the elector had sent an envoy to Cromwell. 'You see how impudent a hypocrite the rogue is become.'[32]

Through her family and household Elizabeth was also heavily involved in cruder forms of political display, not least the aggressive and sometimes violent acts of defiance through which English Royalists sought to intimidate republican envoys from England. In the complex, crowded political space of The Hague, ritualised harassment could be particularly threatening. Followers of the Marquess of Montrose, abetted by associates of Elizabeth, were responsible for the assassination of Isaac Dorislaus, the Dutch-born ambassador of the English Commonwealth, at The Hague in May 1649.[33] The English embassy, headed by Oliver St John and Walter Strickland and sent to The Hague in March 1651 to negotiate a treaty or even a union with the Dutch, feared similar reprisals, especially as they had, provocatively, included Dorislaus's son as a member of their party. The English press indignantly reported:

> As we came along in our coaches, they cald us Traytors, Rebels, and St Johns Bastards all the way we came; some spit in our faces: My L. Strickland sent his Page home to his own house, and they had like to have stoned him; he was constrained to get into a house. They enquire much after yong Dorislaus, and some have dared to say, That they hope my Lord St John will fare no better then his father.[34]

Although a botched assassination attempt was thwarted, the embassy was faced with many insults and threats of violence, as the London press reported: 'many are the dangers we daily go through, we dare hardly peep out of dores'. *Mercurius Politicus*'s language stressed the performative aspects and the political purchase of such incidents:

> the Cavaliers rant as if they intended to act some tragedy or other before we depart: More and more of them come still into the Town, where many of the Dutch themselves likewise are very bitter against us.[35]

While regular reporting in the English press aimed at discrediting Royalists, it inevitably added to the impact of exile defiance. All the spaces of The Hague – courts, streets and parks – served for rival demonstrations of political commitment.[36] Among the first to intimidate the embassy were two children of Elizabeth of Bohemia. The ambassadors and many of their attendants, walking in the 'wood set with many fine walks of trees, to take the air', encountered Prince Edward, 'walking on foot, with the Princess his sister, by the hand'. He shouted at the ambassadors that they were 'Rogues ... grinding his teeth at them, and calling them Dogs'. At home he boasted to his mother 'what a brave business he had done, and how he had served the English Traytors'. The English newsbook indignantly noted that the affront was done 'by the Petty paltry thing called Prince, whose very Nursing was paid for out of the purse of England'. On another day the 'Princess Royal' (*sic*) rode past the ambassador's house 'with six horses all in mourning'; on another, the Duke of York, recently arrived from England with 'as many Cavaliers as they could scrape together, came thrice by my lords door in their Coaches'.[37] When one of the attendants on the ambassadors visited an acquaintance who lived at Elizabeth's court:

being taken notice of, and known to belong to my Lords, he was hist out of dores. The Queen (to shew her thanks to England, and zeal to her wretched Family) declared hereupon, that if any durst come into her Court, she would have them flung down stairs, and kickt out of dores.[38]

Defiance of England's Puritan republic in The Hague was also conducted through religious and cultural patronage. In protecting 'Anglican' religion, or promoting musical and theatrical performance, Elizabeth and Mary were again addressing multiple audiences. They drew on English and French masquing and theatrical traditions to strengthen cultural and social ties between Royalist exiles and Dutch sympathisers while seeking hostile reactions from the regime in England and its representatives in The Hague, as well as from the Dutch reformed churches. Baptisms combined religious ceremony, elite sociability and Royalist cultural display. As Elizabeth reported to Charles and Nicholas in January 1655: 'we had a great feast at P. William's child's Christenin'; 'I was at the supper: my Neece, the Ps dowager, the little Prince and P. Maurice were gossips: the States generall, I meane their Deputies, and the Counsell of State, and my self and Louyse were there as guests. After super was dancing till three a clock ...'.[39] Royalist religious initiatives might also come into conflict with the Puritan practices common in the English and Scottish churches already rooted in Dutch cities. When Hatton reported on the condolences coming from The Hague after the Regicide he added to Nicholas that 'the English minister att the Hague would not name the King in his church', while at Rotterdam the English merchants 'shut up their church dore because the English ministere there had told them that he meant to pray for the king; and leaving their owne meeting they went to the Brownists, amongst whom thanks was given to God for the kings murther and, as is reported, they feasted for that reason'.[40]

The English church at The Hague had long been established on reformed lines but Samuel Bamford, its strongly Puritan minister, became increasingly unpopular in the later 1640s as English politics divided émigré communities and Royalist exiles became involved in church affairs. In 1650 Bamford was replaced by George Beaumont, who acted as Elizabeth's chaplain, one of a series of Anglican figures sponsored by Elizabeth and Mary in the 1650s.[41] In 1644 Elizabeth had been forced to dismiss her Anglican chaplain Sampson Johnson, a man suspected of Arminian and Socinian opinions, when Parliament threatened to remove her pension, but from 1649 she had nothing to lose, and William Stamp, George Beaumont and Hyde's friend George Morley all served her household. Anglican ceremonies were also performed in Mary's chapel, under the ministry of Thomas Browne. All this alarmed English republicans and Dutch Calvinists, to Elizabeth's delight. When she reported to Charles on 'a new divertissement of little plays after supper' at her own and Mary's court she added, 'I hope the godlie will preach against it.'[42] The

Dutch synod questioned Stamp's orthodoxy as it had challenged Johnson's, accused Browne of schism because he would not subscribe the articles of the Dutch church, and failed to limit Mary's ceremonialism.[43] In 1658 the English resident in The Hague, George Downing, condemned the English church as a 'nursery of cavallierisme' and finally managed to prevent Beaumont praying for Charles II. At this point Elizabeth, who used the English church at The Hague for her own services as well as occasionally attending the main services, withdrew, taking her hangings and cushions with her.[44]

In Middelburg also, Royalist involvement had a significant impact on already established English and Scottish residents. Middelburg in Zeeland was more enthusiastic than the towns of Holland about continuing the war against England in 1653–54, and more sympathetic to Orange and Stuart interests, as the English republican press realised: 'the Zealanders being cooled, the interest of young Orange and Charles Stuart lie close by the walls'.[45] As one of the chief bases of the Dutch East India Company, Middelburg was a European thoroughfare and a centre of global trade. Along with nearby Flushing it was a common point of entry and departure for the Netherlands. Thus Sir Edward Hyde lingered there in 1648, hoping to meet up with Prince Charles.[46] The seemingly prosaic accounts of the charitable donations of the English congregation at Middleburg offer vivid evidence of the impact of the British Civil Wars. In 1644 3s was paid 'to a ministers widow and 3 children driven out p. the bloody Irish having good testomy by the parlament', while in November 1647 6d was given 'to a solgier which came from the kings syde'. Inevitably gifts to defeated Royalists featured frequently in the 1650s, such as those in August 1650 to 'a gentlewoeman, a wydowe whose husband followed the king', and in January 1655 to '2 poor Scotch gentlemen with the king passing'.[47]

Middelburg's affiliations were not wholly Orange and Stuart. An English garrison in the town bolstered the revolt against Spain in the 1580s, and English and Scots Puritans found refuge there. From the 1590s many English Puritan books were printed at Middelburg at the press of Richard Schilders, the printer to the States of Zeeland, including John Rainolds's *Th' Overthrow of Stage Playes* (1599). The upheavals of the 1640s and the increasing influence of exiled Royalists challenged these godly traditions. In nearby Veere, the Scottish church held two days of prayer for Charles II and the Scots army in 1651, but this presumably did not compromise its Presbyterian commitment. In Flushing, divisions over events in 1651 were managed only through a laissez-faire policy: the elders of that church 'tooke into consideration some passages which had happened in our church, tending to a breach amongst us, in regard of intermeddling of the affaires of England and Scotland', and decided that 'strangers if they preach amongst us, shal have the liberty to pray or not to pray for the King as their conscience shal lead them unto'.[48] In Middelburg itself, reformed practices were qualified by Anglican ceremonialism as

Royalist influence balanced that of the ministers, including the Scots Presbyterian William Spang, who moved from Veere in 1652. In 1655 'Christ's daye of
nativitye' was celebrated, and sermons were preached on 25 December in 1656
and 1657 although the day was not labelled as Christmas. In 1658, however,
25 December was described as 'Crismas day', and twice as much money was
collected for the poor as on a normal Sunday.[49] Records of baptisms in the
1650s begin to list godparents rather than simply parents and witnesses,
perhaps indicating Anglican ceremonies of which Thomas Browne would
have approved rather than simpler reformed occasions. It is clear that exiles
were involved. On 26 April 1654 Charles, the son of Sir William Quirinson
and Dame Alethia Carey, was baptised with godparents, including 'Lord Georg
Goring' and Lord Craven as well as the 'Queen of Bohemia'. Elizabeth and the
others may well have attended this ceremony in person, for at a subsequent
baptism of a Quirinson child in November 1656, the godparents included
Mary Stuart, the 'Princess Royal of Orange' and Charles 'the King', but Lady
and Lord Wentworth stood in for them.[50] Quirinson was a prominent Anglo-
Dutch merchant who was named as one of the gentlemen of Charles II's privy
chamber at the Restoration, while his wife was from an English family with
established Dutch connections.[51]

Breda was geographically and jurisdictionally a borderland. Nearer to
Antwerp than to The Hague, it had been held by the Spaniards between 1625
and 1637.[52] English, Scots and Irish forces had served on both sides in the great
sieges of the early seventeenth century, and a substantial English community
had long been resident there. What made it a particularly attractive residence
for Royalist exiles and an ideal setting for crucial Royalist political enterprises
in 1649, when the treaty with the Scots Presbyterians was signed, or in 1660,
when Charles and Hyde negotiated the Restoration, was its status as an
Orange patrimony. Politically less exposed than The Hague, it was a refuge
and a source of practical support. Mary's liminal position between Stuart and
Orange is indicated in the register book of the Breda magistrates, where she
is described as 'Mary, by the grace of God, Princess of Great Britain, Dowager
Princess of Orange' when confirming the appointment of magistrates; the last
element was omitted when she adjudicated the affairs of the English church.[53]

Mary's influence was mobilised to secure accommodation for Sir Edward
Hyde's wife and children in 1653. Heenvliet wrote on the Princess's behalf to
Professor van Renesse, the principal of the Orange college in Breda, recommending Elizabeth Hyde as a responsible tenant. Heenvliet pre-empted anxi-
eties about unreliable English tenants, emphasising that she was known as a
respectable woman and a reliable householder who would use the property
well.[54] In practice Lady Hyde was provided with a free residence in Breda.[55]
An exile's life depended on this world of references and recommendations,
permissions and permits, and Heenvliet always stressed that he was writing

at the behest of the Princess Royal herself. In December 1656 he assured van Renesse of Mary's pleasure at the favours shown to Lady Hyde.[56] She had the use of five basement rooms and a kitchen belonging to the college in the complex of buildings around the area of St Catharindal, known as 'Het Clooster', where the English Royalists tended to take lodgings.[57] As late as 1663 the college was still being rewarded for its kindness to 'Madame Heyd' during the 1650s.[58] Elizabeth Hyde's father, Sir Thomas Aylesbury, also settled in Breda after the death of his daughter Barbara, and Mary's protection ensured that Edward Hyde was able to visit his wife regularly after 1654, when the main exiled court had to move to Cologne.[59] The connections between the Hyde family and Princess Mary's court were strengthened by Anne Hyde's service there from 1654 and by association through godparenthood.[60] Breda as a place, then, provided some Royalist women in particular with a degree of stability during a period of uncertainty and turmoil, political and personal. Within Breda careful negotiations with the host community were often undertaken on behalf of Royalist exiles, female and male, by intercessionaries from both the pre-existing English expatriate community and the Dutch hosts.

Like that of Middelburg, Breda's English community had godly traditions. The stadholder Frederick Henry had promoted zealous Calvinism in the town after its recapture by the Spanish in 1637. In 1646 he established the Orange college, an advanced school where boys would be trained for the church or other public service, and where orthodox Calvinist teaching would counteract any surviving Spanish influences. Among the first governors were Constantijn Huygens and Heenvliet, and there was also a significant English presence. Heenvliet's stepson, Philip Stanhope, was among the first pupils, and the first professor of philosophy and mathematics was the Englishman John Pell, a key figure in those 'networks of association and communication through which knowledge was generated and circulated'. Pell's networks included leading continental thinkers such as Marin Mersenne, and a broad spectrum of English figures from the Royalist Charles Cavendish (in Antwerp) to the Puritan Samuel Hartlib in England.[61] Pell himself had Puritan associations and served the republic after 1652, but his social world in Breda suggests a culture where godliness was being modified by the Royalist presence. He was close to the minister Sampson Johnson, who was protected by Mary after he was forced from The Hague. Mary and Johnson promoted more ceremonial 'Anglican' practices in the English church.[62] Pell also moved in musical circles led by Johan Brosterhuysen, the professor of botany and greek, who was an accomplished musician and a friend of Huygens. Another talented musician was Utricia Swann, a member of a long-established Anglo-Dutch family and yet another of Mary's ladies in waiting. Swann's mother was Dutch, while her father Sir John Ogle had served the Dutch republic as governor of Utrecht (hence her name). Utricia's brother John and her husband, William, also served in the Dutch army.[63] Utricia featured in Huygens's major poem inspired by his country estate:

> I name you paramount, Utricia, first of all,
> Most swan-like, Lady Swann, whichever name best names you
> I heard her singing here, I think I hear her still
> Out-sing the nightingale, eclipse the nightingale.[64]

From 1648, with Spain and the United Provinces at peace, sustained contact between Breda and Antwerp was possible for both the Dutch and the exiled English. Geographical proximity fostered personal and cultural exchange despite religious and political contrasts. Earlier connections – such as the kinship ties between Utricia Swann and the Cavendishes – could be revived.[65] Elizabeth Hyde's father and brother moved between Antwerp and Breda while Huygens and Swann featured in the musical life of both cities.[66] In Antwerp they had close ties to the musical family of Gaspar Duarte, a banker, connoisseur and leader of the Portuguese community there.[67] Swann moved as easily in the salon culture associated with Beatrice de Cusance, Duchess of Lorraine in the Spanish Netherlands, as she did at the Dutch courts of Elizabeth and Mary.[68] Sir Balthazar Gerbier's extremely murky career in the 1650s spanned Antwerp and Breda, as well as shifting dubiously between Royalist and republican allegiance.[69] Elizabeth too visited Antwerp (and Brussels), sending excited reports to Nicholas in December 1654: 'I saw the Queene of Sueden at the play, she is extravagant in her fashion and apparel, but she has a good well favoured face, and a milde countenance. One of the players who knew me tolde her who I was, but she made no shew of it.' Although she was later told by Gaspar Duarte that Christina wanted to meet her, Elizabeth avoided contact 'since I heard how unhandsomelie she had spoken on the King my deare Brother and of the King my deare Nephue, and indeed of all our nation', and confined herself to sending 'a complement' through Sir William Swann.[70]

Antwerp was a particularly attractive base for Catholic Royalists like Sir Endymion Porter, but many others found it congenial, especially once Charles and the main Royalist court moved to Bruges and then Brussels after the alliance with Spain in April 1656.[71] The most prominent exiles were, of course, the Marquess of Newcastle, William Cavendish, and his wife Margaret, who maintained a defiantly aristocratic, ceremonial and theatrical presence despite precarious finances at the imposing house they rented from Rubens's widow. William Cavendish had long been an important patron and author, and in exile his interests were enriched by the baroque culture of the Spanish Netherlands and the increasing influence of France in Antwerp. His Caroline comedy *The Country Captain* (a collaboration with James Shirley) had been published in The Hague in 1649, and in Antwerp he promoted theatrical and musical entertainments and published an elaborate horsemanship manual.[72] Cavendish's entertainments brought together exiled figures and members of host communities. Huygens and Swann were frequent visitors, the Catholic poet Richard Flecknoe stayed with the Cavendishes after he quarrelled with his patron, the Duchess of Lorraine, and the master of the king's music, Nicholas Lanier, provided music for the Cavendishes. The Duarte family, as well as the duchess, were present at an ambitious entertainment and ball in honour of Charles II in February 1658, attended also by his sister Mary and his brothers.[73] Newcastle's theatrical initiatives in Antwerp displayed Royalist aspirations in hard times. In February 1658 English 'country dancing' as well as more elaborate verses and banqueting combined nostalgia for a non-Puritan England with hope for the future. Two days earlier another characteristic Royalist ceremony had taken place when Charles II, with Newcastle and the Earl of Bristol in attendance, installed the commander of his army as a knight of the Order of the Garter.[74] Courtly ceremonial, feasting and dancing maintained Royalist networks and morale abroad and perhaps sent defiant messages to the regime at home.

III

Newcastle's literary reputation was made before the Civil War, whereas his wife Margaret became a writer during her time in Antwerp. The experience of exile featured in many of her works, sometimes recounted as 'history', on other occasions fictionalised. In the *Life* of her husband she recounts how he first lodged at Antwerp in 'a publick Inn' until he was rescued from this indignity by Endymion Porter, who was 'not willing that a Person of such Quality as my Lord should lie in a publick-House'. Porter offered his lodgings in his own house, before Newcastle secured the lease on the Rubenshius, helped by a generous loan from Hyde's brother-in-law William Aylesbury. This may be 'history' but inn-house storylines, featuring plotlines of escape or concealed identity, were a standard element in romance fiction and romantic drama in the seventeenth century, and the literary filter through which place was understood is an important element in the cultural geography of exile.[75] Sharp distinctions between 'fact' and 'fiction' are not useful for understanding Margaret Cavendish's writing, and evocative descriptions of Antwerp can be found in her fictionalised epistles, the *Sociable Letters* (first published in 1664). The practical and emotional impact of the weather is one theme, expressed in military metaphors recalling the trauma of civil war:

> we have here at this time Cold with all its Potent Strength, as an Army of Flakes of Snow with Ammunition of Hail for Bullets, and Wind for Powder, also Huge Ships of Ice, which Float in the Main Sea, and Stop up all the Narrow Rivers.[76]

Cold is opposed by an 'Army of Furs', a massive military munitions store of logs, faggots, and bellows, and by the rich resources of food emerging from the kitchens of the city figured as sites of counter-insurgence, with cooks steering topside of beef 'men-of-war' through them, 'besides many Pinnaces of Pork, Mutton, and Veal, and Flying Boats, which are Turkies, Capons, Geese and the Like'.[77] However, for all this imaginative staving-off of the cold and in turn the realities of civil war, the letter deflates towards its close to the position of fireside melancholia with which it began: 'yet for all this', she adds, 'we are Beaten into the Chimney-corner, and there we sit Shaking and Trembling like a Company of Cowards, that dare not stir from their Shelter ...'.[78] Such passages suggest a particular exilic sensibility, attempting to engage with all that is new and different in an adopted homeland, while the discursive strategies are continually permeated by what has been left behind, sacrificed or lost. In another letter, having witnessed skaters on the ice on the outskirts of the city, Cavendish retreats from the cold into her own imagination only to find that it has to a certain extent become the very ice from which she strives to escape: 'being alone to my self, I found I had a River, Lake or Moat Frozen in my Brain, into a Smooth, Glassy Ice, whereupon divers of my Thoughts were Sliding'.[79] Exile brought novel stimulation as well as stresses which contributed to Margaret Cavendish's development as an author. Katie Whitaker has pointed to the influence of the Duchess of Lorraine's salon at Beersel Castle near Brussels, while Flecknoe is another significant connection.[80]

Places were suffused with meaning during the Royalist exile, imagined and constructed as much as simply 'experienced', through the interactions of established and recent émigrés, English and continental figures. Exile had its paradoxes and contradictions; cultural and political defiance co-existed with accommodation and adjustment. Scientific, musical and literary interests cut across political and religious divisions as well as reinforcing them. John Pell was close to Samuel Hartlib as well as Charles Cavendish and claimed that the Anglo-Dutch War prompted his return to England in June 1652 (although it had clearly been in his thoughts for some time). He served the republic thereafter.[81] The relatively comfortable exile of Margaret and William Cavendish in Antwerp was made possible by the compromises with English republican regimes made by William's adult children, while Lady Stanhope's trip home to England in 1651–52 to preserve the Chesterfield estates that were the inheritance of the children of her first marriage aroused much suspicion in Royalist circles. Hyde, however, defended her against attacks by Nicholas, insisting it was not unreasonable for Heenvliet and Stanhope to maintain contact with the Cromwellian regime when the Dutch were about to make peace with them.[82] Margaret Cavendish made a similar trip to London which proved fruitless in financial terms, but most productive for the development of her literary career when participation in Henry Lawes's musical salon gatherings opened up to her a space for female creativity.[83] The Catholic Flecknoe, like the Puritan Pell, returned permanently to England, while even Elizabeth of Bohemia petitioned her brother's murderers for money.

Our research reveals a complex matrix of interactions and intersections between the epistemological categories of gender, place and exile. Changing political geographies rendered places more or less hospitable. The Anglo-Dutch War of 1652–54 made English Royalists more welcome while the peace brought dislocation. Cromwell's alliance with France and the consequent war with Spain made life difficult for some English residents even as it benefitted Royalists more generally.[84] We would also stress the importance of journeys and reunions – movements between England and continental Europe, and within the continent – in maintaining solidarity and Royalist morale. Women usually had greater freedom of movement and were especially prominent travellers between home and the continent. Epistolary networks functioned in similar ways. The letters of Elizabeth of Bohemia have been mentioned, and other examples might be the letters that Huygens wrote to Henrietta Maria in Paris and the emotional correspondence between Edward Hyde and Anne, Lady Morton (previously Lady Dalkeith), the governess to Henrietta Anne.[85] Finally, of course, England as a place of regret, nostalgia and anticipation loomed large in Royalist women's experiences as the most potent of the imagined spaces our research has sought to consider alongside real, mappable places and locations of their exile. The Leiden correspondent of *Mercurius Politicus* mocked the futile exile hopes of return in September 1651:

> the Fugitives of your Nation, they seemed to me ... to be mad drunk with healths and vain hopes, looking big after the rate of Knights and Ladies, the meanest of them; their silly credulous Landlords and Creditors believed now they should be paid all, and rid of their guests; their cry was White-Hall ho.[86]

The Stuarts' return to Whitehall in 1660 reunited exiled Royalists with all the longed-for places of England, so that Richard Flecknoe rejoiced at the imminent return of William Cavendish to the East Midlands:

> Welbeck and Bolsol shall behold again
> Their noble lord as flourishing, and more,
> Than e'er in better times he was before.[87]

Until the better times returned, female Royalists' experience of exile was structured by the distinct opportunities and cultures afforded by the different places, real and imaginary, that they inhabited in the years following defeat. In this respect, gender cannot be separated from place and space in a consideration of the experience and practice of exile. Exile undoubtedly provided for some a space of opportunity: Flecknoe's acquaintance with the Cavendishes was developed in Antwerp, rather than in the East Midlands, and Margaret

Cavendish's works of imagination, creation and publication were all made possible during her period in exile. Other less overt versions of agency can also be traced in the activities of wives, sisters, and mothers, renting rooms, finding employment, arranging baptisms and writing letters. The agency of women at this more quotidian level was clearly fostered by the support and position of Princess Mary and Elizabeth of Bohemia, whose networks of patronage and correspondence created a space for it. Even the more negative aspects of exile for women of all ages and status, the penury and hardship occasioned sometimes by separation from more patriarchal mentors or supporters, in turn required responses of survival and defiance, which were often made possible by engagement with, and often the direct support of, other women. If place conditioned different experiences of exile in the 1650s, then it is equally clear that the response to and understanding of those places was inflected and shaped by gender.

NOTES

1 *Mercurius Politicus*, 33 (16–23 Jan. 1651), p. 540.

2 Hence the common use in the seventeenth century as now of 'Holland' as the description for the whole of the Netherlands. The proper early modern term is 'United Provinces'.

3 Koninklijk Huisarchief, The Hague, Archief Prins Willem III, A16.1.3, fols A1r–E1r. The account in English newsbooks may be derived from this Dutch account. The British Academy awarded us a small grant in 2004–06, which supported research in continental archives. We are grateful to them and to all the libraries and archives that provided assistance in Breda, Middelburg, The Hague, Antwerp and Brussels.

4 Herbert H. Rowen, *The Princes of Orange: The Stadholders in the Dutch Republic* (Cambridge, 1988), pp. 84–94, 99–101.

5 Ann Hughes and Julie Sanders, 'The Hague courts of Elizabeth of Bohemia and Mary Stuart: theatrical and ceremonial cultures', *Early Modern Literary Studies*, Special Issue 15 (Aug. 2007), pp. 1–23; Ann Hughes and Julie Sanders, 'Disruptions and evocations of family amongst Royalist exiles', in Philip Major (ed.), *Exile in the English Revolution and its Aftermath, 1640–1685*, forthcoming.

6 Geoffrey Smith, *The Cavaliers in Exile, 1640–1660* (Basingstoke, 2003), p. 132.

7 Cf. James Knowles's comment that the 'complex appeal to different audiences in different places' is fundamental to any understanding of interactions between Royalist exiles and English culture in the 1650s'. '"We've lost, should we lose too our harmless mirth?" Cavendish's Antwerp entertainments', in Ben van Beneden and Nora de Poorter (eds), *Royalist Refugees: William and Margaret Cavendish in the Rubens House 1648–1660* (Antwerp, 2006), p. 77.

8 *Ibid., passim*; Marika Keblusek, '"A divertissement of little plays": Theater aan de Haagse hoven van Elizabeth van Bohemen en Mary Stuart', in Jan de Jongst, Juliette Roding and Boukje Thijs (eds), *Vermaak van de elite in de vroegmoderne tijd* (Hilversum, 1999), pp. 190–202; Hughes and Sanders, 'The Hague courts of Elizabeth of Bohemia and

Mary Stuart', *passim*; Lisa Jardine, *Going Dutch: How England Plundered Holland's Glory* (London: Harper Collins, 2008), pp 85–6, 188–92.

9 Peter Davidson and Adriaan van der Weel (eds), *A Selection of the Poems of Sir Constantijn Huygens (1596–1687)* (Amsterdam, 1996), p. 198. The letter is quoted in part in Jardine, *Going Dutch*, p. 174.

10 Alastair Bellany, 'Killigrew, Sir Robert (1579/80–1633)', *Oxford DNB*; A.G.R. Bachrach, 'The role of the Huygens family in seventeenth-century Dutch culture', in H.J.M. Bos et al. (eds), *Studies on Christiaan Huygens* (Lisse, 1980), pp. 27–52; Davidson and van der Weel (eds), *A Selection of the Poems*, pp. 15–23. Huygens is a central focus for Jardine, *Going Dutch*; see, for example, pp. 91–8, 110–12, 166–8.

11 KB, KA 46, fol. 45r. We are grateful to Jason McElligott for discussions of the language used here.

12 Davidson and van der Weel (eds), *A Selection of the Poems*, p. 212.

13 Maarten Prak, *The Dutch Republic in the Seventeenth Century: The Golden Age*, trans. Diane Webb (Cambridge, 2005), pp. 250–1; Olaf Mörke, 'The Orange court as centre of political and social life during the Republic', in Marika Keblusek and Jori Zijlmans (eds), *Princely Display: The Court of Frederick Henry of Orange and Amalia van Solms in The Hague* (The Hague, 1997), pp. 58–104.

14 *NP*, vol. I, p. 118.

15 Marika Keblusek, 'The Bohemian court at The Hague', in Keblusek and Zijlmans (eds), *Princely Display*, pp. 47–57.

16 *CCISP*, vol. II, pp. 119, 137, 156, 196, 218, 231, 296, 355; see also Hughes and Sanders, 'Disruptions and evocations of family'.

17 *CCISP*, vol. II, pp. 298, 139, 149; *NP*, vol. I, pp. 299, 308; William Bray (ed.), *Diary and Correspondence of John Evelyn* (n.d), p. 828. Among her male household Nicholas Oudart, who had served Sir Edward Nicholas before becoming Mary's secretary, was a trusted figure: *NP*, vol. I, p. 133.

18 Sarah Poynting, 'Stanhope, Katherine, *suo jure* Countess of Chesterfield and Lady Stanhope (*bap.* 1609, *d.* 1667)', *Oxford DNB*.

19 *CCISP*, vol. II, p. 340.

20 Davidson and van der Weel (eds), *A Selection of the Poems*, p. 196.

21 *TSP*, vol. I, pp. 185, 189–90. A similar attempt to get her interests included in the peace negotiations of 1653–54 was contemptuously rebuffed by the Dutch: *ibid.*, pp. 546, 558.

22 *NP*, vol. I, pp. 280 (Nov. 1651), 318 (Nov. 1652).

23 *Ibid.*, vol. II, p. 182 (Feb. 1655).

24 Nadine Akkerman, 'The letters of Elizabeth Stuart, Electress Palatine of the Rhine, and Queen of Bohemia: a scholarly edition of the years 1632–42' (PhD dissertation, Free University of Amsterdam, 2008).

25 KB, 121 A11 (4).

26 Smith, *Cavaliers in Exile*, pp. 72–3; Bray (ed.), *Diary and Correspondence of John Evelyn*, pp. 831–2, 835.

27 *CCISP*, vol. II, p. 246.

28 *TSP*, vol. I, pp. 672, 675.

29 *Ibid.*, vol. I, p. 700.

30 KB, 121 A11 (4), esp. (4), ii, 18 Mar. 1653, and iii; Bray (ed.), *Diary and Correspondence of John Evelyn*, pp. 828–9.

31 KB, 121 A11 (4), v, vi, Jan. 1654; *CClSP*, vol. II, pp. 288, 175.

32 *TSP*, vol. I, p. 674; *CClSP*, vol. II, p. 328.

33 Jason Peacey, 'Order and disorder in Europe: parliamentary agents and Royalist thugs', *HJ*, 40 (1997), pp. 953–76.

34 *Mercurius Politicus*, 43 (27 Mar.–3 Apr. 1651), p. 696.

35 *Ibid.*, 45 (10–17 Apr. 1651), pp. 724–6, 728–9.

36 *Ibid.*, 44 (3–10 Apr. 1651), pp. 713–15.

37 *Ibid.*, 44 (3–10 Apr. 1651), pp. 713–15; 45 (10–17 Apr. 1651), pp. 724–6; 50 (15–22 May 1651), p. 809.

38 *Ibid.*, 45 (10–17 Apr. 1651), pp. 724–6.

39 Bray (ed.), *Diary and Correspondence of John Evelyn*, p. 836; cf. a similar account sent to Charles II, *TSP*, vol. I, pp. 674–5.

40 *NP*, vol. I, p. 118.

41 Keith Sprunger, *Dutch Puritanism: A History of English and Scottish Churches of the Netherlands in the Sixteenth and Seventeenth Centuries* (Leiden, 1982), pp. 152–3.

42 *TSP*, vol. I, p. 672 (Dec. 1655); Hughes and Sanders, 'The Hague courts of Elizabeth of Bohemia and Mary Stuart'.

43 Sprunger, *Dutch Puritanism*, pp. 155–6, 382–3; W.P.C. Knuttel, *Acta der Particuliere Synoden van Zuid-Holland 1621–1700* (The Hague, 1910), vol. III, pp. 228, 278.

44 Sprunger, *Dutch Puritanism*, pp. 145, 152–3, 156, 257–8, 387; A.G. Matthews, *Walker Revised* (Oxford, 1988), pp. 58, 156, 377–8.

45 *Mercurius Politicus*, 154 (19–26 May 1653), p. 2467; *TSP*, vol. I, p. 487.

46 Bodl., Clarendon MS 31, fol. 232r.

47 Zeeuws Archief, Middelburg, Engelse Gemeende, Inv. 1721/43, 44: accounts of the English church, 1644–52, 1652–60 (unfoliated). There are also records of many donations to casualties of continental conflicts.

48 Sprunger, *Dutch Puritanism*, pp. 210, 203.

49 Zeeuws Archief, Middelburg, Engelse Gemeende, Inv. 1721/4.

50 *Ibid.*, Inv. 1721/7: register book of marriages, baptisms and church members of the English community, 1624–1721 (unfoliated).

51 Nicholas Carlisle, *An Inquiry into the Place and Quality of the Gentlemen of his Majesty's Most Honourable Privy Chamber* (1829), p. 168; William Steven, *The History of the Scottish Church, Rotterdam* (Edinburgh, 1833), p. 323. Alethia's brother Sir Robert Carey had fought in Dutch armies and married a Dutch woman.

52 Breda was some thirty-five miles from Antwerp, fifty miles from The Hague and sixty-five from Middelburg.

53 Stadsarchief Breda, Inv. I/1^A/14, register book of the Breda magistrates, fols 256v, 270r, 282r, 289r (trans. from the Dutch).

54 Nationaal Archief, The Hague, Nassause Domeinraad, 1581–1811, 1.08.11/7951, fol. 476r: letter from Kerkhoven (Heenvliet) to Professor van Renesse in Breda from The Hague, 2 Dec. 1653. We are grateful to Alice Cust Hughes for help with the Dutch.

55 *CClSP*, vol. II, pp. 275, 298.

56 Nationaal Archief, The Hague, Nassause Domeinraad, 1581–1811, 1.08.11/7951, fol. 477r.

57 *Ibid.*, fol. 487r. See also A. Hallema, 'De Oranjevorsten en het voormalige Norberti-nesseklooster St Catharinadal en Breda in de zeventiende en achtiende eeuwen 1646–1740)', *Jaarboek 'De Oranjeboom'*, 14 (1961), pp. 115–48, at p. 117. We are grateful to the staff of the Stadsarchief Breda for their assistance with this research.

58 Nationaal Archief, The Hague, Nassause Domeinraad, 1581–1811, 1.08.11/7951, fol. 479r. See also Hallema, 'De Oranjevorsten', p. 125.

59 Paul Seaward, 'Hyde, Edward, First Earl of Clarendon (1609–1674)', *Oxford DNB*.

60 *TSP*, vol. I, p 664.

61 Noel Malcolm and Jacqueline Stedall, *John Pell (1611–1685) and his Correspondence with Sir Charles Cavendish* (Oxford, 2005), pp. 4, 121–30.

62 Sprunger, *Dutch Puritanism*, pp. 181, 272–3.

63 D.J.B. Trim, 'Ogle, Sir John (*bap.* 1569, *d.* 1640)', *Oxford DNB*; Malcolm and Stedall, *John Pell*, pp. 129–30; Lynn Hulse, 'Amorous in music', in van Beneden and de Poorter (eds), *Royalist Refugees*, pp. 84–6. For Swann and Huygens see also Jardine, *Going Dutch*, pp. 163–6, 198.

64 Davidson and Van der Weel (eds), *A Selection of the Poems*, p. 143 ('Hofwijk', esp. lines 403–10).

65 Newcastle's mother was an Ogle.

66 *CClSP*, vol. II, p. 149; see also Bodl., Clarendon MS 37, fol. 86r–v, 1649, for the Hyde and Aylesbury families; Lynn Hulse, 'Amorous in music', pp. 83–9, esp. pp. 84, 86.

67 Ursula Härting, 'Inhabitants of Antwerp: "The civilest and best-behaved people that I saw"', in van Beneden and de Poorter (eds), *Royalist Refugees*, pp. 63–9, esp. p. 68; Jardine, *Going Dutch*, pp. 175–8.

68 Hulse, 'Amorous in music', p. 84; see Bray (ed.), *Diary and Correspondence of John Evelyn*, pp. 83–4 for links to Elizabeth.

69 AGR, I 112/199, Archives du Conseil d'Etat, diplomatic correspondence with England, 21 Oct. 1655.

70 Bray (ed.), *Diary and Correspondence of John Evelyn*, pp. 833–4; Lucy Worsley, Ursula Harting and Marika Keblusek, 'Horsemanship', in van Beneden and de Poorter (eds), *Royalist Refugees*, p. 53; Ursula Harting, 'Inhabitants of Antwerp', in van Beneden and de Poorter (eds), *Royalist Refugees*, p. 66.

71 Smith, *Cavaliers in Exile*, p. 80.

72 Ilja van Damme, 'A City in Transition: Antwerp after 1648', in van Beneden and de Poorter (eds), *Royalist Refugees*, pp. 55–62 (esp. pp. 55–6); Worsley, Harting and Keblusek, 'Horsemanship'; see also catalogue entries on pp. 182–3, 220–3.

73 For more detailed accounts see James Knowles, 'Cavendish's Antwerp entertainments', pp. 70–7, and Lynn Hulse, 'Amorous in music', in van Beneden and de Poorter (eds), *Royalist Refugees*, pp. 81–9.

74 Harting, 'Inhabitants of Antwerp', pp. 66–7; Jardine, *Going Dutch*, pp. 195–8.

75 C.H. Firth (ed.), *The Life of William Cavendish, Duke of Newcastle* (1906), p. 50.

76 Margaret Cavendish, *Sociable Letters*, ed. James Fitzmaurice (New York, 2004), p. 256.

77 *Ibid.*, p. 257.

78 *Ibid.*, p. 257.

79 *Ibid.*, p. 258.

80 Katie Whitaker, *Mad Madge: Margaret Cavendish, Duchess of Newcastle, Royalist, Writer and Romantic* (2002), pp. 122–4.

81 Malcolm and Stedall, *John Pell*, pp. 136–7.

82 For the Cavendishes see Hughes and Sanders, 'Disruptions and evocations of family'; for Stanhope, see *CClSP*, vol. II, pp. 327, 340, and Poynting, 'Stanhope, Katherine'.

83 Hero Chalmers, 'Dismantling the myth of "Mad Madge": the cultural context of Margaret Cavendish's authorial self-presentation', *Women's Writing*, 4 (1997), pp. 323–39.

84 AGR, I 112/1829, proceedings with 'etrangers'.

85 For Huygens see KB, KA 46, fols 75–6, 89–90 (Feb.–Mar. 1651); for Hyde-Morton see, for example, Bodl., Clarendon MS 28, fol. 292; Clarendon MS 38, fol. 11r–v; Clarendon MS 39, fol. 111r.

86 *Mercurius Politicus*, 69 (25 Sept.–2 Oct. 1651), p. 1101.

87 Flecknoe, 'The portrait of William, Marquis of Newcastle' (1660), quoted in Whitaker, *Mad Madge*, p. 239; see Linda Levy Peck, *Consuming Splendor: Society and Culture in Seventeenth-Century England* (Cambridge, 2005), p. 229 on the importance of house and 'home' to exiled Royalists.

Chapter 8

Dramatis personae: royalism, theatre and the political ontology of the person in post-Regicide writing

James Loxley

I

On 28 June 1660, the officially appointed thanksgiving day for 'His Majesties Happy Return to His Kingdoms', William Towers delivered a sermon during the service held at Exeter House, London.[1] The son of one of 'the most combative of Laudian bishops' and a participant in proto-Royalist and Royalist activities as both a cleric and a writer during the 1630s and 1640s, Towers had lost his preferments fourteen years previously.[2] Like others of his stripe, he had relied since the defeat of the Royalist cause on the support of sympathisers still able to offer patronage, yet he was now on his way to renewed institutional preferment as a result of the restored political power of Mountjoy Blunt, the Earl of Newport.[3] Among his other patrons he counted James Compton, the third Earl of Northampton, whose father Spencer, the second earl, had died a Royalist hero at Hopton Heath in March 1643. James Compton's own royalism and literary interests led him to support a number of similarly inclined writers and actors during the 1650s.[4] The patronage of the Compton family had previously benefited William's father John – indeed, William himself was probably named after the first earl, while two of his siblings bore the names Spencer and Compton.

Unsurprisingly, his sermon that June was a steadfast reiteration of Royalist principles. Towers took as his text the beginning of the first verse of Psalm 21, 'The King shall joy in thy strength, O Lord', and developed out of this text an argument summarised emphatically in the sermon's title as printed: *Obedience Perpetually due to KINGS, Because the KINGLY POWER Is Inseperable from the ONE King's Person.*[5] Here, at the monarchy's moment of triumph, one of its long-toothed partisans took the opportunity to insist once more on an article of Royalist faith that had shared in that institution's trials since Charles I had been turned away from the gates of Hull in 1642. For Towers,

149

the restoration of the monarchy permitted or called for the renewed resort to a Royalist language of personal rule that had been the subject of explicit challenge throughout the ideological and military struggles of the 1640s and early 1650s. Its particular anatomy of kingship could again be affirmed as scripturally supported doctrine:

> The *Power* of the King is, in Scripture-stile the very same with the King, his *Authority* and his *Person* but *one, one and the same,* so little can his authority be *virtually* (or any otherwise then *viciously*) be [*sic*] *evangelically* pretended against the commands of his *Person*.[6]

What the Parliamentarians and their successors had sundered and destroyed could now be reasserted, and proclaiming it thus would produce the containment of a certain kind of drama, a kind that Royalists like Towers were presumably keen to see restored to its proper place:

> Either *power* is perpetually in his *Person*, or the authority of a King is devolvable upon some other, *one* or *more* persons; if upon *one*, then there may be *a King and no King* upon the *Throne*, as well as upon the *Stage*; there may be a King upon earth, which, upon the same spot of earth, hath a King above him, and who would not hisse at the man that should say so?[7]

In this passage, Towers's reference to Francis Beaumont and John Fletcher's archetypal tragicomedy and evocation of a theatrical situation is entwined with the resonant issue of the 'personality' of authority. The implication of his claim is that the monarch's person must serve as a singular locus of sovereign power, and in doing so can hold together both the polity he governs and, at the same time, himself. Untune that string, and what follows is an entanglement in constitutional paradox hazardous to both king and country. It is striking that *A King and No King*, and the art form of which it was an instance, should still prove to be the mnemonic through which such issues, and such perils, are called to mind.[8] Equally interesting is the implication that the tragicomic paradoxes of monarchy give a glimpse of a form of drama that not merely is a cultural form endorsed and embraced by royalism or seen as the property of early Stuart court culture, but can also figure the standing threat of that institution's dissolution.[9] If 1660 offered the opportunity to proclaim not just the happy resolution of a tragicomic play, but also the end of a kind of tragicomic theatricality, then royalism's relation to such a drama was bound to be an awkward one.

II

The substance of this tragicomic theatre – a substance that is not necessarily to be divorced from considerations of form or genre – can be found, Towers suggests, in the politics of monarchy that his sermon seeks finally to

put beyond the reach of controversy. Such a politics is perhaps better understood as a 'political ontology',[10] an attempt to set out that which *'essentiates* a
King into the very being of a King', as Towers puts it in his sermon.[11] To talk
of political ontology in this context is inevitably to recall Ernst Kantorowicz's
influential work on 'political theology', work that sought to set out an intellectual and cultural frame not only for English renaissance drama but also for
the ideological conflicts of the 1640s.[12] Kantorowicz famously suggested that a
mythic, monarch-centred doctrine of the 'king's two bodies' was an animating
presence in English constitutional thought up to and including the debates
of the Civil War, and that it was in such a doctrinal distinction between the
monarch's 'immaterial and immortal body politic and his material and mortal
body natural' that Parliament found the constitutional rationale and justification for its armed resistance to Charles during the 1640s.[13] More recent historians have also felt justified not only in referring to such a doctrine but also
in endorsing its relevance to Civil War controversies and even to the Restoration political imagination. Not without challenge, though: others have cast
doubt on the credibility of any assertion that a theologically derived conception of kingship sat at the heart of English constitutional debate during the
early modern period.[14] To deploy a label such as 'political ontology' here is to
keep hold of some aspects of the Kantorowiczian perspective without thereby
endorsing his peculiar methodological and intellectual presuppositions.

Certainly, the question of what constitutes 'the very being of a king' was
a central point of contest in mid-seventeenth-century politics and culture. It
arose forcefully in the impassioned war of declaration and counter-declara-
tion preceding the raising of the king's standard in 1642, and animated the
different layers of disagreement in which the *Answer to the XIX Propositions*
participates. In these debates, the issue of what makes a king a king, of how
his authority is to be understood, was a prominent feature.[15] The promulgation
of the Solemn League and Covenant a year later placed a particular emphasis
on the status of the king's 'person', and required the kind of exegesis that is to
be found in works such as Samuel Rutherford's *Lex, Rex* of 1644.[16] While Rutherford's particular object was the doctrinal certitude of Bishop John Maxwell,
a wide range of variously Royalist writers and theorists sustained the debates
with definitions and arguments forged in the king's capital at Oxford.[17] After
the defeat of the Royalist armies in the field, the issues were given another
vigorous airing in the debates around Thomas Chaloner's so-called 'speech
out of doors' in 1646; later still, the king's trial for treason, the abolition of 'the
kingly office' and the proscription of Charles's elder sons, as well as the promulgation of the Engagement to the republic's new citizens, obviously required
claims about the nature of monarchy and monarchs.[18] To this extent, ontology
was an urgent business. Yet the fact that so many of these controversies were
impelled by the status of both Charles I and Charles II as kings of more than

one kingdom, that they were therefore picking up on, re-writing or reaffirming positions debated even before the union of the Scottish and English crowns and using languages other than that of English law, points to the longevity and pedigree of this discussion.[19]

This might well sound merely like a reiteration, in different terms, of Kantorowicz's model. The difference in terms is important, though: it recognises that no clearly established 'two bodies doctrine' can be found here, and that the debate about the nature of kingship is in fact a struggle to establish the validity or legitimacy of a set of terms. Indeed, to speak of political ontology is to focus on the ways in which the composite or complex notion of 'king' can be reduced, polemically and with much immediately at stake, to supposedly more primary notions or elements that might well draw on non-monarchical forms of political and more broadly philosophical thought. Far from being the most fundamental of any such notions, the body might well be only one among a number of competing alternatives. In exploring the debate in this way, historians have sometimes posited a distinction between (private) person and (public) office as an alternative to the 'two bodies' approach. [20] But in positing an assured and available distinction between person and office, they are in danger of mirroring those applications of Kantorowiczian 'two bodies' analysis which see in it a settled and more or less common-sense difference between the natural and the civil or the private and the public. One of the strengths of Kantorowicz's argument was his acknowledgment of the lability – the figurative *energeia*, to put it in terms which are not his – of the body, across both civil and natural aspects. Among the most telling aspects of Calvin's Case, an effort early in James's dual reign to establish the way in which English law would seek to interpret the polity's subsumption within a dynastic union, was a recognition from the prevailing participants that to speak of two distinct kingly bodies was perhaps heuristically viable but potentially misleading. As Francis Bacon put it, in a speech published for a fresh audience in 1641:

> The Naturall body of the King hath an operation and influence into his body politique, as well as his body politique hath upon his body Naturall, And therefore that although his body politique of King of *England*, and his body politique of King of *Scotland* be severall and distinct: Yet neverthelesse, his Naturall person, which is one, hath an operation on both, and createth a privity betweene them.[21]

Bacon is insisting on the political and constitutional force of the king's 'natural capacity', what he here also calls his 'person'. He goes on to insist on the admissibility of a 'true and legall distinction' between the two aspects of the king, arguing in effect for the legal substantiality of his person, 'for they that maintaine the contrary opinion doe in effect destroy the whole force of the Kings naturall capacity, as if it were drowned and swallowed up by his politique'.[22] Insofar as this sort of claim contributed to the winning arguments in Calvin's Case it 'repudiated both the idea of a fully abstract state and the impersonal conception of allegiance that it entailed'.[23] So the 'two bodies', if such they are, cannot simply be counterposed to each other: for monarchs at least (and Bacon maintains that the 'Crowne utterly differeth from all other corporations within the Realme'[24]), the personal is also political, or civil, or constitutional. Royalist heirs of this element in the Baconian position are drawn to the same kinds of claims, just as their opponents are driven to find ways in which certain of the king's actions or utterances might be effectively stripped of legal or political force. The debate in which they are participating is in part a debate about whether, as well as how, any such distinction between natural and politic capacities can be upheld.

What, then, of a person–office distinction? Clearly, as Sarah Barber has demonstrated, it can be articulated and it has its uses.[25] She shows how the capacity to draw such a distinction specifically with reference to the Crown enabled Thomas Chaloner and Henry Marten to challenge the terms on which the Scots commissioners based their claims about what to do with the defeated king in 1646. For Chaloner, this is a philosophical question, a matter of logic or definition. As he argues:

> Remember, this word King is of a various signification, sometimes it is taken in *abstracto*, that is for the Royall power, Function and office of a King, sometimes it is taken in *Concreto*, that is for the man or person whom we call King.[26]

Going on to talk of the royal office in terms that do in fact resemble Kantorowicz's account of the 'king body politic', Chaloner is nonetheless keen to strip this figure of any essential relation to a 'man or person' and in so doing to produce an account of a much-diminished Scots king in particular. And as Barber points out, the fact that this version of kingship can cite in its support Rutherford's *Lex, Rex* – a canonical document of Scots Presbyterian political thought – makes it all the sweeter for the Scotophobic Chaloner.[27] It is from Rutherford that the apparently logical and legal distinction between the abstract (official) and the concrete (personal) king most immediately descends, 'an evident and sensible distinction' although 'rejected by Royalists'.[28]

Yet the fact of and basis for its rejection, beyond the 'operation and influence' between capacities asserted by Bacon, are worth noting. A dispute over whether 'abstract' and 'concrete' can be mapped on to person and office in this way forms a minor theme in the controversy over Chaloner's speech, with pamphlets in his defence suggesting that 'this distinction of *Abstractum* and *Concretum* is as ancient as Logicke it selfe' and denouncing those 'pedantick people' who would quibble at it.[29] Opponents, by contrast, insisted that the alignment of 'concrete' and 'person' offended against the very logic to which Chaloner's defenders appealed, and John Cleveland reiterated this objection in his *Character of a Country Committee-man* when he described the notion of '*persona in concreto*' as 'the Solecisme of a moderne Statesman'.[30] Such objections amount to more than the pedantry of an overly precise Latinist, though: instead they assert the rather more fundamental claim that office is by definition personal. As Conal Condren has demonstrated, in early modern languages of duty or social role a 'persona' is precisely the form of an office, not its natural, merely human or extra-civil substrate, and therefore cannot without logical strain be defined against it.[31] At the same time, a political 'persona' could not simply be differentiated from 'some authentic residuum of selves and individuals left over from a limited, usually political world of office'.[32] To speak of person and office, therefore, was not to articulate an accepted and stable opposition of kinds, but instead to invoke concepts that could be seen both as contrasting and overlapping.

Consequently, it would be an error to suggest that a person–office distinction presents a clear alternative to the arcana of 'two bodies' theory as a language for making sense of kingship, or that republican and anti-Royalist political actors could simply use such a two-handed engine to break the spell of mystical monarchy. In Kantorowicz's account, the term 'body' coincides with the word 'king' in extending across the levels of the political and the natural, confounding or articulating them even as it is marked by their difference, opening law on to a sense of the political that exceeds it. It therefore situates kingship as the keystone in the grand arch of constitutional thought.[33] Chaloner and Rutherford recognise that much is at stake here: their logical straightening-out of these confusions, and their suggestion that the difficulty is indeed a matter of logic, seek to master both the word and the power that appears to come with it. Subsequent efforts at working out what a king is, as Joad Raymond has shown, continue to be marked by this ambition.[34] But the perils of the term 'person', perils to which such efforts at conceptual mastery are still exposed, are if anything even more awkward. Here, in a concept to which that of 'king' is held to be reducible, we find the same instabilities. They mark the subsequent debates leading up to and out of the Regicide, and have often been contextualised in a narrative of the development of an 'impersonal' state.[35] Yet the analyses of the ideological turmoil around the beginning of the 1650s also show just how fraught these fundamental concepts could be. In the movement from condemning a bad king to condemning the institution of monarchy itself, in refusing any longer to distinguish between kings and tyrants, regicides and incipient republicans share this sense of a failure of distinction between person and office. If, as Barber puts it, 'the collapse of confidence in the person facilitated a critique of the office which that person had fulfilled', then the critique participated in the very flaw it was attempting to extirpate.[36]

In this, some of the difficulties attendant on the demand for a conception of office defined against the personal, and aligned therefore with a distinction between the public and the private destined to be in its own way difficult for Western political thought, become apparent. It is not an unproblematic enterprise even for the staunchest champions of the Regicide and the abolition of the kingly office. *The Tenure of Kings and Magistrates*, for example, presents a fundamental re-writing – or writing-out – of kingship, while forcefully attacking Presbyterian critics of the proceedings against the king in particular. So the tract presents its own critique of monarchy, while accusing the Presbyterians of inconsistency or incoherence in their own actions and utterances. To this end, Milton follows Rutherford in anchoring the distinction between person and office in the logical difference between 'concrete' and 'abstract', and cleaves too to the implications of such a distinction for the understanding of kingship.[37] At the same time, he also shares Chaloner's hostility to the Presbyterian regard for the royal person expressed in the Solemn League and Covenant. Again like Chaloner, he attempts to defeat his opponents by arguing not only that the actions they most abhor are in fact justified by their own doctrines, but also that according to their own definitions of monarchy they have long since deposed the very king whose fate they now bewail. In a rhetorically complex move, Milton borrows the Presbyterians' affect as well as quoting their arguments in turning their horror at the Regicide against them, while simultaneously mimicking a Royalist horror at their accomplishments in the years between 1641 and 1647. This ambitious strategy, though, leads him into his own difficulties. To argue that those 'who by deposing him have long since tak'n from him the life of a King, his office and his dignity … in the truest sence may be said to have killd the King' is to emphasise as its 'truest sence' a startlingly personalised, vitalist understanding of the kingly office that would sound unsurprising coming from Shakespeare's Richard II.[38] A king deposed is not just a man out of office, since he has lost his 'true life'; in stripping Charles of 'all that could be in him of a King', the Presbyterians 'left in his person, dead as to Law, and all the civil right either of King or Subject, the life onely of a Prisner, a Captive and a Malefactor'.[39] Here, the abstractions of authority or office are to be talked of in the personal terms of life and death, and what exists beyond office is not so much a person as 'an underspecified residuum', as Condren puts it, a '"private" person' – if 'private' here carries the familiar sense, as it does for Milton in this passage, of privation or deprivation – 'or a pillar of salt'; yet when earlier Milton charges the Presbyterians with having covenanted to preserve only 'the meere useless bulke of his person', his language suggests instead that such lumpen concretion, 'dead as to Law', is what a person is.[40]

So Milton's polemical intervention was itself caught in urgent political debate that continued to require the assertion of different claims regarding the political status of personhood, but whose participants could not easily climb free of the problems they were addressing. In the subsequent exchanges

over the Oath of Engagement, the republic's opponents insisted on the inter-
mingling of the constitutional and natural entities that the oath's proponents
are trying to hold apart: the nature of allegiance, title, and lawful succession
demonstrate for them that the 'politic capacities' of both ruler and subject
are intelligible and practicable only through natural or personal relations. To
insist that the king never dies is not in this context to conjure up an abstract
dignitas or *universitas* that might then be counterposed to a natural or personal
existence, a separation between office and office-holder, but instead to situate
the civil bond of allegiance back before all ceremonies or oaths: 'he is our
natural Lord, his person is King'.[41] Kings and subjects are born, not made.
At the same time, though, the significance for this debate of *de facto* thinking
ensures that the oath's opponents have to posit a new division between 'Naturall or Corporall possession', the *de facto* power of the new republic, and the
'Civill possession' or proper title still maintained by the young king.[42] If, then,
'the problems of separating, or conceptually distinguishing, man from office
[were] a constant for the troubled Stuart dynasty', they were not necessarily
less of a problem either for its strongest supporters or for its opponents.[43]

It is this context that can perhaps shed some light on Hobbes's attempt
in *Leviathan* to fix the place of the person within what he calls civil science,
an attempt that highlights one of the prime sources of its conceptual instability. In the last chapter of book I, he re-writes the political significance of
the person in order to resolve etymologically the 'proper signification' of the
word, in tune with his customary method, and in so doing to find a way past
the confusions of personhood in the political theories of others. The concept
of the person becomes the means through which 'authorisation' takes place,
a way of introducing substitution or representation into politics. Thus he sets
up a distinction between an author, the locus of responsibility for any action,
and an actor, who carries out an action in the other's name. At the same time,
he introduces a difference between 'natural' and 'artificial' persons, and these
distinctions could be lined up with each other to produce yet another account
of a personhood distributed or differentiated across distinct natural and politic
levels. No wonder, then, that 'it has come to be widely agreed that Hobbes's
distinction between natural and artificial persons is equivalent to the distinction between represented persons and their representatives', as Quentin
Skinner has claimed.[44]

Such a position, though, would not necessarily amount to a resolution
of any of the convoluted distensions of personhood already evidenced here.
Simply asserting that some persons are able to represent others does not in
fact even register such difficulties. Suggesting that political representatives
inhabit a personhood that is somehow artificial, though, does begin to do so:
we return, it seems, to a distinction between kinds of bodies, like the contrast
between concrete and abstract kings. More food for thought is offered by

Skinner's subtle and 'hermeneutically daring' reading, in which this sense of the relation between natural and artificial is combined with another running counter to it:

> Natural persons convert themselves into artificial persons ... by agreeing to be represented in different ways. But natural persons who agree to serve as representatives also convert themselves into artificial persons, since the act of making such an agreement is at the same time the act of turning oneself from a private individual into a public person discharging a recognised role.[45]

In this version, the artifice can reside at either end of the relation between represented and representative. One possibility is that the representative can be an entity defined within the language of personhood without thereby being a person as such. So the magistrate or the king might act in a certain way, demonstrating or using certain capacities, but does not do so as a person in his or her own right. The familiar Civil War argument that tyrants are monarchs who exceed the bounds of their trust, able to blur an important distinction between their own powers and property and those of the office they exercise because of a shared language of persons, depends on just such a sense of artificial personhood. Milton's critique of the role accorded by the *Eikon Basilike*'s Charles to his own conscience is an attempt to insist that in Stuart practice the artificial personhood of the monarch had been denied, neglected or over-ridden.[46] An alternative interpretation suggests that the personhood of the represented is artificial when it is that of a corporate or institutional entity such as a church, hospital or bridge – to cite Hobbes's own examples – which has a representative to act or speak on its behalf, as if he or she were acting for another person. In Skinner's reading, the Hobbesian state combines these ways of being artificial: it is marked both by the artifice of the representative, in that it is the corporate entity or agent created by the coming together of a multitude, and by that of the represented, insofar as it empowers a sovereign to act on its behalf.[47] Artificial personhood, then, would appear to be the condition that obtains under conditions of representation, and both this and natural personhood are unthinkable outside an already civil society that has established property relations. Natural persons, Hobbes avers, are those who own and represent themselves, who act in their own right and behalf; as soon as they enter into the relation of representation with another, separating an actor from the behalf on which he acts, they are variously affected by artifice. Under the concept of subjective right or entitlement, representation and authorisation coincide.

Working within this frame, Hobbes strives to trace all instances of artificial personhood, however configured, back to an origin in a natural, self-authorising person, and in his doing so the significance of property or dominion becomes particularly evident. A representative who acts for a hospital is in fact ultimately representing a natural person who has authorised that representative. The same, Hobbes suggests, goes for 'Children, Fooles, and Mad-men that have no use of Reason': their personhood is underpinned by that of 'he that hath right of governing them'. Hobbes also acknowledges that 'an Idol, or meer Figment of the brain' has at times 'held Possessions, and other Goods, and Rights' and thus been treated as a person. But 'Idols cannot be Authors; for an Idol is nothing'. Therefore, 'the Authority proceeded from the State'.[48] All of these persons are ultimately backed by other persons, whose status as their masters or guardians, and therefore as authors of other's actions, is made possible by the existence of 'Civill Government'.

Hobbes's containment of representation within the context of dominion, and of the concept of the person within the frame of representation, is perhaps a response to the various significations that the word 'person' carries in the debates of his own time. But the etymological account of the person that Hobbes gives at the beginning of chapter 16 points to problems with this attempt to configure its meaning. Here he remarks on an origin to which Rutherford's and Chaloner's quibbling opponents made implicit reference:

> The word Person is latine: insteed whereof the Greeks have προσωπον, which signi-fies the *Face*, as *Persona* in latine signifies the *disguise* or *outward appearance* of a man, counterfeited on the Stage: and sometimes more particularly that part of it which disguiseth the face, as a Mask or Vizard: And from the Stage, hath been trans-lated to any Representer of speech and action, as well in Tribunalls, as Theaters. So that a *Person*, is the same that an *Actor* is, both on the Stage and in common Conversation; and to *Personate* is to *Act*, or *Represent* himselfe, or an other, and he that acteth another, is said to beare his Person, or act in his name.[49]

This invocation of a theatrical origin is crucial in revealing the fundamental complexities in the notion of the person that Hobbes is seeking to untangle. The fact that his account is still capable of generating such contrasting read-ings three and a half centuries later suggests that this resort to etymology cannot quite do the job he wants. For a start, associating the person with the outward appearance, mask and even disguise implies that personhood is much more the property of the representative than of the represented. The association of person with actor merely confirms this, as does the apparently parallel suggestion that personating is acting, but the following claim that to act another is 'to bear his person' appears to complicate matters again. In this sense, personation is the process of bearing another person, from another time or place: it is carried across in the action of the actor, animates his face with its own.

But if a person is an actor, then personation is the process of actively ascribing the quality of personhood to something which does not neces-sarily have it, being inanimate, notional or dead – the process or trope of personification, what Greek and Renaissance rhetoricians call *prosopopeia* – or that of giving personhood to something which, like the god represented by an idol or a character represented in a play, 'is nothing'. Personhood is not derived from a source and 'borne' by an actor: it is what the actor brings to the process of representation. Such an understanding is encouraged by Hobbes's own reference in the chapter's opening sentence to persons as 'fiction'. As Skinner notes, he returns to this topic in *De Homine*, explicitly linking ficti-tious persons to the characters played by actors on stage:

> For it was understood in the ancient theatre that not the player himself but someone else was speaking, for example Agamemnon, namely when the player, putting on the false face [*faciem fictitiam*] of Agamemnon, was for the time being Agamemnon. At a later stage, however, this was understood to be so even in the absence of the mask, namely when the actor declared publicly which character [*personam*] he was going to play.[50]

This passage clearly indicates some of the tangles of this theatrical notion of personhood (evident perhaps in its avoidance of the word 'persona' for 'mask', confining it to what we would call 'character'; to use it for both, as might be expected, would precisely risk confusion). On the one hand, the actor is a substratum who does not speak for himself, bearing the person of Agamemnon. Actors are not persons; they 'personate', and persons are what they play in doing so. On the other hand, the character is nothing unless given personhood by the actor – Agamemnon is only a character or part to be personated by someone else, a fiction. Most importantly, he and other stage characters evade the frame of authorisation: Hanna Pitkin was there-fore right to suggest that the theatrical example was an awkward model for Hobbes's theory of representation.[51] Skinner argues that the English profes-sional theatre's dependence on government authorisation before 1642 and its subsequent prohibition by Parliament demonstrate the model's fitness for Hobbes's purposes.[52] But as Hobbes might be expected to know, especially given the aptitude and fondness for both professional and non-professional drama demonstrated by his patrons, the Cavendish family, not all performance required such authorisation in order to take place.[53] And there is anyway a manifest difference between playing the part of Agamemnon and performing with the authority of the master of the revels: it is to the former, dramaturgical capability that Hobbes looks in order to make sense of political representation, not the latter. To attempt to explain authorisation via an instance of authorisa-tion would simply be to beg the question.

So the theatrical sense of the person is a problem, and its problematic nature appears perhaps most fully in the Hobbesian claim that personating can be playing oneself as well as another, especially given the potentially worrying conjunction of face and disguise in the conjunction of 'persona' and *prosopon*.[54] If the natural person is here an actor playing himself, then a natural person is as much constituted through the activity of personation as the artificial, and matters become as potentially comic, and in this context disturbing, as when Dick Robinson is substituted for himself in Jonson's *The Devil is an Ass*, or when any boy played a girl playing a boy on the pre-war English stage.[55] Nature, too, depends on the artifice of representation: the figure whose person the actor bears cannot ever appear as such, and all the world shares in the ontology of the stage. What is queried here is the claim that Hobbes makes so forcefully in the cases of bridges, madmen and idols: that there is an apparently necessary and ultimately apparent relation to an original, authorial instance of the person in all personation. The fundamental reason why this is hard to maintain is that the concept and the dramatic inheritance to which Hobbes appeals in fact posits personation as a transformative process in which personhood can be both given and taken.[56] The constitution even of natural persons through this process ensures that even in the last instance personhood might be not the ground but the effect of representation, and might therefore always be fictional. Hobbes's recourse to the concept of the person is not the resolution, but rather another instance, of the mid-century difficulties afflicting the thinking of a politically significant personhood.

III

In seeking an explanation in the theatrical experience or rendering of personhood, however, Hobbes demonstrates one of the more striking ways in which this art influenced the political imagination of both Royalists and their opponents. His sense of the relevance of theatre and his investment in an understanding of what happens in performance reveal how the essential characteristics of an art, and issues of artistic form, are interwoven with pressing and fundamental political problems. Such claims are familiar enough in criticism of Shakespearean and early seventeenth-century drama, particularly in relation to the issue of kingship, and a range of critics have explored the ways in which, after 1642, drama and political upheaval are bound together in ways which make the former much more than a mirror in which events are reflected.[57] What can be noted here, though, is the particular, dense conjunction around the beginning of the 1650s of events and their narratives, theatre and theatricality, and pressing demands on the politics of personhood. And the drama of this short period, as much as the political and philosophical writing of Hobbes and Milton, participates in this conjunction.

The narrative of royal fortunes in these years often meets in parts the generic patterns familiar from dramatic exemplars. By late 1651, Charles I and his two eldest sons had all taken to disguise at some point in the previous five years in order to negotiate a path through dangerous circumstances, and in so doing had fitted themselves to the model of the disguised hero of romance, comedy and tragicomedy. Unsurprisingly, this conduct finds an echo in the dramatic writing of the period, especially that which is coloured by Royalist sympathies or permits their articulation. At the beginning of Act 3 of John Tatham's *The Distracted State*, supposedly written in 1641 but published in 1650, the 'Vanquish'd king' Evander comes on stage for the first time and introduces himself in a manner that points up the consonance between his and Stuart circumstances:

> Pursu'd by my bad Fate, whose Cruelty
> I knew would not admit of any Mean
> Should it once seize on me, I struck my self
> Into Disguise ...

His friend Missellus offers him counsel, urging him:

> be but pleas'd to suffer
> Under this Clowd awhile, and you'l appear
> More glorious to your Peoples eyes and hearts,
> When time presents a fitness for discovery.[58]

The language is in some ways conventional, of course, but it chimes with the way in which Charles I's 'clouded majesty' had been framed and described in the later 1640s.[59] In Cosmo Manuche's play *The Just General*, published in 1652, the flight of King Amasius is described in terms that recall the circumstances of Charles I's second escape, from Hampton Court in 1647:

> Antonio: These stormes presage no good. The
> Generall now arrived at Court,
> Whose business with the King requires hast; Delirus
> With confidence conveighs him to the King his
> Closet; where when arrived, instead of King
> They found a letter with his own hand writ ...[60]

Later in the same play, Manuche includes a direct reference to the escape of the Duke of York from custody in 1648. Antonio is out looking for the disguised king, and has been examining each 'stripling of eighteen' he sees. He scruples at searching every 'handsome gentlewoman', though with some reservations; as he says, it is 'now in fashion for Princes to make scapes in / Womens habit'.[61] Given Manuche's own past as a Royalist combatant, and the play's dedication to his patron, the Earl of Northampton, this might seem an unlikely or uncomfortable topic for a humorous aside – but it is precisely its assimilation to the conventions of romance that here makes it humorous and unthreatening.[62] A year later, Henry Killigrew republished his play *Pallantas and Eudora*, which had appeared – unauthorised and uncorrected – in 1638 under the title *The Conspiracy*. Included in Act 3 of this edition, but missing from its earlier publication, is a reference to one of the characters appearing 'disguis'd like a Saylor', a costume Charles II was said to have assumed for part of his journey from Worcester into exile.[63]

Such topical references, though, are only the least consequential element in the conjunction of theatricality and the terms of political debate in the drama written around the beginning of the decade. More significant is the figure of disguise itself, since this is much more than a thematic or performative element within the drama of early modern England.[64] It has a more fundamental reference, as for Hobbes, to the work of personating in general. In the aftermath of Worcester, Charles II's story became entangled with that of Captain James Hind, the highwayman and former Royalist soldier captured in London on 9 November 1651. Hind had become the focus for chapbook attention before his capture and continued to be so during his imprisonment and subsequent judicial proceedings.[65] Among the works that helped to build his persona was a short play entitled *The Prince of Priggs Revels*, which cast some of Hind's most celebrated exploits into dramatic form. Act 5 of the play sees Hind, as was widely rumoured at the time, helping Charles in his escape from Worcester. Interestingly, the first lines that Hind speaks to the young 'King of Scots' are quoted more or less verbatim from a poem written by the most celebrated Royalist poet of the age, John Cleveland, in response to the elder Charles's flight from Oxford in disguise in 1646.[66] In 'The King's Disguise', Cleveland hyperbolically explores the consequences of Charles's divesting himself of his office and going out into his kingdom under cover.[67] The poem imagines Charles's adoption of disguise as figuring the kind of autoimmunity of the royal person that Royalists were so keen to preclude, that Chaloner was using to such notable effect around the time of its composition and that Cleveland also ridiculed in his *Character of a Country Committee-man*. It expresses the highly dangerous wish for precisely what Royalists did not usually seek, 'a State-distinction to arraigne / *Charles* of high Treason 'gainst my Soveraigne', while suggesting that 'What an usurper to his [P]rince is wont, / Cloyster and shave him, he himselfe hath don't.'[68] Tellingly, the king has 'muffled feature[s]'. According to the taxonomy of disguise that Susan Baker has offered for Shakespearean drama, Cleveland's Charles should be classified among those who disguise themselves by obscuring the face rather than by impersonating another. The veil or vizard borne by such figures 'inscribes an absence and an ignorance', making them the de-personified product of personation.[69] For Cleveland, a king disguised is a king 'defac'd' and thereby ruined, his monarchical integration of capacities or elements rendered inconsistent or incomplete. The monarch appears only insofar as he is stretched along an extended line between the face and the defacer, and is fully present as neither.

There is an echo here once again of *Richard II*'s phenomenological account of exploded monarchy, especially the deposed king's figuration of himself as, in quick succession, 'person', 'nothing' and quasi-human clock.[70] In this context, Charles II's association with Hind seems less a simple historical conjunction and more a likeness traceable to shared habitation of the dark territory proper to, but also destructive of, personhood, the abjected status of those 'dead as to Law', as Milton put it, who can live 'the life onely of a Prisner, Captive and a Malefactor'.[71] Hind's capture and imprisonment serve as a placeholder for the 'lowest degradement and incapacity of the regal name', even as the escapades written up and celebrated during that captivity appear to create an 'imaginary yet political space' in which such degradation might be redeemed.[72] It is perhaps significant, given the chapbooks' balancing of these different elements, that *The Prince of Priggs Revels* concludes with the disguised king telling sad stories of the death of 'all bodies politick' while Hind offers him a grimly double-edged promise of bare-faced fidelity. 'Let me be hang'd if I prove false to you,' he says; as 'J.S.', the play's author, could reasonably have surmised, the gallows were indeed Hind's eventual destination.[73]

In this play, then, the figure of the disguised king serves as an emblem for the fraught politics of royal personhood. Elsewhere, disguise is the occasion for related but not identical examination of the issues involved in this politics. In Christopher Wase's allegorical translation of Sophocles' *Electra*, for example, the character of Clytemnestra personifies the Parliament while that of Orestes figures Charles II: he personates him and she them, redoubling the extent of personation in the play.[74] Political representation is therefore even more deeply enmeshed in its rhetorical and theatrical means, and *Electra* also manages to narrate this essential figural element in its construction. Orestes returns home in disguise and confirms the news of his death to his sister, offering her an urn in which, he claims, his own residuum or remains, his 'Funerall reliques', are to be found.[75] He is oddly distended, present on the stage in two defaced or incomplete instances: Electra bewails the fact that she must make do with the 'dust and uselesse shade' of the urn, substituted for Orestes' 'sweet Face', even while her brother stands disguised before her.[76] The revenge of Orestes on his mother then also becomes his own redemption from such a troubled personhood. In the same spirit, a poem entitled 'The Return' appended to the play looks forward to Charles's appearance 'on our Isles', and imagines the 'Royal Stranger' overcoming his enemies.[77] Here, the language of a reintegrated royal personhood, cut free of the difficulties of personation, is given full and defiant rein. In Wase's play, theatrical representation is the scene and the mode of royal suffering, but also the space in which its prospective redemption can be asserted.

This latter potential perhaps helps to explain why some critics have been persuaded that the surviving texts of plays from this period contain evidence of possible performance.[78] These scripts are prospective: they look forward to their actualisation, and in so doing mimic the element of articulate political longing in post-Regicide royalism. While the more scholarly or readerly apparatus of Wase's translation does not enhance this prospective sense, its status as potential performance does mirror its Royalist hopes. The difficulty with this is that a sense of the play as prospective actualisation also resembles the rather darker invocation of theatricality as a tragic condition that we find in the Royalist writing of the time. The play text anticipates a performance with which it is not identical. The imperilled king, too, is theatrically distended, and in adopting disguise he vividly recalls the fundamental elements of theatricality itself, its constitutive dependence on disguise, masking, the processes of impersonation and personification that animate the relation between actor and character, performance and text, and which may not allow personhood to resolve itself into a simple or settled notion.

We can see this somewhat involved manifestation of the Royalist resort to theatre in another of the plays that Cosmo Manuche presented to James Compton, Earl of Northampton, some time in the early 1650s. Unlike *The Just General*, *Love in Travell* was never printed, and survives now only in a single presentation copy. It is also a comedy, rather than a tragedy or tragicomedy, and it features no royal persons. It does, however, concern the trials of Royalist partisans who have fought in the wars and are now living in disguise. Colonel Allworth has been financially ruined as a result of his service and his persisting loyalty; Lieutenant Shiftwell works at an inn in the guise of Bolster, a chamberlain, providing assistance and hospitality when possible to other undercover Royalists. The play handles their disguise with ambivalence: on the one hand, it is a mark of their dislocation from the proper personhood they inhabited prior to a time 'when base Rebellion / Storm'd a Noble Cause', as Shiftwell puts it.[79] And the nature or extent of their disguise differs, too: while Shiftwell personates Bolster, Allworth has an altogether more shadowy or faceless life in disguise. Indeed, like Wase's Orestes, he is sufficiently dislocated to announce his own death. Yet disguise is also the means by which they may escape the penal consequences of their royalism, including the powerlessness of debt. In this, their condition parallels that of the daughter of Sir Peircival Fondlin, who like a classic comic heroine has left her family and her allotted identity in pursuit of Allworth, with whom she has fallen in love. Unlike a classic heroine, however, Arabella is entirely absent until Act 5, when the play stages the resolution of its own plot through a masque ostensibly performed at Sir Peircival's instigation to distract him from his sorrows. This masque becomes the means by which all the players can be returned to themselves: Arabella is introduced in the guise, tellingly, of a veiled gipsy, and then 'discovered' to her astonished and delighted father. Similarly, Allworth and Shiftwell are recognised and reintegrated as full personae. The masque is in this sense an instance of theatre's self-cancelling drive, as it stages the process whereby dramatic personhood – disguise – can be made to give way to self-identity beyond the enforced play of personation.

Yet there is, even in this comedy, something that resists the containment of the awkward condition of personation in the device of a play within the play. Although the masque allows for the emergence from disguise of underlying persons, it also contains some loose ends. Not all the masquers are given the faces both of part and actor. Masquing shepherds and shepherdesses are carefully identified as characters from elsewhere in the play, while the part of Fortune is played by Allworth's sister, Isabella. But two of the veiled 'Antick Gipsies' are not unveiled, and the presiding divine presence of Phebe is similarly untraceable to another, more fundamental, persona. Are these gipsies, then, gipsies in the world outside the masque, somehow playing a part within it? Does their disguise belong to the masque, or to the play? No answer is forthcoming. As Lois Potter has remarked, 'the apparently fictitious interlude merges with the supposedly real events of the play'; the fact that Sir Peircival invokes the aid of Phebe, 'thou Goddess of all tender youth', to protect his wayward daughter towards the beginning of the play might lead us to assume that the later intervention by such a figure is that of the goddess herself, *in propria persona*, rather than that of a character playing her part.[80] So the figure of Phebe would from this standpoint appear to be a person on a level with Sir Peircival, a divinity intervening directly in his world much as the god Hymen plays a part in the resolution of *As You Like It*. In slightly different ways, the strangely undisguised goddess and the veiled gipsies of the masque return to the play the sense of a compromising process of personation, and an accompanying uncanny theatricality, that its resolution would appear to want to banish.

To say this is not to make a claim for the originality of Manuche's drama – the concluding masque, the intervening deity and the disguised heroine among the gipsies all have ample precedent in pre-war English drama. Yet its interest, like that of the other dramatic works touched on here, does not depend on any such claim. Rather, its distinctiveness resides in the way in which the conjunction or mutual influence of embattled and disguised kings or princes, an embattled Royalist political ontology of kingship, and the theatrical problematics of personation can invest particular conventions or kinds of cultural practice with a renewed or fresh urgency. Suddenly, from different but related angles, both disguise and the broader process of personation for which it stands are imbued with an acute political and philosophical force. As the example of Hobbes shows, theatre is much more than a neutral arena in which events or ideas are replayed or represented, or a source of ready analogies: it turns out to be crucial in allowing participants in political or polemical contest to think through their positions, while also proving ultimately to outstrip that thinking. The politics of the person thus remains an issue, a condition, perhaps particularly acutely in a play such as *Love in Travell* that seeks to use a dramatic practice, the masque, to overcome the perils of this condition. This, perhaps, is the tragicomic performance integral to the Royalist cause during its long eclipse, the drama of disguise on which William Towers hoped to be able to bring down the curtain in 1660.

NOTES

1 *A Form of Prayer, with Thanksgiving* (1660); *By the King. A Proclamation for Setting Apart a Day of Solemn and Publick Thanksgiving Throughout the Whole Kingdom* (1660).

2 J. Fielding, 'Towers, John (*d.* 1649)', *Oxford DNB*; James Loxley, *Royalism and Poetry in the English Civil Wars: The Drawn Sword* (1997), pp. 22 and 208.

3 Fielding, 'Towers, John'.

4 William Proctor Williams, 'The Castle Ashby manuscripts: a description of the volumes in Bishop Percy's list,' *The Library*, 6th series, 2 (1980), pp. 392–412; W.H. Kelliher, 'Compton, James, Third Earl of Northampton (1622–1681)', *Oxford DNB*.

5 William Towers, *Obedience Perpetually due to Kings, Because the Kingly Power Is Inseperable from the One King's Person* (1660).

6 *Ibid.*, p. 9.

7 *Ibid.*, p. 6.

8 A number of literary critics and historians have also thought the role of tragicomedy in the Civil Wars worthy of more than a mention, though they have not pursued it in quite the same direction as I do here. See in particular Lois Potter, '"True Tragicomedies" of the Civil War and Commonwealth', in Nancy Klein Maguire (ed.), *Renaissance Tragicomedy* (New York, 1987), pp. 196–217; Lois Potter, *Secret Rites and Secret Writing: Royalist Literature, 1641–1660* (Cambridge, 1989), pp. 100–12; Susan Wiseman, *Drama and Politics in the English Civil War* (Cambridge, 1998), pp. 190–215; and Dale Randall, *Winter Fruit: English Drama, 1642–1660* (Lexington, KY, 1995), pp. 337–68.

9 Lois Potter described the typical Guarini-inspired pre-war English tragicomedy as 'a play whose source might be Greek romance or Italian pastoral, but whose immediate context was the court and its circle of gentlemen amateurs' (Potter, 'True Tragicomedies', p. 196); see also *ibid.*, *Drama and Politics*, pp. 190–202. In the more obviously polarised context of 1647, the publication of the plays of the acknowledged English masters of tragicomedy, Beaumont and Fletcher, was seen and is still understood as a Royalist gesture. See *ibid.*, *Drama and Politics*, p. 194.

10 I borrow the phrase 'political ontology' and its usage most immediately from Philip Pettit, 'Rawls's political ontology', *Politics, Philosophy and Economics*, 4 (2005), pp. 157–74, though it is also in more general circulation with slightly different inflections. See, for example, Pierre Bourdieu, *The Political Ontology of Martin Heidegger* (Stanford, CA, 1991) and Slavoj Zizek, *The Ticklish Subject: The Absent Centre of Political Ontology* (1999).

11 Towers, *Obedience*, p. 10.

12 Ernst Kantorowicz, *The King's Two Bodies: A Study in Medieval Political Theology* (Princeton, NJ, 1957).

13 *Ibid.*, pp. 20–1.

14 Marie Axton, *The Queen's Two Bodies: Drama and the Elizabethan Succession* (1977);Conrad Russell, *The Fall of the British Monarchies, 1637–1642* (Oxford, 1991), pp. 506–9; Paul Hammond, *The Making of Restoration Poetry* (Cambridge, 2006), pp. 107–36; David Norbrook, 'The emperor's new body: *Richard II*, Ernst Kantorowicz and the politics of Shakespeare criticism', *Textual Practice*, 10 (1996), pp. 329–57; and Lorna Hutson, 'Not the king's two bodies: reading the body politic in Shakespeare's *Henry IV*', in Victoria Kahn and Lorna Hutson (eds), *Rhetoric and Law in Early Modern Europe* (New Haven, CT, 2001), pp. 166–89.

15 Michael Mendle, *Dangerous Positions: Mixed Government, the Estates of the Realm, and the Making of the Answer to the XIX Propositions* (Tuscaloosa, AL, 1985); Michael Mendle, *Henry Parker and the English Civil War: The Political Thought of the Public's "Privado"* (Cambridge, 1995); David L. Smith, *Constitutional Royalism and the Search for Settlement, c.1640–1649* (Cambridge, 1994), p. 177; and Norbrook, 'Emperor's new body', pp. 343–4.

16 Samuel Rutherford, *Lex, Rex, the Law and the Prince: a Dispute for the Just Prerogative of King and People* (1644), esp. pp. 265–80.

17 See Smith, *Constitutional Royalism*, pp. 219–55, and Glenn Burgess, 'Repacifying the polity', in Ian Gentles, John Morrill and Blair Worden (eds), *Soldiers, Writers and Statesmen* (Cambridge, 1998), pp. 202–28.

18 Sarah Barber, *Regicide and Republicanism: Politics and Ethics in the English Revolution, 1646–1659* (Manchester, 1998); D. Alan Orr, *Treason and the State: Law, Politics and Ideology in the English Civil War* (Cambridge, 2002); Jason Peacey (ed.), *The Regicides and the Execution of Charles I* (Basingstoke, 2001).

19 David Scott, 'Motives for king-killing', in Peacey (ed.), *The Regicides*, pp. 138–60. See also the essays in Robert von Friedeburg (ed.), *Murder and Monarchy: Regicide in European History, 1300–1800* (Basingstoke, 2004), and Howard Nenner, *The Right to be King: The Succession to the Crown of England, 1603–1714* (Basingstoke, 1995).

20 Barber, *Regicide and Republicanism*, pp. 11–40, 125–63; Norbrook, 'Emperor's new body', p. 344.

21 Francis Bacon, *Three Speeches of the Right Honorable, Sir Francis Bacon Knight, then his Majesties Sollicitor Generall ...* (1641), p. 37.

22 *Ibid.*, p. 40.

23 Orr, *Treason and the State*, p. 49; see also Norbrook, 'Emperor's new body', p. 344.

24 Bacon, *Three Speeches*, p. 40.

25 Barber, *Regicide and Republicanism*, pp. 11–40.

26 Thomas Chaloner, *An Answer to the Scotch Papers ... Concerning the disposal of the Kings Person* (1646), p. 4.

27 Barber, *Regicide and Republicanism*, pp. 11–40; Scott, 'Motives for king-killing'.

28 Rutherford, *Lex, Rex*, p. 265.

29 *The justification of a safe and wel-grounded answer to the Scottish papers, printed under the name of Master Chaloner his speech* (1646), p. 4; *An answer to severall objections made against some things in Mr. Thomas Chaloners speech* (1646), p. 4.

30 *An answer to a speech without doores; Animadversions upon an unsafe and dangerous answer to the Scotch-papers* (1646), p. 3; *The speech without doores defended without reason* (1646), pp. 4–5; [John Cleveland], *The Character of a Country Committee-man, with the Eare-marke of a Sequestrator* (1649), p. 1.

31 Conal Condren, *Argument and Authority in Early Modern England: The Presupposition of Oaths and Offices* (Cambridge, 2006), pp. 6–7.

32 *Ibid.*, p. 26.

33 In this way of thinking about kingship, Kantorowicz is perhaps most clearly showing his uneasy debt to Carl Schmitt's version of 'political theology', outlined in a monograph first published in 1922. For Schmitt the essential notion was that of sovereignty. See Carl Schmitt, *Political Theology: Four Chapters on the Concept of Sovereignty*, trans. George Schwab (Chicago, IL, 2005). On the relationship with Kantorowicz, see Anslem Haverkamp, '*Richard II* and the end of political theology', *Law and Literature*, 16 (2004), pp. 313–26, and Giorgio Agamben, *Homo Sacer: Sovereign Power and Bare Life*, trans. Daniel Heller-Roazen (Stanford, CA, 1998), pp. 1–30, 91–104.

34 Joad Raymond, 'The king is a thing', in Joad Raymond and Graham Parry (eds), *Milton and the Terms of Liberty* (Cambridge, 2002), pp. 69–94.

35 See, for an eminent example, Quentin Skinner, 'The state', in Terence Ball, James Farr and Russell Hanson (eds), *Political Innovation and Conceptual Change* (Cambridge, 1989), pp. 90–131.

36 Barber, *Regicide and Republicanism*, p. 134.

37 John Milton, *Political Writings*, ed. Martin Dzelzainis (Cambridge, 1991), pp. 9, 15.

38 *Ibid.*, p. 30; William Shakespeare, *Richard II*, ed. Charles Forker (2002), 4.1.163–318, and see Kantorowicz, *King's Two Bodies*, pp. 24–41.

39 Milton, *Political Writings*, p. 31.

40 Condren, *Argument and Authority*, pp. 135, 198.

41 [Francis White?], *Majestas Intemerata, or The Immortality of the King* (London?, 1649), p. 22.

42 [Edward Gee], *A plea for non-scribers. Or, The grounds and reasons of many ministers in Cheshire, Lancashire and the parts adjoyning for their refusall of the late engagement modestly propounded* (1650).

43 Condren, *Argument and Authority*, p. 102.

44 Quentin Skinner, 'Hobbes and the purely artificial person of the state', in *Visions of Politics*, vol. III: *Hobbes and Civil Science* (Cambridge, 2002), p. 188.

45 *Ibid.*, p. 190.

46 See John Milton, *Eikonoklastes*, in Merritt Hughes (ed.), *The Complete Prose Works of John Milton*, vol. III (New Haven, CT, 1962), pp. 335–601. That this is a distinction neither James nor Charles was prepared to acknowledge is hardly surprising. See Kevin Sharpe, 'Private conscience and public duty in the writings of Charles I', *HJ*, 40 (1997), pp. 643–65, esp. pp. 660–2, and Smith, *Constitutional Royalism*, pp. 208–18.

47 Skinner, 'Hobbes and the purely artificial person of the state', pp. 199–204.

48 Thomas Hobbes, *Leviathan*, ed. Richard Tuck (Cambridge, 1996), pp. 114–15.

49 *Ibid.*, p. 112.

50 Hobbes, *De Homine*, trans. and quoted in Skinner, 'Hobbes and the purely artificial person', p. 193. Translation slightly, if problematically, amended – 'character' makes sense to the modern reader, but the word's early modern usage differed from ours.

Compare the very different translation of the second sentence here offered in Bernard Gert (ed.), *Thomas Hobbes: Man and Citizen ('De Homine' and 'De Cive')* (Indianapolis, IN, 1991), p. 83; Skinner's rendering makes much better sense of what he himself calls a 'dark passage'.

51 Hanna Pitkin, *The Concept of Representation* (Berkeley, CA, 1967), p. 25.

52 Skinner, 'Hobbes and the purely artificial person', p. 194.

53 Lynn Hulse (ed.), *Dramatic Works by William Cavendish*, Malone Society Reprints, 158 (1996); S.P. Cerasano and Marion Wynne-Davies, *Renaissance Drama by Women: Texts and Documents* (1996), pp. 3–4, 127–54; Emma Rees, *Margaret Cavendish: Gender, Genre, Exile* (Manchester, 2004); Wiseman, *Drama and Politics*, pp. 91–113; Randall, *Winter Fruit*, pp. 313–36; Hero Chalmers, *Royalist Women Writers, 1650–1689* (Oxford, 2004), pp. 132–48.

54 Victoria Kahn has emphasised this element in the Hobbesian account of the person, though to rather different ends: see 'Hamlet or Hecuba: Carl Schmitt's decision', *Representations*, 83 (2003), pp. 67–96, esp. pp. 78–80.

55 Ben Jonson, *The Devil is an Ass*, ed. Peter Happé (Manchester, 1994), 2.8 and 3.4.

56 For an exploration of this in the rhetorical or tropological terms of *prosopopeia*, see James Paxson, *The Poetics of Personification* (Cambridge, 1994).

57 Some classic instances include Jonathan Goldberg, *James I and the Politics of Literature* (Baltimore, MD, 1983), Leonard Tennenhouse, *Power on Display: The Politics of Shakespeare's Genres* (1986), Christopher Pye, *The Regal Phantasm: Theatricality and Power in Shakespeare and the Renaissance* (1990) and Louis Adrian Montrose, *The Purpose of Playing: Shakespeare and the Cultural Politics of Elizabethan Theatre* (Chicago, IL, 1996). On theatre in the Civil Wars, see Wiseman, *Drama and Politics*, Randall, *Winter Fruit* and Nigel Smith, *Literature and Revolution in England, 1640–1660* (New Haven, CT, 1994).

58 J[ohn] T[atham], *The Distracted State, a Tragedy* (1650), p. 14.

59 Loxley, *Royalism and Poetry*, pp. 129–91; Robert Wilcher, *The Writing of Royalism, 1628–1660* (Cambridge, 2001), pp. 247–71.

60 Cosmo Manuche, *The Just General, A Tragi:Comedy* (1652), p. 24.

61 *Ibid.*, p. 46.

62 William Proctor Williams, 'Manuche, Cosmo *(bap.* 1613, *d.* 1673?)', *Oxford DNB*.

63 Henry Killigrew, *Pallantus and Eudora, a Tragoedie* (1653), p. 30. *The True Speech Delivered on the Scaffold by James, Earl of Derby* (1651), p. 6.

64 See, classically, M.C. Bradbrook, 'Shakespeare and the use of disguise in Elizabethan drama', *Essays in Criticism*, 2 (1952), pp. 159–68; and recently Peter Hyland, 'The performance of disguise', *Early Theatre*, 5 (2002), pp. 77–83.

65 Barbara White, 'Hind, James *(bap.* 1616, *d.* 1652)', *Oxford DNB*. See also Karsten Piep, '"The Merry Life and Mad Exploits of Captain James Hind", or, how the popular press created its first outlaw-hero in the wake of the English Revolution', *Comitatus*, 35 (2004), pp. 124–44; Jerome Friedman, *Miracles and the Pulp Press during the English Revolution* (1993), pp. 207–15.

66 J. S., *An Excellent Comedy Called The Prince of Priggs Revells* (1651), p. 13.

67 Loxley, *Royalism and Poetry*, pp. 138–47; Daniel Jaeckle, 'From witty history to typology: John Cleveland's *The Kings Disguise*', in Joseph Summers and Ted-Larry Pebworth (eds), *The English Civil Wars in the Literary Imagination* (Columbia, MO, 1999), pp. 71–80.

68 John Cleveland, *The Character of a London Diurnall: with Severall Select Poems* (1647), p. 31.

69 Susan Baker, 'Personating persons: rethinking Shakespearean disguises', *Shakespeare Quarterly*, 43 (1992), pp. 303–16.

70 Shakespeare, *Richard II*, ed. Charles Forker (2002), 5.5.31, 38, 50–60.

71 Milton, *Political Writings*, p. 31.

72 *Ibid.*, p. 30; Piep, 'Merry Life', p. 135.

73 J.S., *Prince of Priggs Revells*, p. 14.

74 C[hristopher] W[ase], *Electra of Sophocles* (The Hague, 1649), p. 5.

75 *Ibid.*, p. 42.

76 *Ibid.*, p. 43.

77 *Ibid.*, 'The epilogue', p. 1.

78 A particularly forceful instance of this is William Nelles, 'Cosmo Manuche's Castle Ashby plays as theater pieces', *English Language Notes*, 28 (1990), pp. 39–51.

79 Cosmo Manuche, *Love in Travell*, BL, Add. MS 60275, fol. 27r.

80 Potter, 'True Tragicomedies', p. 211; Manuche, *Love in Travell*, fol. 10v.

Chapter 9

Shakespeare for Royalists: John Quarles and *The Rape of Lucrece* (1655)

Marcus Nevitt

I

In 1655 John Grismond, the printer most famous for his work on the *Eikon Basilike*, and the publishers John Stafford and William Gilbertson brought out a new octavo edition of Shakespeare's popular narrative poem *The Rape of Lucrece*.[1] Compared with all previous editions of the poem the book was a lavish production, adorned by a frontispiece depicting Lucrece on the point of suicide beneath a medallion portrait of Shakespeare, who is lauded as 'the incomparable Master of our English poetry'.[2] As well as recounting the events surrounding Lucrece's rape by Sextus Tarquinius, the volume encouraged its readers to make fresh associations between a dead canonical English poet and a living, fervently Royalist one.[3] This is because it contained a fifteen-page continuation of Shakespeare's original poem by John Quarles entitled *The Banishment of Tarquin: Or, the Reward of Lust*. The 1655 *Lucrece* has attracted attention from scholars in recent years principally because of the frontispiece and the role the edition played both in the revalorisation of vernacular poetry in the early modern period and in the canonisation of Shakespeare as the dominating 'Master' of that vernacular.[4] However, such important assessments notwithstanding, there was actually a tendency in the seventeenth century to associate Quarles's name with the 1655 edition as much as Shakespeare's. Even though Quarles's continuation was probably also sold separately as *The Banishment of Tarquin*, the *Catalogue of the most vendible Books in England* for 1657 and 1658 listed 'Mr Quarles, *Rape of Lucretia*' among those poems most likely to find favour with the book-buying public alongside folio editions of the plays and quarto editions of the poetry of 'Mr Shakespear', which are all listed as distinct items by a different author.[5] Whether the result of a printer's misreading of the title page or deliberate convention, this attribution persevered later into the century as evidenced by Peter Parker's advertisements for

'The Rape of Lucrece by John Quarles' among the lists of books printed by him in 1671 and 1676.[6] In what follows, I argue that it is only by restoring Quarles alongside Shakespeare as a key figure in the 1655 edition of *Lucrece* that we can gain a more accurate sense of how the text might have functioned politically during the turbulent early years of the Protectorate.

John Quarles (1625–1665), a son of the poet Francis Quarles (1592–1644), was a loyal follower of Charles I who fought in the Civil Wars and spent a significant period of his life in exile on the continent as a result. The vast majority of his twelve extant works rail against the violence done to the king and his cause during the Civil Wars. Among his most popular poems was an elegy written for the Royalist military hero Sir Charles Lucas in 1649, which was published in a collection which went through six editions by 1655.[7] It was, though, his lengthy narrative elegy 'upon the Martyrdome of Charls, late king of England of blessed memory', *Regale Lectum Miseriae*, which cemented his reputation as a prominent dissident Royalist writer immediately after the Regicide.[8] A matter of days after the poem's publication John Crouch's *The Man in the Moon* alerted its readers to the work of a 'worthy Gent', claiming that the poem would 'distill tears from a Heart of Adamant'.[9] The poem, reprinted twice, surreptitiously, in the 1650s, begins by casting unthinking, maddening devotion to a man and his cause in quasi-erotic terms:

> Oh what dreams
> Have sailed into my sto[r]my mind? And bring
> No other burden with them but a King,
> A King! Could I but kisse that word, and not be thought
> An Idolizer; 'tis too great a fault
> To kisse his hand. Nor can I think it strange,
> For times and manners needs must have their change.
> 'Tis true, I dream'd methoughts my watchful eyes
> Observ'd a King, and then a Sacrifice;
> And ravish'd with that majesty and grace
> I saw united in that modest face
> I ran to kisse his hand, but with a fall
> I wak'd, and lost both King, and kisse, and all.[10]

There is something undeniably illicit – ''tis too great a fault', the speaker himself admits – about this desire to kiss the king after death. The brutality of the king's 'sacrifice', violently sundering that 'modest face' from its body, means that a traditional gesture of loyal obedience now borders on the necrophilic; the scarcely believable political disappointments attending the Regicide resemble, by the last line of the extract, the more familiar disconsolations of sexual frustration. Quarles's devotion to the Royalist cause was such that he was one of only a small handful of authors who dared put his own name to a printed elegy for Charles on a title page in the immediate aftermath of the

But for this Face, the Work had clearely gone
For old smooth Qvarles himself, and not his Sonne;
Who sighing how KINGS fell, and Subjects rose,
Scornes to miſ-spend one single Teare in Proſe:
This Book's his shadowe, Hee's his Fathers Shade
QVARLES is a Poet as well Borne as Made.

Fig. 9.1 William Marshall, a portrait of Francis Quarles from John Quarles, *Fons Lachrymarum* (1649). Reproduced by permission of the Bodleian Library.

Fig. 9.2 A portrait of John Quarles from John Quarles, *Gods Love and Mans Unworthiness* (1651). Reproduced by permission of the Huntington Library.

Regicide, and despite the 'intransigent ultra-Royalist' nature of his verse, his poetry continued to be reprinted throughout the 1650s.[11] His output during this period was diverse. Alongside his popular elegies, plus another edition of the collection including the poem for Sir Charles Lucas (*Fons Lachrymarum*, 1655), and *An Elegie on the Most Reverend and Learned James Vsher* (1656), he also published devotional poetry (*Divine Meditations Upon Several Subjects*, 1655), an attempt at a Royalist rendition of the Fall narrative (*Gods Love and Mans Unworthinesse*, 1651) and a lengthy continuation of his father's popular Sidneyan romance *Argalus and Parthenia* (*The history of the most Vile Dimagoras*, 1658).[12]

Quarles was regarded by contemporaries as a prominent (if not exceptionally gifted) Royalist writer. His elegy for Charles I, for instance, was popular enough to prompt a piece of anonymous republican counter-propaganda from Cambridge. *Somnium Cantabrigiense* vilified Quarles as a 'rhyming elfe', a 'dull gentleman' whose relentless couplets, 'his leaden mace', had profoundly soporific effects.[13] Despite this a number of seventeenth-century Royalists, longing for the return of the Stuarts, held great hopes for Quarles as the spokesperson for their distracted condition. This was not so much because he presented anything new or stridently original in his verse, but because he adhered to forms of governance and poetry that were long established. What to modern eyes might seem tediously derivative – Quarles often seems incapable of writing in anything other than unwittingly bathetic imitations of his father's robust heroic couplets – was to this community of readers reassuringly famous.[14] Thus Samuel Sheppard saw Quarles's inability to step out of the shadows cast by his more talented father in unequivocally positive terms. 'How like thy Father thou dost strike the strings,' he remarked in his *Epigrams* (1651), proceeding to laud John as the 'Heyre' of Francis Quarles's genius. While this tribute might be generous, Sheppard nonetheless thought it 'Treason' not to 'consecrate one Epigram' to Quarles and actively discouraged him from stylistic innovation, predicting considerable rewards for him if he but persevered in his craft: 'go thou but on, / And doubt not of a Chaplet and a Throne.'[15] In a posthumous accolade published much later in the century, William Winstanley also included Quarles in a series of short biographies of England's finest poets. He remembers Quarles's talent residing in his dogged belief in values learned so well that they appeared to have been the result of the mysterious operations of a deity or, in more modern terms, part of his genetic inheritance. Adapting a familiar maxim, Winstanley thought that Quarles 'may be said to be born a Poet, and that his Father's Genius was infused into him; nor was he less Loyall in his Principles to his Prince'.[16] Such ideas were carefully cultivated by Quarles and his publishers throughout his career as they strove to create the impression that the engraved portraiture accompanying his works was the only means of distinguishing John Quarles's poetry from that of his father (see figures 9.1 and 9.2). Thus some of the editions of *Fons Lachrymarum* carried an engraved portrait of Quarles by William Marshall above the following explanatory stanza:

> But for this Face, the Work had Clearly gone
> For old smooth Quarles himselfe and not his son...
> This Book's his Shadowe, Hee's his Fathers Shade
> Quarles is a Poet as well Borne as Made.[17]

The text beneath Thomas Cross's 1651 engraving to *Gods Love and Mans Unworthiness* made much the same point when it claimed that John Quarles 'Seemes to inherit (by Transmigration) his rare Fathers Spirit'.[18] Indeed Quarles's poetics are so retrograde that vernacular language itself is found wanting in their praise; Quarles's chief 'Exc'llencie', we are told later in the same verse, is that 'Hee / Doth Patrizare'. Only the infinitive form of a Latin verb can do justice to the old-fashioned manner in which Quarles takes after his father.

It was Roger L'Estrange, however, the Royalist pamphleteer and Charles II's future press censor, who most clearly expressed the political potential of this idea of Quarles as a guardian of established forms and values. The 1655 edition of Quarles's 1649 volume of elegies, *Fons Lachrymarum*, a work still dedicated to 'Prince Charles, Prince of Wales', reprints L'Estrange's commendatory poem in which he defines his young friend's verse as the poetics of reassuring continuity amid cataclysm:

> The Son begins to rise, the Father's set:
> Heav'n took away one light, and pleas'd to let
> Another rise. Quarles, thy Light's divine,
> And it shall teach, Darkness it self to shine.
> Each word revives thy Fathers name, his art
> Is well imprinted in thy noble heart,
> I've read thy pleasing lines, wherein I find
> The rare Endeavours of a modest mind.
> Proceed as well as thou hast well begun,
> That we may see the Father by the son.[19]

Although L'Estrange's praise of the young Quarles's inheritance of father's abilities has perhaps a faint quality to it – the modesty of a poet's mind is not an unequivocally positive attribute even when situated in opposition to more excessive varieties of Cavalier verse – his sense of Quarles's cultural importance remains undiminished. Its final line in particular rings loud with political resonance, revealing the way in which a belief in exiled sons who are the image of their fathers – be they kings or poets – could become an important prop for Royalists either routed by civil war or astounded by regicide. Quarles is thus presented as being at the heart of a radically conservative poetics which embraces overbearing influences instead of anxiously attempting to repel them. He is a figure who suggests that it is only when we submit ourselves utterly to the authority of our predecessors that the potential of the next generation, the glory of the resurrection and the occluded hopes for Restoration become visible.

II

Although the main body of the 1655 *Lucrece* is almost identical to that of the previous edition of 1632 (in that it followed the recent tradition of dividing sections of the poem up under descriptive headings), it was unlike any other impression of the poem, before or since, in two key respects.[20] Firstly, Shakespeare's flirtatious dedication to the Earl of Southampton was replaced with an infinitely more sober statement of thanks to Quarles's 'absolute friend' Nehemiah Massey for unspecified help received during the recent troubles. More strikingly still, this 'pamphlet without beginning', as Shakespeare modestly described his efforts in the Southampton dedication, becomes a poem with an altogether different ending by courtesy of Quarles's continuation. Tarquin is no longer left to mill uneasily around the reader's imagination in hurried but 'everlasting banishment' as the original poem's final, bathetic couplet has it. Instead he finds himself pursued by pride and guilt for a further forty-seven stanzas until he is finally sung to death next to a river by Ovid's Philomel and a group of rather sinister 'Sylvane Choristers', a flock of super-Ovidian or Hitchcockian nightingales. The birds bring Quarles's continuation of the poem to a close by pecking Tarquin's eyes out as he lies in the dust:

> But Tarquin, not encourag'd to abide
> So hot a Charge, falls down, and falling dy'd
> Which they perceiving presently arise
> And flockt about him, and pickt out his eyes;
> From which sad story we may infer
> That Philomel abhors a Ravisher.[21]

If Quarles's continuation of Shakespeare's poem adds much to the original narrative, a significant amount is also lost. The sober rhythms and stately delays of the rhyme-royal stanza evaporate in the heat of Quarles's much quicker six-line pentameter couplet stanzas. One of the most dramatic aspects of the lurid final stanza to this new edition of the poem, though, is that it also forces its readers to re-evaluate drastically the relationships between *The Rape of Lucrece*, its sources and, most importantly, the relationship between past and present as revealed by those texts.

In Shakespeare's principal sources, Livy's *Romane Historie* and Ovid's unfinished poem on the Roman calendar, the *Fasti*, Lucrece's rape by Sextus Tarquinius is presented as a direct cause of one of the most dramatic political changes in Roman history. In both of these texts the rape is foundational. For Livy, the sexual assault of Lucrece brings about the birth of liberty and the first republican hero, Lucius Junius Brutus, who opposed the tyrannical excesses of the Tarquin dynasty (revealed in Lucrece's rape) by banishing them from Rome, ousting Roman monarchy and replacing it with a form of republican rule.[22] In the *Fasti*, Ovid reaffirmed that Lucrece's rape was an important causal explanation of the origins of Roman consular government when he explored the aetiology of the *regifugium*, the ancient ceremony commemorating the expulsion of the Tarquins, on 24 February.[23] Quarles's edition of *Lucrece*, however, does much to disrupt the interpretation of the rape as either a foundational moment of Roman history or a memorable turning point in the passing year by disassociating it from these historical texts and contexts. By pursuing Tarquin after his banishment to his painful riverside death and then moralising this as evidence of the familiar aphorism that 'Philomel abhors a Ravisher', Quarles suggests instead that Lucrece's most meaningful intertextual relationship is actually with another poem by Ovid. Indeed when Tarquin himself pleads with the vengeful birds to stop singing before he dies, he seems aware that his banishment from Rome has also involved a relocation from the worlds of the *Fasti* and Livy's *Romane Historie* to that of the sixth book of Ovid's *Metamorphoses*. This is the book which recounts Philomela's rape and mutilation by her brother-in-law Tereus, the dire revenge that she and her sister Procne visited upon him and the subsequent transformation of all the protagonists into different varieties of birds. The culmination of Quarles's continuation sees Tarquin, the former tyrant who would subject all to his will and appetite, forced to beg to Philomela (turned nightingale) for the more modest satisfactions of peace and quiet:

> Sweet Philomel forbear thy tyrannies
> Tell me thou woful wretch, doe not deny
> Who was most villain Tereus or I;
> Was it not he did perpetrate thy rape,
> And made thee wish thy self in this shape?[24]

Tarquin's suggestion that tyranny is a matter of acoustics and his attempt to convince the nightingale that he is not as contemptible as another legendary rapist clearly invite the reader's scorn. This is only compounded by his calculated misreading of *Metamorphoses* VI. Part of Tereus's torture of Philomela involved the removal of her tongue so that she could never speak of her rape, but Tarquin wilfully forgets this in a moment of glib misogyny: 'the Gods did doe thee wrong' he tells the nightingale, 'To take thy woman's shape, yet leave her tongue.'[26]

As will be seen shortly, there is a political dimension to this re-routing of the Lucrece narrative, but there is also a related reassessment at work. If

Lucrece's rape was an important aetiological explanation for the replacement of a tyrannical form of monarchical rule with consular government in ancient Rome, Quarles's moralistic continuation adduces it merely as proof of one man's immoderate lust. Whereas moral outrage at the tyrannical excessiveness of Lucrece's rape was what provoked Brutus to endeavour the wholesale political change of the ancient Roman order in all sources, Quarles seems to suggest that the narrative's only exemplary power in the 1650s is as a prompt to moral self-scrutiny or as a reminder that the deficiencies of history can be best countered through the compensatory powers of verbal art. Thus Quarles uses Tarquin's behaviour as the basis for a general admonition against rashness ('judge him wise that loves to spend / Ere he begins, some thoughts upon the end / of his Design') and also informs his readers that:

> I am confident when thou doest seriously consider the unworthiness of the Action, thou wilt not approve of the Actor; for, after he had received those many civilities which the house of chast Lucretia could afford, he with an unheard-of violence, requited her with a most barbarous rape, which caused not only his banishment, but likewise cost the lives of many of the Nobility; nay, and the King himself in defence of his son, the Ravisher, lost his life; and that which was more than all, was the losse of Lucretia's life: for the sense of the fact, made her stab her self; so died poor Lucretia, blameable in nothing but that she was the Author of her own death: So Reader, as thou hast before read Tarquin's offence, thou mayst now read his punishment.[26]

Although Quarles clearly ascribes some causal significance to Lucrece's 'barbarous rape', he tries to banish any memories that it might have brought about fundamental change to the basic structures of Roman politics. In marked contrast to the argument printed earlier in the volume before Shakespeare's original poem, which clearly states that as a result of the rape 'the Tarquins were all exiled and the state government changed from kings to consuls', there is no sense at all in the continuation that republicanism began to dawn over the body of Lucrece after her rape.[27] Instead Quarles presents that rape either as an instance of the self-harming tendencies of aristocracy and monarchy or as the violence inflicted by the incontinent Tarquin on the aristocratic ethos of hospitality. The logical culmination of all of this (stressed in that overburdened 'So Reader'), for anyone who 'seriously consider[s]' the Lucrece narrative as mediated by Quarles's edition, is that change seems less a matter of historical possibility or political transformation than an aesthetic phenomenon, the playful business of imaginative continuation which can bring about new versions of old poems.

We will consider whether this was a politically pessimistic move for a Royalist poet to make in the 1650s in due course, but Quarles's decision to present the ultimate trajectory of the Lucrece narrative as Ovid's violently playful *Metamorphoses* is at least partly justified by Shakespeare's original poem. Shakespeare's *Lucrece* famously refuses to honour the promises of its prefatory Livian argument: whereas Lucrece actually sends one servant to fetch her husband and father after her attack, he is originally advertised as plural 'messengers'; similarly, the argument suggests that Tarquin has prior knowledge of Lucrece's house before the rape, but the poem enhances the violence of his crime by revealing that it was made on Tarquin's first visit.[28] There are also some important returns to *Metamorphoses* VI at key moments in the poem itself, episodes that Quarles replays in his treatment of Tarquin's death. For example, shortly before her suicide at sunrise, Lucrece hears 'lamenting' Philomela's 'well-tuned warble of her nightly sorrow' and, desperate for any means of empathetic identification after the rape, spends some time talking to the nightingale, inviting her to make a 'sad grove in my dishevelled hair'.[29] Such wilful deviation from the prefatory argument and occasional references to *Metamorphoses* VI create the perspective shifts, the ruptures and disconnections vital for the evocation of the trauma of the rape victim throughout Shakespeare's narrative poem.

Quarles's continuation is equally sympathetic to Lucrece's plight. However, the most telling effect of his decision to make the Philomela narrative the carefully considered end of his new design is to discourage readers from interpreting Lucrece's rape as a cause of historical or political change. While there is a superabundance of violence and sexual assault in both of Ovid's poems (ten rape narratives in the *Fasti*, nineteen extended accounts of rape in the *Metamorphoses*), the *Metamorphoses* refuses to accord rape the foundational status it can assume in the *Fasti*.[30] Rather than being a cause of or incitement to reformation, rape in the *Metamorphoses* is merely another expression of change in a universe endlessly transformed by its gods. Thus Jove's rape victims are frequently simply described as 'rivals' with Juno for the unpredictable desires and changeable affections of her husband, while in George Sandys's translation of the Philomela episode rape primarily exemplifies the metamorphic power of unregulated passion.[31] When Tereus rapes his sister-in-law he is transformed from an Athenian liberator to a 'monster', a 'dire Tyrant' whose 'horrid lust' has, simultaneously, turned his victim from virgin into 'adultresse'.[32] Procne's and Philomela's distracted revenge upon Tereus (feeding him his own son, Itys) makes each of them seem more 'Tigresse' than mother or aunt, while Tereus, in this horrific perversion of the moment of consumption, is turned from irrepressibly violent force into final resting place, 'his sonnes vnhappy tombe'.[33] The barbarity of Tereus's mutilation of Philomela is also, disconcertingly, Ovid's opportunity to showcase the transformative potential of the simile. Describing the moment when Tereus wrenches Philomela's tongue from her mouth, pausing to examine the proximity of the mute and the mutable, the narrator notices:

the panting root:
Which trembling, murmurs curses at the floor.
And as a serpents taile, disseuer'd, Leaps:
Euen so her tongue: and dying sought her steps[34]

The grim realisation of these lines is not that socio-political structures have to change in order to prevent such abuses recurring, nor is it simply a wry celebration of the shape-shifting, credulity-stretching powers of the imagination. It is more a dispassionate awareness that to be human is to be acutely vulnerable in a world of unpredictable flux; modifiable by violence, by language, by passion and time, the contours of the body are entirely provisional. The final metamorphosis of the episode's protagonists into different species of birds is one of the most famous and typical motifs from the poem and gives the clearest indication of the reluctance of the *Metamorphoses* to probe the political consequences of rape. It is thus no surprise to discover that the political reorganisation which takes place in Athens after Tereus's outrages is both minor and incidental: Philomela's father, Pandion, dies of grief only at the strange alterations to his family. Erictheus then ascends the throne in a four-line bridging narrative before his own daughter, Orithiya, is raped by the wind-god Boreas, a violation which merely serves as a means of linking books VI and VII.[35]

III

Ovid's self-conscious depoliticisation of rape takes place in a poem which, as critics have long recognised, problematises notions of historical causation and takes considerable delight in instances of chronological dislocation.[36] Quarles's edition of *The Rape of Lucrece* may be usefully regarded as performing similar work. If Quarles's continuation of Shakespeare's poem depoliticised and mythologised the Lucrece legend in 1655, though, it did so for pointedly political ends. Throughout the 1640s and 1650s, as Britain went through its own tumultuous reaction to the excesses of monarchy, the Lucrece narrative became one of the many discourses through which people tried to make historical sense of the conflict and subsequent political upheavals. Parliamentarians and republicans in particular were quick to secure the legend for their own polemical purposes, and indeed an early version of the oath of loyalty to the new regime, the Engagement, written by Henry Marten and other radicals, made self-conscious allusions to Brutus's banishment of Tarquin.[37] Elsewhere, with a former ruling elite in exile on the continent and some dubious legal chicanery surrounding the Regicide to justify, those polemicists loyal to the newly modelled state saw the Tarquins' expulsion from Rome by Brutus as providing fit historical precedent for their own expulsion of the Stuart dynasty. In *Eikonoklastes* Milton reasoned that Parliament could draft legislation which permitted the regicides' actions after the fact on the basis that there was an important precedent for this from antiquity: 'In Rome the Laws made by Valerius Publicola soon after the expelling of Tarquin and his race, expell'd without a writt'n Law, the Law being afterward writt'n.'[38] Central to Milton's arguments throughout this period was that Charles I was a tyrant, and when he returned to these issues in his 1651 *Defence of the People of England* he rounded on Salmasius, in intemperate Latin, for what he perceived to be his dubious reading of Tarquin's treatment: '"But how", you say, "did they expel Tarquin? Did they summon him to court? Not at all; they shut the gates against him when he came" Ridiculous fool, what could they do but shut the gates when he was speeding there with part of his troops?'[39] By the time of his *Second Defence* it was enough for Milton to remind his readers that Cromwell was a 'liberating Brutus'.[40] William Prynne also found the narrative a useful means of describing the tumultuous changes of the period. By 1660, long disillusioned by the Regicide, he was quoting Seneca to refer to Cromwell as a Tarquin.[44] Early in the Civil Wars, from a different political perspective, however, he used the Lucrece story to justify Parliament's armed resistance against the king on the basis that Lucrece's kinsmen, Brutus and Lucretius, had done exactly the same in response to Tarquin:

> It is lawfull ... to call the people to Arms, and not onely to defend themselves and others against such a one, but plainely to deject him from his Throne ... For if the Prince do ought against his oath, they [Parliament] are not absolved from their Oaths, but rather then especially ought to manifest their fidelity, when the Republicke requires it, because they were specifically instituted for that end ... Hence Brutus the Tribune and Lucretius the Governor of the City called the people to Armes against Tarquin ... and by their authority expelled him from the Kingdome.[42]

Undoubtedly the publication which did most to popularise the political topicality of the Lucrece legend and anchor the significance of 'Tarquin' as a meaningful political term in the 1650s was the Commonwealth's own licensed newsbook *Mercurius Politicus*. In issue after issue *Politicus*'s editor, Marchamont Nedham, expressed his distaste for the Stuart line by comparing it directly to the Tarquins, with 'Tarquin' operating as imaginative short-hand for the inherently tyrannical tendencies of monarchical government. In the early issues, particularly, with the Commonwealth eager to urge its political legitimacy, anyone associated with the Stuart line – Prince Charles, Prince James, Mary Stuart, Prince Rupert – was tarred with the brush of Tarquinian excess:

> The young Tarquin is coming with a world of Majesty and Vermin, and ther's not a Royalist in England but dreams of an Office (Sir Reverence) to be at least Groom of the Stool.
> They say young Tarquin is Landed among his gude people, and must once more

be Proclaimed King by the sound of Bagpipes, that he may be sent after his beloved Cousin Montrosse.

Charles Tarquin being already a Catholick, swore he would turn Turk too, but he would be revenged upon the English; James Tarquin is to be a Cardinal, and Rupert Tarquin is as a good as the best in the Bunch, having been a Thief in two Elements, and a Runnangate in divers Countries.

It is very possible, young Tarquin may lick up again the late vomit of the sins of his Family.[43]

Some Royalists naturally took umbrage with such comparisons, as evidenced by the fact that a Restoration anthology of 'horrid Blasphemies against the Kings Majesty' recorded thirty-five instances of them as examples of the offensiveness of Nedham's hyperbole.[44] Such reactions, though, and those of Royalists of different persuasions, clearly indicate that the politicisation of Tarquin's treatment, especially the designation of the Stuart dynasty as the latest in a line of corrupt Tarquins, was extremely successful in the 1650s. Indeed there were moderate Catholic Royalists, like Sir Percy Herbert, who clearly suspected that there was some substance to this parallel. Herbert found the fate of 'licentious Tarquin ... convincing enough to shew the judgments of God upon sensual and luxurious Countries in the general' and traced the causes of the Civil Wars to the abuses of Charles I and his administration. Like Tarquin's Rome, Caroline England 'abounded with all manner of vice, before these late troubles began ... [and] the sins of the Nation without limitation, have been the chiefest causes of our misfortune and present miseries'.[45]

There was, though, a continual attempt by those sympathetic to the Stuarts throughout the revolutionary decades and Restoration to nullify the success of this dominant politicisation of the Lucrece narrative. Philosophers and political theorists such as Robert Filmer and Thomas Hobbes, for instance, sought to present the expulsion of the Tarquins as a supremely foolish rather than honourable exemplary act in which the appropriate punishment of a culpable individual had become unwarranted revenge against an entire political caste.[46] Hobbes contended that 'indignation carrieth men, not onely against the Actors and Authors of Injustice; but against all power that is likely to protect them; as in the case of Tarquin; when for the Insolent Act of one of his Sonnes, he was driven out of Rome, and the monarchy itself dissolved.'[47] Filmer agreed that the banishment of the Tarquins was an inappropriate response to the sins of one man: 'It is said, that Tarquin was expelled for the rape committed by his sonne on Lucrece; it is unjust to condemn the father for the crime of his Son; it had been fit to have petitioned the Father for the punishment of the offender.'[48]

Other Royalists resignified the political significance of the rape of Lucrece and its consequences by presenting it as a comic interlude. Richard Lovelace's 'Mock song', carefully withheld until the posthumous 1659 edition of *Lucasta*, sought to invalidate the imaginative comparison of Charles I with Tarquin by placing the designation at the heart of a series of losses and reversals:

> Now Whitehalls in the grave,
> And our Head is our slave,
> The bright peal in his close shell of Oyster;
> Now the Miter is lost,
> The proud Praelates, too, crost,
> And all Rome's confin'd to a Cloyster:
> He that Tarquin was styl'd,
> Our white Land's exil'd,
> Yea undefil'd
> Not a Court Ape's left to confute us:
> Then let your Voyces rise high,
> As your Colours did fly,
> And flour'shing cry,
> Long live the brave Oliver-Brutus.[49]

With the social order inverted, with social space itself dramatically restructured – Whitehall has become a grave, Rome has become a cloister – signification itself has fallen into disrepair. Charles I, once 'Head', has become a Tarquin, while Cromwell looks every inch Milton's brave liberating Brutus. The ludic quality of the mock song form, though, plainly suggests the absurdity of such comparisons at the same time as it reveals their durability. Margaret Cavendish also treated the Lucrece narrative as a source of some amusement. In the *Sociable Letters* the eminently polite, well-connected Lady D.C. and Lady G.B. meet to discuss whether 'Lucretia was the best wife that History ever mentioned' but disagree over whether such an accolade can be bestowed upon a suicide. When they fail to agree they almost fall to blows and the narrator, 'afraid they would have Kill'd each other', has to intervene:

> give me leave Ladies, said I, to ask you what Lucretia was to either of you? was she of your Acquaintance or Kindred, or Friend, or Neighbour or Nation? and if she was none of these, as it was very probable she was not, Living and Dying in an age long afore this ... therefore Allay your Passions, for why should you two Ladies fall out, and become Enemies for Lucretia's sake, whom you never knew or heard of, but as in an old Wife's Tale, which is an old History ... leave Lucretia to live and dye in History, and be you two Friends in present Life.[50]

To counter the Lucrece narrative's threat to this community of Royalist women, Cavendish offers a humorous model of aristocratic sociability and politeness which asks those women to disregard the applicability of historical narratives to contemporary disputes and identify with each other rather than eminent examples of femininity from antiquity. In a message that must have had some resonances for her Restoration readers, her ladies must become oblivious to the disorders of the past in order to live peaceably in the present.

A less appealing comic return to the Lucrece narrative came from the Royalist poet Henry Bold in a volume also printed after the Restoration. His 'Song 36' is a love lyric in which the speaker tries to persuade the courtly Florilla to succumb to his advances and surrender herself to a Cavalier world of the flesh. The last stanza of the poem is the speaker's final argumentative assault as he struggles to convince his mistress of the futility of post-coital distress by styling her sexual awakening as reassuringly guilt-free and pleasurable:

> Nor do thou Florilla, as Lucrece hath done
> Lay hands on thy self! cause thy Tarquin is gone!
> For when with rich Wines, I have heighten'd my Vein
> Full fraught, I'le return to my dearest again,
> And Lucrece, ne're dy'd, for her being a whore,
> But, for thought, she should see her young Gallant no more.[54]

The pleasure in question here is clearly that of the Cavalier speaker, and Florilla's discovery of sexuality comes rather to resemble her vulnerability to repeated alcohol-fuelled rape. If these lines are principally intended to delight a male or courtly readership, they are also lines which are politically knowing, since the triumph of sensuality comes only with a reversal of historical causation so striking that it causes the tetrameter to become entirely anapaestic in its concluding line: in the libertine's reading of the *regifugium* Lucrece's suicide is borne of Tarquin's banishment, rather than the reverse. The poem's celebration of Cavalier values, therefore, is reliant upon the awareness and subsequent renunciation of an historically accurate reading of the Lucrece narrative.

IV

Quarles's continuation of Shakespeare's poem should be read in dialogue with these Royalist readings of the Lucrece legend. By eschewing the misogynistic tenor of Bold's lyric and directly moralising the conclusion of his version of the narrative as the peculiarly violent 'reward of lust', Quarles appears to suggest that libertine values offer no beguiling or meaningful escape routes from political defeat for Royalist communities in the mid-1650s. Even so, Quarles's continuation does share Bold's poem's preference for fanciful, speculative endings above the claims of historically accurate representation, a preference which should be read alongside the views of Filmer and Hobbes as a broadly Royalist reaction to the Parliamentarian and republican insistence upon the historical applicability of the Lucrece legend in the 1650s. In order to counter the successful and popular claim that the Tarquins were actually Stuarts *avant la lettre*, Quarles presents us with a Tarquin who is more at home in the mythic narratives of change and renewal offered by the *Metamorphoses*. Situating Lucrece's rape in that more playful context, where rape is neither political nor foundational, and historical causation itself is problematised – rather than amid the annual calendar of events commemorated by Ovid's *Fasti* or in those pages of Livy so favoured by republicans in the period – permits Quarles to co-opt Lucrece's rape for an exemplary moral narrative about the punishment of an individual's licentiousness rather than a broader account of political defeat.

This need not seem far-fetched when we realise that as early as 1649, Quarles was already politicising Lucrece and Tarquin in an arrestingly anti-Parliamentarian way. In *Regale Lectum Miseriae*, Quarles figured what he perceived to be Parliament's unstoppably violent arbitrary authority – represented by its execution of Lord Arthur Capel in March 1649 – in striking terms. Addressing Parliament directly, the speaker of the elegy rounds upon it in vituperative mood:

> You lust-obeying Tarquins, that permit
> And tolerate your pleasures, to commit
> Adulterated actions, and command
> England, our poor Lucretia, to stand
> Subject to your libidinous desires,
> And cannot help her self, heaven grant your fires
> May soon expire, that at the last we may
> (Like Tarquins) see you banish'd quite away.
> Say, will your hungry appetites receive
> No satisfaction? have ye vow'd to leave
> No noble blood?[52]

As the composure of the elegist finally gives way amid the surrounding violence, Quarles reveals a painful sense of a nation levelled, drained of its noble blood, by unrestrained appetite. Struggling with a living nightmare as much vampiric as it is Hobbesian, the speaker takes refuge in (and is floored by) spectacular inversions: parliamentary orders and executions are not law but libido; the English nation, styled a virtuous Lucrece, is prey to the adulterous desires of a parliament, rather than a Stuart king, closely resembling Tarquin.

With his 1655 edition of *Lucrece* Quarles took his disruption of the dominant, topical readings of the legend in a new direction. This was a period when the recently settled Protectorate authorities were acutely sensitive to the ruses, plots, poetics and polemics of dissent and resistance. In 1655, in particular, Cromwell's administration came under attack from several local Royalist insurrections and also had to defend itself against forceful republican polemic expressing considerable disaffection at the apparently authoritarian, quasi-monarchical turn of events following Cromwell's proclamation as Lord

Protector in the previous year.[53] During this period, as David Norbrook has demonstrated, the first book of Ovid's *Metamorphoses*, which recounts the universe's creation from Chaos, became a key text for republicans who wished to express their distaste for Cromwell's aggrandisement by pointing out that Ovid's first humans only ever asserted themselves above animals, never above each other.[54] 1655 also saw the Presbyterian Thomas Hall using his translation of the tale of Phaeton from the second book of the *Metamorphoses* to set 'forth the Nature of rash, ambitious, inconsiderate Rulers, who being inflamed with a desire of Government, aim at things above their reach'.[55] Despite such politicisations of Ovid, and despite the fact that the myth of Philomel, Procne and Tereus also contains material that might very easily have been transported to the political ferment of the mid-1650s – Tereus was, after all, a one-time liberator turned overbearing tyrant – no consistent polemical move was ever made with the sixth book of the *Metamorphoses*.[56] Aware, therefore, that the Ovidian metamorphic world of his remodelled ending was very unlikely to be read as having any transparent political meanings in the mid-1650s, Quarles offered his readers a version of an immensely popular, intensely topical Shakespeare poem which seemed to be resolutely inapplicable to contemporary politics.

This was possible because the narrative of Philomela, Procne and Tereus was pressed into service of a bewildering number of very different discourses during the revolutionary period. Thomas Browne, in the spirit of many earlier Ovidian commentators, suggested that it was simply the fictionalisation of ornithological fact. 'The Nightingale hath some disadvantage in the tongue; which is not acuminated and pointed as in the rest, but seemeth as it were cut of; which perhaps might give the hint unto the fable of Philomela, and the cutting off her tongue by Tereus.'[57] Francis Rous, by contrast, used it as a focal point for a discussion of the semiotics of the Attic dining table: 'usually it [the table] was made with Three leggs ... Of whatever fashion soever it was, they used to reverence it with a greate deale of religion ... The first that ever dared to profane the table, were the Women that killed Tereus his sonne, and served him up in the dish.'[58] By 1644 the story had even been conscripted into a history of gesture when John Bulwer situated it as a crucial text in the geneaology of the handshake: 'Ovid no way ignorant of any matter of manuall expression, brings in Pandion taking his leave of Tereus, and his daughter Philomel demanding this pledge and pawn of faith: Ut fidei pignus dextras untraq, positit / Inter seque dat as junxit [he asked both their right hands as a pledge of promise].'[59] Richard Yonge used the myth in a homily against drunkenness, but there were more politically loaded readings.[60] It was the Laudian minister Alexander Ross who first suggested that Philomela's plight was representative of the wider losses of a nation at war. In a non-partisan argument about the futility of armed conflict, he saw the Civil Wars as a period when 'the Muses are ravished, Scholars are robbed and plundered;

their tongues are cut out, that they may not complain'. [61] Thomas Fuller, on the other hand, saw Tereus as the tyrannical anti-type to Charles I, contrasting conditions in Caroline England with those in the 'Profane State' where tyrants, like Tereus, 'wronged and abused the times they live in, [and] endeavour[ed] to make them speechlese to tell no tales to posterity'.[62] Another politicised reference to the figure of Tereus came in more oblique form in 1653 when the Fifth Monarchist John Rogers used a short Latin tag from *Metamorphoses* VI to reflect upon the irreligious duplicity of the Commonwealth's political cadre. Curiously, however, Rogers attributes the quotation – 'ipso sceleris molimine Tereus Creditur esse pius' (they (the people) think Tereus good and praise him for his crimes) – to Machiavelli rather than Ovid. This is because he was care-lessly part-plagiarising a popular Royalist anti-Engagement pamphlet, *Modern Policies Taken from Machiavel, Borgia and Other Choice Authors*, which used the same quotation to give added colour to its contention that the Civil Wars and their aftermath were best described according to a series of Machiavel-lian precepts. The first of these is that 'The polititian must have the shadow of Religion, but the substance hurts', and Tereus, the rapist who pretends to be a noble kinsman, features as an archetype for the duplicitous statesman.[63]

Even if some Royalists regarded swearing allegiance to the Commonwealth in the form of the Engagement as an example of perfidiousness worthy of a Tereus, the fact that the myth of Philomela, Procne and Tereus was trans-ported in so many, frequently contradictory directions in this period means that it is very unlikely that it was read as having the kind of immediately recog-nisable analogies as those attached to the Lucrece narrative.[64] It was certainly never used with anything like the same frequency in debates surrounding the legitimacy of monarchical or non-monarchical forms of government in the 1650s. Quarles's decision, therefore, to transpose his ending to Shakespeare's narrative poem of Lucrece's rape into its odd mythic key may be read as an attempt on his part to draw a dead canonical author, a favourite text, away from the dominant political controversies of the revolutionary decades. Tempting as such a pattern of retreat in defeat might seem, it is distinctly at odds with the passionate commitment to royalism and its leaders that Quarles exhibited throughout his life and writings. In 1655, the same year in which his *Lucrece* edition appeared, Quarles reissued a corrected imprint of his 1649 elegies *Fons Lachrymarum*. In addition to a reprint of the William Marshall engraving of Quarles, the volume also included, verbatim, his original dedication to Prince Charles, Prince of Wales, the current Charles II:

> There is nothing that can make me esteeme my self unhappy, but that the severity of
> these times will not permit me to tender Your Highness that service which my heart
> is ambitious to perform, and my duty binds me to acknowledge: I have nothing that
> I can stile my own but a fidelious heart, which shall alwaies pray for Your prosperity;
> and that Your successes may (like waves) ride in one upon the back of another; and

that at last, You may, like the Sunne, break through the Clouds of Opposition, and once more shine in Your proper Hemisphere: ... grant that You may not Hide Your Counsels in the Bosomes of them that honour you with their lips, when their hearts are far from You. These are the serious and fervent Prayers of him that desires to live no longer than he is willing to devote himself to Your Highnesses commands, and is

Your Highnesses most obliged servant,

John Quarles.[65]

In the 1655 edition these lines appear after, rather than before, an address to the reader which complains of the printer's errors. Wherever they are placed, though, they are hardly the meek murmurings of the vanquished. The familiar images of Royalist cosmology are given a fresh apocalyptic force by the rhetoric of devotion and dispossession of the would-be insurgent. Quarles is so intent on achieving his ends that he refigures the closure of a traditional valedictory flourish as a desire for the altogether more glorious finale of a self-sacrificing political death. His edition of *Lucrece* is not, of course, as explicit or as threatening as this. But by restyling Shakespeare's great poem as a masterwork borne of the sixth book of *Metamorphoses* rather than a master text recounting a formative moment in the history of republicanism, Quarles refuted one of the dominant anti-monarchical discourses of his day. In his fanciful conclusion to *The Rape of Lucrece* he offered his readers a version of Shakespeare which might permit them to forget the recent past.

NOTES

I am grateful to Jason McElligott and the audiences of research seminars at Leeds University, Keele University and Sheffield University for comments on earlier drafts of this chapter.

1 *The Rape of Lucrece, Committed by Tarquin the Sixt; and The remarkable judgments that befel him for it. By the incomparable Master of our English poetry, Will: Shakespeare Gent. Whereunto is annexed, The Banishment of Tarquin: Or, the Reward of Lust, by J. Quarles* (1655).

2 Stafford and Gilbertson also issued an octavo edition of the poem without the frontispiece in the same year.

3 *The Rape of Lucrece* (1655), sig. A4v.

4 See, for instance, Sasha Roberts, *Reading Shakespeare's Poems in Early Modern England* (Basingstoke, 2003), p. 126. For a different reading of the frontispiece see Susan Wiseman, *Conspiracy and Virtue: Women, Writing and Politics in Seventeenth-Century England* (Oxford, 2006), pp. 42–3.

5 *A Catalogue of most vendible Books* (1657), sigs Fr, Fv; *A Catalogue of most vendible books* (1658), sigs Fr, Fv. Quarles's continuation has a separate title page and pagination. Thomason collected two editions of the poem: one including the continuation, the other with only *The Banishment of Tarquin*. The items are listed separately in the Thomason

collection as E1672[3] and E 1672[4]. References to pages in the second section of the compiled edition have the prefix [2].

6 Donald W. Rude, 'A Shakespearean ghost in the catalogues of Peter Parker', *Notes and Queries*, 47:2 (2000), pp. 187–8; Hyder E. Rollins (ed.), *A New Variorum Edition of Shakespeare: The Poems* (1938), p. 412.

7 John Quarles, *Fons Lachrymarum, Or a Fountain of Tears: From whence doth Flow Englands Complaint ... and an Elegy Upon that Son of Valour Sir Charles Lucas* (1649).

8 John Quarles, *Regale Lectum Miseriae or A Kingly Bed of Miserie* (1649). The volume went through six editions between 1649 and 1659.

9 *The Man in the Moon* (16 April, 1649), p. 8.

10 John Quarles, *Regale Lectum Miseriae: Or a Kingly Bed of Misery* (1649), pp. 1–2. Further editions of the poem appeared in 1658 and 1659.

11 This assessment of Quarles's *Regale Lectum Miseriae* is from Nancy Klein Maguire, *Regicide and Restoration: English Tragicomedy, 1660–71* (Cambridge, 1992), p. 5. For Quarles's place among Charles I's elegists see Lois Potter, *Secret Rites and Secret Writing: Royalist Literature, 1640–1660* (Cambridge, 1989), pp. 184–6.

12 In Quarles's version of the Fall narrative Satan is compared to a conspicuously Parliamentarian 'bold-faced general', and the poem ends with God's promise to a Cavalier elect that they are 'free to revel in my courts': John Quarles, *Gods Love, Mans Unworthiness* (1651), pp. 34, 60.

13 *Somnium Cantabrigiense, Or A Poem Vpon the death of the late King brought to London* (1649), pp. 2, 12.

14 There is one exception. Quarles's *Divine Ejaculations*, which appeared in some editions of *Gods Love and Mans Unworthiness*, is composed of six-line stanzas of iambic tetrameter rhymed ababcc.

15 Samuel Sheppard, *Epigrams* (1651), p. 161. The generosity of this tribute can be seen by Quarles's own assessment of his poetry as 'a Homely Vessel' far inferior to the work of 'a Cowley or a Milton; the very footsteps of either of which, thought art not like here to find': John Quarles, *Triumphant Chastity: Or Josephs Self-Conflict* (1684), sig. A3v.

16 William Winstanley, *The Lives of the Most Famous English Poets* (1687), p. 194. An eighteenth-century annotation in the 1649 edition of Quarles's *Fons Lachrymarum* held in CUL makes much the same point: 'This Mr John Quarles was son of the famous Mr Frances Q author of the Emblemes, and seems to have possesst his Father's Spirit rather than his Genius': John Quarles, *Fons Lachrymarum; or Fountain of Tears* (1649), sig. A6r; classmark 8.40.76.

17 John Quarles, *Fons Lachrymarum* (1655), no sig.

18 Quarles, *Gods Love and Mans Unworthiness*, no sig. By 1658 there were several versions of three engraved portraits of Quarles in print by Thomas Cross, William Faithorne and William Marshall. For Faithorne's version see John Quarles, *Regale Lectum Miseriae* (1658).

19 John Quarles, *Fons Lachrymarum, Or A Fountain of Tears* (1655), sig. A6r.

20 For *Lucrece*'s publication history see Rollins (ed.), *Variorum*, pp. 406–13; Colin Burrow (ed.), *William Shakespeare: The Complete Sonnets and Poems* (Oxford, 2002), pp. 40–5.

21   *The Rape of Lucrece* (1655), [2] sig. G4v. Some signatures and pagination are repeated in the expanded 1655 edition of *Lucrece*, the prefix [2] refers to Quarles's continuation of Shakespeare's poem.

22   Philemon Holland, *The Romane Historie Written By T. Livius of Padua. Also the Breviaries of L. Florus: with a Chronologie to the whole Historie: and the Topographie of Rome in old Time Translated out of Latine into English by Philemon Holland* (1600), pp. 40–3.

23   John Gower, *Ovids Festivalls, Or Romane Calendar, Translated into English verse equinumerally* (1640), pp. 41–6.

24   *The Rape of Lucrece* (1655), [2] p. 11.

25   *Ibid.*

26   *Ibid.*, no sig.

27   *The Rape of Lucrece* (1655), sig. A4v.

28   Burrow (ed.), *Complete Sonnets and Poems*, pp. 47–9.

29   Shakespeare, *The Rape of Lucrece*, lines 1080, 1129, in Burrow (ed.), *Complete Sonnets and Poems*, pp. 301, 303. The switch is also partly prompted by the *Fasti* since Ovid concluded his version of the Lucrece narrative with a linking verse paragraph invoking Procne and Tereus in the swallow's song of spring. See Gower, *Ovids Festivalls*, p. 46. On Shakespeare's use of the *Metamorphoses* in *Lucrece* see Jane O. Newman, '"And Let Mild Women to him Lose their Mildness": Philomela, female violence and Shakespeare's *Lucrece*', *Shakespeare Quarterly*, 45:3 (1994), pp. 304–26; Jonathan Bate, *Shakespeare and Ovid* (Oxford, 1993), pp. 65–82; Katherine Eisaman Maus, 'Taking tropes seriously: language and violence in Shakespeare's *Rape of Lucrece*', *Shakespeare Quarterly*, 37:1 (1986), pp. 66–82; Laura G. Bromley, 'Re-creating Lucrece', *Shakespeare Quarterly*, 34:2 (1983), pp. 200–11.

30   See Amy Richlin, 'Reading Ovid's Rapes', in Amy Richlin (ed.), *Pornography and Representation in Greece and Rome* (New York and Oxford, 1992), pp. 158–79. While there are a number of troublingly comic rapes in the *Fasti*, Ovid also demonstrates the ways in which some of the ceremonies of Roman religion and politics are founded upon such acts of violence. Alongside the rape of Lucretia, which Ovid presents as direct cause of 'the last Monarchick day', there is also the account of Lara, who had her tongue ripped out by Jupiter and was raped by Mercury as a punishment for her talkativeness. Lara's treatment was commemorated in the religious observances to Muta and the Lares. See Gower, *Ovids Festivalls*, pp. 39, 46.

31   For rape victims as love 'rivalls' see George Sandys, *Ovid's Metamorphosis Englished, Mythologizd and Represented in Figures* (Oxford, 1632), pp. 56, 118, 243.

32   *Ibid.*, pp. 213, 214.

33   *Ibid.*, p. 215.

34   *Ibid.*, p. 213.

35   *Ibid.*, pp. 215–16.

36   The poem's opening account of historical degeneration, for instance, refuses to provide any causal explanation for the transitions from the golden age of blissful plenitude to the iron age of 'blushless crimes': Sandys, *Ovid's Metamorphosis*, pp. 3–4. For the poem's ludic take on causes and chronology see Denis Feeney, '*Mea tempora*: patterning of time in the *Metamorphoses*', in Philip Hardie, Alessandro Barchiesi and Stephen Hinds (eds),

Ovidian Transformations: Essays on Ovid's Metamorphoses and its Reception (Cambridge, 1999), pp. 13–29; Sara Myers, *Ovid's Causes: Cosmogony and Aetiology in the Metamorphoses* (Ann Arbor, MI, 1994).

37 David Norbrook, *Writing the English Republic: Poetry, Rhetoric and Politics, 1627–1660* (Cambridge, 1999), p. 192.

38 John Milton, *Eikonoklastes* (1649), p. 219.

39 John Milton, *A Defence of the People of England* (1651), in Martin Dzelzainis (ed.) and Claire Gruzelier (trans.), *John Milton: Political Writings* (Cambridge, 1991), p. 169.

40 John Milton, *A Second Defence of the English People* (1654), in Don M. Wolfe (ed.), *Complete Prose Works of John Milton* (New Haven, CT, 1966), vol. IV part I, p. 682.

41 See William Prynne, *Conscientious, serious theological and legal quaeres, propounded to the twice-dissipated, self-created anti-Parliamentary Westminster juncto, and its members* (1660), p. 20.

42 William Prynne, *The Soveraigne Power of Parliaments and Kingdomes* (1643), p. 189.

43 *Mercurius Politicus*, 5 (4–11 July 1650), p. 65; 4 (27 June–4 July 1650), p. 49; 14 (5–12 Sept. 1650), p. 211; 15 (2–19 Sept. 1650), p. 30.

44 *A Rope for Pol or A Hue and Cry after Marchemont Nedham, the late Scurrulous Newswriter* (1660), pp. 5–14, 18, 20.

45 Sir Percy Herbert, *Certaine Conceptions, or Considerations of Sir Percy Herbert* (1650), pp. 29–30.

46 Although the arguments of *Leviathan* could appeal to people of diverse political opinions Hobbes was adamant that he remained loyal to the Stuarts during the Interregnum. In his verse autobiography he described the period of the Commonwealth and Protectorate as a time when 'Perfidious Fate / Exil'd the Good and Helped the Profligate'. He was particularly incensed that his detractors 'accused me to the King, that I / Seemed to approve Cromwell's impiety, / And countenance the worst of wickedness'. *The Life of Mr Thomas Hobbes of Malmesbury. Written By himself in a Latine Poem. And now Translated into English* (1680), pp. 10–11.

47 Thomas Hobbes, *Leviathan, Or The Matter, Forme and Power Of A Commonwealth Ecclesiasticall and Civill* (1651), pp. 182–3.

48 Robert Filmer, *Observations Upon Aristotles Politiques* (1652), p. 21.

49 Richard Lovelace, 'A mock song', in *Lucasta, Posthume Poems of Richard Lovelace Esq* (1659), pp. 33–4.

50 Margaret Cavendish, *CCXI Sociable Letters Written by the Thrice Noble, Illustrious and Excellent Princess, the Lady Marchioness of Newcastle* (1664), p. 110.

51 Henry Bold, 'Song XXXVI', in *Poems Lyrique, Macaronique, Heroique* (1664), p. 49.

52 Quarles, *Regale Lectum Miseriae*, p. 58.

53 See Austin Woolrych, *Penruddock's Rising, 1655* (1955); David Underdown, *Royalist Conspiracy in England, 1649–1660* (New Haven, CT, 1960), pp. 97–177; Andrea E. Button, 'Penruddock's Rising, 1655', *Southern History*, 19 (1997), 99–111; Barry Coward, *The Cromwellian Protectorate* (Manchester, 2002), pp. 51–8.

54 See Norbrook, *Writing the English Republic*, pp. 467–72, 490.

55 Thomas Hall, *Phaetons Folly, Or, The downfall of Pride: Being a Translation of the Second Book of Ovids Metamorphosis, Paraphrastically and Grammatically* (1655), p. 2.

56 Most early modern commentators remembered Tereus's heroic liberating actions. See Sandys, *Ovid's Metamorphosis*, p. 225; Patrick Hannay, *The Nightingale, Sheretine and Mariana* (1622), sig. Br.

57 Thomas Browne, *Pseudoxica Epidemica or Enquiries into very many received tents and commonly presumed truths* (1646), p. 368.

58 Francis Rous, *Archaeologiae Atticae Libri Septem* (1654), p. 298.

59 John Bulwer, *Chirologia: Or the Naturall Language of the Hand* (1644), p. 94.

60 Richard Yong, *The Drunkard's Character, or, a True Drunkard with such sinnes as raigne in him* (1638), pp. 511–12.

61 Alexander Ross, *Mystagogvs Poeticus, Or the Muses Interpreter explaining the historicall mysteries and mysticall histories of the ancient Greek and Latine poets* (1647), p. 251.

62 Thomas Fuller, *The Holy State* (Cambridge, 1642), pp. 426–7.

63 See John Rogers, *Sagrir, Or Doomes-day drawing nigh with thunder and lightening to lawyers* (1653), p. 141; *Modern Policies Taken from Machiavel, Borgia, and other Choice Authors By an Eye-Witnesse* (1652), sig. B3v.

64 The Royalist journalist and astrologer George Wharton also regarded the taking of 'the curst Engagement which renounced our king' as an example of 'tender-hearted Tereus['s] Leiturgy': George Wharton, *Select and Choice Poems Collected out of the labours of Captain George Wharton* (1661), p. 83.

65 Quarles, *Fons Lachrymarum* (1655), sig. A5r.

Chapter 10

'The honour of this Nation': William Dugdale and the *History of St Paul's* (1658)

Jan Broadway

In June 1657 William Dugdale travelled through the Fens to view the region's recently completed drainage works. He had been commissioned to write a history of these works by the Parliamentarian projectors. The book that resulted was published after the Restoration, dedicated to Charles II and shorn of its associations with the period of the Protectorate. It has been suggested that Dugdale's enthusiasm for this project casts doubt on the staunchly Royalist image that he later promulgated through his autobiography.[1] Yet a close examination of Dugdale's literary output during the Interregnum shows him deliberately forging an identity as a Royalist scholar. In the six months following his visit to the Fens, this process culminated in the publication of the *History of St Paul's*. This was a celebration of St Paul's Cathedral in London, a building that had become a charged political and religious symbol, in which Dugdale did not attempt to disguise his royalism or his support for an episcopal church. In the *History of St Paul's* he castigated the 'Presbyterian contagion' that had seized the country, while making clear his support for the Caroline policy of 'beauty of holiness'.[2] The book is an overtly Royalist and Anglican work published in London during the Protectorate, which advertised Dugdale's alignment with the circle of Midlands Royalists associated with Sir Robert Shirley.[3] In studies of this period, it is inevitably the Royalists in continental exile and those who rose in violent revolt that attract the most attention. Dugdale provides a useful counter-example of a pragmatic, domestic Royalist. An analysis of the circumstances that surrounded the development of his scholarly identity and the publication of the *History of St Paul's* serves to illustrate how a practical accommodation with political realities could be combined with a continuing, fierce support for the Royalist cause.

There is no doubt that during the 1650s William Dugdale reached an accommodation with the political authorities that allowed him to conduct his scholarly life unmolested. Having followed the king to Oxford and remained there until the city fell, he compounded for his estate in November 1646 and took no further part in the conflict. In the aftermath of the king's execution he was confined to his home in Warwickshire, and his friends had some difficulty in acquiring him a pass to go to London in 1651. However, from the following year he spent increasing amounts of time in the capital, and he remained there despite the orders for Royalists to leave London in July 1655, September 1656 and March 1658.[4] It seems to have been a characteristic of antiquarian circles in Stuart England that they were able to lay aside differences of religious and political opinion in the pursuit of their scholastic interests. Consequently Dugdale had close friendships with a number of antiquaries who supported Parliament during the Civil Wars. During his confinement to his home, Blyth Hall in Warwickshire, the two most important of these were Roger Dodsworth and Edward Bysshe. Dodsworth, a client of the Fairfax family, made strenuous efforts to acquire Dugdale a pass to London in 1651. He had been working for many years on a collection of monastic charters, and the antiquarian community seems to have been generally agreed that Dugdale's assistance was required to bring the work to fruition.[5] Edward Bysshe presided over the College of Arms during the Interregnum. He acquired a reputation for assisting scholars and was referred to as 'the host on the hill' by Dodsworth in his letters to Dugdale.[6] It has generally been assumed that the hospitable Bysshe allowed Dugdale to stay at the heralds' office in the 1650s in the interests of promoting antiquarian scholarship. However, a letter that Dodsworth wrote to Dugdale in 1650 following the reorganisation of the College of Arms suggests that his friends were hopeful that Dugdale would take up a position as a herald. Under the new arrangements there were to be six heralds. One of the existing heralds, Edward Norgate, was very ill, and Dodsworth was being urged to replace him should he die. He observed in this respect: 'I see ther is no hope of alteration, whatsoever you may beleeve ... I am confident ther wilbe no change, whilst you and I live ... Every man must stand or fall by his own resolves.'[7] This may be read as reflecting Dodsworth's own uncertainty as to whether he should accept the post. However, it seems more likely that Dodsworth, a man of sixty-five in possession of a reasonable pension and not hampered by the financial burden of royalism, was attempting to persuade the younger and financially insecure Dugdale that he should seek such employment. He would not be the first herald to transfer his allegiance. Edward Norgate had himself served the king until the fall of Oxford and then gone into exile, before returning to London and accepting service in his old position within the College of Arms in 1648. Two other former colleagues, George Owen and William Ryley, had accepted service with Parliament in 1646 and would continue as heralds after the Restoration. Comparatively few records survive in the archive of the College of Arms for the period of the Interregnum, so it is impossible to be certain whether Dugdale accepted an official position.

However, a letter concerning the appropriate arms to be used following the death of Diana, the wife of the Earl of Elgin, makes it clear that Dugdale was actively involved in the work of the office in the spring of 1656.[8]

Although Dugdale may have preferred in later life to give the impression that he had never accepted the usurper's shilling, Dodsworth's argument that a practical man should not expect any change in the immediate future would have resonated with him in the aftermath of the Royalist defeat at Worcester. He was not a man of large estate. His property was valued at a pre-war income of £84 per annum when he compounded in 1648, which placed him in the lower ranks of the gentry.[9] At the same time he was the father of an extensive family. His last child was born in 1650, by which time he had three sons and ten daughters living. None of his daughters were married, and he hoped to place some of them with families 'principled with loyalty'.[10] While confined to the vicinity of his home at Blyth Hall, Dugdale sought the assistance of his antiquarian friends in London to find positions for his daughters. In March 1650 Roger Dodsworth spoke to Sir Simon Archer, the Warwickshire antiquary who had patronised Dugdale in the 1630s and whose son and heir had married the daughter of a London merchant. Having initially taken a neutral stance in 1642, when forced to take sides Archer had served on the Parliamentarian subcommittee for accounts in Warwickshire and two of his sons fought against the king. A godly gentleman, but not a Presbyterian, Archer was a moderate Parliamentarian who regretted the execution of Charles I.[11] Approached by Dodsworth in London, he promised that his daughter-in-law would take one of Dugdale's daughters into her service. Dodsworth and Bysshe then began to seek places for Dugdale's other adult daughters among their acquaintances. The Royalist poet Sir Robert Stapleton 'engag'd his reputation' that all his friends would assist in the quest, and Lord Dorchester promised to remember Dugdale 'for your Da. upon the first opportunity'.[12] Stapleton and his cousin Lord Dorchester met Dugdale's criteria of loyalty to the king, but they also had the advantage of good contacts with the parliamentary authorities. William Pierrepoint, Dorchester's younger brother, was an intimate friend of Oliver Cromwell, and it was his action that had saved Dorchester from financial ruin after the Civil War. In 1653 Dugdale's son John joined the household of Pierrepoint's cousin the Earl of Rutland, a moderate Parliamentarian who supported ceremonial religion.[13] Dugdale, Lord Hatton, another of his pre-war patrons, and Dorchester had been part of the same bibliophilic circle in Oxford during the Civil War, and all three had compounded for their estates under the terms of the city's articles of surrender. Hatton subsequently went into exile in France, but returned to England at the end of 1656. All three were drawn by economic necessity into some degree of accommodation with the republican authorities, as were many of their former comrades. This did not undermine their belief in monarchy or in its restoration in England 'in God's good time'.[14]

During the Interregnum Dugdale applied his antiquarian abilities to improving his income. He could earn small amounts from finding records for use in lawsuits and rather larger sums for researching pedigrees.[15] His ambition, however, was to be a published author, and it was his tenacity in preparing manuscripts and seeing them through the press that made his anti-quarian friends anxious that he should be able to spend time in London. The collection of monastic charters over which Roger Dodsworth had laboured for many years was finally declared ready for the press in the summer of 1651. Dugdale was not optimistic about its commercial success, since 'learning growes to a lower ebbe every day' and only pamphlets filled the stationers' stalls.[16] The collection in print would form two substantial folio volumes in Latin, illustrated with expensive engravings. Unsurprisingly no bookseller could be found who was willing to take on such a substantial commercial risk, so Dodsworth decided to 'play the stationer' himself with the encouragement of friends, who helped to find sponsors for the engravings. It may have been necessity that led him to decide to control the publication of the first volume of the *Monasticon Anglicanum* with Dugdale's assistance, but this involvement in the production process allowed them to retain control of the manuscript and to influence the context of its presentation to the public. Dugdale went on to retain such personal control over the two further works that he published during the Interregnum. This enabled him to shape his own identity as an author and reduced the influence of external censorship.

The role of the stationer was of vital importance in managing the produc-tion of books and their reception. Although it is doubtful that any attempt would have been made to censor such a monument to antiquarian scholarship as the *Monasticon Anglicanum*, awareness of the Cromwellian regime's repres-sive potential may have worked in combination with economic factors to discourage members of the Stationers' Company from taking on such work.[17] Dugdale took charge of organising the printing of the text, the engraving of the illustrations and the bringing of the whole together. Initially he clearly saw himself as the midwife to another author's work. In October 1652 he described the *Monasticon Anglicanum* as 'the work that my freind Mr Dodsworth hath in the presse' when he found himself importuned by several friends to make an unscheduled visit to London as it 'doth want my assistance'.[18] The book was still not published when Dodsworth died in August 1654. In his will written four years before, Dodsworth had appointed John Rushworth to oversee the publication and suggested that Dugdale might be asked to write a dedication to Lord Fairfax. Rushworth had other ideas. He secured the services of the Royalist scholar John Marsham to write a learned preface in Latin. On reading this, William Somner, who had translated Saxon manuscripts for Dodsworth, became worried that his own and Dugdale's greater contribution were to be forgotten. Rushworth, however, elevated Dugdale from research assistant to co-editor, insisting that his name appear below Dodsworth's on the title page.[19] The *Monasticon Anglicanum* appeared in the spring of 1655 and by the summer had sold some 400 copies, of which around half had gone abroad. At the time Dugdale was defensive about his own contribution, repeatedly insisting that at least a third of the collection was his and that 'the ordering and methodizing thereof lay totally upon my shoulders'.[20] Subsequently he has been criticised for claiming the credit for Dodsworth's work. The supervision of the work's production was, however, undoubtedly greater than the contribution of many modern editors to works that bear their names. Moreover in 1654 the wily John Rushworth appears to have decided that an antiquarian work on monastic foundations would achieve better sales if associated with two known Royalists in addition to the deceased Dodsworth.

As the *Monasticon Anglicanum* wended its slow way through the press, Dugdale sent his own *Antiquities of Warwickshire* hard on its heels. Printing began early in 1655 and the work was ready for distribution at the beginning of May 1656. Once again there was no bookseller prepared to take on the work, and it was largely financed by persuading members of the gentry to sponsor engravings of their family monuments and coats of arms. Sir Simon Archer, who had been involved in the project since its inception two decades earlier, was tireless in persuading the Warwickshire gentry to contribute. The lavish illustrations in the volume were intended to increase its appeal, but they also complicated the printing process. While engravings could not be finalised without confirmation from the sponsor, the text also continued to change. Dugdale was still revising the section on the Fieldings in consultation with the Earl of Denbigh in August 1655 when Viscount Conway decided to send him some material for inclusion in the account of his own family.[21] When the work was finally published, it was a paean to the Warwickshire gentry, representing an image of a united county society which ignored the disruption that had been caused by the Civil War. The allegiances of individual gentlemen were not divulged and very few references to the destruction the county had experienced were included. The book carried two dedicatory epistles, the first to the gentry of Warwickshire, including a paragraph acknowledging Archer's contribution, and the second to Lord Hatton. Although Hatton had been Dugdale's patron for some of the time when he had been working on the *Antiquities*, he was not as instrumental as Archer in ensuring that the book was finally published. By dedicating the work to Hatton, however, Dugdale was able to include the name of the late king in equal-sized print in a reference to his patron's service on the Privy Council and to mention 'our sad distractions', which had sent Hatton into exile.[22] The *Antiquities of Warwickshire* was not an overtly Royalist publication, but the political sympathies of its author would not have been in doubt to his readers.

In his later description of the genesis of the next publication to bear his name, the *History of St Paul's*, Dugdale presented it as a way of preserving the surviving records of the cathedral which had happened to come into his hands. This represented his role as a preserver of documents associated with symbols of the Stuart dynasty, analogous to Dean Wren's preservation of the records of the Order of the Garter.[23] However, it also followed with inexorable logic from his involvement in the *Monasticon Anglicanum* and the related volume of engravings published by Daniel King as *The Cathedrall and Conventuall Churches of England and Wales* (1656). Although the inclusion of the text made the *History of St Paul's* a scholarly work, on which Dugdale could happily place his name, it is the engravings that are the heart of the book. In May 1656 Gerard Langbaine of Queen's College, Oxford, referred to his promise to finance an engraving 'to help out' with 'your Edition of the monuments of Pauls' and in September Thomas Barlow, the Bodleian librarian, in reference to his own plate wrote that 'Mr Hollar is an excellent person and deserves all incourage-ment'.[24] This suggests that the work was initially conceived as a volume of engravings which would provide gainful employment for Wencelaus Hollar, who had produced engravings for the *Monasticon Anglicanum* and the *Antiquities of Warwickshire*.[25] The usual procedure with such a volume seems to have been to get the artist to produce a sample engraving showing how the sponsor would be acknowledged and to use prints of this to encourage further sponsor-ship. Thus in 1654 Dugdale had circulated Hollar's view of Kenilworth Castle to demonstrate to potential sponsors of the engravings for the *Antiquities of Warwickshire* what they would get for their money. The first engravings to be made were probably the four views by Hollar sponsored by John Robinson in 1656. Indeed Robinson, a London alderman and nephew of Laud, seems likely to have been the instigator of the *History of St Paul's*, perhaps by initially commissioning Hollar to produce the set of engravings from drawings he had made in the 1640s of the building with which Laud was so closely associated.

The engravings seem more likely to have been the original inspiration for the work, than Dugdale's chance encounter in the street, described in his auto-biography, with John Reading, the Inner Temple lawyer who had acquired the St Paul's papers. In his *Life* Dugdale describes Reading as a gentleman and offers no explanation as to how he came to acquire the papers of St Paul's. In fact Reading was a godly lawyer who supported Parliament and had the papers because he was counsellor to the Commissioners for Sequestrations. Like many lawyers in early Stuart England, he had compiled transcripts of legal records, which could be utilised for a fee by people pursuing lawsuits, and he had consequently had contacts with Dugdale's antiquarian circle before the Civil Wars.[26] It is unlikely that he appreciated that Dugdale was inter-ested in publishing the St Paul's papers. Antiquaries collected and transcribed vast volumes of documents, a very small percentage of which ever found their way into print. While Reading's legal position explains his possession of the manuscripts, his motives for retaining them probably involved a combination of a wish to preserve vulnerable documents and an appreciation of their potential monetary value. He clearly thought the documents were his property sufficiently to entitle him to lend them to Dugdale and to allow him to take them out of London into the country. Nor did he take steps to ensure that the entire archive would be preserved intact, either to assist his successors in office or against an eventual restoration of episcopal authority.[27] In 1656 there seemed to be no prospect that the monarchy and bishops would be restored and, consequently, little reason to preserve the collection of manuscripts intact against that possibility. Dugdale's account of how he preserved the collection was written after the Restoration, when such acts of apparent piety towards the Stuart dynasty were appreciated.[28]

While the expansion of the project to include the text may indeed have been due to a chance encounter in the street, it seems more likely to have resulted from an awareness within the antiquarian community that Reading had acquired the papers and was willing to allow access. He lent Dugdale a number of documents in the summer of 1656 to take home to Blyth Hall. When Dugdale returned to London in October 1656, he found that Reading had died. Through the good offices of the executor – very probably encouraged by John Robinson – he acquired the remainder of the documents that Reading had saved and decided to preserve them in print. When Dugdale returned to Blyth that Christmas, he was joined by Elias Ashmole, who also became a subscriber to the work. Once all the manuscripts preserved by Reading were in his possession, Dugdale decided to extend his account to include the controversial developments at the cathedral in the 1630s. In his quest to acquire testimony about more recent work on the cathedral from surviving witnesses, he was assisted by Edward Bysshe, through whom he received material from Henry King, former bishop of Chichester, in January 1657.

With the work on the *History of St Paul's* well under way Dugdale spent three weeks in the early summer of 1657 travelling with Elias Ashmole in the Fens of Cambridgeshire, Norfolk and Lincolnshire in order to observe the drainage work that had been carried out there. Following the publication of the *Antiquities of Warwickshire* Dugdale had been commissioned by the company responsible for the works to write a history of land drainage to promote its interests. Precisely how he obtained this commission is uncertain. In his autobiography he described it as having come from Lord Gorges, Sir John Marsham 'and others', thus obscuring the association with the Interregnum since both men remained involved in the company after the Restoration.[29] The obscure 'others' may have included John Thurloe, who knew Dugdale through their mutual involvement in the Uxbridge negotiations of 1645. By whatever means he secured the commission, the £150 he received for undertaking it was a very welcome contribution to his finances.[30]

The trip to the Fens was reminiscent of two earlier tours that Dugdale had made at Hatton's instigation through London, the Midlands and the north of England in 1640 and 1641 accompanied by a herald painter, recording the monuments and arms they found in the churches and cathedrals.[31] In the dedication of the *History of St Paul's*, Dugdale referred to 'this veiw' [sic] that he had taken of the country's ecclesiastical monuments and the encouragement he had received to 'communicate it to the World'. With the benefit of hindsight he associated the tours with Hatton's premonition of the destruction that the coming civil war would wreak on the country's churches, although the contemporary evidence does not bear out this interpretation. The collection of church notes was a common antiquarian activity and part of the accepted duties of heralds. In the years immediately before the Civil Wars Hatton had been in a financial position to place this activity on a more systematic footing. The preface to the *History of St Paul's* explained that Dugdale had thought it appropriate to begin the publication of his record of England's great churches with St Paul's, 'as one of the most eminent Structures of that kinde in the Christian World'.[32] As this suggests, he was considering the publication of a series of cathedral histories, if the *History of St Paul's* was successful. In 1655 he had referred to 'those Monuments of St Pauls and other places' in a letter to a Royalist friend,[33] and two years later he and Ashmole tacked a detour north to York, where they visited the minster, on to the end of what was already an exhausting tour. Dugdale had already collected epitaphs and details of the stained glass in the cathedrals of Ely, Peterborough, and Lincoln, and York Minster on his earlier tours, and his 1657 visit gave him the opportunity to check his notes and to survey the damage caused by the war. Through a contact at Lichfield, he was actively investigating the availability of materials for a history of his local cathedral, which was symbolic for Midlands Royalists as the place from where the Parliamentarian commander Lord Brooke was shot dead during a siege. The records of the bishop and of the dean and chapter had remained in the hands of Royalists out of favour with the new regime, who lived 'obscurely in the Countrey' following their ousting from the cathedral, complicating the process of finding and examining them.[34] Dugdale's success in obtaining subscribers for the *History of St Paul's*, and earlier in finding sponsors for the engravings of ecclesiastical buildings in the *Monasticon Anglicanum*, suggested that well-illustrated cathedral histories would prove popular. Moreover, when Sir Roger Twysden received his copy of the *History of St Paul's* he wrote to him: 'I wish you might have some good incouragement to doe the like for Westminster, where I could tell you of the like for the Abbots there to bee had, which in truth deserves to be put out.'[35] Unlike his previous works which had required lengthy research, cathedral histories offered Dugdale the possibility of relatively rapid publication.

A month after his return to Blyth from Yorkshire, and only around a year after embarking on the project, Dugdale wrote the dedication of the *History of St Paul's*. The book was printed during the autumn of 1657 and was ready for distribution in February 1658. The publication was managed personally by Dugdale using the printer Thomas Warren, who had printed the *Antiquities of Warwickshire* the previous year. This meant that he purchased the paper, delivered it to the printer, checked the proofs, had the books bound as his customers requested and arranged for their delivery. The *History of St Paul's* did not achieve the anticipated commercial success. This was presumably due to a combination of Dugdale's lack of experience as a publisher and book-seller and the cost of this lavishly illustrated folio work.[36] The print run was probably around 500 copies, of which a tenth were required for subscribers and as presentation copies, such as those sent to the libraries of Oxford and Cambridge.[37] Such works, however, had a limited market and were liable to lie on a bookseller's hands. When Dugdale left the heralds' office in March 1659 to move in with his newly married daughter, he still had 359 copies in his possession. Two months later he offloaded 340 copies on to his son-in-law, a Paul's Yard bookseller, at 6s 8d each, which suggested that he had by this time exhausted his own immediate market for the work. In 1666 some 300 copies of the edition were destroyed in the Great Fire.[38] In the light of these poor sales figures, Dugdale's enthusiasm for further volumes seems to have diminished, although he continued to work periodically on a single-volume history of the cathedrals until the manuscript of that too perished in the Great Fire, never to be resurrected.[39] The support of his subscribers meant that he did not need the *History of St Paul's* to sell well to a wider public, and what it did achieve was the reinforcing of his reputation as a scholar. By the end of the Interregnum he was receiving further offers of commissioned work and his financial position was sufficiently secure to allow him to begin printing the second volume of the *Monasticon Anglicanum*.[40]

Dugdale's comparative success in Interregnum London is at odds with the persistent image of Royalists during this period as marginalised. Frances Willmoth has argued on the strength of his acceptance of the commission to write the *History of Imbanking and Drayning* that we should not necessarily accept that Dugdale was as consistently and determinedly Royalist during the 1650s as he later presented himself. However, there is plenty of contemporary evidence that he was always a Royalist and always a supporter of the established church. His correspondence with Royalists in England and abroad reveals that he was not reconciled to the 'evil times' in which they were forced to live, and that he took a keen interest in the fate of Royalists and of ministers who fell out with the parliamentary authorities.[41] Antiquarian research provided Dugdale with the perfect excuse to visit prominent Royalists in their homes and to examine their papers, and in 1653 he visited Staunton Harold, where Sir Robert Shirley was beginning to build a new Gothic church. Shirley was one of the leading Royalists in the Midlands, and the church was a symbol of his linking of loyalty to the king with support for the episcopal church. The circle that gathered around Shirley at this time overlapped with the Laudian circle to which Dugdale and Hatton had belonged in Royalist Oxford.[42] When working among the archives kept in the Tower of London, Dugdale took advantage of the opportunity to visit Royalist prisoners there; while he was working on the *History of St Paul's*, they included Shirley, who died in the Tower in November 1656. In August 1657, immediately after completing the *History of St Paul's*, Dugdale visited Hatton and the former Royalist prisoners Sir Geoffrey Palmer and Sir Justinian Isham at their homes in Northamptonshire.[43]

The *Antiquities of Warwickshire* and the *History of St Paul's* were both dedicated to the prominent Royalist Lord Hatton. The financial burden of his support for the king precluded Hatton from resuming his status as an antiquarian patron, but he was able to act as a surrogate for Charles II as dedicatee of Dugdale's scholarship until the Restoration. Dugdale described the people who encouraged him to publish his records of church monuments, as those 'whose hearts, notwithstanding a multitude of discouragements, are still much affected to the honour of this Nation'.[44] In the circles associated with Hatton and Shirley the honour of the nation was held to depend upon both monarch and church, as a significant proportion of the people who read Dugdale's book would have been aware. It is apparent that Dugdale and others like him were not concealing their royalism during the Interregnum, but were assuming their right to acceptance within London society despite their refusal to deny their monarchical beliefs. In this respect parallels may be drawn between Royalists during the Interregnum and Catholics before the Civil War and after the Restoration. It is possible that Dugdale's unusually tolerant attitude towards Catholics in the reign of Charles II was prompted by this experience. The Cromwellian authorities seem to have demonstrated a similar tolerance of Royalists in their midst to that which Charles I had shown towards recusants. The publishing of an expensive volume destined for the libraries of gentlemen did not arouse their wrath, and the greatest restriction on the antiquarian writer was almost certainly self-censorship.

The *History of St Paul's* could be read as a neutral celebration of a historic building and a record of its monuments. As the cathedral of the City of London, St Paul's had been an ecclesiastical tourist attraction second only to Westminster Abbey, until the building had become unsafe to enter. Dugdale reminded his readers 'with what venerable respect, the most eminent men amongst us, for learning and knowledge' visited Westminster Abbey to observe the monuments and had formerly visited St Paul's for the same reason.[45] 'Out of a sad contemplation, therefore, that so glorious a structure, thus rais'd, inricht, and beautified by the piety of our deceased Ancestors, should be utterly destroyed, and become a wofull spectacle of ruine', Dugdale undertook 'to give some representation, as well to the present age, as future times, of what it hath been'.[46] The engravings included one showing Hollar's recreation of how he imagined the cathedral looked before it lost its spire, while none of the views depicted the actual, dilapidated state of the building. The cathedral was also portrayed in splendid isolation without the bookshops and other buildings or the milling crowds of people that surrounded it in mundane reality. Significantly the external views of the building do not show the preaching cross, which figured so prominently in earlier depictions of St Paul's. This engraving presented the cathedral as a memorial to the dead, not as a place of active worship.[47]

Dugdale could have represented his motivation as purely antiquarian, but he chose to make it explicit that he regarded the work as a duty laid upon him 'as I am a son of the Church of England'.[48] Despite the controversy over the renovation of the cathedral during the reign of Charles I, two of Hollar's engravings were prominently dedicated to William Laud.[49] The archbishop, who had been executed by Parliament little more than a decade before, was also praised in the text as 'a person of great parts, and a most publick Spirit'. The dedication to Hatton spoke of his having foreseen the 'Presbyterian contagion', prevalent in the Long Parliament, which had led the country into trouble and caused such damage to its churches. [50] While Presbyterianism might have fallen somewhat from favour in London following the incursion of the Scots army into England, this was hardly conciliatory towards Parliamentarians. Unlike the *Monasticon Anglicanum* and the *Antiquities of Warwickshire*, where each engraving must be examined to identify the sponsor, in the *History of St Paul's* the forty-one individuals and one livery company who contributed plates were conveniently listed at the end. An analysis of this roll-call of contributors provides an insight into Dugdale's circle during this period and the sort of people who were willing to be associated with a work in favour of the Church of England.

The subscribers to the *History of St Paul's* fall into several, overlapping groups. The least interesting for the purposes of my argument are those subscribers whose antiquarian interests, connection to a particular individual or family piety led them to sponsor an engraving. Sir Simon Archer, the Staffordshire historian Walter Chetwynd and Charles Neville, vice-provost of Cambridge University, were old friends who had all previously contributed to Dugdale's *Antiquities of Warwickshire*.[51] Christopher Clapham's motivation was an interest in genealogy.[52] His wife, Margaret, paid for an engraving of the tomb of John Donne, whose preaching she admired. Katherine Baskerville sponsored the engraving of the monument to her husband, a royal physician who had died in 1641.[53] The Mercers' Company paid for an engraving of the tomb it had provided for its former member and benefactor John Colet, the humanist founder of St Paul's School.[54] Among those prompted by family piety to sponsor the engraving of an ancestor's tomb the political views of Sir Edmund Bacon, John Herbert and John Leigh are unknown. Sir Thomas Hewit's receipt of a baronetcy at the Restoration suggests that he was a Royalist. Heneage Finch, Earl of Winchilsea, who contributed the plate of his grandfather's monument, certainly was one. He provided financial support to Charles II in his exile until he was forced to flee to the continent after the abortive coup of 1655.[55]

The subscribers who provide the immediate context for the publication of the *History of St Paul's* are the friends with whom Dugdale was in frequent contact when in London. Such meetings have left little trace in the archive, but one surviving letter from his engraver does throw light on Dugdale's London circle. In January 1656 Hollar was in trouble over having attended mass at the Venetian ambassador's chapel and needed the assistance of his friends. Dugdale arranged to see Hollar and John Aubrey after he had called on Sir Wingfield Bodenham, a Royalist antiquary interested in the history of Rutland. However, the friends missed their meeting, which led Hollar to write his letter. From this we learn that Edward Bysshe and his brother-in-law James Green (or Greene) had acted as Hollar's legal representatives before the justices. While Hollar had plenty of legal assistance, he needed the money that Dugdale owed him for the *Antiquities of Warwickshire* to resolve his problems with the court officials. Some ten days later Dugdale paid him £10.[56] All four of the friends mentioned in this letter – Bodenham, Aubrey, Bysshe and Green – appear in the list of the subscribers to the *History of St Paul's*. The snapshot of Dugdale's London life provided by Hollar's mishap also indicates how he drew his friends from both sides of the political divide in the 1650s, although the Royalists predominated. Bodenham was a Royalist gentleman from Rutland, who had been imprisoned in the Tower in the late 1640s. Aubrey was also a Royalist. Bysshe had been a Parliamentarian and alleged Presbyterian, but was implicated in Royalist conspiracy in 1651. James Green came from a Parliamentarian family, his father having been a judge in the sheriff's court in London throughout the conflict and a sergeant of the Commonwealth for three years before his death in 1653. Green's own political views are unknown.[57] As we have seen, Elias Ashmole was one of Dugdale's closest friends, and they spent a great deal of time in each other's company in London and the country. His friendship with Ashmole brought Dugdale into association with the alchemist and astrologer William Backhouse and his son-in-law William Bishop, who both became subscribers to the *History of St Paul's*. Although the details of Backhouse's life are obscure, his support for the episcopal church is indicated by his employment of William Lloyd, future bishop of St Asaph, as tutor to his children in the late 1640s.[58] From his later correspondence we know that Dugdale saw the Yorkshire antiquary Richard Gascoigne at the London home of the second Earl of Strafford during the 1650s, while associated with

299

Catalogus perfonarum, natalibus & virtute proprià illuſtrium quæ pro ſuâ in ædes Paulinas (mole & majeſtate ſacrâ venerandas) benevolentiâ , ad editionem hanc promovendam , Iconibuſq; ſummâ arte accuratis ornandam , ſumptus ultrò erogârunt ; quarum nomina , Honorumq; titulos , juxta Iconiſmorum ordinem , ſeriemq; Paginarum , præſens tabella ut infrà exhibet.

pag.

THomas *Chichley* de **Wimpole** in agro *Cantabr.* Arm. 40

Carolus Nevill Arm. Vice-præpoſitus Collegii Regalis *Cantabr.* 52

Jacobus Green, filius natu minor, *Johannis Green* ſervientis ad legem. 60

Maria uxor *Chriſtophori Clapham* de **Bemeſley** in agro *Ebor.* Arm. 62

Cuſtodes & aſſiſtentes *Mercerorum Lond.* ſocietatis 64

Thomas Hewit de **Piſhaw-Bury**, in Com. *Hertf.* eques aur. 66

Prænobilis *Carolus* Vicecomes *Cullen*, (de **Ruſhton** in agro *Northampt.*)68

Edmundus Bacon de **Redgrave** in com. *Suff.* Baronettus 70

Willielmus Haward de **Tanridge** in agro *Surregienſi* eques aur. 72

Franciſcus Compton, filius natu quintus *Spenſeri* nuper Comitis *Northampt.* 74

Ricardus Gaſcoigne de **Bramham-biggin** in agro *Ebor.* arm. 76

Brome Whorwood de **Holton** in agro *Oxon.* arm. 78

Gerardus Langbaine PræpoſitusCollegii Regin. *Oxon.* 80

Prænob. *Chriſtophorus* Baro *Hatton*, de **Kirby** (in agro *Northampt.*) 82

Prænob. *Coniers* Baro *Darcy* & *Coniers* (de **Hornby** caſtro in agro *Ebor.*) 84

Edwardus Waterhouſe de **Greeneford** in agro *Middleſex.* armig. 86

Johannes Herbert, filius natu minor *Philippi* nuper Comitis *Pombrochiæ* & *Montegomerici.* 88

Chriſtophorus Clapham de **Bemeſley** in agro *Ebor.* armig. 90

Prænobilis *Iſabella*, uxor *Jacobi* Com. *Northampt.* 92

Robertus Maſon LL.D. & *Regi Carolo*, ejus nominis primo, à Libellis ſupplicibus. 94

Johannes Aubrey de.... in agro *Wilton.* armig. 96

pag.

Robertus Porey de **Compton** *parva*, in agro *Glouc.* armig. 98

Orlandus Bridgeman eques aur. interioris Templi *Lond.* ſocius 100

Tho. Stanley de **Cumberlow** in agro *Hertford.* arm. 102

Walterus Chetwynd primogenitus *Walteri Chetwynd* de **Grendon** in agro *Warw.* arm. 104

Katherina relicta *Simonis Baskervile*, eq. aur. ib.

Johannes Leigh, filius & hæres *Wollai Leigh*, nuper de **Wickham** in agro *Cantiano* arm. 106

Prænobilis *Heneagius* Comes de **Wincheley.** 108

Simon Archer de **Tanworth** in agro *Warw.* eques aur. 110

Wingfeldus Bodenham de **Ryhall** in agro *Rutl.* eq. aur. 112

Guil. Backhouſe de **Swallowfield** in agro *Berrocenſi* arm. 114

Guil. Biſhop de **South-Warnborow** in agro *Hantonienſi* arm. 116

Prænobilis *Albericus* Comes *Oxon.* 127

Thomas Barlow Collegii Regin. ſocius & Proto-bibl. *Bodleianus Oxon.* 133

Edwardus Biſhe de **Smalifield** in agro *Surr.* arm. 161

Johannes Robinſon Civis & Senator *Londinenſis* 162,163,164;165.

Johannes Walpole de **Pinchbeck** in agro *Linc.* Eq. aur. 166.

Samuel Collins. Medicinæ Dr. 167.

Henricus Compton, filius natu minimus *Spenſeri* nuper *Comitis Northamptoniæ* 168.

Elias Aſhmole medii Templi *Lond.* ſocius 169

Willielmus Walter primogenitus *Willielmi Walter* de **Sarſden** in agro *Oxon.* eq. aurat. & Bar. 170

Johannes Porey Civis *Lond.* 258.

Yyy 2

THE

Figure 10.1 Published list of those who paid for engravings in William Dugdale's *History of St Paul's* (1658). Reproduced by permission of the Dean and Chapter of St Paul's Cathedral.

Figure 10.2 View of St Paul's from the north dedicated to William Laud, from William Dugdale's *History of St Paul's* (1658). Reproduced by permission of the Dean and Chapter of St Paul's Cathedral.

the College of Arms was the heraldic writer Edward Waterhouse. After the Restoration Waterhouse was persuaded by Archbishop Sheldon to take holy orders.[59] Thomas Stanley, a poet and classical scholar, was an ardent Royalist and founder of the order of the Black Riband, whose supporters had worn black mourning bands on their arms during Charles I's captivity to demonstrate their loyalty to the king. He was related by marriage to John Marsham, who had written the preface for the *Monasticon Anglicanum*.[60] The physician Samuel Collins was presumably also one of Dugdale's London acquaintances. He was a fellow of King's College, Cambridge, where his Laudian uncle was provost until deprived by Parliament in 1645.[61] During 1657 Dugdale was also frequently in the company of Lord Hatton, newly returned from the exiled court in Paris. As well as being the dedicatee of the volume, Lord Hatton sponsored the engraving of the grand monument to his namesake, Elizabeth I's Lord Chancellor.

A significant group of subscribers to the *History of St Paul's* were Royalists with whom Dugdale had become acquainted in Oxford during the Civil Wars. These included Francis and Henry Compton, two of the younger sons of Spencer Compton, Earl of Northampton and commander of the Royalist forces at Hopton Heath, and their sister-in-law Isabella, the wife of the third earl and daughter of Lady Anne Clifford.[62] Sir William Haward was a gentleman of the privy chamber to Charles I and had antiquarian interests. Sir John Walpole had been standard-bearer to Charles I and knighted for his military service, while Charles Cockayne had been created Viscount Cullen after raising a troop of horse for the king. Conyers, Lord Darcy, had served as a colonel of a Royalist regiment of foot and Brome Whorwood was the husband of Jane, who formed a close friendship with Charles I during his captivity.[63] Aubrey Vere, Earl of Oxford, had been in the Tower in 1654 suspected of conspiring against the protector, at a time when Dugdale was able to combine research among the records with visits to Royalist prisoners. Sir Thomas Chicheley of Wimpole, who had sat for Cambridgeshire in the Long Parliament, was involved in various Royalist conspiracies and in 1655 had been imprisoned in Great Yarmouth.[64] Sir Orlando Bridgeman appears to have worked more circumspectly for the restoration of the monarchy. Similarly cautious were the two Oxford academics among the subscribers, Thomas Barlow and Gerard Langbaine, who had both retained their positions in the university after the departure of the Royalist garrison by careful concessions to the parliamentary authorities. Their continuing sympathy for the Royalist cause is shown by their contributions to the secret collection in support of exiled bishops in 1654.[65]

A further group of subscribers was associated with William Juxon, the bishop of London. Juxon had taken no part in the Civil Wars, but retired to the quiet life of a rural parson. Nevertheless he had defended Laud at his trial and attended Charles I on the scaffold. Robert Porey (or Pory) of Little Compton, Gloucestershire, was an ejected minister and Juxon's chaplain, living with him in his rural retreat. John Porey, citizen of London, who sponsored the engraving of the Dance of Death, was presumably a brother or other close relation. Another subscriber, William Walter, had a sister who married Juxon's nephew and heir. To this group may be added Robert Mason, the chancellor of the diocese of Winchester until the Civil War.[66]

The *History of St Paul's* was not a work directed at a mass readership. It was destined for the libraries of the gentry and wealthy antiquaries. For such contemporaries the pro-Royalist, pro-Anglican tenor of the *History of St Paul's* would have been reinforced by looking at the list of subscribers to the engravings (see figure 10.1). Although comparatively few of the subscribers are known to have been actively engaged in Royalist conspiracy, many had been imprisoned or confined to house arrest during the Interregnum. It is doubtful that the government would have been at all concerned about the publication of such an elite antiquarian work; its importance lay in creating a sense of community among the embattled supporters of the episcopal church. In 1658 the structure of St Paul's Cathedral was in a sorry state of repair. The inner scaffolding that supported the vault having been removed, part of the roof had collapsed, and it was unsafe to enter the building for fear of falling masonry. However, the cathedral depicted in Hollar's engravings displayed none of this decay; the views represented the building in splendid isolation, not jostled by houses and shops (see figure 10.2), and the plans imposed a uniformity of construction, which the medieval builders had never achieved. To an embattled circle of Royalists the *History of St Paul's* presented an idealised image of the cathedral, standing as a metaphor for the Church of England. William Higgins, a member of the chapter of Lichfield Cathedral, saw the author as another Atlas, bearing up 'strenuously what base erthly minded Sacriledg beates down'.[67] When Dugdale began to compile the *History of St Paul's*, there can have seemed little prospect that the monarchy and the episcopal church would be restored in his lifetime. While the majority of attention has been focused on the Royalists who went into exile or who plotted violent insurrections, this work stands as a reminder to us that there were many ways of keeping the Royalist flame alive. By refusing to hide their beliefs, while interacting with the situation as they found it, men like Dugdale helped to make the restoration of the Stuarts and of the Church of England eventually appear a reasonable idea for reasonable men.

NOTES

1 F. Willmoth, 'Dugdale's *History of Imbanking and Drayning*: a "Royalist" antiquarian in the sixteen-fifties', *HR*, 71 (1998), pp. 281–302.

2 Psalm 29, v. 2; P. Lake, 'The Laudian style: order, uniformity and the pursuit of the beauty of holiness in the 1630s', in K. Fincham (ed.), *The Early Stuart Church, 1603–1642* (Basingstoke, 1993), pp. 161–85; K. Fincham, 'The restoration of altars in the 1630s', *HJ*, 44:4 (2001), pp. 919–40; K. Sharpe, *The Personal Rule of Charles I* (New Haven, CT, 1992), chapter 6; J. Eales, 'Iconoclasm, iconography, and the altar in the English Civil War', *Studies in Church History*, 28 (1992), pp. 313–27.

3 M. Dorman, 'Shirley, Sir Robert, fourth baronet (1629–1656)', *Oxford DNB*. Shirley produced proposals for the identification of support of the Church of England with royalism in 1656. The term 'Anglican' may be considered anachronistic before the Restoration. It is used here to indicate those people who supported the idea of the re-establishment of an episcopal church. Although Dugdale was himself a Laudian, not all those who supported the idea of a Church of England held the sacramental and ceremonial beliefs associated with the former archbishop.

4 W. Hamper (ed.), *The Life, Diary and Correspondence of William Dugdale* (1827), pp. 253–5, 291–2, 316–17, 330–2; *CSPD 1655*, p. 592.

5 Birmingham Reference Library, Warwickshire MSS L/3, fol. 87.

6 A. Wood, *Athenae Oxonienses* (1692), pp. 483–4; Hamper (ed.), *William Dugdale*, pp. 226–8.

7 Hamper (ed.), *William Dugdale*, pp. 233–7. Edward Norgate died in December 1650.

8 Wiltshire RO, 1300/2755/A+B.

9 Warwickshire RO, Z13/4.

10 Staffordshire RO, D868/5/2.

11 R. Cust, 'Archer, Sir Simon (1581–1662)', *Oxford DNB*; P. Styles, *Studies in Seventeenth Century West Midlands History* (Kineton, 1978), pp. 1–41.

12 Hamper (ed.), *William Dugdale*, pp. 226–8.

13 *Ibid.*, p. 99.

14 *Gentleman's Magazine* (June 1838), p. 592. This sentiment is expressed in a letter from Dugdale to Sir Edward Nicholas at Antwerp in February 1660. At the time of Charles I's trial and execution Dugdale wrote to Sir Simonds D'Ewes that he was sure that 'the great hand of God is eminently in this worke', although the two men could not understand his purpose: Hamper (ed.), *William Dugdale*, pp. 218–19.

15 See, for example, Warwickshire RO, Z13/8 and CR2017/F101; BL, Add. MS 6396, fol. 17.

16 Hamper (ed.), *William Dugdale*, pp. 263–4.

17 A. Johns, *The Nature of the Book* (Chicago, IL, 1998). On Cromwellian censorship, see D. Hirst, 'The politics of literature in the English republic', *Seventeenth Century*, 5 (1990), pp. 133–55; J. Peacey, 'Cromwellian England: a propaganda state?', *History*, 91:302 (2006), pp. 176–99; Jason McElligott, *Royalism, Print and Censorship in Revolutionary England* (Woodbridge, 2007), chapters 6, 7 and 8.

18 Birmingham Reference Library, Warwickshire MS L/3, fol. 87.

19   Hamper (ed.), *William Dugdale*, pp. 282–5.

20   *Gentleman's Magazine* (June 1838), pp. 590–1. Dugdale's letter is not clear on this point, but it appears that the sales were to bookseller intermediaries on credit.

21   Warwickshire RO, CR2017/F101; Hamper (ed.), *William Dugdale*, pp. 291–2; W. Dugdale, *The Antiquities of Warwickshire* (1656), pp. 57, 621.

22   Dugdale, *Antiquities of Warwickshire*, pp. a3–a4v.

23   Lisa Jardine, *On a Grander Scale* (2002), pp. 44–5.

24   Hamper (ed.), *William Dugdale*, pp. 313–14, 316.

25   Twenty-nine of the forty-five engravings in W. Dugdale, *The History of St Paul's* (1658) are signed by Hollar, while the remainder are unsigned.

26   Bodl., Eng Lett b 1, fol. 29; C. Markham and J. Cox (eds), *Northampton Borough Records*, 2 vols (Northampton, 1898), vol. II, p. 117; G. Aylmer, *The State's Servants* (1973), p. 418; HMC, *Manuscripts in Various Collections*, vol. II (1903), p. 115.

27   N. Ramsay, 'The library and archives to 1897', in D. Keene, A. Burns and A. Saint (eds), *St Paul's: The Cathedral Church of London 604–2004* (New Haven, CT, 2004), pp. 418–19.

28   John Rushworth's similar claim concerning the preservation of Privy Council papers is typically regarded with more scepticism: J. Raymond, 'Rushworth, John (c.1612–1690)', Oxford DNB. Dean Wren, however, did recover the registers of the Order of the Garter from the parliamentary commissioners in order to ensure their preservation: C.S.L. Davies, 'Christopher Wren (1589–1658), dean of Windsor, his family and connections: patronage and careers during the Civil Wars, Interregnum and Restoration', *Southern History*, 27 (2005), pp. 24–47.

29   Hamper (ed.), *William Dugdale*, p. 28 mentions Lord Gorges only, but Sir John Marsham is mentioned in the version of his life published in Dugdale, *History of St Paul's*, 2nd edn (1716), p. xviii.

30   Hamper (ed.), *William Dugdale*, pp. 28, 104–5; A.W. Skempton et al., *A Biographical Dictionary of Civil Engineers* (2002), p. 232; J. Thirsk, 'Plough and pen: agricultural writers in the seventeenth century', in T.H. Aston et al. (eds), *Social Relations and Ideas* (Cambridge, 1983), pp. 295–318; C. Josten, *Elias Ashmole* (Oxford, 1966), vol. II, pp. 704, 706. Walter Blith was a neighbour of Dugdale's in Warwickshire, while Ashmole was friendly with Jonas Moore, the company's surveyor.

31   BL, Add. MS 71474 is an incomplete record of the tours.

32   Dugdale, *History of St Paul's* (1658), pp. a3v–a4.

33   Staffordshire RO, D868/5, fol. 8.

34   Hamper (ed.), *William Dugdale*, pp. 205–8, 319–21, 333–4.

35   Twysden was a supporter of what he described in 1658 as the 'afflicted Church of England': *ibid.*, pp. 330–1, 335–7.

36   The lack of repeat editions of comparable antiquarian works suggests that the market was always limited: see Jan Broadway, *'No historie so meete': Gentry Culture and the Development of Local History in Elizabethan and Early Stuart England* (Manchester, 2006), p. 37.

37   The size of the edition was dictated by the engravings, since for a larger print run the etchings would have needed retouching: P. Nash et al. (eds), *Early Printed Books 1478–*

1840: catalogue of the British Architectural Library Early Imprints Collection (1994), vol. I, entry 932.

38 Hamper (ed.), *William Dugdale*, p. 104. Dugdale reported that his son-in-law was bankrupt in August 1660, which may have hampered sales of the book: Staffordshire RO, D868/5/13.

39 Hamper (ed.), *William Dugdale*, p. 104; F. Maddison et al., *Sir William Dugdale* (Warwick, 1953), p. 70; College of Arms, London, 'Dugdale's visitation papers for Yorkshire': Nathaniel Johnston to William Dugdale, Nov. 1666.

40 Each subscriber seems to have paid a minimum of £5 for his or her plates. HMC, *Manuscripts of the Earl of Westmoreland and Others* (1885), pp. 204–7; Hamper (ed.), *William Dugdale*, pp. 330–1; *Gentleman's Magazine* (June 1838), pp. 591–2.

41 For example, Hamper (ed.), *William Dugdale*, pp. 293–4, 302–3 and Staffordshire RO, D868/5. Only a few letters from Dugdale's correspondence with exiled Royalists survive, but he was certainly in correspondence with Hatton, whom he visited in France in 1648, with the Arundel circle and with Sir Edward Walker. One letter from Francis Junius at The Hague refers to Dugdale conferring with Joseph Jane, intelligencer to Sir Edward Nicholas, about 'Cornubian and other businesses'.

42 Hamper (ed.), *William Dugdale*, pp. 269–72. For example, Peter Gunning, who had been tutor to Hatton's son in Oxford, subsequently became chaplain to Shirley.

43 Leicestershire RO, DE2191; J. Wake and G. Isham, 'Sir William Dugdale in Northamptonshire', *Northamptonshire Past and Present*, 2 (1955), pp. 8–12. Isham was also a high churchman and supported deprived clergy during the Interregnum.

44 Dugdale, *History of St Paul's* (1658), p. a4.

45 *Ibid.*, p. 44.

46 *Ibid.*, p. 192.

47 See the illustrations in P. Tudor-Craig, '*Old St Paul's': The Society of Antiquaries Diptych, 1616* (2004).

48 Dugdale, *History of St Paul's* (1658), p. 192.

49 On the controversy see Sharpe, *The Personal Rule of Charles I*, pp. 322–8; D. Crankshaw, 'Community, city and nation, 1540–1714', in Keene et al. (eds), *St Paul's*, pp. 45–70. The other engravings are not dedicated, but each carries an acknowledgment of the sponsor.

50 Dugdale, *History of St Paul's* (1658), pp. a3–4, 157, 163, 164.

51 Chetwynd, whose father had been closely associated with the Earl of Essex, maintained a strict neutrality during the Civil War although many of his friends and family were Royalists: H.E. Chetwynd-Stapylton, *The Chetwynds of Ingestre* (1892), pp. 193–200.

52 Merevale Hall, Atherstone,Warwickshire, HT 3G. Roger Dodsworth had worked on the Clifford archive.

53 Margaret's first husband was Robert Moyle, protonotary of Common Pleas, and she would have had the opportunity to hear Donne preach at St Paul's. T. Cooper, 'Baskerville, Sir Simon (*bap.* 1574, *d.* 1641)', rev. B. Nance, *Oxford DNB*; J.H. Baker, 'Moyle, Robert (1589/90–1638)', *Oxford DNB*.

54 J.B. Trap, 'Colet, John (1467–1519)', *Oxford DNB*.

55 S.P. Anderson, 'Finch, Heneage, Third Earl of Winchilsea (1627/8–1689), *Oxford DNB*.

56 BL, Add. MS 21450, fol. 1, published in G. Tindall, *The Man who Drew London* (2002), pp. 119–20; Warwickshire RO, Z13/8.

57 Leicestershire RO, DE2191; W. Priest, 'Greene, John (1578–1653)', *Oxford DNB*.

58 J. Speake, 'Backhouse, William (1593–1662)', *Oxford DNB*; M. Mullett, 'Lloyd, William (1627–1717)', *Oxford DNB*.

59 Bodl., Top Yorks MS c36, fol. 33; D.R. Woolf, 'Waterhouse, Edward (1619–1670)', *Oxford DNB*. Sheldon was also a member of Sir Robert Shirley's circle during the Interregnum.

60 W. Chernaik, 'Stanley, Thomas (1625–1678)', *Oxford DNB*. John Evelyn recorded being introduced to Marsham, Dugdale and Stanley in November 1659: E.S. de Beer (ed.), *The Diary of John Evelyn*, 6 vols (Oxford, 1955), vol. III, p. 237.

61 N.W.S. Cranfield, 'Collins, Samuel (1576–1651)', *Oxford DNB*; T. Cooper, 'Collins, Samuel (1617–1685)', rev. M. Bevan, *Oxford DNB*.

62 Following the death of Spencer Compton, Hatton became involved in resolving the disputes between the third earl, his mother and his brothers: BL, Add MS 29570.

63 W.H. Kelliher, 'Haward, Sir William (c.1617–1704)', *Oxford DNB*; M.R. Toynbee and P. Young, *Strangers in Oxford* (1973), p. 258; J. Nicholas, *The Topographer and Genealogist* (1858), vol. III, p. 440; P. Newman, *Royalist Officers in England and Wales, 1642–1660* (1981), p. 103; S. Poynting, 'Deciphering the king: Charles I's letters to Jane Whorwood', *Seventeenth Century*, 21:1 (2006), pp. 128–40.

64 V. Slater, 'Vere, Aubrey de, Twentieth Earl of Oxford (1627–1703)', *Oxford DNB*; S.L. Sadler, 'Chicheley, Sir Thomas (1614–1699)', *Oxford DNB*.

65 H. Nenner, 'Bridgeman, Sir Orlando (1609–1674)', *Oxford DNB*; J. Spurr, 'Barlow, Thomas (1608/9–1691)', *Oxford DNB*; A.J. Hegarty, 'Langbaine, Gerard (1608/9–1658)', *Oxford DNB*.

66 William Juxon had retired to Little Compton, which was owned by his brother John. B. Quintrell, 'Juxon, William (bap. 1582, d. 1663)', *Oxford DNB*; S. Wright, 'Pory, Robert (1608?–1669)', *Oxford DNB*; M. Jansson, 'Mason, Robert (1588×90–1662)', *Oxford DNB*.

67 Hamper (ed.), *William Dugdale*, pp. 333–4.

Chapter 11

Atlantic royalism? Polemic, censorship and the 'Declaration and Protestation of the Governour and Inhabitants of Virginia'

Jason McElligott

I

Historians of those who won the Civil Wars have long advocated a 'British' context to the study of the troubles of the mid-seventeenth century. In more recent years, 'British' history has been increasingly challenged by the broader perspective of 'Atlantic history': a burgeoning field of enquiry which, in the Anglophone world at least, has tended to focus on the economic, religious and political links which tied Britain to other states and nations around the Atlantic rim, primarily, but not exclusively, in North America. There are important conceptual and methodological problems with both 'British' and 'Atlantic' history,[1] but they are at least dynamic and energetic attempts to explore new intellectual horizons in the early modern period. In contrast to these innovative methodologies, historians of those who lost the Civil Wars have remained doggedly Anglo-centric in their research interests. This intellectual and methodological conservatism is unfortunate because it will never be possible to present a rounded, nuanced and textured account of royalism as a whole until we know much more about the experience of Royalists outside England: how did the experiences of Irish and Scottish Royalists compare and contrast with each other, and with those of their comrades in England? Could, or did, the nature of royalism differ between the three kingdoms? How did men with such different cultural, religious and political backgrounds interact with each other, particularly during periods of exile on the continent? Work by Geoffrey Smith, Lloyd Bowen, Robert Armstrong and Mark Stoyle suggests that there is a growing interest among scholars in what might be termed the Celtic dimensions of royalism.[2] Furthermore, recent and forthcoming work by (among others) Marika Keblusek, John Cronin, Philip Major, Ann Hughes and Julie Sanders sheds new light on the European contexts of British royalism. Yet we still have little or no concept of an Atlantic dimension to royalism.

The idea of Atlantic royalism might, at first glance, seem preposterous. The literature around the area of Atlantic history is probably as far removed as it is possible to get from the traditionally rather staid study of Royalists and royalism. Yet the lack of an Atlantic dimension to the study of royalism is strange when one considers that six of the twenty-four British colonies in the New World rebelled against the regime that came to power in England in 1649. These rebellions took place in Antigua, Barbados, Bermuda, Maryland, Newfoundland and Virginia.[3] All of these territories were reduced to obedience to the English Commonwealth by early 1652, but during the first years of the republic they provided the authorities in London with a potentially very dangerous problem. The rebellious colonies were sources of refuge for Royalist fugitives; possible sites of new civil strife between colonists for and against the Regicide; potential sources of financial and military aid to Charles II in Europe; and prospective launching pads for attacks on Commonwealth shipping. During the first years of the republic the authorities in London frequently cast a worried eye over developments in the New World. It became common, for example, to allow passengers travelling to the New World to depart only after they had taken the Oath of Engagement to the Commonwealth of England.[4]

Carla Pestana's *The English Atlantic in an Age of Revolution, 1640–1661* has sketched the outline of these revolts, but there is much that is still unknown about how and why these settlers rose, and the nature and extent of their loyalism.[5] The neglect of these conflicts by historians has been due, in part, to the destruction of an enormous amount of historical sources relating to colonial America as a result of the vagaries of climate, fires, war and accidents. In this context, the discovery of a text which purports to be a faithful copy of a declaration made in Virginia abhorring the Regicide of Charles I and committing the settlers in the colony to fight for his son, Charles II, may provide an opportunity to assess the nature and extent of royalism in one particular colony and, by extension, force us to rethink our attitude to royalism in the rest of colonial America. If genuine, this remarkable document sheds new light on three related issues: the nature and extent of loyalism in the British Atlantic world; the nature and changing fortunes of British royalism; and, perhaps most importantly, the trans-oceanic links between the two phenomena.

II

The 568-word alleged declaration from Virginia appeared in London in early January 1650 in issue no. 37 of a surreptitious, underground Royalist newsbook entitled *The Man in the Moon*. This title was one of fifty-one separate Royalist serials which appeared in London in the turbulent thirty-three months between September 1647 and June 1650. Many of these Royalist newsbooks survived for only a few weeks, but a number managed to appear for longer periods of between one and two years. There were a dozen separate Royalist titles in production during the summer of 1648,[6] but thereafter the number of newsbooks declined, as some of the existing titles disappeared and fewer new ones were introduced. The decline in the number of Royalist newsbooks was a result of the demoralising victory of the New Model Army in the Second Civil War, as well as the increased efforts of the authorities in London to arrest those involved with these serials. The months after the execution of Charles I saw a number of new Royalist newsbooks, but most survived for no more than a few weeks: the exception was *The Man in the Moon*, which first appeared in April 1649 and was finally suppressed by the Cromwellian regime in early June 1650. There was little news as such in *The Man in the Moon*; it was mostly devoted to rather coarse attempts to poke fun at the perceived ridiculousness, cruelty, pomposity and hypocrisy of the Puritans. It was primarily focused on events in London, but at the top of page 5 of issue no. 37 the author informed his readers: 'There is a Declaration and Protestation of the Governour and Inhabitants of *Virginia*, which was taken by all, onely some few of the Independent party [excepted]; it came to my hands by a Captain that came in a *New-England* Ship, which I will give you *verbatim*.' He then provided the text of this alleged declaration, which reads:

> *When we do duly consider the late report that hath bin brought in amongst us; That the Schismaticall Faction in* England; *that walk in the name of Independents, have laid violent hands upon the sacred person of the King, and with horror we report it here, usurped the power and formalitie of lawful Iustice, and to depose him, and imbrue their impious hands more than barbarously in his royal blood, whom the lawes both of God and man hath fenced from us, yea, from account or question by any earthly power; we confesse the villanie of this Act exceeds all or any yet whatsoever that beares the name of wickednesse, hoping that though the guilt of so superlative a Treason could not refraine [i.e. restrain?] their madnesse, yet the sense of punishment would affright them, which the whole world of men must threaten against such open sinne, so pernicious, as destructive to humanitie it selfe: yet we call to mind, with what a high and desperate hand this viperous brood have carried on their designs, not sparing the most sacred and most precious blood of Gods Annointed to satisfie their Avarice; nay, defying God himself, by their open Blasphemies and pernicious Lyes: when we have these things in memorie, our fears surpasse our hopes, [and] may allow us the boldnesse to separate from their master-piece of villanie: and though we have not hitherto received other wayes then a bare Report, and not by a lawfull Information, which only injoyneth a publike notice to be taken thereof; yet doubting, though the Information but slight, yet our silence might argue our allowance or approbation of so horrid a Treason, and give the world occasion to suspect our Loyaltie: To vindicate our selves from so hated an Imputation, we thought it our dutie to publish this our Declaration and Protestation, that we have in detestation of Treason so high and horrid, monstrous, impious, and hereticall, according to our Oath, and the many Oathes the Miscreants have taken themselves, that damnable, Jesuiticall, and now Independent doctrine That Princes may be deposed and murthered by their owne subjects.*

That with all reall sinceritie we will prosecute such who shall be in our power; and shall be convinced to have beene Actors and consenting, or in mind approving so horrid a treason: That we wil never submit to any Commission, Act, or Ordinance, from those that call themselves the Parliament of England, who are said to have usurped power over the Kings life; but rather trust our selves to the Woods and Mountaines, nay first to the faith of the Turks, or our neighbour Savages, then yield obedience to these perjured Tray-tors: that in case of the K. death, we do acknowledge the late Prince of Wales his heire and Lawfull successor, and now to be rightfull King of all his Dominions, and of this Country of Virginia; and that laying aside all other interest of Wife, Children, and Estates we will maintaine and defend his Titles to our last blood and latest breath: All this we swear upon the holy Evangelists, and as we do duely and Religiously observe the same, so may the blessing in Gods holy Book contained, fall upon us, our wives, and children, and for the breach thereof, may all the Curses in the same Booke, be the portion and inheritance for us, our wives, and children. So help us God.

At the end of the text *The Man in the Moon* comments, 'I would that this might be a patterne of Loyaltie, not onely for *New-England*, but for old *England* too.' The author seems to have been unaware of, or confused by, American geography; Virginia was not, and is not, part of New England, but he may have been using 'New England' in a loose sense, merely contrasting the colonies with 'Old England'.[7]

The text itself is intriguing. It is a pugnacious, self-consciously Royalist document which both condemns the Regicide and promises to fight for Charles II against the rebels in England. Its strong biblical focus reminds us that Puritans did not have a monopoly on religiosity and piety. It also displays an understanding of the English law of treason, which considered thoughts of violence against the king to be as serious as actual violence against him: '*we will prosecute such who shall be in our power; and shall be convinced to have beene Actors and consenting, or in mind approving so horrid a treason*'. The claim that the colonists would rather join with their '*neighbour Savages*' than yield to the Regicides is striking when one considers that they had fought a brutal war against the Native Americans between 1644 and 1646. That these heathens were less noxious than the English regicides was obviously considered to be an important rhetorical trope.[8] The invocation of the colonists' wives and children was evidently an attempt to stress the contrast between the Royalist concept of a properly ordered society and the unnatural execution of Charles I, who was father of both his immediate family and the nation. In subsequent sections of this chapter, a number of arguments will be presented for and against the authenticity of the document presented in *The Man in the Moon*. At this point, however, it is necessary to provide some background on the man who was governor of Virginia in 1649 and who allegedly promulgated this declaration: Sir William Berkeley.

Sir William Berkeley (1605–77) hailed from a wealthy Somerset family with impeccable Royalist credentials. His brother Charles (1599–1668) was a commissioner for raising money for the royal army during the 1640s, and was arrested in 1651 for his involvement in Royalist plotting in the West Country; he was made a privy councillor after the Restoration, sat in the Cavalier Parliament and had significant financial interests in what later became South Carolina. William's brother John (1607–78) fought with distinction for Charles I during the Bishops' Wars and the First Civil War. He was involved in organising the king's escape from Hampton Court in 1647, and subsequently went into exile on the continent, where he became very close to James, Duke of York.[9] John was an important, if divisive, figure among the Royalists in exile during the Interregnum, and his memoirs were published in 1699.

According to Sir William's biographer, Warren M. Billings, his politics, at least before the Regicide, would be hard to categorise as overtly or enthusiastically Royalist. William was appointed a member of the king's privy chamber in 1632, and later fought against the Scots in the Bishops' Wars. He was knighted by Charles I in 1639, but, in Billings's view, he had 'an abiding wariness of Stuart Kings' and a 'low regard for his master'. With no real prospect of future advancement at the court, and anxious to avoid taking sides in the conflict between Charles and Parliament, he decided to purchase the office of governor of Virginia from the incumbent in 1641. He landed at Jamestown in 1642 and over the succeeding decades amassed a significant personal fortune. Sir William formally committed Virginia to the side of the Crown during the Civil Wars but was pragmatic and flexible enough not to allow civil conflict to erupt within the isolated and impoverished colony itself. His over-riding interest was, it has been claimed, the development of the colony's economy, and to this end he was anxious to continue trading with London-based shipping, and was particularly careful to avoid any conflicts that might lead the rebels in London to embark upon a blockade of the colony.

According to Billings, it was the news of the Regicide that pushed Berkeley into Royalist activism. He is alleged to have 'wasted no sorrow on the hapless Charles', but, as an honourable man, to have been resolutely opposed to the murderous actions of the Puritans. He now began to correspond with Charles II and a number of his advisers in France and the United Provinces, and was determined to hold the colony for the young king. When a fleet from London arrived in the Chesapeake Bay in early 1652, Berkeley was ready and willing to fight. He called out 1,000 militiamen, but after a tense stand-off of a few days, he backed away from armed conflict and negotiated highly favourable terms for the surrender of the colony to the Commonwealth of England. He was restored to the governorship after the Restoration, but all of his efforts to diversify and strengthen the economy of the colony came to nothing. His career ended in ignominy when he was recalled to England in 1676 in the aftermath of an internal rebellion which had been sparked, exacerbated and prolonged by his incompetent handling of a relatively minor matter.[10]

There are at least three powerful arguments for considering that the text presented in *The Man in the Moon* is unlikely to be genuine. Firstly, there is apparently no surviving original copy of it, and no other historical source from the period quotes it. It is true that on 14 December 1649 the Council of State in London took into consideration a 'remonstrance and protestation of the Governor of Virginia'; the members referred it to the 'Committee of the Admiralty' and directed it 'to consider how the government of that plantation may be altered.' No copy of this 'remonstrance and protestation' seems to have survived, and the text was not transcribed into the surviving records of the Commonwealth regime. It may be that the Council of State had merely heard about this 'remonstrance and petition', and did not possess a copy of it.[11] It is possible, but entirely unprovable, that the 'remonstrance and protestation' was identical to the 'Declaration and Protestation' reproduced in *The Man in the Moon*. On the other hand, *The Man in the Moon* may have simply invented his declaration after hearing about a text that was circulating in London and happened to have come to the attention of the Council of State.

Surely if the text presented by *The Man in the Moon* were genuine it would be recorded in some source in Virginia, or perhaps by someone in one of the other Stuart dominions who happened to have read a copy of the declaration? Even if one allows for the substantial loss of historical sources from the colonial period due to the vagaries of climate, carelessness, accidents and the burning of Richmond in the dog days of the American Civil War, one might reasonably expect to find such a pugnacious condemnation of the regicidal regime somewhere among the voluminous private letters and papers of the leading figures of the new regime. One might also expect to find some trace of it among the papers of Samuel Hartlib, who was part of a group of intellectuals which saw the preparations of the Commonwealth to reduce Virginia to obedience as an opportunity to instigate a far-reaching programme of economic and religious reform in the New World.[12] One might also expect it to have survived, or at least been mentioned, somewhere among the largest and most important collection of papers relating to early colonial Virginia: the Ferrar family papers preserved in Magdalene College, Cambridge.[13] Alternatively, the Royalist court in exile on the European continent (or at the very least Sir William's brother John, who at the time was governor to the Duke of York) might have been expected to preserve a copy of the declaration, or at least to be aware of its existence. There was not much good news for English Royalists at home or in exile during the dark days of 1649 and 1650, and this declaration might have given some comfort to the defeated and demoralised Loyalists scattered across Britain and Europe that at least some of their comrades were willing and able to continue the fight against the rebels. Furthermore, the absence of the declaration from the Royalist leader Edward Hyde's *History of the Rebellion*, which discusses the resistance of Virginia in 1651 and 1652 to a fleet despatched by the English Commonwealth, is, one might conclude, extremely telling.[15]

The second reason for doubting the veracity of the declaration concerns the low status, the geographical parochialism and lack of influential connections of those who produced *The Man in the Moon*. The principal author of this title was John Crouch and the printer was his kinsman Edward Crouch. The Crouches were of very low social status, and endured recurring bouts of grinding poverty throughout their adult lives. Both men hailed from Standon in Hertfordshire, some thirty miles from London, and migrated to the capital in their early teens during the 1630s to take up apprenticeships in the book trade. They settled in Smithfield on the north-western fringe of the City, where they apparently spent all of their adult lives, and had a network of relatives in and around the area. As Adrian Johns has noted, the citizens of early modern London 'tended to live for much of their lives in and around one precinct, and such local structures seem to have developed a primacy similar to that found in rural villages of the period'.[15] The Crouches' persistence in the area and the proximity of kin are two indications of the existence of what sociologists term an 'urban local social system': a society where social relationships and bonds are centred on a relatively restricted local area.[16]

There were a number of Royalist polemicists active in London in the late 1640s who had direct or indirect connections with influential Royalist leaders in London and, to a lesser extent, in exile on the continent.[17] All the surviving evidence suggests that the Crouches, by contrast, had no contact with, or input from, leading Royalist figures in London or on the continent.[18] This lack of connection to the Royalist mainstream, and, in particular, the absence of a patron to shelter or protect them, helps to explain a number of related phenomena: the distinctive, colloquial, informal, yet violent style of the prose in *The Man in the Moon*; how and why Edward Crouch was arrested more often by the Cromwellian searchers than any other Royalist printer in London; and why the Crouches' Herculean efforts in support of Charles II were completely ignored after the restoration of the monarchy in 1660.[19] One might say that these impoverished, isolated, angry and hunted Royalists living in the north-western fringes of London are the most unlikely people to have had any sort of privileged information from Virginia.

The third reason to doubt the veracity of the declaration is *The Man in the Moon*'s joyful eschewal of facts in favour of obscenity, sexual libel and wonderfully colourful and inventive lies and misinformation.[20] John Crouch claimed to be privy to information from 'the House of Commons ... the Council of State, the Council of Warrs, [and] the Common Council'. This information enabled him to 'see all their deepest conspiracies, hear their closest debates, [and] understand their slyest plots'.[21] He invented a character, that of a dog called Towzer, which he claimed provided him with much of this information.[22] Towzer, he claimed, could go 'unsuspected through their guards of Musquetters into the House of Commons and Councill of State, and fetch and carry intelligence for his master, without the least suspect'.[23] In addition, Crouch laid claim to an extensive intelligence-gathering network which included Royalists in the Low Countries and Ireland, sympathetic individuals in the armed forces and prostitutes frequented by members of the government.[24] Yet it is obvious from the pages of *The Man in the Moon* that Crouch had no special insight into the corridors of power. The majority of his news items were based on hearsay or rumour. Very often these reports were wildly inaccurate. In June 1649 he falsely claimed, on the basis of 'a letter I saw from a seaman to his wife', that Cromwell's expedition to Ireland had been forced by bad weather to return to Milford Haven.[25] He once printed a letter which purported to prove that Cromwell had joined the Jesuits and entered into secret negotiations with the pope to be recognised as King of England and Ireland.[26]

Crouch's flair for invention reached its zenith during Oliver Cromwell's campaign in Ireland. For more than a month after the fall of the Irish town of Drogheda to Cromwell, Crouch denied that the town had been taken. When he did finally admit that the defenders had been overwhelmed he falsely claimed that more than 3,000 Cromwellians had died during the fighting. In November 1649 he printed a spurious letter from Cromwell to Parliament which claimed that the conquest of Ireland was in jeopardy after the slaughter of over 9,000 Cromwellian soldiers by Royalist troops.[27] The issue of *The Man in the Moon* which contains the alleged declaration from Virginia contains entirely unfounded reports of Royalist successes against Cromwell in Ireland, the great prospects for the Royalist cause in Scotland and progress in the forging of a military alliance against republican England by the United Provinces, 'France, Denmark, Spaine, Sweden, and Germany'.[28] It is little wonder, then, that John Crouch has been universally dismissed as a peddler of dull obscenities and ephemeral, foolish nonsense.[29] Joad Raymond claims that 'a modern reader would probably be reluctant to buy a used car from Crouch'; Marie Gimmelfarb-Brack has described him as an untrustworthy 'journaliste à sensation'; and Lois Potter has expressed doubts as to whether he merits the title of 'writer' at all.[30]

IV

There are, however, a number of compelling reasons for suggesting that the declaration is likely to be authentic. Firstly, one should not assume that the historical record will preserve documents of importance to subsequent generations. Nowadays, scholars tend to assume that the 120,000 or so items listed on Early English Books Online are a fair representation of what was printed and published in Britain before 1700. Tessa Watt's chilling calculation that only one in 10,000 of the ballads printed during the sixteenth century has survived is rarely called to mind.[31] Insofar as it is ever remembered, there is a tendency to assume that such an enormous rate of destruction could not be true for the seventeenth century because of the efforts of collectors such as George Thomason, Narcissus Luttrell and Samuel Pepys. To an extent this is certainly true, but one should not underestimate the scale of the losses during the seventeenth century. In fact, scholars interested in popular culture need to be much more aware of the relationship between price and survival rate; more expensive items survived in greater numbers while the survival of the cheapest sort of print is very rare indeed. What is more, there is a difference between buying a text and reading it. Items that survive in library collections were not necessarily read more than once or even read at all; those items which were actually read and used regularly have tended to disappear at a phenomenal rate. So, for example, John Barnard has shown that there is only one surviving copy of a school primer from the year 1676/77, but it is clear from archival sources that 84,000 copies were printed that year.[32] That represents a frightening survival rate of one in 84,000 copies. The print run of most items varied between 250 and 1,500 copies during the seventeenth century. The obvious question is: how many popular titles – those that were actually read and passed around – have simply disappeared without trace? A genuine text would not necessarily survive in numerous copies. Furthermore, about half a dozen or so issues of *The Man in the Moon* from 1650 survive in only one copy: that collected by the London stationer and bibliophile George Thomason. If Thomason had not been able to locate and buy his copy of issue no. 37 of *The Man in the Moon* in the first week of 1650 there would be no surviving text of this declaration.[33]

'A Declaration and Protestation of the Governour and Inhabitants of Virginia' is a remarkably restrained document in the context of the wild inventions of Crouchean polemic. If John Crouch had invented a story about a loyal declaration from the New World he might have been expected to have claimed that it was but part of a powerful united front of the twenty-four British colonies in the New World, or perhaps even just those six which did publicly condemn the Regicide and declare for Charles II.[34] Crouch would have been inclined to invent actions against the Regicides across the whole of British America, possibly including a series of dramatic stands against the Independents on land and sea. He might also have been expected to claim that the Royalists in the colonies were determined to harass the navy of the new republic, and give some sort of aid to the projected invasion of England by the Scottish and European allies of the exiled king. One would not expect Crouch to have settled for inventing a mere declaration of words from the demographically very small and economically underdeveloped colony of Virginia.

In linguistic and stylistic terms, the declaration is very far removed from the teasing, jocular, railing and often decidedly coarse language of *The Man in the Moon*. It does not read as if it was invented by John Crouch; its biblical overtones do not sit well with the gratuitous obscenities and sexual libels of an author who could pen a story about one of the Regicides falling asleep and dreaming 'that he was in heaven, and there he had carnall copulation with the Virgin Mary, her Son standing and looking on!'[35] Indeed, the declaration sits uncomfortably with the polemical needs of royalism, and the intended audience for these newsbooks, in early 1650. On the first appearance of the Royalist newsbooks in September 1647 the Loyalists themselves admitted that their cause was isolated from the general population and that the majority of their readers would be convinced Royalists. This changed gradually over the next few months, and by February 1648 the Royalists (and a number of other commentators) came to believe that the political climate had become much more favourable to the Stuart cause. For about six months thereafter the polemicists gave the definite impression that they believed they were being widely read by Royalists and non-Royalists alike. During these months they repeatedly tried to convince those who had either previously supported the rebels or remained neutral to declare for the king. Their confidence that they were reaching an increasing number of readers increased over the spring of 1648, and by June they seem to have believed that they were in a position to rally support among the citizens of London for the Royalist insurrections across the country.[36]

Internal evidence suggests, however, that the polemicists believed their readership contracted significantly in the wake of the Second Civil War and the Regicide. During 1649 and 1650 the main intended audience seems not to have been the citizens of London in general, but London Presbyterians who were alienated from the regime and, it was hoped, would support a Scottish invasion of England to restore the Stuarts to the throne.[37] In early 1650 the main priority of *The Man in the Moon*, and the small number of other Royalists who continued to appear in print, was to appeal to these Presbyterians.[38] In this context, the decidedly Anglican nature of the declaration was ill-suited to appeal to the then target audience of *The Man in the Moon*: it was sworn 'upon the holy Evangelists'; asserted that monarchs were accountable to no earthly powers; and condemned the 'damnable' (and entirely orthodox Calvinist) doctrine that princes could, in certain circumstances, be deposed by their subjects. This sort of language could only serve to alienate Presbyterians in London and their allies north of the border, who would have been horrified at the prospect of Charles II returning to the throne at the head of such pugnacious and unrepentant Loyalists. If one were to invent for propaganda purposes a declaration from Virginia in early 1650 it would be very different from the text presented by John Crouch to his readers.

John and Edward Crouch may have been, as argued above, the most unlikely people to have had any sort of privileged information from Virginia, but they did have indirect connections to at least two members of the book trade who had access to information from Virginia and the New World. Over a dozen pamphlets and broadsides were printed in London between 1647 and 1652 which referred to events in, or plans for, the colony of Virginia. The status and provenance of a number of these items is unproblematic: for example, *An Act Prohibiting Trade with the Barbada's, Virginia, Bermuda's and Antego* (1650) was printed by the official printers to the Parliament of England. Several of the items concerning Virginia provide no information as to who printed or published them,[39] but the other surviving pamphlets provide the names of three 'printers': James Moxon, John Hammond and Thomas Harper. The first of these men, James Moxon, was a printer who lived in Houndsditch on the north-eastern fringe of the City. He may have had anti-Royalist politics and certainly had no discernible link to the Crouches.[40] The second man, John Hammond, was not a printer, but a bookseller and stationer, although the title pages of his publications sometimes bore the words 'Printed by John Hammond' rather than the more accurate 'Printed for John Hammond'. Hammond traded at a shop 'over against St Andrews Church in Holborn', very close to Smithfield, and during the first years of the Civil War he published a number of declarations by Charles I, as well as four highly entertaining pamphlets by the self-styled Royalist 'Water Poet', John Taylor.

In April 1649 Hammond published a pamphlet entitled *Virginia Impartially Examined*, which urged the colonists to diversify their economy and reform their government. This tract was written by William Bullock, whose father had returned to England in 1639 after a decade or so in Virginia during which he amassed a substantial estate. William Bullock lived in London during the 1640s, but evidently maintained some commercial interests in the colony; in 1649 he was advising prospective emigrants to come to him for advice at the Middle Temple. Samuel Hartlib believed that Bullock was of the 'royal interest and design',[41] and Hammond, Bullock's publisher, had at least one link to the Crouch family. In 1647 he published an anti-Puritan ballad by the well-known balladeer Humphrey Crouch, who lived in Aldersgate Street in Smithfield and was evidently related in some way to John and Edward Crouch of *The Man in the Moon*.[43] It would be a mistake to construct an imposing edifice upon this single, indirect link between Bullock, Hammond and Crouch. The vast majority of an individual's personal and professional contacts will not be recorded in the historical sources, and those links which we can trace using the surviving fragmentary evidence may not be significant. When examining the biographical links thrown up by print-culture one needs to be mindful of Clyve Jones's warning to those scholars of the early eighteenth century who find evidence of support for the exiled Stuarts in the most unlikely of places that a man cannot be classified as a Jacobite merely because he happened to know, or dine with, a Jacobite.[43]

The one surviving link in the historical record between the Crouches and the second of our persons of interest – the printer Thomas Harper – was stronger and much more significant. Harper was the printer of three separate descriptions of Virginia and its trade which appeared in 1650, as well as Edward Bland's *The Discovery of New Brittaine ... at the Head of Appamattuck River in Virginia* (1651). Edward Bland was a member of a prominent family of London merchants; he had recently returned to England from the colony, and claimed to have been in the company of the Royalist governor of Virginia, Sir William Berkeley, as late as 27 August 1650.[44] Harper's link to the Crouches is provided by a list of recognisances for good behaviour filed by all London printers under the terms of the draconian Printing Act of September 1649. The Act decreed that all printers must post an enormous personal bond of £300 for their future good behaviour, as well as two independent sureties of £300 each. Any man who printed or caused 'to be printed any seditious[,] scandalous or treasonable pamphlet[,] paper[,] booke or picture dishonourable to, or against the State and government' would forfeit his bond and the independent sureties.[45] The two recognisances for Thomas Harper were provided by a surgeon named 'Henock Bostocke' of St Andrew's, Holborn, and a certain Humphrey Crouch of the parish of St Bartholomew the Great.[46] This was, in all likelihood, the balladeer mentioned above in connection with John Hammond, who lived in Aldersgate Street in this Smithfield parish, and was related to John and Edward Crouch of *The Man in the Moon*.[47] This link is particularly significant because one does not generally put up a large bond to get somebody out of trouble with the law unless one has some sort of amicable relationship – whether professional, commercial, personal or political – with that individual. Here one finds evidence of a connection between the Crouches, a London printer with regular access to news from Virginia, and an author (Edward Bland) who seems to have personally known the governor of Virginia, who is alleged to have promulgated the Declaration and Protestation.

The pamphlets by William Bullock and Edward Bland demonstrate that there were channels along which information could travel between Virginia and London at this difficult time, even if those links were likely to be precarious, indirect, intermittent and often unreliable. Bullock's and Bland's pamphlets, as we have seen, were published by John Hammond and Thomas Harper respectively. Both Hammond and Harper had known links with Humphrey Crouch, who, in turn, was linked to those behind *The Man in the Moon*. Bullock seems to have been residing in the Middle Temple in 1649, and Bland was probably in Virginia: he was certainly there in the summer of 1650. It is striking, however, that the five possible members of this network who were involved in the book trade were living and working within a few hundred feet of each other at this time: John Hammond near St Andrew's Church, Holborn; Thomas Harper in Little Britain; Edward Crouch in Hosier Lane; John Crouch in Cock Lane; and Humphrey Crouch in Aldersgate Street.

The Crouches were almost certainly not the intended recipients of Sir William Berkeley's 'Declaration and Protestation'. If Berkeley did send the text to be printed he would undoubtedly have hoped that it would appear in a more reputable publication, and that it would make a greater impact on contemporary events. In 1651, for example, he was able to ensure that his rousing speech in the representative assembly of Virginia against the Navigation Act was sent to The Hague and published by the well-connected Royalist printer in exile, Samuel Browne.[48] In 1649 and 1650, though, Royalists in Virginia did not have the luxury of easy channels of communication with their comrades on the other side of the Atlantic. The hand-written 'Declaration and Protestation' obviously made its way to London on a ship returning from Virginia or one of the other colonies in the New World. It is not clear whether it was consciously sent to London by Berkeley or another, unknown, Royalist, or whether it simply found its way to London because of its newsworthiness. The text may well have circulated freely in London in late 1649 and early 1650, in which case it is possible (but unprovable) that the text published in *The Man in the Moon* on 9 January 1650 was the same as the 'remonstrance and protestation of the Governor of Virginia' discussed by the Council of State on 14 December 1649 (see n. 11). If this were the case, though, one would expect to find other contemporary references to, and quotations of, Berkeley's declaration: there are none. It is, therefore, possible that the Council of State merely heard of the declaration – hence the fact that there is no copy of the text in the papers of the regime and the title is different from that published by Crouch – and that independently of this source of information the text found its way to London and passed through the hands of various Royalists until it reached the Crouches: the men behind one of only two Royalist newsbooks still in production and the only men who were, moreover, brave enough, or foolhardy enough, to publish it.

V

If one accepts the authenticity of 'A Declaration and Protestation of the Governour and Inhabitants of Virginia' one is immediately confronted by a number of important questions. How unanimous were these pugnaciously loyal sentiments among the colonists in 1649? Was the declaration an untypical and exceptional response to an exceptional event: the Regicide? Or was it an early example of the widely diffused and deeply ingrained, almost instinctive, royalism described by Brendan McConville in his recent study of colonial society in the century before the American Revolution of 1776?[49]

Historians of the English Civil Wars have long held negative views of Charles I and have traditionally displayed little interest in either the experience of Royalists or the phenomenon of royalism. The assumption that royalism was an autocratic, reactionary and elitist ideology which could not hold any attraction for the populace outside the rarified milieu of the royal court has meant that scholars have been blind to the hundreds of thousands, if not millions, of men and women in the three kingdoms who supported the Stuarts. What is more, scholars have also missed the fact that at particular periods – and the months before and after the Regicide constitute one such period – the popular mood swang decisively against the Puritans and Roundheads. Recent work on the nature and extent of loyalism in Britain means that it is no longer possible to dismiss royalism as nothing more than an unthinking (and unthinkable) prejudice.[50] If one examines Sir William Berkeley's politics in the context of this evolving literature, it is reasonable to conclude that he is likely to have been as Royalist during the Civil Wars as he was during the Interregnum. If Berkeley was not, as his biographer has claimed, a Royalist during the 1640s is it really likely that he would have enforced so consistently and vigorously the Oath of Allegiance, the Book of Common Prayer and the church 'as by law established' on the colony in the face of dogged resistance from Puritan settlers, both laymen and clergy? If he was only interested in the economic well-being of the colony, as has been claimed, he would not have picked this fight and run the risk of starting a civil war in Virginia itself.[51] If he was anything other than a committed Loyalist he would not have returned to England in 1644 and taken part in military campaigning for Charles I in his native West Country.[52] If he only became a Royalist after the news of the Regicide reached Virginia, it is strange that the authorities in London were advised as early as February 1649 – i.e. before the news of Charles's execution reached the colonies – that they could never hope to exert their power over the colony so long as Berkeley remained governor.[53]

Despite the large gaps in the historical record from this period, there are a number of intriguing indications of Royalist sentiment in Virginia during the Interregnum. There was evidently continuing discord in the colony concerning ministers who would not use the Book of Common Prayer in services.[54] The Council of State in London was anxious to ensure that as few Royalist exiles as possible went to the colony to stir up trouble, but a significant number – perhaps several hundred – poured in.[55] In October 1649 the General Assembly of Virginia made it a treasonable offence to deny the succession of Charles II or to defend the execution of his father, and in March 1651 the governor, Council, and burgesses of Virginia made a public declaration of their loyalism: 'no power on earth can absolve or manumit us from our obedience to our PRINCE, and his lawfull Successors'.[56] The articles negotiated in 1652 for the surrender of Virginia to the Commonwealth of England seem to demonstrate a sincere affinity with the king and the traditional church on the part of

Berkeley and the members of his official Council. These articles stipulated that they would be free for one year to refuse the Oath of Engagement to the Commonwealth; that they would not 'bee censured for praying for or speaking well of the king for one whole yeare in their howses and private Conferences'; and that 'the use of the Book of Common Prayer shall be permitted for one Year ensuing ... PROVIDED that those things which relate to Kingship or that Government be not used Publickly'.[57] These were obviously important issues for the men who had led the colony during the previous decade, and it would be interesting to know how widely diffused this 'prayer book' piety was among the 8,000 or so settlers in the colony.[58] In the light of the call to arms in the 1649 'Declaration and Protestation', it may be necessary to take seriously the plot hatched in Virginia during 1654 to send money to Charles II, buy arms and ammunition and organise a rebellion across the islands of the West Indies.[59] The conspiracy was broken up in the days before Christmas 1654, but it helps to explain why Cromwell's spymaster, John Thurloe, kept such a close eye on events in the colony.

Lest one be tempted to assume that royalism was merely the preserve of a small clique which controlled the colony,[60] it is necessary to note that in June 1653 a nervous General Assembly chose to interpret unrest concerning a commercial matter on the eastern shore as evidence of a revolt by 'delinquents' against the authority of the Parliament of England: they were mistaken as to the nature of the disturbances, but were obviously not as certain as some modern scholars about the impossibility of royalism on American soil.[61] It is important not to fall in to the trap of claiming that everybody in Interregnum Virginia was a Royalist; Charles II's commission of June 1650 ordering Berkeley to dig in and construct a network of 'Castles Forts and Places defensible ... with Walls and Bulwarks' explicitly envisaged that they would be used both to fight off an invasion fleet from England and to put down anti-Royalists in the colony.[62] Most Virginians probably preferred not to have to take sides during the 1640s, and those in the colony who wished to fight for either Charles I or the Parliament were almost certainly a minority. Yet there was nothing particularly Virginian or American about this disinclination to kill one's neighbours, or be killed by them; the same attitude had permeated British society before the activities of relatively small numbers of armed ideologues forced most (but by no means all of the nation) to divide into two mutually antagonistic camps. The colony declared its allegiance to Charles I throughout the 1640s, but its distance from the actual fighting in Britain ensured that the conflict had relatively little impact upon the daily lives of most Virginians. In this the colonists were fortunate; millions of men and women across Britain during the 1640s would have welcomed the opportunity to live in peace under the protection of a local grandee after nothing more than a formal allegiance to one or other party to the conflict.

We do not, and cannot, know exactly how many men and women in Virginia actively considered themselves to be Royalists during the English Civil Wars and Revolution.[63] It is, however, possible to make three statements about politics in the colony, the first two of which are incontrovertible, and the third of which is highly likely: there was nothing about life in this English colony which ensured that it ever could or would be unaffected by the habits, assumptions and ways of thinking of the old country; there was a Royalist faction in control in Virginia during the 1640s which consisted of men and women other than Sir William Berkeley; and if the popular mood in Virginia followed the same trajectory as that in Britain, it is likely that there was an upsurge in Royalist sentiment in the year or so before the Regicide. 'A Declaration and Protestation of the Governour and Inhabitants of Virginia' may well be the product of a genuine sense of outrage among large numbers of the colonists at the execution of their king by a small faction of the political nation in England. The colonists' decision not to fight against the Commonwealth fleet that appeared in the Chesapeake in early 1652 has been interpreted as evidence of their lack of genuine Royalist convictions. Yet it is much more likely to have been the product of an entirely rational desire – scholars tend not to think that Royalists could ever behave rationally, or act logically – not to fight against overwhelming odds in the wake of the complete rout of Charles II's forces at Worcester in September 1651. Defeat forced the same sorts of messy compromises upon Royalists living in the American colonies as it did upon those who remained in Britain.

In a British context, this declaration demonstrates just how desperate the Royalist cause was in January 1650. The security situation was so dire that *The Man in the Moon* was not in a position to maximise the propaganda possibilities of the declaration; there was, so far as we know, no attempt to publish it as a separate broadsheet and paste it about the streets of London to give courage to the Loyalists in the capital and advertise Crouch's newsbook, as would have been standard practice in less difficult times. Instead, it seems to have been simply transcribed, tipped into the text, and not explored or analysed in any depth. Indeed, the publication of the declaration may have been counterproductive in terms of the propaganda needs of that specific moment in time, and it only served to draw yet more attention from the Regicides to Crouch and his comrades. There is nothing particularly new about the statement that the weeks before the first anniversary of the Regicide were a difficult time for the Royalist cause, but the declaration is remarkable for suggesting that there may have been intriguing and unexpected channels of communication between Royalists who at this time were geographically very far apart.

The few modern studies of British royalism during the Interregnum rely heavily on the well-mined papers of a small number of leading courtiers in exile: Hyde, Nicholas and Ormond. The fact that *The Man in the*

Moon's contacts may have bypassed the Royalist court in exile is potentially very exciting. The declaration holds out the tantalising possibility that there are other, less well-mined sources and hitherto unexplored networks which transect the London book trade and the City merchants. A detailed examination of these communities and their trade networks may well shed new light on the Royalist experience across Britain, Ireland, Europe and Colonial America. London has traditionally been seen as the heart of the Puritan beast: unwelcoming, dangerous and unfertile ground for those loyal to the king.[64] Merchants and their capitalistic enterprises are, even now, often instinctively associated in scholars' minds with Parliament, Puritanism and progress: it is simply assumed that such men could never have been attracted to a backward-looking, feudal, aristocratic creed like royalism.[65] One of the most pressing tasks for scholars of royalism is to demonstrate the inaccuracy of these two-dimensional assumptions. In doing so, it will be necessary to access a range of sources that have rarely been explored by historians of royalism, such as, for example, those in the London Guildhall and the London Metropolitan Archives, and the records of various London trade guilds and trading companies. Whatever the future results of this research, one can definitely say that 'A Declaration and Protestation of the Governour and Inhabitants of Virginia' must force us to reassess some of our preconceptions about *The Man in the Moon*. There may well have been, surprisingly, some wheat among the chaff of John Crouch's eminently readable publication.

NOTES

I am grateful to Warren M. Billings, Lloyd Bowen, L.H. Roper, David L. Smith, John Springford and Peter Thompson for their comments on this chapter, earlier versions of which were presented at a conference organised in Swansea in September 2007 by the British Group in Early American History and at the Huntington Library in California in January 2009. I wish to acknowledge the extraordinary kindness and support that I have received from the Warden and Fellows of Merton College, Oxford, and from the Electors to the J.P.R. Lyell Research Fellowship in the History of the Early Modern Printed Book.

1　See, for example, David Armitage, 'Greater Britain: a useful category of historical analysis?', *AHR*, 104:2 (Apr. 1999), pp. 427–45; Conrad Russell, 'Is British history international history?', in Allan I. Macinnes and Jane Ohlmeyer (eds), *The Stuart Kingdoms in the Seventeenth Century* (Dublin, 2002), pp. 62–9.

2　See Robert Armstrong, 'Ormond, the confederate peace talks and Protestant royalism', in Micheál Ó Siochrú (ed.), *Kingdoms in Crisis: Ireland in the 1640s. Essays in Honour of Dónal Cregan* (Dublin, 2001), pp. 122–40, and Robert Armstrong, 'Protestant churchmen and the Confederate Wars', in Ciarán Brady and Jane Ohlmeyer (eds), *British Interventions in Early Modern Ireland* (Cambridge, 2005), pp. 230–51; Lloyd Bowen, 'Representations of Wales and the Welsh during the Civil Wars and Interregnum', *HR*, 77:197 (2004), pp. 358–76; Lloyd Bowen, 'Rediscovering difference? Nations, peoples and politics in the British Civil Wars', *History Compass*, 4:5 (2006), pp. 836–51; Geoffrey Smith, *The Cavaliers in Exile, 1640–1660* (Basingstoke, 2003); Mark Stoyle, *West Britons: Cornish Identities and the Early Modern British State* (Exeter, 2002).

3 Carla Gardina Pestana, *The English Atlantic in an Age of Revolution, 1640–1661* (Cambridge, MA, 2004), pp. 86–122. I use the term 'British' here because twenty-three of the colonies were English and one was Scottish.

4 A few of the many possible examples will be found at TNA, SP 25/90/263; SP 25/95/148; SP 25/115/482–3; SP 25/146/93; SP 25/146/98; SP 25/92/7; SP 25/146/123; SP 25/146/138; SP 25/146/165; SP 25/146/229; SP 25/36/80.

5 Pestana, *English Atlantic*, pp. 86–122.

6 On these newsbooks see Jason McElligott, *Royalism, Print and Censorship in Revolutionary England* (Woodbridge, 2007).

7 *The Man in the Moon*, no. 37 (2–9 January 1650), pp. 297–8.

8 Warren M. Billings, *Sir William Berkeley and the Forging of Colonial Virginia* (Baton Rouge, LA, 2004), pp. 96–8.

9 See D.W. Hayton, 'Berkeley, John, First Baron Berkeley of Stratton (*bap.* 1607, *d.* 1678)', *Oxford DNB*; and Andrew Warmington, 'Berkeley, Charles, Second Viscount Fitzhardinge of Berehaven (1599–1668)', *Oxford DNB*.

10 This account of Berkeley's life is based on Billings, *Forging of Colonial Virginia*, pp. 21, 29, 30, 40, 101, 102–3, 106–7; Warren M. Billings, 'Berkeley, William (1605–1677)', *Oxford DNB*; Warren M. Billings (ed.), *The Papers of Sir William Berkeley, 1605–1677* (Richmond, VA, 2007). Carla Pestana concurs with this view of Berkeley's politics during the 1640s: *English Atlantic*, pp. 26, 27, 34, 45, 65. All other histories of Berkeley's governorship stress his staunch royalism and attachment to the Loyalist cause. See, for example, Edward L. Bond, *Damned Souls in a Tobacco Colony: Religion in Seventeenth-Century Virginia* (Macon, GA, 2000), pp. 146–54.

11 TNA, SP 25/146/389.

12 Robert Brenner, *Merchants and Revolution: Commercial Change, Political Conflict and London's Overseas Traders, 1550–1653* (2003), p. 588.

13 For this archive see the excellent www.virginiacompanyarchives.amdigital.co.uk

14 *CHR*, vol. V, p. 263. Berkeley and Hyde had known each other in the late 1630s: Billings, *Forging of Colonial Virginia*, pp. 21, 34.

15 Adrian Johns, *The Nature of the Book: Print and Knowledge in the Making* (Chicago, IL, 1998), p. 63.

16 Jason McElligott, 'Crouch, John (*b.* c.1615, *d.* in or after 1680)', *Oxford DNB*; Jason McElligott, 'Crouch, Humphrey (*fl.* 1601–1657)', *Oxford DNB*; Jason McElligott, 'Edward Crouch: a poor printer in seventeenth-century London', *Journal of the Printing Historical Society*, new series 1 (2000), pp. 49–73; McElligott, *Royalism, Print and Censorship*, *passim*; TNA, PROB 11/454, fols 30–1.

17 TNA, SP 29/63/144; TNA, SP 25/63/282–4.

18 McElligott, *Royalism, Print and Censorship*, chapters 4, 5 and 6.

19 Jason McElligott, 'John Crouch: a Royalist journalist in Cromwellian England', *Media History*, 10:3 (2004), pp. 139–55; McElligott, 'Edward Crouch'.

20 Jason McElligott, 'The politics of sexual libel: Royalist propaganda in the 1640s', *HLQ*, 67:1 (2004), pp. 75–99.

21 *The Man in the Moon*, unnumbered (16 April 1649), p. 3.

22 *Ibid.*, no. 18 (15–23 Aug. 1649), pp. 147–8; no. 40 (23–31 Jan. 1650), p. 319.

23 *Ibid.*, no. 41 (30 Jan.–6 Feb. 1650), p. 322.

24 *Ibid.*, no. 16 (1–8 Aug. 1649), p. 138; no. 55 (8–23 May 1650), p. 410.

25 *Ibid.*, no. 18 (15–23 Aug. 1649), p. 153.

26 *Ibid.*, no. 8 (28 May–5 June 1649), pp. 70–1.

27 *Ibid.*, no. 25 (10–17 Oct. 1649), p. 207; no. 28 (31 Oct.–7 Nov. 1649), pp. 228–9.

28 *Ibid.*, no. 37 (2–9 Jan. 1650), pp. 293, 298–300.

29 S.R. Gardiner, *History of the Commonwealth and Protectorate*, 4 vols (1988), vol. II, p. 83; J.B. Williams, *A History of English Journalism to the Foundation of the Gazette* (1908), p. 145; Hyder E. Rollins, *Cavalier and Puritan: Ballads and Broadsides Illustrating the Period of the Great Rebellion, 1640–1660* (New York, 1923), p. 58; W.M. Clyde, *Freedom of the Press in England from Caxton to Cromwell* (New York, 1934), p. 215; Joseph Frank, *The Beginnings of the English Newspaper, 1620–1660* (Cambridge, MA, 1961), p. 230.

30 Marie Gimmelfarb-Brack, *Liberté, Egalité, Fraternité, Justice! La vie et l'oeuvre de Richard Overton, Niveleur* (Berne, 1979), p. 282; Lois Potter, *Secret Rites and Secret Writing: Royalist Literature, 1641–1660* (Cambridge, 1989), p. xiv; Joad Raymond, *Making the News: An Anthology of the Newsbooks of Revolutionary England, 1641–1660* (Moreton-in-Marsh, Gloucestershire, 1993), p. 20. For a reassessment of John Crouch's political career see McElligott, 'John Crouch'.

31 Tessa Watt, *Cheap Print and Popular Piety, 1550–1640* (Cambridge, 1991), p. 141.

32 John Barnard, 'The survival and loss rate of Psalms, ABCs, psalters and primers from the Stationers' stock, 1660–1700', *The Library*, 6th series, 21:2 (June 1999), pp. 148–50.

33 For more on this see my 'Calibrating early-modern print culture' (forthcoming).

34 Pestana, *English Atlantic*, pp. 86–122. There is, of course, no evidence he ever realised that six colonies had risen for Charles II.

35 *The Man in the Moon*, no. 53 (1–9 May 1650), pp. 303–4.

36 McElligott, *Royalism, Print and Censorship*, chapter 1, section 4.

37 *Mercurius Pragmaticus*, no. 1 (17–24 April 1649), sig. 3v; no. 42 (12–19 Feb. 1649 [i.e. 1650]), sig. 4v; no. 38 (15–22 Jan. 1649 [i.e. 1650]), sig. 2v.

38 *The Man in the Moon*, no 37 (2–9 January 1650), pp. 293–4.

39 See *The Virginia Trade Stated* (*c*.1647); *Copy of a Petition from the Governor and Company of the Sommer Islands* (1651).

40 *Short-Title Catalogue … 1641–1700*, vol. IV: *Indexes* (New York, 1998), p. 635.

41 See Peter Thompson, 'William Bullock's "Strange Adventure": a plan to transform seventeenth-century Virginia', *WMQ*, 3rd series, 61:1 (Jan. 2004), pp. 107–28.

42 Humphrey Crouch, *Come buy a mouse-trap, or, A new way to catch an old rat* (1647). McElligott, 'Crouch, Humphrey'. For Humphrey's residence in this vicinity in 1638 see T.C. Dale (ed.), *The Inhabitants of London in 1638* (1938), p. 207.

43 Clyve Jones, '1720–3 and All That', *Albion*, 26:1 (1994), 45n. Cf. Jason Peacey, *Politicians and Pamphleteers: Propaganda during the English Civil Wars and Interregnum* (Aldershot, 2004), *passim*.

44 Edward Bland, *The Discovery of New Brittaine … at the Head of Appamattuck River in Virginia* (1651), 'To the Reader' (unpaginated) and p. 1; Alan V. Briceland, 'The search for Edward Bland's New Britain', *Virginia Magazine of History and Biography*, 87:2 (Apr. 1979), pp. 131–57.

45 TNA, SP 25/120, fol. 6.

46 *Ibid.*, SP 25/120, fol. 11. On the usefulness of this list of printers and recognisances see my 'Printers' networks in Cromwellian England' (forthcoming).

47 McElligott, 'Crouch, Humphrey'. A possible further link between the Crouches and Harpers is that Edward Crouch served his apprenticeship under a Smithfield bookseller named Richard Harper who published a number of ballads in the 1630s written by Humphrey Crouch. There is no evidence that this Richard Harper was related in any way to his near neighbour Thomas Harper, but it is a possibility. See H.R. Plomer, *A Dictionary of the Printers who were at Work in England, Scotland and Ireland between 1641 and 1667* (1907), p. 91; *Short-Title Catalogue … 1641–1700 … Indexes*, pp. 425–7; D.F. McKenzie (ed.), *Stationers' Company Apprentices, 1605–1640* (Charlottesville, VA, 1961), p. 78; D.F. McKenzie (ed.), *Stationers' Company Apprentices, 1641–1700* (Oxford, 1974), p. 72.

48 *The Speech of the Honourable Sr William Berkeley … Together with a Declaration of the whole Country, occasioned upon the sight of a printed paper from England, Intituled An Act,&c* (The Hague, 1651).

49 Brendan McConville, *The King's Three Faces: The Rise and Fall of Royal America, 1688–1776* (Chapel Hill, NC, 2006).

50 See McElligott, *Royalism, Print and Censorship*, pp. 1–16; Jason McElligott and David L. Smith (eds), *Royalists and Royalism during the English Civil Wars* (Cambridge, 2007), pp. 1–12.

51 Allyn B. Forde (ed.), *Winthrop Papers*, vol. V: *1645–49* (Boston, MA, 1947), pp. 273–4, 277; Steven D Crow, '"Your Majesty's Good Subjects": A reconsideration of royalism in Virginia, 1642–1652', *Virginia Magazine of History and Biography*, 87:2 (Apr. 1979), pp. 158–73, at p. 163; Robert M. Bliss, *Revolution and Empire: English Politics and the American Colonies in the Seventeenth Century* (Manchester, 1990), p. 76.

52 Bliss, *Revolution and Empire*, p. 51.

53 Billings, *Berkeley and the Forging of Colonial Virginia*, pp. 102–3, 109.

54 TNA, SP 25/115/482–3.

55 See n. 5 above, and Lyon G. Tyler, 'Virginia under the Commonwealth', *WMQ*, 1:4 (Apr. 1893), pp. 189–96, at p. 190; Bond, *Damned Souls*, p. 133.

56 Tyler, 'Virginia under the Commonwealth', pp. 189–90; Bliss, *Revolution and Empire*, p. 87; *The Speech of the Honourable Sr William Berkeley … Together with a Declaration of the whole Country* (The Hague, 1651), pp. 8, 9–10, 11.

57 Billings (ed.), *Papers of Sir William Berkeley*, pp. 102–5.

58 Bond, *Damned Souls*, pp. 158, 264–8.

59 Billings, *Forging of Colonial Virginia*, pp. 118–19.

60 This claim was made in a letter to Samuel Hartlib in London from Ben Worsley in Amsterdam dated 3/13 Aug. 1648, Sheffield University, Hartlib Papers Online, Hartlib MS 33/2/1A. This statement should be contrasted with the belief of the republic's Council of State in September 1651 that a section of the settlers would not submit to the regime, and that London might only be able to exert its control after a civil conflict within the colony: see *TSP*, vol. I, pp. 197–8.

61 Tyler, 'Virginia under the Commonwealth', pp. 192–3; Billings (ed.), *Papers of Sir William Berkeley*, p. 129.

62 Billings (ed.), *Papers of Sir William Berkeley*, pp. 91–4.

63 This is the innovative definition of royalism put forward in McElligott, *Royalism, Print and Censorship*, pp. 1–16 and McElligott and Smith (eds), *Royalists and Royalism*, pp. 1–12.

64 Ian Roy, '"This proud unthankefull city": A cavalier view of London in the Civil War', in Stephen Porter (ed.), *London and the Civil War* (1996), pp. 149–75.

65 See, for example, Brenner, *Merchants and Revolution*, *passim* and Jerome de Groot, *Royalist Identities* (Basingstoke, 2004), *passim*; and the passing, but very telling, reference in Mark Jenner, 'The roasting of the rump: scatology and the body politic in restoration England', *PandP*, 177 (2002), pp. 84–120, at p. 108.

Chapter 12

The Earl of Southampton and the lessons of Interregnum finance

D'Maris Coffman

I

Most modern narratives of the Restoration financial settlement and the fledgling Restoration treasury emphasise their essential conservatism. Thomas Wriothesley, fourth Earl of Southampton and Lord Treasurer from September 1660 until his death in May 1667, emerges from these studies as a principled and magnanimous caretaker, if a far from enterprising or imaginative one, who laboured unsuccessfully to teach the virtues of economy to a spendthrift king.[1] Modern scholars echo Burnet and Clarendon in their approval of Southampton's concern for the rule of law, his generosity and his incorruptibility.[2] The Lord Treasurer's financial policy appears in these accounts as an adjunct to a larger Clarendonian project, which envisioned a Restoration built upon a commitment to the rule of law, a moderate religious settlement and rehabilitation of the ancient constitution.[3] Unlike his successors, Southampton did not seek to aggrandise the powers of his office by extending control over departmental expenditures. Although he advised the king, both in and out of Council, of the necessity of curbing outflows, his constitutional mandate was to ensure the smooth functioning of the Exchequer.[4] He never exceeded it. To his modern detractors, this made Southampton lazy, weak, irresponsible and even incompetent.[5] In such versions, government finance limped along until Sir George Downing arrived to 'new-model' single-handedly the treasury establishment from his post as treasury secretary.[6] After Southampton's death, the 'rougher hands' of the treasury commission and its shrewd secretary created an independent treasury.[7] In one recent verdict, Downing had perceived in Dutch finance the potential of what Joseph Schumpeter termed the modern 'tax state'.[8]

In broadest outline, elements of this argument retain their explanatory power. By making the case for abrupt change in 1667, emphasis on Sir George

Downing unwittingly highlights the continuities between the Protectorate and Restoration regimes in matters of finance. However bitter their differences, both Cromwell and Clarendon were Elizabethans, that is to say, admirers of the Tudor polity. For Cromwell, that had meant both an uneasy relationship with the established London financial and mercantile communities and a cautious, even conservative, approach to financial policy.[9] When the Protector re-established the Exchequer in 1654, the only innovation upon the 'ancient course' was the inscription and recording of tallies in English.[10] Each time the Protectorate regime continued the excise or imposed new assessments, the preambles to the legislation maintained that the revenue raised in such a manner would be applied either towards the public debt or to extraordinary expenses. The excise, in particular, would be continued no longer than necessary to satisfy the charges laid upon it. Despite the purported unpopularity of commodity taxation, the Cavalier Parliaments retained the excise. They granted half the duty on excisable liquors to the Crown in perpetuity to replace the Court of Wards and the revenues associated with the rights of purveyance. The Commons had intended that the other half, voted to the monarch for life, would ensure that the Crown's ordinary revenues were sufficient for this king to 'live on his own'.[11] As one scholar has noticed, this settlement very nearly achieved the aims of Salisbury's Great Contract of 1610.[12] The Convention Parliament of 1660 may have ignored Fortescue's preferences for re-endowing the Crown via subsidies and the skilful application of the rights *primer seisin* or escheat, but the Commons laboured to retain the underlying assumptions of a *demesne* state.[13]

Southampton faced the Herculean challenge of making such a financial settlement work. From the very beginning (and in marked contrast to the financial settlement of 1690), the Crown faced the reality of chronic undersupply.[14] Despite Parliament's efforts to ensure an adequate settlement, the actual revenue yields were nowhere near the £1,200,000 per year considered necessary to support the king.[15] One more miserly might have made do with less, but Charles II famously was not such a man. To succeed, his new Lord Treasurer needed to maximise revenue while preaching thrift. To accomplish the first, Southampton oversaw extensive investigations of the financial records of the Interregnum regime. A detailed exploration of those efforts should go some modest distance towards rehabilitating Southampton's reputation. If nothing else, his tenure as Lord Treasurer has left modern historians with the only surviving records of the first twenty years of the excise, by far the most important of the fiscal innovations of the Civil Wars. Understanding Southampton's efforts also furnishes an example of how a moderate Royalist, who spent the Interregnum in internal exile only to emerge as a leading figure after the Restoration, grappled with the evidence of its financial experiments. To a surprising degree, Southampton was able to both diagnose and avert the structural problems associated with the Protectorate excise farms, and to protect the interests of loyal Cavaliers in the counties.

II

In his last public act during the Civil Wars, Southampton served as pallbearer to the late king. Afterwards, he retired to his estates in Hampshire. Although the details of this period are scant, several things seem clear. First, he refused to have anything to do with the new regime. As his most recent biographer notes, the earl did not take the Engagement, nor did he receive Cromwell when he ventured into the New Forest on a hunting trip. By keeping a low profile, Southampton escaped both the financial exactions of Parliament's compositions, which though imposed were never collected, and those of the Protectorate's Decimation Tax. After the Restoration, he refused to hear petitions from returning Royalists on the grounds that he had spent the Interregnum in England and did not know the merits of their cases. In the same vein, he was reluctant to impose harsh measures on the Crown's enemies; he encouraged leniency after Venner's uprising by insisting that those who were exempted from the general pardon be given ten days to leave England. In this, his generosity stands in sharp contrast to the zeal with which Sir George Downing arrested three regicides in exile and returned them to England to meet their grizzly fates.[16] By 1666 the ageing Lord Treasurer had grown very ill, a condition that Clarendon thought worsened by his refusal to exercise, and thus left the majority of the business to his secretary, Sir Philip Warwick.

The early years of Southampton's ministry paint a picture of a much more energetic man. Southampton worked within his narrow constitutional remit to reconstruct the ancient Exchequer and to settle the revenue. In the case of the excise, an innovatory and unpopular tax only reluctantly retained by Parliament, Southampton laboured to ensure the co-operation of local officials and to discipline the excise establishment. The records of his attempts reflect not so much lack of imagination as a principled and often nuanced appreciation of the lessons to be gleaned from the recent regime's experience of commodity taxation. Because the excise was a constitutional innovation, the administrative apparatus could be supervised directly by the Lord Treasurer. His aggressive management of the excise commission suggests something of Southampton's approach to treasury business in the absence of the explicit constitutional limits he so studiously observed elsewhere. To a surprising degree, the Lord Treasurer succeeded in forging workable compromises among numerous competing interests.

In these efforts, Southampton looked to his able comptroller for assistance. Following the recommendation of one of the secretaries of state, Sir Edward Nicholas, the Lord Treasurer backed the appointment of Elias Ashmole to replace Samuel Bartlett as excise comptroller. Ashmole received his commission, to be shared with his business partner Thomas Chiffinch, in April 1661.[17] In reality, he had held the post since October 1660, when Bartlett had resigned it to him.[18] Within a few years, Ashmole's vigilance paid real dividends. Although the sectional farming of the excise was reintroduced in 1663, aggressive comptrol gave the state the evidentiary base through which to contest the representations of private parties. Meanwhile, the Lord Treasurer had more pressing problems.

Southampton had evidently hoped that the general pardon would facilitate the settling of the revenues. In late February 1661 he issued a 'warrant to the Auditors of the Excise to take the accompts of the Commissioners'.[19] This addressed those who had not declared their accounts before the Exchequer by 24 September 1660, despite being covered by 'his Majesties' gracious Act of Free and General Pardon and Oblivion' in August. While the stated objective was to ensure that his Majesty was 'true and really informed what sums of money are remaining in the hands of the commissioners or governors of the excise or by their sub-commissioners respectively for the said duty of excise', Southampton expressed his particular interest in the 'facts' of the accounts, including (but not limited to) the 'sum or sums' of these revenues that had been disbursed to service debt. The warrant demanded the accounts of not only 'all and every' of those 'commissioners, governors and collectors [or farmers] of the excise', but also their subordinates (and their subordinates' subordinates) who had 'from the time the excise had been raised [in 1643] to the 25th of December last [i.e. 1660] whose accompts are not declared or discharged as aforesaid'. These 'sub-commissioners, officers, and clerks and all other persons therein concerned' were ordered to 'deliver unto such accompts, ledger books, accompt books, and their books of accompt, warrants, acquittances, and all other vouchers and papers that may pertain to the true and clear rating of the said accompt'. The auditor, John Birch, was authorised to employ as many clerks as necessary to ensure that the accounts could be declared in the Exchequer before 1 June 1662. Birch and his subordinates had about fifteen months to conduct their investigations.

Southampton did not sit on his hands while he waited for the accounts. The day after his warrant to Birch, he wrote to the lords and justices of the assize 'recommending' that they mention in their charges the 'due payment of the excise'. To these correspondences he attached letters that he had already written to the justices of the peace detailing for them their duties in this matter. Southampton reminded them that the revenue had been settled by an Act of Parliament and was now 'the law of the realm'. Collection of the excise 'therefore [was] deserving of the said judges' particular care', since, upon their reflection, they would see 'in lieu of what ancient and considerable flowers of the Crown it was granted'.[20] Southampton used his position to try to avert an intractable problem that had plagued the Protectorate excises in the last years of Oliver Cromwell's reign, namely the refusal of the justices of the peace to co-operate in the issuing of warrants for search and distraint.

In February 1658 the farmers of the excise on 'beere, ale, perry, cyder, meade & metheglin in the several counties of England and Wales' had humbly petitioned the Lord Protector for relief.[21] The twenty-two names affixed to the petition were not those of minor players in government finance. Together they held the farms of Berkshire and Hampshire, Buckinghamshire and Oxfordshire, Cornwall and Devon, Derbyshire and Nottinghamshire, Dorset, Kent and Sussex, Lincolnshire and Ely, Norfolk, Suffolk and Essex, Wiltshire and the East Riding of Yorkshire. These contracts represented at least £147,500 of the nearly £220,000 per annum in county beer farms.[22] The list included Esau Rigby and Richard Best, who, in addition to their county obligations, had the contract for another £128,400 in annual rents for the same commodities in London and Westminster. These men already 'for security of the payment of the said several and respective rents have together with other securities acknowledged to your Highness before your barons of your highnesses' exchequer several recognizances of very great penal sums'. No doubt the farmers had anticipated healthy profits. Yet having 'thus embarqued in this great undertaking together with all that is neere and deare unto us, we have in our very first setting ... discovered several very great and dangerous wrecks against which not only we and ours are in danger inevitably to be splitt and shipwrecked'. More ominous still, they alleged, 'the Publique Revenue (where of the excise is so considerable a part) is in hazard of very great diminution unless prevented by greater wisdom of your Highness and your most honourable counsels'.

They blamed their misfortunes on specific legislation that had unexpectedly interfered with their ability to collect the excise. In June 1657 Parliament had passed 'An Additional Act for the better improvement and advancing the Receipts of the Excise and New Impost', which relieved the commissioners of their supervisory responsibility for the farmers. This transferred the 'executive and coercive' powers to enforce collection of the duties from the sub-commissioners to the justices of the peace. Since the first farms of 1651, the farmers, who worked alongside the respective sub-commissioners in the counties, had gone to the sub-commissioners to impose fines and to issue warrants to enter premises or to distrain goods for non-payment of excise duties. As the petitioners explained, the result of this administrative change was disastrous. Part of the problem was practical: 'we are enforced (although with all due regard to the quality of their persons and places) humbly to represent unto your Highness that partly through their remoteness of habitation from one another and difficulty of procuring [the JPs] to meet and sit together upon this affair ...'. But their troubles went even further: 'partly through their general dissatisfaction touching the extent of the power itself (that we may abstain from calling it otherwise) we find our selves by this proviso itself utterly disabled to levy the said duties and consequently to raise wherewithal to satisfy the rents unto your Highness'.[23] The taxpayer was, they explained, 'being encouraged thereby almost universally to withhold and withdraw the same'. The farmers feared for their livelihoods, as '[they] having no means otherwise to leavy and recover them are in danger to be rest into great arrears with your Highnesse many thousands of pounds in the mean time standing out in debts in the hands of the said persons more than sufficient to satisfy the said Arrears'. Worse still, according to the farmers, while the sub-commissioners had been interested in their discoveries of ingenuous new 'frauds and circumventions', the justices of the peace were not. Prohibitive legislation was not, in itself, sufficient to deter evasion, especially if the justices were unable or unwilling to co-operate.

To redress the situation, the petitioners asked for 'further assurance of the permissions and such further powers and authority agreeable to Law for levying and collecting of the said duties'.[24] They also wanted acknowledgement that the legislation (and not their own negligence) had disabled them from performance of their contracts. The Council of State responded on 9 March 1658 by issuing a proclamation reminding justices of the peace that they had a duty to co-operate with the farmers. When that failed to produce results, in June the Council issued a temporary order authorising the Commissioners for Appeals and Regulating the Excise to issue warrants for forced entry into the premises of brewers. The commissioners could also authorise confiscation of brewing instruments until the outstanding duties were paid.[25] Yet the Protectorate did not grant the petitioners' requests for forbearance of their contractual obligations. Within eighteen months many of the farms had failed.[26]

The original legislation had been a response to the Protectorate Parliament's growing hostility to the arbitrary powers of the regime. Over the course of the 1650s farming had progressively replaced direct collection of the liquor excise. To supervise the farmers and continue direct collection of the foreign and industrial excises, the excise establishment had continued to employ sub-commissioners in the counties, and in the absence of farming contracts for a given county, the sub-commissioners collected the excises themselves. As Luke Robinson, MP for the North Riding of Yorkshire, put it: 'I like not to put an arbitrary power in a person, much less in inferior officers, to imprison men and seize their goods, and enter into their houses. We shall have a muster-master come into our houses every quarter, to disturb us and reckon over our families.'[27]

The Restoration Excise Act of December 1660 kept the judicial functions in the hands of the JPs but gave the sub-commissioners the authority to impose fines and forfeitures if unable to secure timely co-operation.[28] Southampton's letter to the justices of the assize anticipated resistance from the JPs. Some measure of the Lord Treasurer's success in securing the JPs' co-operation can be inferred from the fact that even though the 'Additional Act for Better Ordering and Collecting the Duty of the Excise and Preventing the Abuses Therein' of July 1663 enlarged the penalties for frauds and evasions, it cemented the role of the JPs in the judicial process. Not only could sub-commissioners not serve in lieu of the JPs, but also individuals were no longer even permitted to hold both posts.[29]

III

A week later after his intercession with the justices of the assize, Southampton issued two sets of instructions to the commissioners of the excise. The first outlined for them procedures to be followed in their London office; the second consisted of instructions to be given to their sub-commissioners.[30] The details of Southampton's instructions reflected a further awareness of the specific failings of the Protectorate excise establishment. The first three articles dealt with routine matters, including the administration of oaths and the taking of good security from the receivers and the cashier. The fifth article required the London office to make weekly reports to the Lord Treasurer of the cash received in the previous week. The requirement of weekly reporting dated from May 1656, but had grown irregular in December 1658 and appears to have lapsed thereafter.[31] Southampton imposed the further requirement that the cashier, receivers-general and tellers could receive monies only in the presence of the comptroller or one of his deputies, who was to take immediate account and issue a signed receipt. The instructions also mandated close supervision and monitoring of brewers. The commissioners were allowed to negotiate 'compositions' (a practice by which the excise office and the producer agreed on a sum in lieu of the gauging of vessels) with producers of strong waters, cider, perry, mead, metheglin, coffee, chocolate, tea and sherbet, but were required to take bonds in exchange for allowing them to pay in quarterly instalments.[32] The Lord Treasurer also ordered the commissioners to appoint from among their number an auditor who was to produce weekly reconciliations of the brewer's accounts with the returns from gauging furnished by the excise officers and another who was to perform a similar function on a quarterly basis for the lesser excises. A third commissioner was to supervise the receivers-general and cashiers, and a fourth was to serve as correspondent with the sub-commissioners and county accountants, thereby assuring that their letters and petitions would be answered. This excise commission was no sinecure.

The Lord Treasurer sent even more detailed instructions to be passed along to the sub-commissioners in the counties. The first provision dealt with a frequent complaint of the Protectorate excise auditors. Sub-commissioners, upon appointment, were to demand from the previous sub-commissioners their ledger books 'with all other books, bonds, papers, and entries belonging to the excise'.[33] The sub-commissioners were to account for current arrears and to undertake the collection of them, but to show arrears paid as distinct from subsequent charges in their accounts. They were to account for all monies on the day on which they received them and were given detailed instructions governing the declaration of their quarterly accounts before the commissioners. After those declarations, they had six weeks to balance their grand account and their account of the fines, and to transmit those with the outstanding bills of exchange to the London office. They were obliged to take careful record of all judicial proceedings according to the requirements of law. Upon undertaking employment, they were required to notify all concerned within their districts of their offices and that 'they report conformity according to law so that none may protest ignorance'.[34] Those who refused to make entry or payment were to be proceeded against at law. The sub-commissioners were to give delinquents adequate notice of summons and to arrange for witnesses and the collection of evidence. This ensured that upon default, the sub-commissioners could then 'proceed to judgement according to law'. This emphasis on legality meant that the complaints could be heard by the justices of the peace and, failing them, at the quarter sessions.

The sub-commissioners, like the commissioners, were also to oblige their gauging officers to make weekly reports. The most surprising requirement came at the end. The sub-commissioners were to record all of the cities, towns, villages and parishes in each hundred, and to record the names of the common brewers or brewing victuallers liable for the duty and, in the case of common brewers, to note whether or not they paid by composition or on the gauge, and the quality of beer or ale so brewed. This information they were to attach to their receipts. Failure to comply in 'method and form' in their accounts would cause the sub-commissioners to forfeit their bonds. Rather than netting out revenue and expenses, they were also obliged to account for each separately. Departure from these principles could also trigger forfeiture of their bonds.[35]

These strict accounting controls survived the shift from direct collection to sectional farming of the revenue in 1663. Under the new scheme, the farmer advanced a sum (usually 40 per cent of the contracted annual rent) upon commencement of the lease, paid the rest at regular intervals and received repayment out of the revenue or out of the funds advanced for the successive farm. In 1665, during the second farm (they customarily ran for three years), the farmers had secured for themselves a 6 per cent interest on their advances and a 2 per cent gratuity.[36] The farmers also kept as profits all revenue above the contracted rent. Should their profits prove unreasonably great, the rent would be raised the next time the farm was let. This model, known as absolute farming, had the advantage of ensuring the king a fixed and certain revenue, a sizeable percentage of which he received as advances. Moreover, the Crown could borrow on advances owing in subsequent years of the lease. The argument most often given in the modern literature for farming is minimisation of risk: if the economy does well and tax revenues are high, the farmer makes money; should it take a downturn and revenues are below expectations, the farmer loses his shirt and the government's coffers are none the worse for wear. In the early years of the Restoration excise, that principle did not hold in practice. Farmers were permitted 'defalcations', which in the early modern period meant 'defaults' as well as the modern connotation of 'frauds', some of which were quite considerable, for unforeseen events like the Plague. In 1665–67, these defaults amounted to £87,000, making the average annual increased yield of the excise for 1665–68 less than a third of what could be expected from the rent increase.[37] To ensure that the leases were negotiated accurately, the county farmers were obliged to make returns on actual excise duties charged. Elias Ashmole monitored these accounts closely.[38]

The farming system was both an expedient to deal with a complex problem of revenue collection and an elaborate mechanism of patronage. As noted earlier, the initial act establishing 'A Grant of Certain Impositions Upon Beer, Ale and other Liquors, for the Increase of his Majesty's Revenue during His Life' (Anno. 12 Caroli II Regis) provided that 'the said duty shall not be let to any other person or persons, then to the person or persons recommended by the Justices, under the Rate that it shall be tended to, and refused by such person or persons recommended'.[39] That provision, in itself, was hardly new. The House of Commons had imposed a similar requirement in December 1652 when it shifted responsibility for naming farmers from the commissioners to the local justices of the peace in their respective counties. In a brief order to the excise commissioners, the Rump instructed 'that it be referred to the Commissioners of the Excise to permit each County to take the Excise to Farm, if they please; and in such Cases not to let it to particular Persons: And that the Committee for regulating the Excise do see this Vote put in Execution'.[40] When the Protectorate showed a willingness to usurp parliamentary power over appointments, the House curtly informed the Council of State that parliament had affirmed that it 'shall name commissioners for the excise, as it seems it always was in the customs, tonnage, and poundage'. It further declared the excise was '*subsidium*, an aid, a tax upon the people, wherein the Protector had no negative'.[41]

Under the Cavalier Parliaments, these provisions were ostensibly to ensure 'the aforesaid duty may be paid with most ease to the people'.[42] In reality, this meant that those persons named by the justices of the peace held considerable powers of patronage over the farms. In this important sense, the Restoration settlement was not just an 'act of pardon for the king's enemies and oblivion for his friends'. Those who held the farms in the early years did very well out of them, but the king's credit needs soon eclipsed the legal niceties of the Act. The 'Home Counties' lease of London, Middlesex and Surrey was awarded in 1665 to a consortium led by William Bucknall, who represented the London Corporation of Brewers, under the rationale that 'their expertise would increase efficiency and reduce opposition'.[43] After Southampton's death, the treasury commission took the strategy even further. When Bucknall's group promised in 1668 to make significant loans in excess of the advance, they were re-confirmed in their lease, but the country excise was put open to competitive bid. Three years later the gentry farmers faced the loss of their leases. In their remonstrance of 1671, they argued: 'the present farmers are many of them such as have ventured their lives & fortunes in his Majesty's services in the late wars & the rest are not only justices of the peace, but most deputy lord commission officers, & commissioners in several counties where they dwell'. In effect, they maintained that the profits they made as excise farmers cross-subsidised their activities in the localities, 'so that what they get by their farms, they expend in his Majesty's service in those employments'.[44]

In the 1670s Danby and his associates offered an opposing analysis of what had transpired from those provisions in the original Acts: 'by absolute farms, the farmers of this branch had from the king's happy Restoration to that time shared among them some 1,200,000 l. clear profit whereas 10,000 l. a year might suffice and the king have the over-plus, which in 15 years had been but 150,000 l. so that a million at least had been lost for want of due regards'. Worse still, in the new Lord Treasurer's review, 'the very men who grew rich by this means, turned country gentlemen to that degree as oppose the court with all their might'.[45] To advance such an argument at all, Danby needed the accounts furnished by the excise comptroller. Twenty years before, the Council of State had lacked the financial data needed to judge the farmers' requests for defalcations in view of the reassignment of judicial powers.

IV

What did Southampton learn once the surviving Interregnum commissioners had complied with his order to produce the accounts so that they might be declared before the Restoration Exchequer? The first, and perhaps most alarming, lesson was that there was no consistent accounting of arrears.[46] Some accountants listed total accrued arrears; others listed them only for the given accounting period. Under the Protectorate, the subsequent year's account did not necessarily match that of the preceding one, especially where the county sub-commissioners were concerned. The accounts also did not distinguish payments on arrears in subsequent accounting periods from receipts from new charges, nor did they specify returns of fines and forfeitures by counties. Instead, those entries were grouped as lump sums. Southampton addressed all three of these limitations in his initial instructions to officers in March 1661.

The defects of these accounts encouraged one scholar to insist that 'it should be remembered that the figures do not represent so much the actual sums passing through the hands of the farmers as an effort on the part of their clerks to present a balanced account which would if possible clear the farmers of all liability on account of those farms'.[47] That view was mistaken. Under the Commonwealth, the Committee for Regulating the Excise made a distinction between accounts it wanted to 'inspect' and those it intended to 'discharge'.[48] It frequently demanded that the auditor present an abstract of the monies paid out as orders, salaries, incident charges and gratuities. In other instances, it ordered the auditor to 'bring in' accounts so that they might be discharged. The committee's refusal to discharge accounts in view of disagreements over arrears should not be read as evidence that they did not exist. The Protectorate Commission for Appeals and Regulating the Excise, which replaced the parliamentary committee under the Commonwealth, had a similar practice. The conclusion that the declared accounts were simply fabricated after the Restoration by commissioners eager to escape liability appears to be without merit.[49] Nevertheless, declaring the accounts before the Exchequer permitted the Lord Treasurer to proceed with the collection of arrears and to mediate between different claims about the relative merits of a general excise versus one restricted to the native liquors and a handful of related commodities.

For the sake of this discussion, the Interregnum excises can be grouped into three classes. The most important (which dated from the Grand Ordinances of 1643) were the duties on victuals: beer, ale, cider and mead.[50] To these, flesh and salt were added in January 1644. The second most profitable excises were the additional duties on specified imports (later others not specifically mentioned were taxed *ad valorem*) and a handful of exports. Of these, the exports were taxed primarily as a punitive measure against Royalist strongholds.[51] Except insofar as the duties were paid by the 'first buyer' (usually the retailer) rather than the 'importer', these 'foreign excises' on imports were, in economic terms, equivalent to customs duties. After the Restoration, the foreign excises were merged with the customs, but during the Interregnum, they remained distinct, in part because of the political clout wielded by the great merchants. The third category includes all the impositions on a host of domestic manufactures: alum, copperas, monmouth-caps and other haberdashery, hops, saffron, starch and silks. These were the commodities that had been assessed via crown prerogative taxation (the royal imposts, licenses and grants of monopolies) under Charles I and were thus closely associated with arbitrary government. They were not part of the initial legislation but were added in April 1644. A related ordinance followed in November 1645 on lead, gold, silver and copper thread and wire; glass; linseed, whale, pilchard and other oils; silks, soap, imported woollen cloth and, however improbably, lamperns or eels, which were used in large quantities as fish bait and in smaller ones as food. The collection of this third class of duties was confined to the few areas in which the items were produced. Despite economic expansion in the 1650s, the excises on these commodities contributed less to government coffers than they had in the 1630s,[52] but they generated the most popular hostility and elite resistance. In spite of attempts to make these duties profitable by leasing them as kingdom-wide farms, their collection had all but lapsed by the late 1650s.

After the Restoration, Southampton and his secretary investigated the merits of a general excise. A scribal memorandum, copied by Treasurer Southampton's secretary, contained a draft response to various proposals. It considered 'Reasons against the excise of native commodities other than ale and beer'.[53] The author judged that 'the Clamor, Charges and other Inconveniences of the Excise of native commodities is far more than the profit thereof'. Part but not all of the blame rested, in his view, with the last round of farmers: 'the way of farming the excise of native commodities hath all ready been found by experience to be both unprofitable – burdensome and very vexatious, and therefore the late farmers thereof were turned out of the said farms before the expiration of their contract which they could not perform, but are still in great arrears'.[54] Worse still, he argued that most native commodities were 'doubly charged', and that 'the clamor thereof arises not only from the makers and owners particularly concerned, but also from above 100,000 poor employed in the manufacturing thereof whose work and wages are daily diminished and in danger to be lost by the burden of excise'.[55] He ended by offering calculations for half a year's excise (29 September 1659 to 25 March 1660) and the conclusion 'that the receipt of the excise of native commodities will not probably amount to about 20000 pounds per annum there, and as it hath formerly will still decrease if continued as a burden to manufacturers thereof'.[56] Although these calculations were rough and even crude by the standards of what would become regular treasury practice within even a decade or two, they appear to have convinced the treasury not to press for an extension of the excises once the shortfall in the financial settlement became clear. The Exchequer's accounts confirmed the author's claims about the insignificance of the revenue raised from the industrial excises by providing hard data (see Appendix I). Although the Declared Accounts did not bother to break down the categories of commodities within the Grand Ordinance for the counties, the data from the London office further confirmed that beer, ale, cider, mead, perry, wine and tobacco made up the majority of the revenues (see Appendix II). These data help explain why Southampton consistently opposed the introduction of a general excise despite pressure from other members of the court party.[57]

If Southampton's investigations confirmed the conventional wisdom about the lack of profitability of the industrial excises, they also provided valuable insight into the reasons behind the failure of the Protectorate excise farms. The net revenue from the Protectorate excise remained relatively constant despite the sharp increase in contracted rents. Arrears grew steeply under Richard Cromwell's regime, but as far as the excise is concerned it would be an exaggeration to term even the period after March 1659 as a full-blown 'tax strike'. Appendix III confirms the finding that the contracted rents had grown to unrealistic levels. The regime could expect to extract gross annual revenues of approximately £450,000. Anything in excess of that threshold went uncollected. The evidence also suggests that despite the suspension of their judicial powers, the sub-commissioners remained in place. As the excise farms failed during the winter and spring of 1659, the sub-commissioners were positioned to resume collection of the excisable liquors from the farmers. At the county level (though not in the London office), decisions to farm or collect the duty could be seamlessly managed.

These findings support Michael Braddick's thesis that the success of the excise turned on its brokerage.[58] Under the Protectorate regime, 'gauging' worked best as a check on under-valuation by common brewers, brewing victuallers and vinters in their weekly declarations to the county excise offices. Once gauging became obligatory in June 1657 and the brewers became legally liable for the results of the gauge, the extent of the 'compromise' between taxpayer and tax collector became apparent. In effect, what this data reveals is the gap between nominal and real tax rate during the first fifteen years of the tax. In some counties, the real tax rate was no more than a third of the nominal one.

Attempts to 'improve' the liquor excises to something approaching the nominal tax rate failed. The total of county rents, coupled with the London and Home Counties farm of £128,400 and the all-England farms of native commodities held by the rogue financier Martin Noell and his associates (totalling £65,000), represented nearly £400,000 in contracted revenue plus another £200,000 in anticipated foreign excises from London and the outports. Once the Declared Accounts for this period were discharged in 1662, it became clear that the figure represented almost twice the actual gross yield of £665,399 for the period from 25 March 1658 to 18 August 1660.[59] The actual number was far more in line with the net revenues throughout the Interregnum period.

The over-valuation of the farms represented a failure of financial forecasting. The Restoration financial settlement retained the excise on native liquors, but the debates about the excise suggest widely divergent estimates of its probable yields. Southampton had no choice but to resort to direct collection of all excises until he could investigate what had happened. By allowing the practice of compositions in the counties in his instructions to officers in 1661, the Lord Treasurer returned to a negotiated duty. The sub-commissioners had the authority to put brewers on the gauge if the duty was too low, which was usually enough of a threat to guarantee a reasonable valuation.[60]

V

Although the excise was but one branch of the public revenue, Southampton's attempts to make sense of the Interregnum experience of commodity taxation reflect a pragmatism which has more often been ascribed to his opponents. Forensic accounting was far less glamorous than the Restoration fashion of 'projecting', or lobbying for a pet project, but it revealed important information. In this case, it provided the 'facts' to support three significant shifts in policy. Firstly, it would now be impossible to contest the benefits of better comptrol, especially over arrears. Secondly, shifts in jurisdiction over disputes between taxpayers and farmers or commissioners might have deleterious consequences, but better accounting procedures could at least mediate among competing claims about who was to blame for arrears. Thirdly, gauging revealed the gap between the nominal and real tax rates, but it also furnished the sub-commissioners with a powerful weapon in their negotiations with brewers for compositions. A general excise was not realistic in England. The Lord Treasurer could argue that the Long Parliament's experiment with collecting industrial excises was not worth repeating. Part of his opposition might have been solidified by his own experiences during the Interregnum, but Southampton now had the evidence to justify his beliefs.

Nothing in this account refutes the consensus that Southampton was a man with uncommon principles. Bishop Burnet noted after his death that he was 'an incorrupt man, and during seven years of the management of the treasury he made but an ordinary fortune out of it'.[61] As one modern scholar has put it, the Lord Treasurer never compromised his 'constitutional scruples'.[62] The evidence presented in this chapter suggests this analysis might be taken even further. If Southampton disapproved of the insufficient constitutional limitations placed upon Charles II at the Restoration, then his tenure as Lord Treasurer left him in a position to impose some indirect limits. By authorising compositions and introducing farming, he ensured that the tax was brokered through local elites and that it cross-subsidised their activities in the localities. The Lord Treasurer also all but guaranteed that the revenue would fall short of optimistic targets or even its potential. In far less scrupulous hands the excise would be used to turn under-supply into over-supply in the 1680s. The shift back to direct taxation in the summer of 1683 brought immediate gains, an increase in the yield from £565,000 per annum in 1680–83 to £635,000 in 1683–84, £670,000 in 1684–85, and £725,000 per annum in 1686–88.[63] By the Revolution, the excise had proved an 'easy and productive' tax indeed. Southampton's twenty-page report on the information to be gleaned from the declared accounts may not have convinced the king in 1663 'that the revenue is the centre of all your business'.[64] But the records that the Restoration's first Lord Treasurer left to his successors showed them where ministers so inclined might strengthen the sinews of monarchy.

APPENDIX I: BREAKDOWN OF GROSS EXCISE REVENUE BY ORDINANCE[a]

Ordinance by date of imposition	1647–1650			1650–1653		
	London	Country	Total	London	Country	Total
11 Sept. 1643 (Grand Excise)	£453,995 (53% of total excise revenue)	£332,820 (39%)	£786,815 (92%)	£520,199 (47%) (except tobacco pipes)	£308,132[b] (28%) + £221,447 (farms) (20%)	£1,049,778 (95%)
9 Jan. 1644 (flesh and salt)	£6,924 (<1%)	£15,933 (2%)	£22,857 (3%)	£1,662 (foreign) (<1%)	£7,728 (foreign) (<1%)	£9,390 (<1%)
8 July 1644 (industrial excises)	£21,015 (2%)	£11,337 (1%)	£32,352 (4%)	£21,486 (2%)	£19,428 (2%)	£40,914 (4%)
24 Nov. 1645 (industrial excises)	£5,720 (<1%)	£5,687 (<1%)	£11,407 (1%)	£8,772 (<1%)	£7,825 (<1%)	£16,557 (1%)
Total			£853,431			£1,116,679

Notes: a See TNA, E 351/1295–1296 for data. Summarised in Fine, *Production and Excise*, p. 17.
b Direct collection by sub-commissioners.

APPENDIX II: COMPARISON OF THE GRAND ORDINANCE (LONDON, 1647–50 V. 1650–53)[a]

	1647–50		1650–53	
	(London) sub-total	(Counties) sub-total	(London) sub-total	(Counties) sub-total
Beer, ale, cider, mead and perry	£128,214		£182,643	
Wine and tobacco	£140,613		£134,622[b]	
Linen drapery	£49,295		£56,858	
Grocery	£59,730		£70,018	
Old and new drapery	£26,227		£16,886[c]	
Mercery/silk	£23,423		£27,713	
Soap and strong waters	£6,237		£4,589[d]	
The foreign excise	£20,252		£26,868	
Total	£453,995	£332,830	£520,199	£308,132

Notes: a See TNA, E 351/1295–1296 for data. Summarised in Fine, *Production and Excise*, p. 17.
b Excludes the £500 farm of tobacco pipes.
c The excise on woollen drapery was suspended from January 1653.
d Excludes the £13,000 from the soap farm for May 1651–May 1653.

APPENDIX III: PROTECTORATE EXCISE REVENUE, 1654–59

Gross and net revenue, September 1653 to March 1660[a]

Date	Arrears (A)	London	County sub-committee	County farms + England[b]	Total less arrears (B)	Net Exchequer payments (C)	Fines
29 Sept. 1653 to 29 Mar. 1654[c]	£111,492[d]	£97,197	£67,437	£58,049	£222,683	[not applicable][e]	£1,275
Mar. 1654 to Mar. 1655[f]	£108,495	£227,366	£92,906	£100,818	£423,496	£369,021[g]	£2,406
Mar. 1655 to Mar. 1656[h]	£87,142	£189,562	£87,974	£139,890	£419,838	£347,324	£2,412
Mar. 1656 to Mar. 1657[i]	£99,525	£205,625	£73,804	£150,982	£434,502	£359,247	£4,091
Mar. 1657 to Mar. 1658[j]	£101,600	£242,271	£64,830	£168,814	£479,715 (£587,161)	£430,477	£3,800
Mar. 1658 to Mar. 1659[k]	£123,546	£128400 £155,001[k]	£42,833	£276,260	£605,774	£427,052	£3,280
Mar. 1659 to Mar. 1660[l]	£177,867	£128,400 £159,567	£118,476	£276,260	£681,851	£389,608	£2,148
Total[m]						£2,322,729	
Average					£525,437	£387,121	

Notes: a See Fine, *Production and Excise*, p. 41a for a similar presentation. For the estimate of net revenues used in the table, see Bodl., Carte MS 74, fol. 232, and Carte MS 73, fol. 67 for contemporary reports of revenue figures; this material is also available in TNA, E 405/289, fols 1–19 (previously fols 391–410) and BL, Add. MS 32471, fols 1–21. Ashley, *Financial and Commercial Policy*, pp. 68–9 abstracts the Carte Manuscripts, though his arithmetic on p. 69 is incorrect.

b These include the all-England farms for salt, soap, glass, alum, copperas, gold, silver and copper wire, and imported linen, paper and timber.

c TNA, E 351/1297; see AO 1/889/3 and AO 1/890/4 for figures in columns 2–6.

d In the parchment roll, this figure is too badly smudged to be read. James Scott Wheeler, *The Making of a World Power: War and the Military Revolution in Seventeenth Century England* (Stroud, 1999), gives the figure (p. 163) as 'around £120,000'. My figure was obtained by subtracting the total less arrears from the total including arrears, which the Audit Office account (TNA, AO 1/889/3) gives as £334,175.

e The Protectorate Exchequer was established in May 1654 and consolidated the separate funds into one receipt. As far as can be ascertained, this applied retroactively to the accounting period from March 1654 to March 1655 in the Audit Office series.

f TNA, AO 1/890/4.

g Although this figure technically consists of the period from July 1654 to March 1655 (because of the aforementioned merger into a single receipt), it would appear that the cash remaining in the excise funds was paid into the Exchequer.

h TNA, AO 1/890/5. TNA, AO 1/890/6 is a duplicate but in poor condition.
i TNA, AO 1/891/7 and AO 1/891/8.
j TNA, AO 1/891/9 and AO 1/891/9A.
k TNA, AO 1/892/10 and E 351/1298.
l Farm of £128,400 plus imports.
m TNA, AO 1/892/11 and E 351/1299, E 351/1300.
n Excludes partial year from September 1653 to March 1654.

PROTECTORATE EXCISE REVENUE

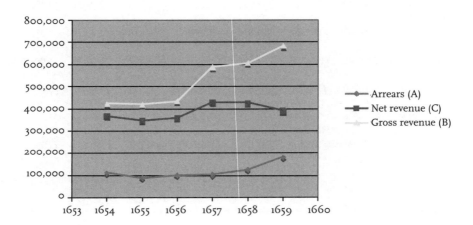

NOTES

1 David L. Smith, *Constitutional Royalism and the Search for Settlement, c.1640–1649* (Cambridge, 1994), p. 298; Paul Seaward, *The Cavalier Parliament and the Reconstruction of the Old Regime, 1661–1667* (Cambridge, 1988), pp. 103–30.

2 David L. Smith, 'Wriothesley, Thomas, Fourth Earl of Southampton (1608–1667)', *Oxford DNB*.

3 Smith, *Constitutional Royalism*, pp. 298–9; Seaward, *Cavalier Parliament*, pp. 103–9; Cecil D. Chandaman, *The English Public Revenue, 1660–1688* (Oxford, 1975), pp. 196–205.

4 *CTB*, vol. I, pp. xxxv–xxxvii.

5 Stephen B. Baxter, *The Development of the Treasury, 1660–1702* (Cambridge, MA, 1957), pp. 9–10; Henry Roseveare, *The Treasury: The Evolution of a British Institution* (1969), pp. 54–8; Henry Roseveare, *The Treasury 1660–1870: The Foundations of Control* (1973), pp. 17–26.

6 Jonathan Scott, '"Good Night Amsterdam": Sir George Downing and Anglo-Dutch state-building', *EHR*, 118:476 (Apr. 2003), pp. 335–56; Henry Roseveare, 'Prejudice and policy: Sir George Downing as parliamentary entrepreneur', in D.C. Coleman and Peter Mathias (eds), *Enterprise and History: Essays in honour of Charles Wilson* (Cambridge, 1984), pp. 135–50. Joseph A. Schumpeter, 'The Crisis of the Tax State' [1918], *International Economic Papers*, 4 (1954), pp. 5–38. For a discussion of the evolution of the Schumpeter thesis in the literature, see the introduction to Michael J. Braddick, *Parliamentary Taxation in Seventeenth-Century England: Local Administration and Response* (Woodbridge, 1994).

7 D.M. Gill, 'The Treasury, 1660–1714', *EHR*, 46 (1931), pp. 600–22; Roseveare, *Foundations of Control*, pp. 18–19; and Roseveare, *British Institution*, pp. 58–62.

8 Scott, 'Good Night Amsterdam', pp. 355–6; Jonathan Scott, 'What the Dutch taught us: the late emergence of the modern British state', *Times Literary Supplement* (16 Mar. 2001), pp. 4–6; Jonathan Scott, *England's Troubles: Seventeenth-Century English Political Instability in European Context* (Cambridge, 2000); J.A. Schumpeter, 'The crisis of the tax state', *International Economic Papers*, 4 (1954), pp. 5–38. See also Charles H. Wilson, *England's Apprenticeship, 1603–1763* (1965). For a rebuttal of Wilson, see M.T. Hart, 'The devil or the Dutch: Holland's impact on the financial revolution in England 1643–1694', *Parliaments, Estates and Representations*, 11 (1991), pp. 39–52.

9 Maurice Ashley, *Financial and Commercial Policy under the Commonwealth and Protectorate*, 2nd edn (1962), pp. 1–6.

10 Roseveare, *British Institution*, p. 54. For the legislation, see 'September 1654: an ordinance for bringing several branches of the Revenue under the managing and government of the commissioners for the treasury and Court of Exchequer', *A&O*, vol. II, pp. 1016–19, www.british-history.ac.uk/report.aspx?compid=56587 (accessed 12 June 2009).

11 Chandaman, *English Public Revenue*, pp. 38–44.

12 Roseveare, *British Institution*, p. 55.

13 Sir John Fortescue, *On the Laws and Governance of England*, ed. Shelley Lockwood (Cambridge, 1997), pp. 106–8. For the significance of Fortescue's formulation, see Gerald L. Harriss, 'Medieval doctrines in the debates on supply, 1610–1629', in Kevin Sharpe (ed.), *Faction and Parliament, Essays on Early Stuart History* (Oxford, 1978), pp. 73–103, esp. pp. 76–7.

14 Clayton Roberts, 'The constitutional significance of the financial settlement of 1690', *HJ*, 20:1 (1977), pp. 59–76.

15 Chandaman, *English Public Revenue*, pp. 196–215.

16 Smith, 'Wriothesley, Thomas'.

17 BL, Harley MS 7423, fols 1–3; C.H. Josten (ed.), *Elias Ashmole (1617–1692): His Auto-biographical and Historical Notes, his Correspondence, and Other Contemporary Sources Relating to his Life and Work* (Oxford, 1966), vol. III, p. 817.

18 Josten (ed.), *Elias Ashmole*, p. 801. See TNA, T 51/11, fol. 31 (11 Mar. 1661).

19 TNA, T 51/11, fols 22–3; *CTB*, vol. I, p. 215.

20 TNA, T 51/11, fol. 22. See also *CTB*, vol. I, p. 215.

21 BL, Stowe MS 185, fols 117–18.

22 Three more farmers, who were not included in the petition, had trouble paying their rents in December 1659. See BL, Add. MS 4197, fol. 114 for correspondence between the commission and the Hertford farmers William Rance, Humphrey Taylor and William Gardiner.

23 *Ibid.*

24 BL, Stowe MS 185, fol. 118.

25 *CSPD 1657–58*, pp. 262, 322; *CSPD 1658–59*, pp. 42–3. Ashley, *Financial and Commercial Policy*, p. 65.

26 In some cases, the farmers could pay their instalments when threatened with proceedings against their security. See BL, Add. MS 4197, fol. 114.

27 J.T. Rutt (ed.), *Thomas Burton, Diary of Thomas Burton* (1828), vol. I, pp. 291–4.

28 *Statutes of the Realm*, vol. V: *1628–80* (1819), pp. 255–9.

29 *Ibid.*, pp. 488–92.

30 *CTB*, vol. I, p. 219.

31 TNA, SP 18/131A, SP 18/160 and SP 18/186.

32 Gauging dated from 1649. The practice entailed an excise officer measuring the production of a common brewer or brewing victualler by inspecting the vessels and later also the mash tuns rather than relying upon the weekly declarations made to the local office.

33 TNA, T 51/11, fol. 26. For the difficulty with collection after personnel changes during the Interregnum, see Thomas Fauntleroy, *Lux in tenebris, or, A clavis to the treasury in Broad-Street* (1653).

34 TNA, T 51/11, fol. 27.

35 *Ibid.*, fol. 30.

36 Chandaman, *English Public Revenue*, pp. 54–5. For particular provisions, see TNA, CUST 48/1 (entry books, 1668–82).

37 Chandaman, *English Public Revenue*, p. 57; TNA, E 351/1303–5 (declared accounts).

38 See Josten (ed.), *Elias Ashmole*, p. 1079 for Ashmole's success in February 1667 at re-establishing comptrol over the London farmers, which had been suspended in November 1662. He had retained it over the county farmers.

39 *A collection of all the statutes now in force, relating to the excise* (1696), p. 17.

40 *CJ*, vol. VII, pp. 225–6 (4 Dec. 1652).

41 Rutt (ed.), *Diary of Thomas Burton*, vol. I, p. 344 (13 Jan. 1657).

42 Chandaman, *English Public Revenue*, p. 42.

43 *Ibid.*, p. 56.

44 BL, Add. MS 28078, fol. 450.

45 *Ibid.*, fols 392–4.

46 TNA, E 351/1295–1301; AO 1/889/1–892/13.

47 William P. Harper, 'Public borrowing, 1640–60' (MSc dissertation, University of London, 1927), p. 143.

48 Bodl., Rawlinson MS C386, fol. 30b (21 Feb. 1651).

49 Harper, 'Public borrowing', p. 140.

50 For the original Grand Ordinance, 'July 1643: An Ordinance for the speedy Rising and Leavying of Moneys, set by way of Charge or new Impost, on the severall Commodities mentioned in the Schedule hereunto annexed, Aswell for the better securing of Trade, as for the maintenance of the Forces raised for the Defence of the King and Parliament, both by Sea and Land, as for and towards the Payment of the Debts of the Common-wealth, for which the Publique Faith is or shall be given', *A&O*, vol. I, pp. 202–14, www.british-history.ac.uk/report.aspx?compid=55838 (accessed 12 June 2009). The following September, the Long Parliament passed a revised version which remained in effect until 1660. See 'September 1643: An Ordinance for the speedy Raising and Leavying of Moneys by way of Charge or New-Impost, upon the severall Commodities, in a Schedule hereunto annexed contained, as well for the better securing of Trade, as for the maintenance of the Forces raised for the defence of the King, Parliament, and Kingdom, both by Sea and Land, as for and towards the payment of the Debts of the Commonwealth, for which the Publike Faith is, or shall be ingaged', *A&O*, vol. I, pp. 274–83, www.british-history.ac.uk/report.aspx?compid=55862 (accessed 12 June 2009).

51 For a brief mention of this, see Selma E. Fine, 'Production and excise in England, 1643–1825' (PhD dissertation, Harvard University, Radcliffe College, 1937), p. 1. For the initial legislation regarding Newcastle coal, see *CJ*, vol. II, p. 957 (4 Feb. 1643).

52 For a comparison, see Frederick C. Dietz, 'The receipts and issues of the Exchequer during the reigns of James I and Charles I', *Smith College Studies in History*, 13:4 (1928), pp. 146–53 for the earlier period and BL, Lansdowne MS 1215 (fol. 7) for Mr Barnard's accounts of the excise for the year ending in March 1655.

53 BL, Add. MS 33051, fol. 188. Mentioned in Edward Hughes, *Studies in Administration and Finance 1558–1825 with Special Reference to the History of Salt Taxation in England* (Manchester, 1934), p. 129.

54 BL, Add. MS 33051, fol. 188.

55 *Ibid.*

56 *Ibid.*

57 For the pressure from the court, see Chandaman, *English Public Revenue*, pp. 40, 44.

58 Braddick, *Parliamentary Taxation in Seventeenth-Century England*, pp. 168–229.

59 TNA, E 351/1298, E 351/1299, E 351/1300 and E 351/1501.

60 Braddick, *Parliamentary Taxation*, p. 202.
61 Quoted in Smith, *Constitutional Royalism*, p. 299.
62 *Ibid.*
63 Chandaman, *English Public Revenue*, p. 75.
64 BL, Harley MS 1223, fol. 202.

Index

Index